AFRICAN ETHNOGRAPHIC STUDIES
OF THE 20TH CENTURY

Volume 3

THE BASUTO

THE BASUTO

A Social Study of Traditional and Modern Lesotho

HUGH ASHTON

LONDON AND NEW YORK

First published in 1952 and as a second edition in 1967 by Oxford University Press for the International African Institute.

This edition first published in 2018
by Routledge
2 Park Square, Milton Park, Abingdon, Oxon OX14 4RN

and by Routledge
711 Third Avenue, New York, NY 10017

Routledge is an imprint of the Taylor & Francis Group, an informa business

© 1967 International African Institute

All rights reserved. No part of this book may be reprinted or reproduced or utilised in any form or by any electronic, mechanical, or other means, now known or hereafter invented, including photocopying and recording, or in any information storage or retrieval system, without permission in writing from the publishers.

Trademark notice: Product or corporate names may be trademarks or registered trademarks, and are used only for identification and explanation without intent to infringe.

British Library Cataloguing in Publication Data
A catalogue record for this book is available from the British Library

ISBN: 978-0-8153-8713-8 (Set)
ISBN: 978-0-429-48813-9 (Set) (ebk)
ISBN: 978-1-138-48710-9 (Volume 3) (hbk)
ISBN: 978-1-351-04306-9 (Volume 3) (ebk)

Publisher's Note
The publisher has gone to great lengths to ensure the quality of this reprint but points out that some imperfections in the original copies may be apparent.

Disclaimer
The publisher has made every effort to trace copyright holders and would welcome correspondence from those they have been unable to trace.

Photo: Constance Stuart

A Mosuto looks over the Lowlands

THE BASUTO

A SOCIAL STUDY OF TRADITIONAL
AND MODERN LESOTHO

by

HUGH ASHTON

Second Edition

Published for the
INTERNATIONAL AFRICAN INSTITUTE
by the
OXFORD UNIVERSITY PRESS
LONDON   NEW YORK   TORONTO
1967

Oxford University Press, Ely House, London W.1

GLASGOW NEW YORK TORONTO MELBOURNE WELLINGTON
CAPE TOWN SALISBURY IBADAN NAIROBI LUSAKA ADDIS ABABA
BOMBAY CALCUTTA MADRAS KARACHI LAHORE DACCA
KUALA LUMPUR HONG KONG TOKYO

New material in this edition
© International African Institute 1967

First published 1952
Second edition 1967

Printed in Great Britain

CONTENTS

	INTRODUCTION	vii
	INTRODUCTION TO THE SECOND EDITION	xii
I.	HISTORICAL INTRODUCTION	1
II.	SOCIAL BACKGROUND	10
III.	CONCEPTION, BIRTH AND CHILDHOOD	26
IV.	EDUCATION	41
V.	MARRIAGE	62
VI.	SOCIAL ROUTINE AND ACTIVITIES	88
VII.	OLD AGE, DEATH AND RELIGIOUS BELIEFS	100
VIII.	AGRICULTURE	120
IX.	ANIMAL HUSBANDRY	134
X.	LAND TENURE	144
XI.	MISCELLANEOUS OCCUPATIONS AND PURSUITS	158
XII.	TRADE, EXCHANGE, WEALTH AND PROPERTY	166
XIII.	POLITICAL ORGANIZATION	186
XIV.	JUDICIAL ORGANIZATION	222
XV.	LAW	249
XVI.	MEDICINE, MAGIC AND SORCERY	282

APPENDICES

I.	GLOSSARY OF SESUTO WORDS	317
	BOTANICAL NAMES	318
	COLLOQUIALISMS	322
II.	KINSHIP TERMS	324
III.	KINSHIP MARRIAGE	327
IV.	CASES TRIED IN NATIVE AUTHORITY COURTS	338
V.	NATIVE AUTHORITIES, 1949	342
	BIBLIOGRAPHY	347
	SUPPLEMENTARY BIBLIOGRAPHY	351
	INDEX	355

LIST OF PLATES

A Mosuto looks over the Lowlands		*Frontispiece*
		Facing page
I.	(a) General view near Matsieng	32
	(b) View from the top of Thaba Bosigo	32
II.	(a) Young girl acting as nurse to baby brother	33
	(b) Mother and child	33
III.	(a) Mother making porridge with baby on her back	48
	(b) Children round hearth	48
IV.	Boys' initiation	49
V.	Girls' initiation	96
VI.	(a) Boys' initiation	97
	(b) Girls' initiation	97
VII.	(a) Women fetching water	112
	(b) Women winnowing at sunset	112
VIII.	(a) A Mothepu belle	113
	(b) Clerk of the Court at his desk	113
IX.	(a) Funeral of Chief's son	160
	(b) Herd-boys racing cattle	160
X.	(a) Woman carrying kaffir corn-heads	161
	(b) Girl carrying maize	161
XI.	(a) Harvesting	176
	(b) Threshing mealies in private courtyard	176
XII.	(a) Gathering for a national *pitso* on the outskirts of Maseru	177
	(b) Women returning from the fields	177
XIII.	(a) Sheep	288
	(b) Scene at Paramount Chief's village—Matsieng	288
XIV.	(a) The late Paramount Chief Seeiso Griffith	289
	(b) Basuto type	289
	(c) Basuto blanket and grass hat	289
XV.	Native court scenes	304
XVI.	(a) Girl initiate	305
	(b) Female witch doctor	305

INTRODUCTION

NINETY years ago, Eugène Casalis (of the Société des Missions Évangeliques, Paris) was the first to write a full account of the customs and beliefs of the Basuto, an interesting and forthcoming Bantu people living in South Africa. He was in a unique position to do so, and being one of the earliest Europeans to live amongst them, he could observe and describe their culture before the disrupting influences of Western civilization began to take effect. He was followed some fifty years later by two more of the French missionaries to whom Basutoland owes so much, Dieterlen and Kohler, who wrote on the Basuto of "Yesterday" and "To-day" in the *Livre d'Or* published in 1912, to celebrate the mission's Golden Jubilee. About that time appeared two historical publications, Ellenberger and MacGregor's collection of tribal traditions and Lagden's two-volume political history. Since then, save for Dutton's slight sketch, there have been no comprehensive descriptions of the Basuto's changing culture, although there has been a spate of articles on different subjects. Of these the best include those written by Laydevant, another French missionary, but of a different persuasion from his predecessors, and some admirable technical surveys such as Staples's on the ecology and Stockley's on the geology of Basutoland. In this book I have attempted to synthesize all this published material together with the results of my own field work, and to present an all-round picture of the Basuto as they are to-day.

Casalis wrote his book to arouse his fellow-countrymen's interest in the Basuto with a view to enlisting their material support for the work of the mission in its far-flung foreign fields. I, too, hope to interest the general public, not for any particular institution or policy, but for the sake of mutual understanding and enjoyment. I think it is fun to know how other people live, think, and tackle the fundamental human problems of education, sex, earning a living, law and order; but I also believe it is of paramount importance for the sake of peace and mutual accommodation, in a race-ridden society such as we have in Southern Africa, that there should be mutual respect and understanding. It is comparatively easy for the African to learn about the European way of life—in fact he can scarcely escape getting some ideas on the subject—but the European has to make more of an effort as he has little direct contact with African life and little access to the available literature. I have therefore tried to make this a straightforward and readable account of the Basuto way of life and I must seek the indulgence of my fellow-anthropologists for eschewing jargon and adhering to common forms of spelling such as "Basuto" (instead of the technically correct but awkward-sounding "BaSotho") and for omitting all theoretical discussion.

There are, however, two theoretical points that I should have liked to work out in detail. One is that culture is not a homogeneous, integrated whole. There is obviously a central pattern which gives a particular culture its general character and distinguishes it from other cultures; but it is not a rigid pattern nor yet all-embracing. It has all sorts of deviations and exceptions, some of which are due to individual aberration or choice, to changes of time, place or circumstance, while others are due to differences between whole sections of the community. This applies to the Basuto. There is undoubtedly a Basuto culture as distinct from the culture of the Zulus or the Bechuana—quite apart from that of Europeans—but it varies in detail from one area to another, from one group or one individual to another. Up in the mountains the Batlokoa still observe many of the old Basuto customs described by Casalis, and are closer than other Basuto to the traditional culture of pre-European times; but even here, there are wide variations between chiefs and commoners, rich and poor, educated and untutored; in the lowlands a few Basuto still follow the old ways, but most have left them and are living by a hotchpotch of old and new customs, and some have largely adopted European customs and modes of thought.

The second point concerns the theory that the function of some institutions and aspects of culture is to satisfy certain basic human needs: that systems of magic and religion provide reassurance regarding future life, allay man's fear of death and give him confidence to face the natural forces of storm and drought, pestilence and famine; the economic system directs his efforts to feed and clothe himself; the political and judicial systems provide for social order and stability. When societies were in a state of equilibrium, as many primitive ones were before the coming of the white man, it could reasonably be assumed that these systems effectively achieved their objects. Now that most primitive societies are changing and unstable, such an assumption is no longer valid and it behoves the anthropologist to assess the effectiveness of these institutions and aspects of culture: to judge the extent to which the economic system does satisfy the people's material needs, in terms of health, physical development, and decent living; how far their political institutions are satisfactory, judged by such indices as stability of family and social relations, expressions of contentment or misery, grumbling and complaint, and the prevalence of crime. These are not easy assessments to make and many of them require the many-sided approach of a team of experts; but they should be attempted and to a limited—too limited—extent I have tried to assess the worth of Basuto economic and judicial institutions.

The material for this book came from two sources: the publications

INTRODUCTION ix

and manuscripts listed in the bibliography and various spells of fieldwork. The first period covered two months in the winter of 1934, at Phamong in southern Basutoland. I lived at a Roman Catholic mission and worked in the neighbouring villages, occupied mostly by Baphuthi. I was in fairly close touch with Chief Bereng Griffith, a son of the then Paramount Chief and one of the most important chiefs in Basutoland. I worked partly through an interpreter and partly directly in Sesuto, which I learnt passably well, having been born and brought up in Basutoland; I also used some texts and records written by my interpreter who was a school teacher, and the diaries kept for me for several months by two young girls.

My next period of field-work, lasting from October 1935, with a short break, to April 1936, was among the Batlokoa, whom I revisited for a few days in 1949. They live in the mountain area and are generally recognized by the Basuto to be the closest living exponents of the old Basuto culture. For my first three weeks I lived at a trading store, visiting the neighbouring villages daily. Thereafter I settled in the chief's village. I lived in one of his huts and was looked after by 'Makhamelo, one of his father's widows, having all my meals in her household and contributing in kind to her commissariat. I was thus able to establish friendly and personal relations with a wide range of people, and became particularly friendly with Mokete Lethunya, a fellow-boarder who was president of the chief's court and a doctor. I did the usual round of ceremonies, being lucky in that several important ones occurred while I was there; but I sometimes sent my personal assistant or other literate informant to cover them for me, because they took up a lot of time and I was more interested in the ordinary life of the people and the way these events affected it, than in details of ritual. I spent most of my time at the courts, in the fields or in the villages, chatting with the people and noting down their activities, and interrogating those who dropped in at my hut to visit me. Throughout my work I relied almost entirely on friends and acquaintances to volunteer information and only rarely employed paid informants. This was made possible by my living so closely among the people and being able to work almost entirely in the vernacular without an interpreter, thanks to the inestimable aid of the Mabille-Dieterlen Sesuto-English dictionary. Two informants stood in a special category, Tapotsa and Borikhoe. The former was my personal assistant, and he kept records of court cases, local events and ceremonies, wrote texts on various subjects and investigated specific points and problems. He was able and conscientious, well connected through his father, who had been the old chief's principal warrior and doctor to the army, and held in high esteem for his own character and abilities; he later acquired a position of importance in the tribe. He continued to work for me for nine months after I left the field, keeping records of court cases and a commentary on tribal and his own personal affairs, and making inquiries on various questions I asked him. Unfortunately, he died very suddenly about a year later. Borikhoe was a lad of about thirteen who attached himself to me as groom and general factotum; he was friendly and very bright, a mine of information on child life and interests and an exuberant reporter of local gossip.

Since these two field trips I have revisited Basutoland on numerous occasions, in various capacities, and so collected further information and kept in touch with political and administrative developments. Thanks to the kindness of the Resident Commissioner, I spent a week in March and nearly three weeks in August 1949, examining all the relevant official documents dealing with "ritual" murders and inquiring into the various factors that may have contributed to them.

I have dwelt on the nature of my field-work at some length because I am conscious of its briefness. Compared with the long periods that most anthropologists spend in the field, my few months are negligible. The only justification that I have for believing that this is a reasonably accurate book, which should be judged by the same standards as other ethnographic works, is that the intensity of my work should have compensated to some extent for its brevity. I am, however, only too conscious of great gaps in my data and inadequacies in my book.

There are three points I should like to make in the matter of presentation. One is that I have reluctantly omitted as many Sesuto terms as possible. This may be regretted by the Basuto, who I hope will read this book, and by others who know Sesuto, but it is done for the sake of those who are not so fortunate and would only find them burdensome. The second is that I have omitted a great deal of detail. This book is already long enough and in any case, as the Basuto put it, *"khomo ha e nye bolokoe kaofela"*—"an ox does not evacuate all at once"; I hope my unused material will appear in a separate publication of field notes. The third is that to avoid endless footnotes and references, I have quoted from other publications or communications only when they mention points I did not come across in the field or differ from my own findings.

In its original form this book was accepted by the University of Cape Town in 1939 as a thesis for a doctorate in Philosophy. Its publication was delayed by the war. I have modified it considerably, amplified it in certain respects, particularly in the sections on kinship and law, and brought it up to date where there have been obvious cultural changes, for example, in political structure and administration. There have undoubtedly been other cultural changes which I have not touched, but I believe that they have been changes of detail only and that fundamentally the Basuto culture and customs are still much as they were.

Finally, I should like to thank very sincerely those who have helped me with this work and made its publication possible. My 1935–6 field-

INTRODUCTION

work was financed by a grant from the Rhodes Trust. This was to have covered a two-year programme, but for personal reasons, which I have not ceased to regret, I was unable to complete it. The Basutoland Government and the University of Cape Town have contributed to the cost of publication. For the generosity of these three institutions I am deeply grateful. I am honoured by having this book produced under the auspices of the International African Institute, and am grateful to the Rev. Dr. E. W. Smith for sponsoring it in the first instance, to Professor Daryll Forde for his continued interest, and to Mrs. Wyatt for her endless patience. I am most grateful to government officials for help, information and access to files, and especially to Lieut.-Col. Forsyth Thompson, C.V.O., C.B.E., for his personal interest and support; to the Rev. Jankie for his manuscript "Mosotho e Motona"; to Bethel Mission, Mr. and Mrs. H. Smith and Mr. Warren for much hospitality; and to all my friends at Malingoaneng who helped me to collect my information, especially Chief Mosuoe Lelingoana, my "mother" 'Makhamelo, Mokete Lethunya, Bennet Leshota, Tapotsa Moqhoai and Borikhoe. This book was read in draft by Mrs. Hoernlé, Dr. Ellen Hellman, T. B. Kennan, Ken and Deborah Kirkwood, G. I. Jones, E. Ramseyer and David Mochochoko—to all of them I am extremely grateful for the trouble they took and for the many helpful suggestions and criticisms they made. My mother and my wife have borne the tedium of a tapping typewriter these many years and scarcely ever grumbled. Petronella Clark has twice typed the whole book through and put me deeply in her debt. Bill Lewis and Constance Stuart have very kindly allowed me to use their photographs. Finally, Professor Schapera has, in every crisis, been a tower of strength; without him this book would never have been written.

HUGH ASHTON

BULAWAYO,
31 October 1949.

INTRODUCTION TO THE SECOND EDITION

IN the sixteen years since *The Basuto* was written, Basutoland[1] has ceased to be a backwater, isolated by her mountains from the world at large. She has been exposed to the ferment of world politics, to the pressures of ideological conflicts, to international communication and to other external influences to a degree unprecedented in her previous history. These have wrought inconceivably rapid changes. Although they are mainly structural, and have not yet affected the people's ordinary way of life, these changes reflect new attitudes, and contain within themselves seeds of still further change with profound social and economic consequences.

The country has been exposed to unending inquiries and commissions—G. I. Jones on Medicine Murder; V. Sheddick and Chicago University experts on Land Tenure; numerous hydrological surveys; a population and two agricultural censuses; a social survey; two economic surveys; four constitutional commissions and Lord Hailey's historical and political survey. There have been streams of visitors[2] from all over the world—high officials, politicians, churchmen, journalists, diplomats, economists, educationalists, agronomists and a host of other experts, all probing, questioning, advising and providing stimuli of one sort or another. Political refugees from South Africa,[3] such as Joe Matthews, one-time National Secretary of the Youth League; Patrick Duncan, Editor of *Contact*, journal of the Liberal Party, who retired from the Basutoland Service in 1952; and the renowned African author, Ezekiel Mphahlele, have also had significant influence as well as lesser luminaries. But with the advent of self-rule their influence has waned and they have been associated with terrorists and criminals who have sought political asylum to escape from their own political crimes, and their welcome is wearing thin.

Easier travel has increased the numbers of Basuto, other than migrant workers, who have gone abroad and has widened their range of contact. The Paramount Chief, Constantinus Bereng Seeiso, was educated at

---

[1] Even her name has changed, and "Lesotho", hitherto applicable only to the Lowlands, has been officially adopted as the new name of the whole country. To maintain consistency with the rest of this book, the old name has been retained, as well as the Anglicized Basuto for Basotho.

[2] The first list of visitors in an Annual Report, 1958, p. 7, contained 9 names, including wives. In the 1963 report, p. 9, this had expanded to 53. These are V.I.P.'s only. There were many more visitors unnamed, whose visits were just as stimulating.

[3] Segal, *Political Africa*, pp. 79, 173. See also Hailey, *Republic of South Africa and the High Commission Territories*, pp. 108, 111.

INTRODUCTION TO THE SECOND EDITION xiii

the Catholic College of Ampleforth and at Oxford, and other leaders have been overseas to universities and technical institutions. Chiefs and National Councillors have visited East and Central Africa, Europe and America, studying farming and local government; some have been to the United Kingdom on constitutional negotiations bringing them to the heart of the British political maelstrom, and others to Ghana, Egypt, Russia and China on other political quests.

A growing influence nearer home has been the University. On 8 April 1945, the Catholic University College of Pius XII was opened at Roma. Enrolment was small—6 in 1945, 24 in 1950, 38 in 1955, 167 in 1960—but influential and "the political consciousness of those from the Territory was sharpened by daily contact with students of wider background from South Africa and Rhodesia",[1] and with staff and visitors. In 1963 the College was reconstituted the University of Basutoland, Bechuanaland Protectorate and Swaziland, an autonomous institution, established under Royal Charter. With greater financial backing from Britain and America, it is increasing its student intake and widening its range of Faculties.

Although these influences leave the ordinary man "surprisingly undisturbed",[2] they have provided an incessant succession of stimuli to Government officials, leaders and intelligentsia, making them receptive to ideas of political change, and aware of political, social and economic development elsewhere.

Modern media of communication have also played their part. The wireless has not yet had much influence except among the more advanced and affluent who could afford sufficiently powerful sets to receive South African and overseas broadcasts, but the recent development of cheap portable transistor sets is bringing the medium to an increasing number of listeners. Since 1 January 1962, Bantu Radio in South Africa has offered a Sotho programme of $17\frac{1}{2}$ hours a day. At first it reached only those Basuto who lived and worked in the Republic, but the rapid expansion of its F.M. network has brought most of Basutoland within its range. Since 1964, the Basutoland Government has broadcast short programmes daily over the Catholic Mission transmitter in Maseru. A Government radio was established in 1966.

The press, long an important influence, has also extended its range and, with the spread of education, its readership. Two old independent papers, *Mochochonono* (the *Comet*) and *Mphatlalatsane* (a title that means both "Morning Star" and "Publisher") ceased publication in 1953 and 1954, respectively, giving way before the independent *Naledi oa Lesotho* ("Star of Basutoland"), and the growing circulation of two long-established mission papers *Leselinyane la Lesotho* ("The Little Light of

[1] Stevens, *Southern Africa's Multiracial University*, p. 17.
[2] Clymer, A., *Basutoland progresses, but whither?*, p. 9.

Basutoland", P.E.M.S. 1863, 3,130 fortnightly) and *Moeletsi* ("The Counsellor", R.C. 1933, 4,500 weekly), a spate of local publications of varying endurance, and the influence of South African English papers which are probably read even more widely than Sesotho papers.[1]

The quickening interest in local publications is shown by the comparison that before 1954 only four papers were registered under Proc. 3 of 1917, whereas between that date and 1965, 27 were registered, 19 of them after 1960; 8 can be classified as religious, 3 general, 6 labour and professional, and 11 political, although no exact distinctions are possible, since their interests often overlap. Some of them have lasted quite well, especially the two major political ones, *Mohlabani* ("The Warrior", 1955) and *Makatolle* ("The Revealer", 1960) with irregular issues and unknown circulation and mission-sponsored papers such as the *Sesotho Quarterly Digest* (Catholic, 1959, 3,000); others have already died. The Government has also sponsored some minor publications, such as for farmers, and from 4 January 1963, the *Lesotho* (previously *Basutoland*) *Times*. There may be a few other publications too insignificant to have registered. South African papers include both European and African orientated publications. The former are mainly regional dailies such as *The Friend*, published in Bloemfontein, *The Star* and *Rand Daily Mail*, both published in Johannesburg, and national weeklies such as the *Sunday Times* also published in Johannesburg. The latter include *The Bantu World* called *The World* since 1955, *Drum*, *Zonk*, and *Golden City Post*. Afrikaans papers are read by a minute number of Basuto because few are sufficiently literate in that language. Then there are—or were, for several have been banned in South Africa or otherwise ceased publication—the political party papers in South Africa, mainly those of the Communist and Liberal Parties. There are also church papers with a limited circulation, such as *Southern Cross* and *Sursum Corda*.

Schools and Government offices receive occasional issues of British information posters and hand-outs. There was no external Information Service until 1965, when the British Council opened a centre in Maseru. Western publications generally have been "expensive and difficult to obtain", whereas at one time Soviet and Chinese Communist ephemera and literature were easily distributed and "sold extremely well",[2] but now have little appeal.

The two Mission printing presses at Morija and Mazenod have operated since 1861[3] and 1933, and have recently increased their output of pamphlets and books of all kinds in Sesotho and English; 135 Sesuto books printed or reprinted since January 1961 were exhibited at the

---

[1] *General Report: Third National Conference of Basuto Authors*, November 1962 Conference Report, p. 3.

[2] Rotberg, A., *Africa Special Report*, May 1960, p. 10.

[3] Previously established at Beersheba, 1841.

INTRODUCTION TO THE SECOND EDITION

Third Conference of Basuto authors in November 1962, and the Morija Sesotho Book Depot catalogue, 1965, lists over 140 vernacular publications. They include religious tracts, national and tribal histories, biographies of past Paramount chiefs and other personalities, descriptions of current events, novels and plays. This output of literature is "one of the most prolific in all of Africa".[1]

The film has not been a medium of importance, as there are no commercial cinemas. Basuto working and living in South Africa have access to cinemas on mines and townships; these show the usual newsfilms, but their feature films are confined to Westerns and simple musicals to suit an unsophisticated audience. The Government operates mobile film units which show "official British newsreels, and C.O.L. features and documentaries widely in schools, clubs, missions and villages".[2]

A completely new factor has been the emergence of modern politics. It is nothing new for individuals and groups to air their views, criticize and complain, but what is new is the continuous exercise of political pressures by organized parties, vying with one another and with the British Administration and the chieftainship to influence Government policy, control the administration and acquire positions of power and prestige. Before the present era, there were two political groups, the Progressive Association and the Lekhotla la Bafo.[3] The former was established in 1907[4] by the intelligentsia and educated. It achieved fair prominence in 1922 when it demanded that some members of the Basutoland National Council be elected, and again, in the years before the Native Administration and Courts Proclamations of 1938, when it pressed for reform of the chieftainship. In 1944, it was one of the five Associations to be given the then privilege of nominating a representative to the Basutoland Council, and in 1945 to the District Councils. Although the electoral principle was introduced with the creation of District Councils, it did not campaign as a party or sponsor party candidates beyond the nominees to which it was entitled. Its views were "reasonably and moderately expressed",[5] and though after the Second World War, one of its branches, that in Mafeteng, came under the influence of Phillip Mokhatla "who at various times had trouble with the Police and whose attitude was far less guarded",[6] generally it remained too conservative and staid for the younger generation.

The Lekhotla la Bafo was a more turbulent body. From its establishment it was strongly traditionalist and urged the Basuto to return

[1] Extract from A.R.O.M.I., Rome, January 1963, quoted in General Report of the B.O.S.A. Third National Conference, 1962, p. 1.
[2] *Annual Report*, 1963, p. 121.
[3] Infra, p. 313.
[4] *Report on Constitutional Reform*, p. 36.
[5] Hailey, 1963, p. 102.
[6] Ibid.

to the ways of their forefathers. It was strongly anti-Government, anti-mission and anti-European. It was also anti-chieftainship until the late 1940's when it attempted to turn the medicine murder scandals, then at their height, into political capital against the Government by accusing the latter of faking or perpetrating the murders itself in order to discredit the chiefs and sell the country to European speculators; in so doing, it had to champion the chiefs and make them out to be cruelly misused, misunderstood and misrepresented. It was strongest in the Berea district where it was led by Josiel Lefela, variously described[1] as "eloquent" but "politically unbalanced". Its lack of ideological content or positive purpose and its rejection of modern education, disenchanted the younger post-war militants, whom it might otherwise have attracted, and caused them to seek their political homes elsewhere.

The development of the modern political party—a party with a coherent policy and discipline, and above all with financial backing—took place after the Second World War. It was the product of the great political awakening of Africa and of the Cold War, and it went *pari passu* with democratization of the National and District Councils, a process it helped to accelerate and from which it benefited. It came to a climax in the General Election of 1965, which was contested by four major parties, complete with printed manifestos, loudspeaker vans, news sheets and offices.

The first of these parties was the Basutoland African Congress, which became the Basutoland Congress Party (B.C.P.) in 1959. It was founded in 1952 by Mr. Ntsu Mokhehle, then a teacher at the Maseru Intermediate School, and a graduate from the South African Native College, Fort Hare, with a Master's Degree in Zoology, awarded for a thesis on bird parasitology. He had been a member of the Lekhotla la Bafo and, as a student, had been active in the African National Youth Congress League, whose former Treasurer, Walter Sisulu, had encouraged him to start this new party. It continued to have close ties with the South African National movement, and gained much strength from South Africa, where it established at least three Provincial Councils (Cape, Orange Free State and Transvaal) and several branches from Cape Town to Johannesburg. Its members took part in South African politics and several were deported from that country in 1963 because of their activities. Of its 60 candidates in the 1965 Basutoland elections, at least 22 had originally joined the party in South Africa (5 as early as 1952, and the rest before 1960) and 2 were deportees from that country.

It also gained early strength from the support of a noted Basuto author and teacher, B. M. Khaketla and of his paper *Mohlabani*, started in 1955 with the help of two South Africans, Ezekiel Mphahlehle and Zeph Mothopeng, who were banned in their homeland but found political asylum in Basutoland. It later became estranged from South

[1] Hailey, p. 102. Halpern, *South Africa's Hostages*, 1965.

INTRODUCTION TO THE SECOND EDITION

African National Congress "whom it accused of interfering in Basutoland's affairs"[1] but it remained closely aligned with the South African Pan-African Congress and with Pan-Africanism generally. In December 1958, Mr. Mokhehle attended the first All Africa People's Conference in Accra, and was elected a member of the Steering Committee.

For over a decade, the B.A.C. (and later its successor, the B.C.P.) was the dominant party. It was first in the field and so attracted the young and the educated. It reflected and was able to capitalize on post-war unsettlement and discontent, it expressed growing awareness of the possibility of change, it was able to exploit anti-colonialism, then fashionable in international circles, being fomented, for differing reasons, by the U.S.A. and by Communist countries, and it profited from the British Government's policy of Colonial disengagement which weakened the local administration, and from internal dissension of the chieftainship, which is discussed below. It also had funds and other support from Ghana, Moscow, Cairo, and from British sympathizers, to establish and maintain a proper organization and a cadre of professional politicians and helpers. It also had in Ntsu Mokhehle a leader of courage and great ability.

These sources of strength also contributed to its decline. Its outside support made it suspect at home, and the stature of its leader caused personal dissension and schism. It reached its zenith in 1960, when it won 73 out of 162 seats on the District Council elections, and 29 out of 40 seats on the Basutoland Council, and emerged as the strongest single party. Three years later, Mokhehle fell out with Joe Matthews, who had the disposal of funds from Moscow, so the party turned to Peking for support. Its continued militancy—it chose the knobkerry as its party symbol—its anti-Europeanism and its hostility to the Church and chieftainship and its involvement (18 October 1964) in an armed foray resulting in deaths at Rothe when it flagrantly challenged the authority of the local ward chief, played into the hands of its rivals, and led to its defeat in the 1965 elections,[2] which up to a few months before it had been expected to win.

The first split came in 1955 when Chief S. S. Matete left the party. He was a good all-rounder, a man of education, and an important chief, below the first rank, a leading member of the National Council, where he was one of the Paramount Chief's nominees representing the chieftainship, and an ardent member of the Congress Party. The National Council appointed him in 1954 as one of four advisers to the Regent Paramount Chief and in 1956 as one of its representatives on the chieftainship committee. At the end of that year, he was about to be elected President of the B.C.P. when he resigned both from the Party and from his position as the Paramount Chief's adviser, the former

[1] Rotberg, A., "Basutoland 1962", *Africa Report*, p. 9.
[2] It won only 25 out of 60 seats.

because of disagreement with its growing extremism and because it refused to become involved in the Paramountcy succession dispute that was flaring up again, and the latter because of the Regent's apparent reluctance to retire. In 1957, he formed the Marema-Tlou Party to "unite chiefs and commoners".[1]

For a time it was the second most influential group. In 1960 it won sixteen seats in the District Council elections and five in the National Council, and Chief Matete became a member of the Executive Council, in charge of Local Government and Chieftainship Affairs. In 1962 it, too, split, and many members broke away to join with another party, the Freedom Party, to form the Marema-Tlou Freedom Party. This so weakened it that in the 1965 elections it lost every contest, even Chief Matete himself, in spite of his outstanding personality, position and record.

The second major breakaway from the B.C.P. took place on the 29 December 1960, when B. M. Khaketla, Deputy President of the Party, resigned. He was one of the Party stalwarts, and the only Party member to be elected a member of the Executive Council, where he was responsible for Health and Education. He broke because of personal differences[2] with Mokhehle, and because he disagreed with the Party's demand for ultra-rapid constitutional advance, and with anti-Christian bias, hostility to the chiefs, criticism of Europeans in general and South Africans in particular, which he felt would gravely prejudice Basutoland's economic progress and political independence. The following April, together with others who had resigned or been expelled from the B.C.P., he launched the Basutoland Freedom Party and continued to edit *Mohlabani*, which now became the mouthpiece of the new Party. In 1962, the B.F.P. joined forces with the Marema-Tlou to form the Marema-Tlou Freedom Party (M.F.P.). The Party has little coherence or unity of purpose, and combines within itself elements of the right and left. But it has gradually developed into the "King's Party", supporting and being supported by the new Paramount Chief and the Principal Chiefs, and backing the former's ambition to become an executive monarch rather than a constitutional ruler. It has accepted money both from Moscow, obtaining Communist funds which the B.C.P. forfeited when it fell out with Joe Matthews, and from South African business and mining interests, who felt that its experienced, capable leadership would be an asset to the country. It failed to convince the Basuto voters of its stability and won only four seats, Khaketla himself being overwhelmingly defeated (223 votes to 4,669) in Maseru, another loss to public affairs for he had contributed greatly to Basutoland's constitutional advance. Later, however, he was appointed to the Senate by the Paramount Chief and became its President, a position of some

---

[1] Segal, ibid., pp. 99, 173, 306. The name comes from the proverb *Marema-Tlou a ntsoe leng*, lit: "those who kill an elephant must be unanimous—Union is strength".
[2] See also Segal, pp. 139, 305, 306.

INTRODUCTION TO THE SECOND EDITION xix

prestige though little influence. In spite of its defeat, the Party tried to retain its Janus-like identity, and refused to throw its lot in with either of the two major parties in parliament. But in September 1965, one of its sitting members, Chief Setenane Mapheleba, without crossing the floor, announced his intention "of supporting the government at all times and on all questions", thereby almost splitting the Party again, and possibly heralding future alignments.

The fourth and now the most important Party is the Basutoland National Party. This was formed in direct opposition to the B.C.P. It was established in 1959 by Chief Leabua Jonathan, a junior member of the House of Moshesh through Moshesh's second son, Malapo, ruler of the Northern District of Leribe. Leabua had a distinguished practical career in the administration of the Paramount Chief's office during the Regency, as President of the Basuto Courts and Assessor to the Judicial Commissioner, who was at that time Patrick Duncan. He was a National Councillor, a member of both the constitutional reform and the chieftainship committees which were appointed in 1956 and one of four advisers to the Regent.

The Party was formed "to defend the traditional way of life",[1] to protect the body of the chieftainship, to resist the radicalism of the B.C.P. and to oppose the anti-mission, anti-European extremism of that Party. It later became the main protagonist of the vital need to establish confidence in the country's stability, so as to attract investment and win South African support for development projects such as the Oxbow hydro-electric and water-supply schemes; it gained the support of the Catholic Church, and of political and business interests in South Africa and the United Kingdom. The Party won twenty-two seats in the 1960 District Council elections, and only one in the National Council. During the next five years it so improved its organization and increased its strength that it won thirty-one seats in the 1965 elections, and thereby became the governing Party. Chief Leabua lost his contest, but after winning a by-election, became Prime Minister of the new Government.

Other parties have come and gone. In 1960, an anti-Communist League Mesa-Mohloane (the "Grasshopper Roaster") was founded which ran two papers, *Mesa-Mohloane* and *Toa-Toa*. In spite of its efforts, a Communist Party was started two years later by John Motloheloa who had been deported from South Africa: it found it better to infiltrate other organizations, and was formally disbanded in January 1966. A Basutoland Labour Party, rather conservative and anti-Communist in outlook, was also started but it never caught on and when on 26 October 1964, its leader, Elliott Lethata, announced its support of the B.N.P.,[2] it virtually ceased to exist.

[1] Segal, ibid., p. 306.
[2] *Africa Report*, December 1964, p. 17.

The Trades Unions have also been involved in politics. Legislation providing for their formation was passed in 1942 (The Trade Unions and Trade Disputes Proc. 17/42), not because it was needed at the time but because it was required in order that Basutoland might qualify for assistance from the Colonial Development Fund.[1] It was not till ten years later that the first Unions registered. In 1965, there were seven, viz:

Basutoland Typographical W.U., 1952
Basutoland Commercial Distributive W.U., 1952
Basutoland National Union of Artisans, 1953
Basutoland General W.U., 1954
Basutoland Motor Transport W.U., 1959
Basutoland Workers Union, 1962
Mazenod Union of Printing, Bookbinding and Allied W., 1963

and one "Union of Employers", 1961.

Except for the two typographical unions they were confined almost entirely to the administration centres or Camps, especially Maseru, where the majority of Basutoland's few employees were located, but owing to the fact that these Camps were the main nerve centres of the country, and that these unions were about the only organized bodies, their influence was disproportionate to their numbers and membership. In 1962 a Federation of Labour was formed to try to co-ordinate them and weld them into a political force. Its secretary was Shakane Mokhehle, a brother of Ntsu Mokhehle, who had been secretary of the Union of Artisans since 1956, after previous experience of Trade Unionism in Cape Town, South Africa, and who later became a member of the All African Workers Union. In the same year (1962) he became treasurer of the B.C.P., and through labour associations soundly defeated B. M. Khaketla at Maseru in the 1965 elections.

There have also been professional associations such as the Basutoland National Teachers' Association (B.A.N.T.A.), African Civil Service Association and Expatriate Service Organization. Although precluded from active political participation, they have exercised unobtrusive political pressure so far as their own interests were concerned. They have also provided useful adjuncts in the pursuit of political influence. Mr. Ntsu Mokhehle, for instance, was Chairman of B.A.N.T.A. in 1953, and its nominated representative on the National Council from 1957 to 1959.

Other associations and groups have sprung up to represent or co-ordinate various interests and most of them have had, at some time or other, some political association. They include the:

Basutoland African Students Association
Basutoland Sports Association
Basutoland Agricultural Union

[1] *Annual Report*, 1951, p. 20.

Basutoland Traders Association
Botsabelo Leper Settlement
Basutoland ex-Servicemen.

Each of the last four had one representative on the National Council.

Co-operatives of various sorts have been encouraged by the Administration from 1948 onwards. It is claimed that this movement was encouraged by the Catholic Bishop, J. C. Bonhomme, as early as 1946.[1] They are of several kinds: agricultural credit, which mushroomed in 1963 to 139 with a membership of over 3,400, 21 marketing, 15 consumer, and 11 miscellaneous societies. Few of them were particularly strong and sound, and most of them suffered from lack of managerial skill and understanding and many gave credit too easily and enforced repayments too lukewarmly. But they provided a valuable educational as well as economic function and have given many useful administrative experience. Some were also used for political purposes, notably the Basutoland Co-operation Banking Union which was established in 1958 to bank for member societies, supply goods wholesale, run a transport service and organize the dispersal of produce. After an encouraging start it ran into financial difficulties and was wound up in 1963, and in its place "to save the whole movement from collapsing, the Co-operative Union of Basutoland was formed",[2] with Government membership. In 1960 another society was formed, the Basutoland Co-operation Federation, as a central supply and marketing organization, but was dissolved after a year's operation.

This same period has witnessed the dominating rise of the Catholic Church, which celebrated its centenary in 1962. The Church was second[3] in the missionary field in Basutoland and remained in that position until, with ample funds behind it, it gradually overtook the Paris Evangelical Mission whose parent body was no longer able to give it substantial support financially.

An early major success was the conversion to Catholicism in 1912 of Griffiths Lerotholi, previously baptized into the Church of England,[4] who became Paramount Chief in 1913. This gave the Church a valuable foothold in the political hierarchy of which it made the greatest use. All Griffiths' successors and many of his descendants have been Catholics, and now almost all the leading chiefs belong to this faith.

The Church's educational efforts have been tremendous, and its influence in this field is indicated by the following figures:[5]

[1] *Centenary*, 1962, p. unnumbered.   [2] *Annual Report*, 1963, p. 49.
[3] See p. 8.   [4] Laydevant, *Morena N. Griffiths Lerotholi*, pp. 51, 53.
[5] *Education Reports*, 1961, 1962. *Centenary of the Catholic Church in Basutoland*, 1962, page unnumbered. Where there are slight divergences between the two sources, the official figures have been quoted. The P.E.M.S. still has more lower Primary Schools (422) but falls away rapidly in higher level institutions. The University was originally a Catholic institution, but has been independent since 1963, though still closely linked with the Church.

	Catholic	Other	Total
Training Colleges	4	3	7
Secondary Schools	11	8	19
Higher Primary	55	57	112
Lower Primary	391	571	962
Pupils (boys)	24,555	34,875	59,430
(girls)	43,785	50,713	94,498
	68,340	85,588	153,928

Not all those who go to a Catholic church are Catholics, but the religious effects of such schooling are likely to be profound. The Church can now claim to have the largest following of any religious group in the country, and it is quite remarkable to find large, beautiful churches and pealing bells tucked away in remote parts of the mountains. The 1956 census recorded[1] 33·8% of the population as belonging to it. The actual figures differ slightly from the estimates that had been given by the Mission Headquarters:

	Catholics	Protestants	Church of England
Enumeration	215,921	140,003	60,130
Estimate	261,000	130,000	54,500

Both the Catholic Church and P.E.M.S. have become structurally more closely integrated with the people than before. Basuto have joined several Catholic orders—in 1963[2] there were 35 Oblate Brothers, 28 Brothers of the Sacred Heart and 472 Sisters belonging to seven different categories; 31 have been ordained Priests, and 2 called in 1961 to the high office of the Episcopate are His Grace, the Most Reverend Emanuel 'Mabathoana, Archbishop of Maseru and His Lordship, the Most Reverent Ignatius Phakoe, Bishop of Leribe.

In 1964, P.E.M.S. reorganized its structure and separated the Mission from the Church. The former continued to look to France and Switzerland for personnel and financial support, whereas the latter, in keeping with the times, became the Church of Basutoland, autonomous and self-supporting. The two were linked at various levels by joint committees and at the top by Synod.

In the political sphere, using this term in its sociological sense, there have been considerable developments. The dispute over the Paramount Chief's Regency continued to rumble until ended by the accession of Constantinus Bereng in 1960. It had serious effects, whose ripples are still perceptible. It started in 1940[3] with the death of Seeiso, when his

---

[1] French Protestants 21·92%, Church of England 9·41%, other Christians 5·77%, leaving 28·9% non-Christian or no denomination and 2% unspecified. *1956 Population Census*, p. 99.

[2] *Centenary of the Catholic Church*, 1962, page unnumbered.

[3] See pp. 7, 196–7.

senior widow 'Mantsebo, who had no son, was appointed Regent for her stepson, born of the second house on 2 May 1938, and was challenged by Seeiso's brother Bereng, who had himself hoped to succeed their father. Although their dispute was the subject of a High Court decision, both contestants continued the struggle by various means, including medicines. These necessitated the use of human ingredients thus leading to murder and counter-murder and culminated in Bereng's conviction and execution for one such murder in 1949. This ended the first part of the feud, though not before the chieftainship was deeply divided by the issue (Chief Gabashane, for instance, went with Bereng to the gallows, although he had originally opposed his claims), demoralized by the depths to which it had sunk and gravely weakened by lack of leadership and its own involvement. The Paramount Chieftainship itself was also shaken, and that it did not disintegrate is a measure of its strong emotional and symbolic appeal to the Basuto, the British Administration's continued traditional support, the loyalty and skill of the official advisers appointed by the National Council, and 'Mantsebo's own strength of character. It was nonetheless a very different institution at the end of the Regency from what it had been at the beginning, and though historical events played their part, the changes would not have been so great if the feud had never occurred or the Regent had been a man.

The death in 1949 of her main antagonist gave her an opportunity to repair the damage, but she could not rise fully to the challenge. Nor could she avoid jealousy and disharmony within the family, especially with her ward's mother, 'MaBereng. When his twenty-first birthday came and went without her stepping down for him, co-wifely jealousy, fomented by private ambition, spread accusations that she was planning to prevent his succession. It was rumoured that she intended to usurp the position herself, or to engineer her daughter's succession, citing as precedent the Queen's accession to the British Throne, or even to give it to her other stepson, Leshoboro, who was the eldest son of her stepsister, her husband's third wife of an impeccably correct marriage. In vain did she and her official advisers point out that attainment of majority at twenty-one was an empty and foreign concept, that according to SeSuto custom he should first finish his education (the modern equivalent of initiation, in his case to take his degree at Oxford) and then marry, that his inheritance was intact and his livings had been kept open.

Passions were aroused again, though not to the same fever-heat, and sides taken. The issue assumed party political importance and the immediate succession of Constantinus became a plank of the Marema-Tlou party which was thereby led to becoming the Paramount Chief's party and supporting a return to executive monarchy. It also led to a split among the Paramount Chief's official advisers, with Chief S. S.

Matete resigning to support 'MaBereng and her son, while the others, including Chief Leabua Jonathan, now Prime Minister, supported the Regent.

The impending introduction of the 1960 Constitution brought matters to a head. It was appropriate that the new political era should be heralded by the new Paramount Chief, and it was right that the important nominations to the National and Executive Councils, which the new Constitution entitled the Paramount Chief to make, should be his rather than the Regent's. A special meeting of the Sons of Moshesh and senior chiefs was specially convened on 3 February to consider the question and eventually, by acclamation and almost complete unanimity, urged that Constantinus Bereng be officially declared the rightful heir and installed as Paramount Chief without delay. Effect was given to this a month later, when to symbolize the beginning of the new era, the formal installation took place on Moshesh's Day and immediately prior to the opening of the new Parliament, in which historic event he assisted as his first official function.

The 1965 Constitution now provides (Section 22) specifically for succession to the Paramount Chief, and for the designation of a Regent or Acting Paramount Chief, and assigns this duty to the College of Chiefs. In December 1965, at the Paramount Chief's instance, the College designated his infant son as the person "entitled to succeed" and his wife, 'Mamohato, to be Regent, should he be absent from Basutoland or be incapacitated or die, during his heir's minority. This is now defined as under twenty-one years of age.

The Administrative Reforms that were initiated in 1938 continued, in varying degrees, to work themselves out or were caught up in constitutional changes.

(a) The Courts

The early reduction in numbers of courts and their separation from the chieftainship[1] were only partially successful, and the system continued to cause dissatisfaction. Therefore a Native Courts Reform Committee, consisting of three chiefs and a commoner appointed by the National Council and two Administrative Officers, was set up in 1950. After considerable discussion, its recommendations were brought into effect on 1 January 1954. They reaffirmed "the complete removal from the judicial system of the influence and control of the chiefs" and the establishment of an independent, professional judiciary. Partly to find the money to improve conditions of court personnel, and partly to streamline the system still further, the number of "B" courts was reduced from 85 to 46, "A" courts from 21 to 12, and Appeal Courts from 5 to 4. Some were re-sited at more convenient centres and new staff were carefully selected and given a course of training. Chiefs were

---

[1] See pp. 210, 222.

left with powers of arbitration in civil disputes where both parties were prepared to accept them.

In 1955 and 1962 an additional "B" court was established. In 1956, the practice was started whereby twelve "B" courts sat alternately in two centres to facilitate public access to them.

In 1956, the Court Reforms Committee was reconvened to tidy the whole judicial system still further. It recommended precise rules of procedure and evidence, and sought to replace the three-tiered system by twelve Central (Appeal) and fifty-three Local Courts, in order to streamline it further and line it up with the Subordinate Courts. It also made the contradictory suggestion that the Paramount Chief should be responsible for the courts' administration—a proposal that would have hindered rather than helped their integration with the rest of the judicial system. Although these proposals were incorporated into legislation, the Basuto Courts Proc. No. 23 of 1958, they were not implemented, being overshadowed by concurrent constitutional negotiations and by the last throes of the Regency dispute. Nonetheless they had an effective impact on those responsible for the Courts' operation, consolidated their separation from the chiefs and improved their professional conduct.

In 1963 the Constitutional Commission observed of the Basuto Courts that "their overall position in the judicial system is obscure" and recommended that they should be "united or integrated with the subordinate courts in a single system . . . and any existing limitation of jurisdiction based on race should be eliminated".[1] With the subsequent adoption of the 1965 Constitution, the National Treasury was dissolved, and the Courts' personnel for whom it had been responsible, were transferred to the Department of Justice. Their jurisdiction was also widened to include Europeans, in appropriate cases such as debt and civil contract where traditional laws and customs were not in question. It is now only a matter of time before the Basuto Courts become fully integrated with the rest of the judicial system.

(b) Chieftainship

Increasing political awareness and the medicine murder scandals gave rise to continuing public concern over the chieftainship. In 1950 at the request of the British Government, Lord Hailey examined "certain aspects of Native Administration"; at the same time, ideas of administrative reform began to be interlaced with concepts of parliamentary advance and self-government. A year later, the National Council asked for the appointment of a committee, like the Native Courts Reform Committee, "to examine the present state of the chiefs' administration". Beyond obtaining the High Commissioner's perfunctory approval, nothing was done about it until 1954 when, without any

[1] *Report*, pp. 75, 76.

preliminaries, the Government appointed two ex-Colonial officers, from outside Basutoland, assisted by three chiefs, as an "Administrative Reforms Committee". This was the ill-fated Moore Committee. Its brief, practical, sensible report was vigorously rejected by the National Council, partly because it was aggrieved by not having been consulted about the committee's composition and terms of reference, but mainly because the committee brusquely refused to allow any discussion on and made no reference to possible constitutional advancement, in spite of Lord Hailey's clear hints on the subject[1] published a year before. It was followed by a petition for a "legislative council as a step towards self-government", which bore fruit two years later with the appointment in October 1956 of the Constitutional Reform Committee.

This debacle left the problem of the chieftainship still unsolved, so at the request of the Resident Commissioner and Paramount Chief, the National Council in May 1956 appointed a "Chieftainship Affairs Committee" to deal with this. The committee met at the end of November, five days before the Constitutional Reform Committee, and the two then decided to combine, as their spheres were so interconnected. Their joint report was accepted by the Council in July 1958, and finally translated into the Basutoland Constitution Orders-in-Council at the end of 1959.

The "dilemma of the chieftainship"[2] was still basically the same problem as the 1938 reforms had tried to solve, the proliferation, rapacity and incompetence of the chiefs and headmen. Moore had firmly recommended that their numbers be drastically reduced as had been done in the Courts, their pay improved and based on responsibility and performance, and their discipline tightened up. The joint committee was not as forthright and adopted a more indirect approach in which it relied on the long-term effects of other recommendations, such as the creation of a legislature in which the chieftainship was reduced to a minority, transfer of power from the Paramount Chief to an Executive Council and the addition of executive functions to District Courts. Its only direct recommendation was the creation of a College of Chiefs. This was composed of the Paramount Chief and all Principal and Ward Chiefs, and its functions were to control the recognition and creation of chiefs and headmen, to discipline inefficient, criminous, absentee chiefs and to adjudicate on succession and boundary disputes; it was not a success, and the chieftainship remained unreformed.

The next Constitutional Commission also avoided dealing with the problem directly. It retained the College of Chiefs to deal with the problems of succession, especially of the Paramount Chieftainship, but

[1] Hailey, op. cit., pp. 138–40.
[2] *Report on Constitutional Reform*, etc., pp. 51, 158.

relieved it of its disciplinary functions as "the chiefs have found it embarrassing to discipline themselves".[1] It made tentative proposals for turning the Principal Chiefs into Administrative Agents[2] but these were later dropped and instead the positions of the twenty-two Principal and Ward Chiefs were entrenched in the new 1965 Constitution, leaving the problem of their powers as well as the powers and "the very thorny question of definitely establishing and freezing the areas of jurisdiction"[3] of other chiefs and headmen to be dealt with by the new Government.

The future of the chieftainship was a major issue in the 1965 elections although nothing very explicit was said on either side. Had the B.C.P. won it would have drastically reduced the chiefs' status, functions, authority and salary, and might even have tried to eliminate them altogether. But the present Government is more sympathetic to the middling and lower chieftainship and is also trying to win the Principal and Ward Chiefs' support from the M.F.P., so is unlikely to tackle this "thorny problem" until it is more experienced and secure.

(c) *The Paramount Chieftainship*

The Paramount Chieftainship has changed from a position of ruler with considerable legislative, executive and judicial authority to that of a constitutional monarchy, practically bereft of all real power, though still of immense prestige, from being executive head of an administrative hierarchy that paralleled and rivalled the British Administration to being nominal head of a Unitary State. The process began in 1943 when progressive elements took advantage of the Regent's weakness to wrest a promise from her to consult the National Council before exercising her powers to make rules and regulations. This was carried a stage further in 1948 when her credit was gravely shaken by the *liretlo* murders, by the appointment of official advisers, who were drawn from a panel submitted by the Council. The gradual decrease in the proportion of nominated members in the Council and increase in popular representation[4] also had their effects. The establishment of a National Treasury at the Paramount Chief's village of Matsieng and the creation of a large new class of quasi-civil servants ostensibly under the Paramount Chief's direction temporarily enhanced the position, until negatived by the appointment of a controlling Finance Committee, half of whose members were initially appointed by the Paramount Chief until in 1950 they were whittled down to one out of ten.

The next major change came in 1960, when the Paramount Chief was stripped of all legislative authority, which was thereafter to be

[1] *Report*, p. 63.   [2] Ibid., p. 52.
[3] Ibid., p. 65.   [4] See pp. 218–219 and also next section.

shared between the National Council and District Councils under the new Constitution. He was left with only limited powers of delay. His executive power was also reduced by the creation of an Executive Council which replaced the previous advisers, and whose advice he was now obliged to take. This Council consisted of 8 members. Four were Government officials, 3 Councillors appointed by the National Council and 1 Councillor nominated by the Paramount Chief.

The final step was taken by the next Constitution in 1965. This (Section 21) specifically provides "there shall be a Paramount Chief of Basutoland, who shall be styled Motlotlehi" ("One who deserves praise"—Royal Highness), it emphasizes his dignity by providing that he shall take "precedence over all persons in Basutoland other than Her Majesty". It prescribes his functions in detail and limits them to those of Constitutional Ruler such as appointment or dismissal of a Prime Minister, exercise of prerogative of mercy, appointment of certain senators and other public officers, and carrying out various acts on the advice of his Government. It also refers (Section 88) to his and the Chieftainship's powers over land, held "in trust for the Basuto Nation", which he will continue to exercise "according to custom and tradition", until changed by the Basuto Parliament.

(d) The National Council

The democratization of the Council[1] continued. Moore's recommendations to reduce its numbers and to alter its composition were at first rejected, but eventually accepted in principle by the Joint Constitutional Reform and Chieftainship Affairs Committee and introduced in 1960. Its members were reduced from 100 to 80, 40 being directly elected by the District Councils, 14 nominated by the Paramount Chief, 4 Government officials and 22 ex-officio Principal and Ward Chiefs. In 1965, its composition was again revised, and it became a Bicameral Parliament, comprising a Senate and a National Assembly. The former now consists of the 22 Principal and Ward Chiefs (or their nominees) and 11 other Senators nominated by Motlotlehi. It has limited powers of delay. The latter has 60 members, all elected on universal adult suffrage. *Pari passu* with these structural changes, its functions have also changed, and from being an advisory body it has become an autonomous legislature. In 1960, it was given power to legislate for all persons in Basutoland save a few reserved matters such as external affairs, security, currency, customs and communications. In 1965 this authority was extended, subject to a few limitations during the pre-Independence period. Once Independence was achieved (October 1966) it became the supreme lawmaking body, unfettered

[1] See pp. 218–19.

except by such clauses as were entrenched in the Independence Constitution.

With Parliament becoming Sovereign, executive powers passed from the British Administration and the Executive Council, referred to above, to Motlotlehi's Government, subject to pre-Independence reservations vesting certain responsibilities in the British Government's Representative. It follows the British Democratic pattern and consists of a Cabinet, comprising the leader of the Party with a majority in the National Assembly, who is appointed by Motlotlehi as Prime Minister and not less than seven Ministers chosen by him. Its functions officially are "to advise Motlotlehi" (Section 67(a)), but in reality, to govern.

(e) District Councils

Democratic principles were also extended on the Local Government level. District Councils were started in 1944 and constituted an innovation, based on principles, such as popular election "hitherto unknown in tribal law".[1] During the next few years, continued attempts were made to extend their functions and importance while at the same time preserving the chieftainship although the two institutions were essentially incompatible. In 1951, for instance, the High Commissioner announced that "the Government, in consultation with the Paramount Chief was considering how to balance the need for increased popular representation and participation in the conduct of affairs with the unquestioned need to maintain authority of the chieftainship". Moore tried to resolve the contradiction by recommending that the Councils be given considerable executive and bye-law making powers, and at the same time that the chieftainship be brought in by making the Principal or Ward Chiefs their deputy chairman. This solution was rejected, along with the rest of his report, but was later adopted in principle, though without acknowledgement, by the Joint Constitutional Reform and Chieftainship Affairs Committee and incorporated into the 1960 Constitution. At the same time, the National Treasury was decentralized, as Moore had also proposed, and its functions added to the District Councils.

As it turned out, the Councils did not affect the chieftainship as much as they might have done. A few successfully ran minor services which were transferred to them by the Central Government. But for the rest, they were not interested. They had fallen into the hands of the B.C.P. and become irresponsible debating chambers concerned with political harassment of their opponents rather than constructive Local Government. Nonetheless, in 1962 and 1963, on the initiative of the newly created Ministry of Local Government, they all passed model bye-laws which replaced the Paramount Chief's Rules which they had inherited

[1] See pp. 219–20.

but never operated, dealing with a wide range of subjects, including soil erosion, protection of crops, control of grazing. Although they made no attempt to use these powers, this "unleashed an unbridled opposition from the traditional leaders"[1] who suddenly realized how seriously their authority might be challenged.

The 1963 Constitution Commission was obviously disenchanted by them and recommended that their future "requires close study because the limited financial resources of the territory should not be burdened with too elaborate a governmental structure".[2] The incoming Government took the hint and its first legislative act, apart from technical matters, was to provide for their suspension without preliminary inquiry. This was implemented at the beginning of 1966 by suspending every one of them, as a preliminary to their abolition. Whether anything takes their place remains to be seen—there is some talk of forming Ward Councils to assist Principal and Ward Chiefs as District Administrative Secretaries, but nothing is likely to be done until the "dilemma of the chieftainship" has been solved.

(f) Land Tenure

The considerable growth of population in spite of considerable emigration to South Africa[3] has increased the pressure on land that was already serious enough to warrant concern thirty years ago.[4] This has led to questioning the validity of the traditional system of tenure and some observers, such as Hailey, flatly considered it "no longer suited to conditions in which the increase in population has created competition for the possession of arable holdings, while the rise in the cost of living has made cultivation uneconomic"[5] except with the application of

[1] *Annual Report of the Sec. for Local Government*, 1953, p. 6.
[2] *Report*, p. 79.
[3]

Year	Basuto Population	Total Population	Absentees
1868 (Nil)	130,000*		Not included in population figures
1875	127,523†		
1891	218,324	219,082	30,000
1904	347,731	348,848	—
1911	401,807	404,507	
1921	495,937	498,781	
1936	559,223	562,311	101,273
1946	561,209	563,854	
1956	638,857	641,674	154,782
1960 (agric)	681,834		205,424

* Kuczynshi, R. R., quoted by Sheddick, p. 34.   † Lagden (*The Basuto*), p. 484.

[4] Supra, p. 174 et seq. The 1960 Agricultural Census documents the position in detail. In 1960 24% of the families had no land and 44% had no stock.
[5] Op. cit., p. 145.

INTRODUCTION TO THE SECOND EDITION

capital and intensive labour. It has been closely studied[1] and various recommendations made for its improvement by outside persons[2] as well as the appropriate Government Departments but so far without effect. As the Constitution Commission noted "it has long been recognized that the system requires revision, but at the same time we have little doubt that the overwhelming majority of the Basotho people—for good and sufficient reason—are neither willing nor indeed ready, to jettison fundamental principles of their land law".[3]

The 1965 Constitution formalizes the traditional system of land allocations and hearing of disputes, but provides that elected Advisory Boards should assist headmen, chiefs and the Paramount Chief in their duties, and that a National Planning Board may be established to "prepare plans for the economic development of Basutoland, including in particular the development, conservation and use of land and other natural resources".[4] Both these innovations are rather artificial and are likely to be disregarded. The first Advisory Board elections in 1965 were turned by the B.C.P. into political tussles, and so are likely to suffer the same fate as the District Councils. Moreover, the Regulations constituting them[5] are so loose that they will be ineffective. No Planning Board has yet been appointed.

The present Government is unlikely to make any great changes. The defects of the system are not so great as to justify any upheaval and if its administration were improved through tighter control of the chieftainship it could be suited to the Basutos' present needs. The Government will, however, doubtless make some changes of which the most likely are:

(a) to grant special security of tenure to industrialists;
(b) to modify the position in Maseru and possibly other Camps;
(c) to transfer to itself the Paramount Chief's last remaining executive functions concerning land and so complete the transition of his position to that of Constitutional Ruler.

My thanks are due to those who have helped towards the production of this new edition—to those whose kindly reception of the original work has called for a new issue; to the International African Institute for undertaking it; to Professor Daryll Forde for his patient encouragement during its long gestation; to Professor Schapera for helpful advice

---

[1] Douglas, A. J. A. and Tennant, R. Y., *Basutoland Agricultural Survey, 1949–50*; Sheddick, V., *Land Tenure in Basutoland*, 1954; Marojele, C. M. H., 1960, *Agricultural Census Basutoland* in seven detailed volumes; Chicago University Survey, 1963 (unpublished).

[2] Hailey, op. cit., p. 145. Moore, op. cit., p. 10. The Morse *Economic Survey Mission*, pp. 242–4. *Constitution Commission Report*, pp. 67–9.

[3] *Report*, p. 67.

[4] Section 85, 2(a).

[5] Land (Advisory Board Procedure) Regulations No. 15 of 1965.

at the beginning and at the end; to Motlotheli Moshoeshoe II for his support in Basutoland; to many Basuto and Basutolanders for sharing their knowledge and experience; to Walter and Mary Stanford; and to Miss Olive Lycett for being the perfect secretary.

I should like to conclude by expressing every good wish to Lesotho that she will enter the latest stage of her history with peace and prosperity.

HUGH ASHTON

BULAWAYO,
25 March 1966.

CHAPTER I

HISTORICAL INTRODUCTION

BASUTOLAND lies more or less in the heart of the Union, and is surrounded by the Provinces of Natal on the east, the Orange Free State on the north and west, and the Cape on the south. It has an area of 11,716 square miles (about that of Belgium), and a population of about 553,827.[1] About two-thirds of the country is mountainous and above 6,000 ft., and is known as the Highlands or *Maluti*. The remaining third is a narrow strip on the west, lying between 5,000 and 6,000 ft., known as the Lowlands or *Lesotho*. The bulk of the population is concentrated in the latter area giving a higher density than anywhere else in rural southern Africa.

The topography is governed by the drainage[2] of the Caledon and Orange rivers which flow to the south-west. The Caledon forms the north-western boundary. Separating one main valley from another are high mountain ranges, attaining an altitude of 10,000 ft., with subsidiary valleys, separated by ridges rising to 8,500–9,000 ft. The highest point so far recorded is Mont-aux-Sources, 10,763 ft., which is also the highest mountain of the Drakensberg range and of the Union of South Africa. The Drakensberg forms the eastern and south-eastern boundaries of Basutoland. The main rains occur between November and March; snow may fall in the mountains at any time of the year and often lies continuously for weeks in winter, and may occasionally fall in the Lowlands between March and December. This and the well-distributed rainfall account for the numerous perennial streams, and also for the absence of serious droughts, although two periods of such drought have been known in one hundred and thirty years. The weather is nevertheless variable enough to cause intermittent and partial crop failures in one part of the country or another, due to late or inopportune rains, and unseasonable or early frosts. The climate is temperate, bracing and healthy.

Basutoland is a British colony. It is administered by the British Government through the Commonwealth Relations office, and is governed by the High Commissioner through the Resident Commissioner, Secretariat, Technical Officers and District Administration.[3]

The first inhabitants of the country, so far as historical times are

---

[1] The 1946 Census figures give 553,827 Basuto in the Territory and 70,778 absent at "labour centres". The 1936 Census figures were 559,273 and 101,273 respectively.

[2] This short description is adapted from Stockley, 1947, who briefly indicates the close relationship between population and geology. See also Sayce, 1924.

[3] For further details see Ashton, 1949.

concerned, were Bushmen.[1] They were never numerous and have now died out as a people, although their blood still flows in the veins of the Basuto,[2] and individual Bushmen may still be found. They have also left their memorial in fine rock paintings scattered about the country, and in the names of several mountains and other geographical features. Boys' initiation rites and the "clicks" which occur in Sesuto are also attributed to them, but the validity of this is questionable.[3]

The first Bantu to enter Basutoland were three Nguni groups,[4] who crossed the Drakensberg from the east in three waves and settled south of the Caledon river. They were the Phetla (the "pioneers"), the Polane and the Phuthi. Some years later they were joined by the "First Basuto" who were the Peli, Phuthing, Sia and Tlokoa. They were followed by other clans or tribes, of whom the most important were the Fokeng, Koena and Taung. The Tlokoa were at one time the most powerful military group, particularly in the days of the famous "Queen" Mantatisi and her son Sekonyela, but they have long lost this ascendancy and are now mainly of interest as the last repository of the old Sesuto culture. The other tribes are still important, and practically all the principal chiefs to-day belong to the Koena, and many are related on the maternal side to the Fokeng.

All these groups were scattered and more or less independent of one another. For the most part they lived at peace with one another, disturbed only by intermittent cattle raids, punitive expeditions and internal intrigues. This relatively peaceful existence was rudely and irretrievably shattered early in the nineteenth century. Chaka, a young Zulu, fired by the value of proper military discipline, perfected the organization of his impis, and spread war and destruction far and wide. Neighbouring tribes fled before him and burst across the Drakensberg with his regiments in pursuit, ravaging and plundering. The Tlokoa bore the brunt of the first invasions, but eventually they broke under

---

[1] Ellenberger and MacGregor, 1912
[2] Intermarriage with groups such as the Fokeng and Phetla is mentioned: Ibid., pp. xxi, 11, 18, 21, 56.
[3] In spite of references to Bushmen which occur in some of the initiation songs, I doubt whether these rites were derived from them, for it is difficult to see how so important an institution could have been taken over by the Basuto from a people whom they regard as being of very low standing, and how the Bushmen should have given them an institution whose details differ so greatly from those of their own. (See Schapera, 1930, for a description of Bushmen initiation rites.) Similarly, with regard to the adoption of the "click", it remains to be explained why they should have adopted only this "click" from the latter's many "clicks", the more so that the Tswana who have been in longer and closer contact with the Bushmen have no "clicks". That many of the words with a "click" also appear in Zulu suggests rather that they may have originated from Nguni elements incorporated into the Basuto. See Lestrade, G. P. Introductory article on the South Basotho in *The Bantu Tribes of S. Africa*, 1933, vol. iii, sect. iii, pp. 66-7.
[4] Ibid., pp. 31-52.

the strain and plunged southward. Fighting became general, whole tribes were broken, fields were destroyed or left uncultivated, famines broke out and some of the people became cannibals. Eventually a young Koena chief, Moshesh, one of the most brilliant native statesmen of Africa, gathered round him the remnants of former tribes at Butha Buthe, where he fortified the Butha Buthe Mountain and held it against the Tlokoa for some time, until he withdrew and went to Thaba Bosiu. With the impregnable mountain fortress of Thaba Bosiu as his base, he moulded the remnants of the tribes into a fighting unit and slowly beat back the invaders. In 1831 the last of them was repulsed. Within a few years Moshesh became the acknowledged leader of the Basuto, except for the Tlokoa to the west of him, who remained completely independent, and the Phuthi and Taung in the south who were more or less autonomous.

As soon as the Nguni menace had passed, Moshesh set about restoring the peace and prosperity of his people. He also foresaw new difficulties and dangers from the south, where there were strange stirrings among the Whites. So, hearing of the great services rendered by missionaries to tribes in Bechuanaland, he determined to get similar help for his people and gave his informant, Adam Krotz, 100 head of cattle to "procure in exchange, a man of prayer".[1] Three missionaries of the Paris Evangelical Missionary Society, Messrs. Arbousset, Casalis and Gosselin, lately arrived from France, responded to the appeal and, after a long trek by ox wagon, arrived at Thaba Bosiu in June 1833. They were warmly welcomed by Moshesh and a few days later founded the first mission station at Morija. Thus was started a new relationship for the Basuto which has been of incalculable importance to them. The missionaries have stood by them through all the critical times of the last hundred years and have profoundly influenced their ways of life.

About the same time as the missionaries arrived, bands of other Europeans began to pass through the country. This is how they were described in early folk-tales: "The people of this tale are light-coloured people, with hair like hair on a cob of maize. They eat meat with big needles; they eat stooping down. They have a white hut; you may see it from afar. It is drawn by oxen with their tails. There are many goods in it. Their huts are very large huts, full of goods; their pots are of iron; they have much brass and lots of beads."[2] At first they came in their tented wagons as hunters and traders, travelling light and returning to their homes in Cape Colony. Later they began to come with their families and still were granted the usual rights of travellers—grazing and land for temporary cultivation. But it soon became apparent that they were not mere birds of passage and that they intended to settle. With different ideas of land tenure, different political loyalties and different

[1] Casalis, 1861, p. 9.   [2] Jacottet, 1909, p. 62

racial origin, it was obvious that trouble lay ahead between them and the Basuto.

Moshesh was convinced that the only hope of "existence and independence" for his people lay in the protective support of the British Sovereign, so he tried to gain British protection. He experienced heartbreaking setbacks—protection was granted in 1848 and withdrawn in 1854—and he had to fight desperately for his country's freedom from the invading Boers, and even had to manufacture his own gunpowder and cast his own cannon. But encouraged by the loyalty and advice of the French missionaries, he struggled on until, in 1868, Basutoland was declared British territory and the Basuto were proclaimed British subjects. The Boers, who were on the point of over-running the whole of the western Lowlands protested vigorously against this interference, but in vain, and the old warrior chief was able to die in 1870 content that his people were "folded in the arms of the Queen".[1]

Before he died, Moshesh also succeeded in consolidating his own people and ridding himself of the Tlokoa. Under the madly warlike Sekonyela, the latter heeded neither the preachings of their Wesleyan missionary nor the signs of the times and persisted in raiding Moshesh's country, allying themselves with anyone likely to be of use, whether British, Boers, Bastards or rebel Basuto. After several abortive efforts, Moshesh attacked them in 1853 with overwhelming force and after a ferocious battle captured their fortress at Joala Boholo. The tribe was shattered; some of the people stayed where they were and joined Moshesh, some went to Natal and the rest, under Sekonyela, fled south, after "proudly declining a liberal offer of land from Moshesh on the sole condition of fealty".[2] Sekonyela settled in the Cape Colony, where he died two years later. The tribe then moved to Mount Fletcher, a secluded corner below the Drakensberg, where they remained quietly until 1880. In that year, under Sekonyela's grandson, Lelingoana, they joined in the revolt against the Cape Government's proposed disarmament of all native tribes, crossed into Basutoland and assisted Moshesh's successor, Letsie I, in his war against the Cape Government. On the cessation of hostilities they were rewarded for their services by being given an area in the bleak and hitherto unoccupied Maluti Highlands, where they have lived in peace and prosperity ever since, except for their recent struggle to maintain their tribal integrity, which will be discussed in due course.

For the Basuto generally, the period following British protection was one of unrest and gradual unification, followed by growing contact with European civilization. In 1871, without proper consultation, Basutoland was annexed to the Cape and a small British administration was established. A magistrate was appointed to each of the three districts into which Moshesh had divided Basutoland under his sons,

[1] Lagden, 1909, p. 462.   [2] Ibid., p. 170.

HISTORICAL INTRODUCTION

Letsie, Molapo and Masupha. Their unsuccessful attempts at direct rule created considerable dissatisfaction which flared up into the Gun War of 1880-3, when the Cape Government tried to disarm the people. Peace was established in 1883 when the Basuto humbly petitioned that British protection should not be removed and the chiefs tactfully promised to obey the Government. Their petition was granted: Basutoland was detached from the Cape and placed under direct Imperial control. A new administration was set up and the High Commissioner was empowered to make such laws as were necessary "for the peace, order and good government" of the territory.

A repetition of past occurrences was not to be risked and the new Governor's Agent was instructed that "nothing more could be attempted at first than the protection of life and property and the maintenance of order on the Border", and that "the Basuto were to be encouraged to establish internal self-government sufficient to suppress crimes and settle inter-tribal disputes".[1] These instructions for long remained the keynote of the Administration which initially comprised only two British officials. The three divisions made by Moshesh were retained at first, but as this tended to promote quarrels, intrigues and armed disturbances, Letsie I, Moshesh's senior son, was encouraged to regain his father's pre-eminence. Lerotholi succeeded him in 1893; he was a stronger character and in 1898, with the Government's continual moral support, he defeated the last of the recalcitrant Sons of Moshesh (as Moshesh's descendants were coming to be called) and enjoyed "for the first time undisputed supremacy".[2] Since then he and his successors have been regarded as Paramount Chief of Basutoland, and as the head and representative of the Basuto people. The nature of this supremacy and the ways in which it operates and is maintained will be discussed in subsequent chapters.

With the assertion of the paramountcy of the principal House of Moshesh went the unification of the Basuto which Moshesh had with difficulty initiated through an astute combination of tact, cunning benevolence and force, and which had threatened to break down during the rivalries of his descendants. The Basuto did not intervene in the Boer War (1899-1902) in any militant way, although they helped the British forces with medical supplies, horses and military intelligence. They were, however, torn between their loyalty to the Queen and their fear of reprisals by the Boers should the British be defeated and withdraw, as had happened in the past—as recently as 1881 after Majuba—and as the initial Boer victories indicated might happen again. Lerotholi remained steadfastly loyal, but many of his people opposed him and one strong chief openly allied himself with the Boers. However, this was but a temporary setback and thereafter their loyalty and

---

[1] Lagden, p. 560.   [2] Ibid., p. 597.

unity were not seriously jeopardized. In 1903 a National Council was formed, consisting mainly of chiefs, to deal with national affairs in consultation with the Government. This was the culmination of a project which had been conceived twenty years before and which was given statutory recognition four years later. The extension of the railway in 1906 to Maseru, the capital, was strenuously resisted by the younger chiefs as a potential threat to the country's independence.

In 1908 the projected unification of the four South African colonies revived these fears and caused the Basuto to ponder on their own future. On the publication of the schedule to the draft Act of Union, providing for the transfer to the Union of any native territory at some future date, they became alarmed lest their land and institutions were thereby threatened. A deputation of chiefs, therefore, went to England in 1909 and petitioned the King that in the event of Union "Basutoland may not be included in such union but may remain outside it, as far as possible, independent as it is now", but that should their inclusion become inevitable, their position might be suitably safeguarded. In reply, the deputation was informed that it might "assure the Paramount Chief and the Basuto people that it is the purpose of His Majesty and of His Majesty's Government, who are his advisers, that they should continue in the enjoyment of those privileges which they have hitherto possessed".[1]

Since then the political history of Basutoland has been quiet and uneventful. In the 1914–18 war "the Basuto displayed marked loyalty"[2] and several thousand men volunteered for service with the South African Labour Corps. A last flare up of the old internecine feuds occurred in 1915 when Jonathan, son of Molapo Moshesh, and a powerful chief in charge of northern Basutoland, created a disturbance and was fined in open court 4,000 head of cattle, and ordered to pay compensation for the damage he had caused. The Paramount Chieftainship and the chieftainship system as a whole waxed even stronger until it threatened to become less an instrument of government than a means of personal aggrandisement and of despotism. Attempts at reform were made in 1926 and 1927, and were strongly opposed by the chiefs themselves in the National Council. After the publication of the Pim Report in 1935, which clearly showed how closely the political organization affected the economic development and welfare of the country, these attempts were renewed and led to the successful promulgation of the Native Administration and Courts Proclamations, Nos. 61 and 62 of 1938. At the same time considerable sums were spent from the Colonial Development and Welfare Fund on economic rehabilitation and development, especially on anti-soil erosion work and the improvement of agriculture and animal husbandry. The outbreak of war in 1939 checked further develop-

---

[1] Lagden, p. 624.   [2] Pim, 1935, p. 22.

ment. Thousands of Basuto enlisted[1] and saw active service in North Africa, the Middle East and Italy, many being drafted as combatants to British fighting units. After their demobilization in 1946, a further batch enlisted for garrison duty in Egypt and the Middle East, and finally returned to Basutoland in 1949.

The Paramount Chief Seeiso died in 1940 and was succeeded by his widow 'Mantsebo, who became regent for his infant son and the first woman to be head of the Basuto nation. Her succession was challenged in court in 1943 by Bereng, Seeiso's junior brother. The judgment went against him and was accepted with resentment which simmered until his conviction and execution in 1949 for "ritual murder".

Towards the end of the war, several political changes took place. Elected District Councils were established in 1944 (introducing a completely new element into Basuto life), and the basis of the Basutoland National Council was widened. In 1946, the number of native courts was drastically reduced from over 1,300 to 121 and other fundamental innovations were introduced through the separation of the chiefs' judicial and administrative functions. That same year a National Treasury was established which introduced yet another fundamental change by virtually turning the chiefs into salaried public officials; two years later the modified Basutoland Council and the District Councils were given statutory recognition.

All these changes, combined with the unsettling effects of the war and of the bitter disputes over the Paramount Chief's succession, have had disturbing effects on the people and their leaders. There have been no open conflicts and the tumultuous reception given to the Royal Family during their visit to Basutoland on Moshesh's Day, 1947, demonstrated their continued loyalty to the British connection. The discord seems to have introverted and encouraged a return to their traditional beliefs and customs. One manifestation of this is the shocking outbreak of ritual murder (at least fifty cases have been perpetrated and revealed between 1944 and 1948), that has cast a shadow over the fair name of Basutoland, hitherto regarded as the most enlightened and progressive African country in the southern continent.

Apart from the political influences just described, the main impact on the Basuto has been that of the missions and of European trade and industry. The first brought a new religion and a revolutionary form of education to the Basuto, and the latter profoundly altered their traditional economy, widened their horizons and opened up still further spheres of European contact.

The French mission rapidly grew from the single station founded

[1] 21,462 Basuto enlisted in the African Pioneer Corps and approximately 2,500 in the Native Military Corps. The former was part of the British Forces, the latter a branch of the Union Defence Force.

among a nation of heathens. In fifty years, despite destruction caused by the incessant wars with the Dutch in which it suffered with the Basuto, it blossomed into 81 stations, with 86 Basuto evangelists, 5,000 adherents and 42 schools.[1] It was joined in 1864 by the Roman Catholics[2] and in 1875[2] by the Anglican Church, which had already been working among the Basuto from a nearby mission station for some years. In 1936, 45 per cent of the population was recorded[3] as being Christian. Each of these missions has its own schools, subsidized by the Government, and they have done great work in creating a literate people. The French mission has been specially responsible for the excellent Sesuto literature which has been produced, and has also greatly contributed to their material development by introducing new agricultural methods and new crops, such as wheat and fruit trees. Its early missionaries, unfortunately, were strict Calvinists who tried to abolish, as un-Christian, many Basuto customs, not only among their converts by example and precept, but also among the people generally by proclaimed law—and so, incidentally, helped to precipitate the 1880 revolt which in other ways they had valiantly sought to prevent. Their successors, realizing that much of this antithesis between Basuto custom and Christianity was artificial and shallow, have pursued a more tolerant policy. But irreparable damage has been done to much of the old Sesuto culture. Apart from this, the balance is all on the credit side, and what the Resident Commissioner said during their 1908 jubilee celebrations is still true to-day: "If one influence more than another had helped the Basuto it was the missionary influence which began seventy-five years ago."[4] The Paris mission, which is now known as the *Kereke ea Lesotho* (the Basutoland Church), still leads the way, but it has been crippled financially by the Second World War and the Roman Catholics who are very much wealthier have recently rapidly come to the fore.

Economic contact with Europeans dates back to the early days when a trader established himself at Morija and began to exchange goods of European manufacture against Basuto produce. At much the same time the Basuto began to take their wheat, maize and cattle to the Cape Colony, bringing home in exchange, guns, improved livestock and ordinary trade goods. When the diamond fields opened at Kimberley in 1870, they provided transport, produce and labour. Since the discovery of gold in 1886 they have gone to the Rand in their thousands (over 30,000 were away from the country in 1893, 78,000 in 1908,[5] and 35,138 in 1947[6]). Their production has increased vastly as the

---

[1] Lagden, p. 636. [2] Ibid., p. 638. [3] Basutoland Census, p. 27.
[4] Ibid., p. 638. [5] Lagden, pp. 580 and 642.
[6] Annual Report. The drop from 78,000 in 1908 to 35,138 in 1947 is due partly to changed methods in computing the returns of passes issued and partly to the longer absences the Basuto now indulge in.

result of improved methods of agriculture and animal husbandry. The volume of trade has also grown enormously, as is reflected by the number of stores which rose from six in 1868 to about two hundred in 1938, and also by the revenue which increased from £97,000 in 1904-5 to £350,000 in 1936-7 and £908,457 in 1948-9. Local production has not kept pace with the people's demand for imported goods and, as is shown later, they largely depend on their earnings as labourers in South African mines and industries.

These economic factors have had far-reaching effects on Sesuto culture. They have profoundly altered its material aspect and have facilitated social changes by forcing men and women to work in a European environment where they have come in contact with new ideas and ways of life. Some of them, dissatisfied with, and intolerant of, their old customs which appear backward and uncivilized, may become impatient of tribal authority and domestic discipline. At the same time, others react against excessive European influence and encourage the revival of old traditions and the readoption of old customs.

CHAPTER II

SOCIAL BACKGROUND

There are four principal social groups to which the Basuto normally belong: the nation, the clan, the village and the family. There are other groups to which the Basuto may also belong, such as the church, school and various associations, but membership of these is voluntary and terminable at any time, whereas membership of the former is a permanent and essential feature of a Mosuto's life.

The Nation

The nation[1] is essentially a political group and is composed of all who acknowledge the authority of the Paramount Chief. It includes everyone living in Basutoland, for such domicile automatically implies political adherence, as well as Basuto living outside the territory who pay Basutoland taxes.

Children automatically acquire their father's nationality. Others may acquire it through admission into the country, the formal grant of a residential site and payment of local taxes. It may be lost through residence elsewhere combined with failure to pay local taxes. Many Basuto live for years in the Union of South Africa, but, by paying their dues at home and keeping in occasional touch with their chief, maintain their status and are assured of being received when they eventually return and of being given lands and other political rights.

The nation is not an ethnic group, for not all nationals are Basuto, and not all Basuto are nationals. The nation includes both true Basuto and members of other tribes. The true Basuto are those who have always been Basuto, that is, for as far back as their own traditions go. They believe they are all of common stock,[2] and though this is possible, it cannot be proved. Their genealogies reach back only three or four generations and, except in the case of chiefs, cannot be linked to the genealogies recorded by Ellenberger and MacGregor, which extend further back than living memory now goes. The historical accuracy of the belief is only of academic interest, but it is sociologically significant in that it creates a feeling of unity. This feeling is further fostered by the claim that all true Basuto originated from the same place, namely, a reed bed at Ntsuanatsatsi, where the first man emerged. This legend, which is almost universally held, has many variations and is

---

[1] This term may sound pretentious when applied to so small a group, but it is commonly used in Basutoland itself. It is also convenient and has, therefore, been retained.

[2] N. J. van Warmelo "Grouping and Ethnic History" in *Bantu-Speaking Peoples*, Schapera, 1937, pp. 58–60.

sometimes combined with Biblical stories of the creation or with appropriate incidents from the Old Testament, such as that the Basuto are descended from a group of people who hid in the rushes on the River Nile when the Israelites were leaving Egypt.

Those who were not originally Basuto belong to two main groups. One group is that of the Natal Nguni which includes the Phetla, Polane and Phuthi, mentioned earlier, and other small groups. The latter, collectively called *Matebele* by the Basuto and Zulus by Europeans, are scattered throughout the country, with concentrations among the Tlokoa with whom they mingled at the beginning of the nineteenth century, and in the Leribe and Butha Buthe districts where they were stranded before and during Chaka's wars. They have now become more or less completely absorbed and are practically indistinguishable from Basuto. Ordinarily little reference is made to their origin, which they usually try to hide. Most of them are inferior in status to true Basuto and are often to be found occupying menial positions, though a few reach high social and political positions.

The second group consists of other Natal Nguni, such as the Mahlape at Butha Buthe, and of Cape Nguni, such as Fingoes, Pondoes and Thembu, collectively called *Bathepu*. They have maintained their own cultural identity and language and are regarded as "Basuto" solely in virtue of their political attachment. The true Basuto have little to do with them socially and treat them with even more contempt than they do the *Matebele*. The *Bathepu* also include a group of true Basuto—Voova's Bafokeng—who at one time left Basutoland and mixed intimately with Thembus in the Cape Colony many years ago and absorbed the Thembu culture. They have since returned to Basutoland and are living in the Quthing district.[1]

Excluded from the Basuto nation are many Basuto living outside Basutoland in neighbouring parts of the Union of South Africa. They have the same common culture and speak the same language as the Basuto but are not regarded as belonging to the nation on account of their political independence.

The boundaries of Basutoland are defined for the most part by clear natural features and are politically significant in that they should not be crossed without special formalities. Within this "enisled seclusion"[2] the Basuto are subject to legal, political and economic institutions which differ from those existing in the Union of South Africa. Their attachment to their own form of government and their loyalty to their British connection lead them to dislike the thought of their country being transferred to the Union of South Africa, and help to foster the feeling of national unity.

Their national unity is based on a common history and culture. Their language is remarkably uniform and there are only a few minor

[1] See Ellenberger and MacGregor, p. 19.   [2] L. Barnes, *The New Boer War*.

dialectal differences. The smallness and compactness of the country facilitates continual movement of people, visiting friends and relations or going about on business, and this movement helps to break down inter-tribal prejudices and creates a feeling of unity. This is reflected in the tendency, referred to above, to claim that they all originated at Ntsuanatsatsi. They also call themselves *"Bakoena"*—a ceremonial form of address used in public meetings and vernacular newspapers as well as in every-day greetings, which implies a common kinship through fictitious adherence to the Paramount Chief's clan, the *BaKoena*. The emblem of this clan, the crocodile, has become the national emblem. Another verbal link of the same kind is the term *Basotho ba ha Moshoeshoe* —Moshesh's Basuto—by which they are known to other South African tribes.

The political unity of the nation is expressed in a centralized organization under the Paramount Chief. He is its representative, the head of the local judicial and political systems, and the trustee for the land and other natural resources of the country. The fact that geographically the British Administration coincides with his authority reinforces this unity.

Nevertheless, the nation is culturally and administratively divided. One division includes clans, families and villages; the other comprises districts, sub-districts and wards, and will be described in Chapter XII.

The Clan

All Basuto are divided into clans.[1] These are primarily social groupings or affiliations distinguishable by name and also sometimes by totem and other cultural features The most common clans to be found at present in Basutoland are the Fokeng, Hlakoana, Khoakhoa, Phuthing, Tlokoa, Sia, Taung, Tloung, Kholokoe, Phetla, Polane and Phuthi. Some of these have subdivisions, distinguished by the name of one of their early leaders, e.g. Ba-Taung ba Moletsane, found in the Mafeteng district, Ba-Taung ba Molete and Ba-Taung ba Motesaoana found among the Tlokoa, and the Ba-Koena ba Monaheng and Ba-Koena ba Molibehi.[2]

The clan name (*seboko*) in some cases is that of its founder, e.g. the Sia were founded by Mosia and the Hlakoana by Mohkaloana. In other

---

[1] Many people, including Ellenberger, MacGregor and Casalis, speak of tribes and /or clans indiscriminately. Both terms are unsatisfactory as each has special anthropological connotations which the Sesuto groups do not always possess; e.g. some of them are kinship groups, real or fictitious, some are political units and become identical with the tribe; others again have no political significance whatever. For convenience, I shall use the word "clan" when describing social groupings and the word "tribe" only when describing pre-eminently political units. But attention should be paid less to terms than to descriptions, for the nature of these groups lies in their effect on social behaviour and this is too fluid to be expressed in a single word.

[2] Ellenberger and MacGregor, pp. 54–86.

SOCIAL BACKGROUND

cases it is derived from an incident connected with the clan's establishment. For instance,[1] a group of Khatla broke away from the main clan and shortly after came upon a land teeming with duiker (*phuthi*) and thereupon called themselves MaPhuthing. In other cases again, it is taken from the clan emblem (also *seboko*), for example, the BaFokeng, whose emblem is the dew (*foka*).

Most clans have their own emblems, commonly called totems. That of the Tlokoa is the wild cat (*qoabi*), of the Phuthing and the Phuthi the duiker (*phuthi*), of the BaKoena the crocodile (*koena*). Some clans have more than one, the totems of the Fokeng are the dew (*foka*), the wild vine (*morara*) and the hare (*'mutla*). In several cases, such as the Taung and Koena, the totem is the same as the clan name, but no particular significance is attached to this, and whatever the position may once have been, no Mosuto now believes in a genetic relationship between the totemic animal and the clan. Arbousset records a belief that when they came out of the marsh at Ntsuanatsatsi, each "tribe" received a different animal as an emblem which would be for it a god-protector,[2] but he does not say what this really meant and its significance and the belief itself are now lost. The reasons for the adoption of a particular totem are obscure in many cases, but in a few it was connected with some historical event. For instance, the Tlokoa adopted the wild cat as a mark of respect and friendship for the Sia, whose emblem it was, and with whom their chiefs intermarried.[3] Another example is that of the Phuthi, given above.

According to earlier authorities, these totems were regarded as sacred. "Their stock bear its mark as a sign of protection. They put it on their shields, on their domestic utensils, on their skin mantles; they swear by these animals, and by them they conjure evil spirits. If any one ate such an animal during famine he was looked upon as sacrilegious and worthy of punishment by the gods."[4] The Koena considered themselves under the protection of the crocodile, calling it their father a'd swearing by it.[5] These "emblems—whether metals, trees, animals or insects —symbolize a mysterious being, a god, all the more to be feared because he was a *molimo*, that is an invisible being".[6] "The Bafokeng of Mangole did not mind taking advantage of the shade of the vine, but they never touched its fruit, and still less would they use its wood. On the contrary, if some stranger did use it as fuel, they feared to use even the embers to light their own fires, but would religiously collect the ashes, placing them on their temples and foreheads in sign of sorrow."[7]

[1] Ibid., p. 34. See also pp. 12, 19 *et seq.* and Laydevant, 1931, pp. 209-12.
[2] *Journal des Missions*, 1844, p. 474. "Tribe" here clearly refers to "clan".
[3] Ellenberger and MacGregor, pp. 33 and 34.
[4] *Journal des Missions*, 1844, pp. 474.
[5] Ellenberger and MacGregor, p. 241.
[6] Ibid., p. xx.
[7] Arbousset, *Relation d'un Voyage d'Exploration*, p. 212, quoted by Ellenberger and MacGregor.

"Other Bafokeng who venerated the hare would, when they caught one, assemble in the village court, and then, beginning with the chief, they would each in turn bite the end of the animal's ears; then they rubbed their foreheads with the carcase, as if by that means they could be endowed with all the virtues and material benefits which their *seboko* was able to grant."[1] The totems are said to have been held in great regard. The people used to "honour and venerate them, they sang and danced in their honour, they glorified, praised and swore by them".[2] Unfortunately, we are not given any details of their "virtues and material benefits", nor any further account of the beliefs attaching to the totems or the degree of veneration in which they were really held. Nowadays the totems have little significance; most of these old observances have died out and the few that remain are unimportant. Clansmen are still not supposed to hunt, kill or eat their totemic animals; but, as animals are practically extinct in Basutoland, this taboo means very little, although the Tlokoa still punctiliously brush their eyes with the fur of a wild cat they may chance to see, lest they be blinded. Cattle are earmarked with a mark called *koena*, a zigzag cut resembling crocodile teeth, but this is no longer confined to members of the Koena clan. The totem name is still occasionally used to strengthen an oath, and in a few praise-songs of a non-religious character. It is also used as a formal term of address.

Several clans have ceremonial and minor cultural differences. Thus small variations are to be found in the treatment of pregnant women, in the decorations (colours and shapes of beads) worn by infants, in certain phases of initiation[3], marriage and mortuary ritual. Some clans, such as the Taung ba Moletsane and the Tlokoa have minor differences of vocabulary, grammar and pronunciation, and the Phuthi still speak a distinct dialect of their own.

The status of various clans also differs. Ordinarily pride of place is given to the politically dominant Koena, the clan of the Paramount Chief, but strictly speaking, the Fokeng is senior. The Tlokoa, in their own area, do not recognize this and claim to be superior. In practice the question of seniority seldom arises, and when it does as, for example, at initiation, it has to be settled by amicable agreement. The position is very confused and I have never seen a list of clans in order of seniority which meets with general approval.

Membership of the clan is determined by birth and is theoretically acquired only through the father. But there are exceptions. For instance, illegitimate children belong to their mother's clan, unless they are acknowledged by their father. So, too, children deserted by their father and brought up by their mother's people may become members of her clan, if it is advantageous for them to do so. Laydevant[4] records

[1] Ellenberger and MacGregor, p. 244. [2] Ibid., p. 241.
[3] See also Sekese, 1931 pp. 20-2. [4] Laydevant, 1931, p. 208.

that people may change their clan to that of the chief, either with his permission on payment of a fee of six or eight head of cattle, or by his order. The reason in the first case is their wish to identify themselves with the dominant clan with whom they are sojourning, and in the second the chief's desire to create a feeling of tribal and political solidarity.

There are two other exceptions. The first is that travellers in a strange area, where few of their own clan live, may pass themselves off as belonging to the same clan as the local inhabitants. They do this to make themselves less conspicuous in the hope of being better received than they would be otherwise and also of avoiding being chosen by the "bones" to be the victims of a ritual murder. The second case occurs where a chief provides his close personal retainer with a wife. The children of such a marriage become full members of their father's clan; at the same time they become partially affiliated to the chief's clan on account of their close connection with him through the marriage cattle, and though they do not take his clan's name, they must respect all taboos and observances connected with the clan.

Fellow-clanspeople may intermarry: such marriages are neither admired nor disliked and there is no obligation[1] either to marry or to avoid marrying a person of the same clan as oneself. Similarly, there is no obligation either to marry or to avoid marrying a person of a different clan. In actual fact most people marry outside their clan. The reason is not that they deliberately choose partners from a clan other than their own, but that their choice is influenced by many factors, and as there are many clans, the chances are considerable that the chosen partner will be of a different clan. Clanship is however relevant where important families are concerned: they should not marry beneath them and therefore should not choose a senior wife from a much inferior clan. So, too, there should be no intermarriage between important members of clans whose forebears have used one another for medicine: for instance, the Tlokoa should not intermarry with Koena descended from Moshesh, as parts of a Motlokoa, killed in battle about 1840, were used in Moshesh's war medicine. Here it is difficult to say whether kinship or clanship is the dominant factor.

Clanship is an attenuated and fictitious form of kinship. Clansmen believe they are descended from a common ancestor, although they cannot prove it. They are supposed to be friendly and helpful to one another and a stranger who is a fellow-clansman should be welcomed and treated better than an outsider. When human flesh is needed for a chief's *lenaka* (see glossary, p. 317), the victim should belong to a different clan from his own—for Koena chiefs, the victim should preferably be a Sia or Fokeng; but in one recent instance, involving an

---

[1] Laydevant, 1931, p. 208, states that clan endogamy is prescribed, but I think he is confusing this with preferential marriage of the father's brother's daughter type (q.v.).

important Koena chief, the victim was said to be a fellow-Mokoena, chosen, presumably, to intensify the medicine's potency.[1]

Sometimes clans are no more than lineages. As the common ancestor is no more than three or four or five generations removed, they have comparatively few members. All the lineages that I came across are of Matebele origin, the ancestor from whom the present people trace their descent having joined the Basuto about a century ago. The earliest of those I found among the Tlokoa joined them about the time of Mokotjo, around 1775. They have their own distinctive names, such as Masako, Lekhomalo, Khala, Koenehatsi, Thutsi and Sekhosana, and many have little peculiarities and taboos, just as proper clans have. I have no data at all about those of Thepu descent.

Sometimes clans and lineages form appreciable territorial groups and certain areas are occupied mainly by members of a clan or lineage. In the Butha Buthe district there are Khoakhoa and Kholokoe; in Leribe, Koena; in Mafeteng, Taung ba Moletsane and Fokeng; in Mohale's Hoek, more Taung ba Moletsane and Phuthi; in Quthing, more Phuthi and Voova's Fokeng; in Maseru, Fokeng, Koena and Tlokoa; in Mokhotlong, Tlokoa, who have pockets of Taung, Tloung, Phuthing, Sia, Koena, Fokeng and lineages such as those just described. In all these areas, the predominant clan is mixed with male members of other clans (they naturally have many females of other clans brought in by marriage), but the smaller the group, the purer it is. Sometimes the head of the group has some political authority as headman or subchief and, in such cases, the clan or lineage acquires some of the attributes of a political group: the land is said to belong to it and that area may even be given the clan or lineage name.

Formerly, many clans were large enough political units to merit the term tribe. Most of them have been broken up, but four remain: the Tlokoa, Khoakhoa, Taung ba Moletsane and Phuthi—and the last two of these are fast disintegrating. The composition of these earlier tribal groups is not clear. They may have been homogeneous clans, which had grown powerful enough to maintain their independence, and Ellenberger and MacGregor often give the impression that this was the case. But it is also possible that they consisted of heterogeneous units who adopted the name of the dominant or nuclear clan, though they were actually composed of different clans, and this I think was the nature of many of the tribes. Ellenberger and MacGregor frequently refer to "clans" breaking off from the principal groups and joining up with other tribes. For instance, "many strangers and masterless men joined

---

[1] This is so unusual that I should have liked to check the accuracy of the report (Rex v. Pitso Ramatlali, etc., No. 253-45). More consistent with the conventional belief, is the rumour of an undetected murder in Mokhotlong in 1945, where the victim was discovered, too late, to be a Mokoena and so could not be used, as the person for whom medicine was being made was also a Mokoena.

Ratsebe (chief of the Phuthing), including a whole clan of Bahlakoana who, living near, became entirely absorbed by marriage and other means".[1] Laydevant's record of people being forced by their chief to change their totem indicates that in some tribes members belonged to different clans. But whatever was the constitution of the old tribes, that of the few which exist to-day is distinctly heterogeneous and closely similar to that of the Tswana tribes.[2] The Tlokoa may be taken as an example as I have more data about them than about others, and they have remained the best organized tribe in the country.

The true Tlokoa comprise a nucleus of three clans: the Ba-Tsotetsi or Ba-Mokhalong, the Ba-Lefe and a group who just call themselves Tlokoa. (They are probably Malakeng,[3] but I did not meet this term.) The Ba-Tsotetsi are genealogically the senior group, but political authority has passed from them to the junior branch, the Ba-Lefe. The head of the Ba-Lefe is chief of the tribe. Incorporated with them to form the Tlokoa tribe are clans, such as the Taung, Tloung, Phuthing, Sia, Koena and Fokeng, and Tebele lineages such as those described earlier, plus a few Thepu. All these clans and lineages, whether of Sesuto or Nguni origin, regard themselves as Tlokoa and call themselves *Batlokoa*: they distinguish themselves as a group from other Basuto, and dub the latter *Bakhalahali*. As a tribe, they share various cultural peculiarities, they all speak the Tlokoa dialect and clansmen are not obliged to live in any particular clan area. At the same time, each of these clans, including the Ba-Lefe and Ba-Tsotetsi, has an individuality of its own and maintains its own characteristics within the tribal framework; some of them live as fairly distinct groups within the tribal area and have defined villages or wards of their own.

It is difficult to estimate the significance of clan affiliation to the Basuto. It is unobtrusive and enters subtly into many types of relationship and many situations, and though often taken for granted, is a factor to which they attach importance.

Family and Kinship

The family is less clearly defined than the clan, but more important. It does not consist of a particular or limited group, but shades away from the nucleus of parents and children to indefinite and obscure individual kinsmen. It is less a group than a complicated and ever-widening tangle of relationships, involving specific attitudes and obligations towards people with whom one is connected by blood and marriage. The range of effective relationships fluctuates according to circumstances—contracts during everyday life and widens during crises. It also varies with individuals; a rich or important man recog-

[1] Ellenberger and MacGregor, p. 36. See also pp. 69 and 70.
[2] I. Schapera, *Handbook of Tswana Law and Custom*. Oxford, 1938.
[3] Ellenberger and MacGregor, p. 40.

nizes more distant kinsmen than a poor obscure man. The relationships also differ in kind. Some are clear, formal and specific, and involve reciprocal obligations, rights and attitudes between particular kinsmen on particular occasions or in particular situations; others are less formal and relate to what might be called "family" affairs, which affect and require co-operation between relatives in general rather than with any particular sets or types of relations; others again do not necessarily concern kinsmen—they affect "anyone", but in many cases, although the criterion is friendship, the friends are found to be kinsmen. All in all, kinship is a powerful and persuasive factor that enters into almost every social situation in a Mosuto's life.

The basic family group is the biological family of parents and children. This widens out to include parents' parents and children's children, together with the brothers and sisters of all these individuals and their wives and children in ever-widening circles. One's close kinsmen are known as "*ba heso*" (the people of our place). They form what is primarily a patrilineal group, composed loosely of one's parents, paternal grandparents, paternal uncles and their wives and children. One is usually brought up amongst these people, lives and works with them, assists them in ceremonies and domestic and agricultural activities, is helped by them to marry and bring up one's own children. For a woman this connexion with her own people is weakened by marriage, for she has then to go to her husband's village and identify herself with his people; but it should not be entirely severed and in case of trouble with her husband and his people, a woman seeks refuge and help among her own.

Relationship within the paternal group should be one of friendship, coloured with respect and obedience to the older generation. Nevertheless, there is a danger that claims and counter-claims to property and other rights, the closeness of the relationship and physical propinquity, will create rivalry and friction between members of the group which may erupt into quarrels and illnesses attributed to sorcery. Peace may be restored after the protagonists have blown off steam in family discussion or in legal proceedings, but sometimes mutual antagonisms are so strong that they break up the village. The avoidance of such conflict, which is almost inevitable where the issues are greater, is the main reason for separating chiefs and their senior sons and placing the latter in their own villages. This also induces some clans, such as the Fokeng and Tlokoa, to favour smaller villages where kinsmen can be more or less on their own.

Relationship with the distaff side of the family should be one of good feeling and friendship. There are a few enjoined obligations between them, such as that the maternal uncle should provide his nephew or niece with food and clothing at initiation and should help at his or her marriage. Reciprocally, he should be given some of his nephew's first earnings or findings (such as wild honey) and one or more of his niece's marriage cattle, and should ultimately inherit his nephew's intimate personal property, provided in each case that he had previously fulfilled his obligations to them. In general, one is expected to be friendly and helpful to one's maternal kinsmen and to keep on close, intimate terms with them, and this expectation is often realized. Children are sometimes brought up by their maternal relatives—mother's parents or brother—and are always encouraged to visit them regularly, especially when they return home after an absence, such as at school or work, and they should always be able to count on a warm welcome. This general characteristic of friendliness applies to all one's mother's relations (reckoned patrilineally from herself) and extends to her brothers' children, i.e. one's cross-cousins, and to their children and other members of her "home group".

Both these types of kinship are with blood relations. A third type is with one's in-laws. This bond is not as strong as the others and is more tinged with formality and restraint which are most marked between a man or woman and his or her parents-in-law. A woman should not call her father-in-law or her son-in-law by his name or use it in conversation, and should even avoid using words associated with it; she should not touch his clothing or uncover her body in his presence. A man should visit his parents-in-law occasionally and take his mother-in-law a formal present; he will be well received and honourably treated, but he should not stay long with them lest they get "accustomed to him and cease to respect him". Moreover, the formality and restraint that have to be observed are irksome and should not be prolonged.

Between in-laws of the same generation relations should be friendly. Between a man and his wife's younger sisters, who are potential wives, considerable freedom of behaviour short of sexual intimacy is permitted. Brothers-in-law are a little more formal with one another than with ordinary friends, and salacious topics and jokes should be excluded from their conversation. Parents of married couples are expected to be friends and should keep on good, though not intimate, terms.

The strongest of these three types of kinship ties is between patrilineal kinsmen and the weakest between in-laws. This is reflected in people's genealogical interests and in the suppression of the weaker relationships where these conflict with the others. Generally speaking people know most about their paternal relations and ancestors, and least about their in-laws. Chiefs and other family-proud people can trace their patrilineal ancestors for six generations, whereas on the mother's side they usually fall short of this by at least two generations, and in each case they can trace the male line further than the female. Similarly with their in-laws' ancestry although, by reason of their closer association, a woman usually knows more about her husband's ancestry than he does about hers.

Conflict between different relationships or prescribed patterns of behaviour occurs in cases of intermarriage between kinsmen. Here the new in-law relationship conflicts with the previous cognatic one. For instance, when a man marries his mother's brother's daughter, the intimate friendliness that previously subsisted between him and his maternal uncle should now be modified by the formality due to his father-in-law; the change is even greater for the woman. The Basuto do not carry the change to its logical conclusion, but adopt a sensible practical attitude towards the whole situation, and avoid or ignore awkward points that may arise. Those primarily affected by the marriage, namely, the couple and their parents, should observe the in-law relationship between themselves, but where others are concerned, this rather irksome relationship may be suppressed in favour of the freer and friendlier one that existed before. The same applies when kinship conflicts with status and age. For instance, a boy of five correctly calls his elder brother aged sixty *aubuti* (brother), but the latter answers *ngoanaka* (my child); the boy also calls his elder brother's child (aged twenty) *aubuti* instead of the correct term for brother's child, *ngoanake*. Again, when a man marries as a junior wife his senior wife's brother's daughter, the former continues to call the latter "aunt" (*rakhali*) instead of *mohalitsong* (co-wife) and to call the former's children who are roughly of the same age as herself, "cousin" (*motsoala*), rather than "child" (*ngoanake*), although they correctly call her "*mangoane*" (little mother) rather than the reciprocal "*motsoala*": at the same time the children of these women call one another brother and sister instead of by more distant kinship terms. A further inconsistency is occasioned by individual preferences. Some people prefer to stress blood relationship (*tsoalo*—birth), others relationship due to marriage (*ka likhomo*—through cattle). The former will minimize in-law kinship terms and patterns of behaviour whereas the latter will accentuate them.

The Basuto observe the widespread classificatory system of kinship terms and apply the same terms to different classes of kinsmen standing to one in the same general relationship. Thus one's mother's sister is called *mangoane* and the same term is applied to all those whom she calls "sister". A table of terms is given in Appendix II. As already shown, kinship terms are not always used with strict regard to genealogical relationship and are often modified to suit the social situation. An aged and distant patrilineal cousin, for instance, would be called *ntate* (father) out of respect for his age, rather than by the more familiar *ngoaneso* (cousin). This also applies to close kinsmen where their social relationship conflicts somewhat with their actual relationship—for instance, a young orphan brought up by his much older brother called him "father" and his wife "mother" as they had actually been more like father and mother to him than brother and sister. At the same time, the Basuto often distinguish between "real" and classificatory kinsmen by qualifying the relationship in terms of parentage. For instance, one's real father is the "father who begot me" (*ntate ea ntsoetseng*). So, too, ortho-cousins (*ngoaneso*) are distinguished as "child of my father's sister" or "child of my mother's sister".[1]

Kinship terms are also extended to non-kinsmen to express appropriate social relationships and mutual behaviour patterns, similar to those existing between kinsmen properly covered by those terms. Thus a father stands in authority over his son and is entitled to expect obedience and respect from him. This general pattern of behaviour is expected between all older and younger men, and is reflected in the general term of address *ntate* (my father) used by younger to older men and by men who, though older than the man they are addressing, are inferior in status. Other kinship terms similarly used are *'me* (my mother), *ngoanake* (my child), *ngoaneso* (child of our place), *aubuti* (my brother: applied by boys and girls or young men and women to older males of roughly the same generation), *ngoaneso* or *ausi* (my sister: applied by boys and young men to women of roughly the same age and by girls and young women to other slightly older girls or women), *soare* (my brother-in-law: between men of roughly the same age, or by young girls and women to men of the same age—in both cases to express close friendship), *mokhotsi* (reciprocal term between parents of a married couple—used between older men and women of roughly the same age who are on friendly terms).

The Village

Villages vary widely in size. Some consist of no more than one family, others have four or five hundred. The average is between about thirty and fifty families. Small villages are mainly to be found in the Highlands and intrusive river valleys where arable lands are scattered and suitable sites for large settlements rare; large villages in the Lowlands on open plateaux. Clan characteristics may occasionally influence the matter; for instance, the Koena prefer to have large compact villages, whereas the Tlokoa and the Fokeng prefer small family groups. The largest Tlokoa village was the chief's at Malingoaneng, and had only twenty-four families (including several polygynous households) whereas on the other side of the Orange river the villages of even minor Koena sub-chiefs had forty families or more.

Most villages are picturesque. They directly reflect their environment and the simple line of the huts, their patterns and curves, their dark brown roofs and brown and grey walls harmonize with the grey-brown of the rocky landscape. In the Lowlands, many villages are surrounded by trees and aloes which add to their attraction.

The choice of a site is determined mainly by practical reasons, al-

[1] *Ngoana' rangoane* and *ngoana' mangoane* respectively.

though occasionally aesthetic or other factors enter in. Formerly the best site was a defensive position on the top of or near an easily defensible hill or cave. There the chief lived permanently while most of his people lived in small, lightly built villages scattered about the neighbourhood, within easy reach of his village. Nowadays, most villages are built on level ledges or natural terraces, away from the arable lands in the valleys and the grazing areas on the hill-tops. This situation also avoids the cold drainage air at night and yet is cool in summer. In some cases, the suitability of a site is obvious; in others, it is chosen because of the presence of suitable building stone, a fine spring of water or a beautiful view. It is occasionally dictated by custom—the chief's successor should build a new village on the right-hand side of his father's village (Mosuoe built on the left, to the displeasure of the old men); and a village, if shifted following some calamity, should not be taken far from the old site. I have not heard of a site being chosen by divination, although its abandonment may be so advised.

Normally, villages are permanent and many have been continuously occupied for over a century. They are moved only rarely, and then as a result of some disaster, such as an epidemic or frequent lightning strokes, or to vacate an area which is needed for cultivation.

Villages are usually called after their headmen, or a prominent member who outshines his headman, or the predominant clan. For instance, Matsieng and Malingoaneng were called after their founders, Letsie I and Lelingoana respectively; Masakong, a village next to Malingoaneng, was so called because it was occupied by the Masako lineage. They may also be named from some natural feature (Makaleng—"confluence of rivers"), or some incident associated with its founding, e.g. Thabang—"Rejoice", a name ironically chosen by Seeiso for his new village placed over a group of disgruntled subordinates.[1] They may also be referred to simply as "At So and so's"—*ha Makutla*.

The village itself is divided into households. The basic household group consists of a man, his wife and children. This becomes more complicated in the case of polygynists and still more so when the head of the family has his father's widows, their families and one or two married servants living with him. Some households have only one hut, but the majority have several—a living hut, and one or more outhouses, storerooms and cooking huts. These are either separate or closely grouped together and joined by a reed fence or mud walls. Friends and close relations tend to congregate together and their huts are either contiguous or, as in many Lowland villages, divided by small enclosed gardens, varying from a few square yards to over an acre.

Some villages may have a school or church; the schools are usually built in the same style as the dwelling huts, although here and there,

[1] For an interesting list of place names and their meanings, see Kennan, T. B., in tockley, G. M., *Report on the Geology of Basutoland*, pp. 113-14.

near a mission station, they may be large and imposing. The only other constructions are kraals (*lesaka*) and the court (*lekhotla*), both of which are open and extremely simple.

The lay-out of the village follows very rough principles, which are frequently modified through personal preferences and local topography. The chief's or headman's own private hut is usually in the centre, with that of his principal wife next to it, and those of his junior wives ranged in rough order of seniority round them. The court is in front of this and next to it are the cattle kraal,[1] calves' kraal and stables. The huts of the chief's retainers and relatives are usually at the back, the remoter connexions being farther away. Where possible, the principal dwelling huts face east to catch the morning sun and avoid the prevailing cold west wind.

The huts are simply and efficiently designed, solidly and warmly constructed—as indeed they have to be with temperatures falling below zero. The old type of hut (*mohlongoafatse*) was oval with an elongated entrance and was built of mud and grass over a framework of sticks.[2] Many of these may still be found, but more modern and popular types which have been in vogue for nearly a hundred years are circular or rectangular (the latter called *huis*) and are built of turf, Kimberley brick or dressed stone. The area of these huts varies from about 30 to 300 sq. feet and many of the rectangular ones have two or three rooms. They are usually roofed with thatch laid on a layer of reeds. Where thatch is not available, as in the Highlands, wheat straw or Khaki-bush is used instead. The roof may be crowned with a sheet of zinc or tin, or with bundles of straw tied in a particular way, or else left open to save work and let out smoke. The huts of the chief or of wealthy commoners may be roofed with corrugated iron, which is much admired as a symbol of wealth. Some chiefs and wealthy commoners have neat bungalows built on European lines.

The hut walls are smeared with mud plaster inside and out. The mud is mixed with chaff or fresh cattle- or horse-dung to make it strong and lasting, and for the final coating, which should be smooth, the earth is sifted. The walls are sometimes decorated with simple patterns and designs, either drawn by hand when the last coating is applied, or painted with washes of coloured earths, red, yellow, cream or brown. Outer walls may also be decorated with a simple mosaic of stones. Frequently clay or plaster cupboards and shelves are built into the walls.

Most households have two kinds of hut, one large and the other small. The latter (*mokhoro*), of which there may be more than one, is

[1] Formerly in the centre of the village, surrounded by huts for protection of the cattle. Casalis, p. 125; for a detailed account see Ashton, 1946.

[2] For a detailed description of hut building, see Laydevant, 1931, pp. 218-20 and Casalis, pp. 126-7.

used as a storeroom and kitchen, and as a dormitory for bachelors and herd-boys; it is black with smoke and is seldom furnished. The larger hut is the "living room" and is used as a living room, dining-room, meeting-room, bedroom—for practically everything except cooking. It is here that the parents and young children sleep. Older girls sleep with a grandmother or aunt, and boys in the *mokhoro* or in a bachelor hut (*thakaneng*) in the chief's household.

The decorations described above are to be found in the large hut and, to avoid blackening them, fires are rarely lit there. Nevertheless, a hearth is usually provided—a shallow, saucer-like depression, made of specially hardened clay. In this hut, grain is stored in sacks or bales, and a battery of pots, varying from large twenty-gallon ones to small water jars, drinking vessels and cooking paraphernalia, is kept on the low platform built against the back wall. Across the top of the walls a pole is slung on which clothes, blankets and sleeping rugs are hung during the day. The roof is used for storage and is festooned with spears, walking-sticks, switches, heads of kaffir-corn and sweet-cane kept for seed, spoons, old calabashes and a bunch of roots.

In the Highlands, the only furniture most people have consists of low chairs and stools, but the wealthier people are beginning to acquire European furniture, such as tables, bedsteads and cupboards. In the Lowlands, even the poor have many articles of European furniture and the homes of the wealthy are very well equipped. Most households also possess iron pots and pans, enamel and china plates, cups, teapots and other domestic utensils.[1]

Most huts have a courtyard (*lelapa*) which is provided with a hearth and often with a low earthen platform built against the hut. It is usually surrounded by a strong reed fence (*seotloana*).[2] If this fence should be temporarily removed, people are still expected to enter the courtyard by the old entrance—to do otherwise is exceedingly ill-mannered. In fine weather most of the domestic life is lived and work done in this courtyard. Each house has its own ash-heap immediately in front of it, though in the larger villages this may be placed just on the outskirts.

Many people protect their huts from sorcery by means of pegs and stones smeared with medicine, which are sunk level with the floor and placed opposite the entrances of the courtyard and hut. They may also smear medicine on the door above the lintel, or inconspicuously behind the door or in some dark corner. *Mofifi* sticks may also be stuck in the roof as a protection against lightning; some Christians use wild olive

[1] These articles were described as "necessities" as far back as 1910, which indicates the extent to which the material culture of the West has been accepted. *Livre d'Or*, p. 460.

[2] A good reed fence is now a rarity owing to the ploughing up of reed beds and the tremendous demand for the few reeds there are. Except in a few remote places, almost the only people who still have a *seotloana* are the chiefs. Khaki-bush may be substituted for reeds but is less neat and attractive.

branches, blessed by the mission priest or sprinkled with holy water and placed inside the roof, for the same purpose.

Practically every village has one or more kraals. These are unroofed enclosures. Formerly they were circular and built of wooden pallisades, but they are now rectangular, built of raw or roughly shaped stone, and vary in size from about 20 to over 100 sq. yards, with a narrow entrance closed by heavy logs. Nearby there are usually smaller kraals for calves and small stock, and very occasionally there may also be a covered stable for horses. Sometimes each family group has its own set of kraals.

Villages of chiefs and headmen have a court or public meeting-place (*lekhotla*). Usually, this is nothing more than an open space adjoining the kraal, consisting of no more than a circle of stones, perhaps half-fenced with reeds on the windy side, and provided with a few loose stones for seats. Very occasionally a well-grassed enclosure may be found, neatly fitted with stone benches. The court and kraals may also be protected with medicine by burying besmeared stones at the entrance and corners. The *Monkhoane* tree[1] may be used to give shade and to bring the village luck. Some chiefs have a hut set aside as an office where records and files are kept, meetings held in inclement weather and where visitors may sleep. At Matsieng, large barn-like buildings are used as courtrooms for meetings and for hearing cases.

---

[1] E. P. Phillips, *Flora of Leribe Plateau*, p. 106. Moshesh was born at Menkhoaneng near Pitseng in Leribe district and the tree was adopted as a sign of authority and used to be planted at the court of the principal chief of Moshesh's family and cases were decided under its shade. It is also known as the tree of Moshesh.

CHAPTER III

CONCEPTION, BIRTH AND CHILDHOOD

THE act of sexual intercourse is recognized as necessary for conception: virgin birth, as propounded in Christian doctrine and as found in some Sesuto legends, is regarded as an inexplicable miracle (*mohlolo*). The mechanics of conception are explained as follows: during copulation, semen (*mali*, which also means blood), which is the vital substance, is thrown into the woman's womb (*popelo*: the moulder). Thereafter, the mouth of the womb closes and so bottles up the normal menstrual flow which fuses with and is vitalized by the semen and is then moulded by the womb into the shape of a child. According to some, the vital essence comes from the Spirit of God. These two elements, the man's semen or "blood" and the woman's blood, are not necessarily of equal potency and the child will take after the parent whose "blood" is the stronger. The foetus lies in a vertical position, and its movements, especially when it turns round just before parturition, are one of the causes of pregnancy pains.

Failure to conceive may be due to a number of causes. One is purely mechanical, namely that the semen does not reach the womb, and so is ineffective; another is promiscuity. If a woman has intercourse with different men before her womb has "closed", their semen struggle for sole possession of the womb until all are ejected so that no fusion with the woman's blood takes place: hence the notorious barrenness of prostitutes and of female sexual maniacs; hence, too, the seriousness of a wife's adultery which may thwart her husband's procreation and lead to her sterility, quite apart from the danger of her introducing her lover's "strange" blood into the family.

Sterility may also be due to physical abnormality, to the malevolent action of departed spirits or to sorcery. The first may be incurable—("God has made her womb incapable of conceiving")—or may be due to some remediable incapacity, such as poor blood. There is no method of diagnosing the cause and time alone will tell whether it is curable or not. Various medicines are tried in the hope that it may be. For instance, the woman may be given a concoction to drink night and morning and enjoined to sleep regularly with her husband, and with him only—"to keep herself from adultery". Her husband may also have to take this medicine to purify his blood and so facilitate conception. Sometimes, though rarely nowadays, she may also be given a doll made of clay or rags, a calabash or a large bulb which she carries about with her as she would a child.[1] Formerly, prayer was often resorted to in this

[1] Segoete.

connexion. The praise-songs of the ancestors and of famous doctors, such as Ntili,[1] were sung and they were asked to mediate between the afflicted couple and their ancestor-spirits or God, and to try to procure a child for them: they were also besought to strengthen the medicines used in ordinary cases of physical incapacity. If sorcery was suspected steps were taken in the ordinary way to combat it and protect the woman.

As a result of these physiological ideas, sterility is regarded as primarily due to the woman and is rarely attributed to the man. The fact that some wives of a polygynist are childless bears this out. To suggest, therefore, that the husband may be responsible for his wife's childlessness would insult him deeply, for to ignore the more obvious explanation that she is unfaithful or unfortunate would question his virility and suggest that he is some sort of a freak.

Other complaints connected with birth are also amenable to medical treatment. For instance, a woman whose children are all of one sex can be helped to produce children of the opposite sex by taking medicine to "change her hip". In normal cases she should be able to regulate this quite easily: if she lies on her right side during and immediately after intercourse she should produce male children, if on her left, female. Women whose previous pregnancies ended in miscarriages should take medicine to "support the child". This is such delicate medicine that the patient should take care, when crossing a river, to rinse her mouth out with river water, or to smear her forehead with mud lest its potency be spoiled.

Conception does not at first interfere with the woman's domestic routine. This is gradually modified, and, as her time approaches, she drops her heavier tasks. Her ordinary marital life continues until about the sixth month when her husband may cease to co-habit with her on the grounds that she is becoming lazy, dirty and unattractive. Normally she receives no special treatment, but when her pains or sickness begin she may be given medicines, such as *mohlapiso, mohato* or *mothaleho*,[2] with which she is vaccinated on her hips and breasts to help her pregnancy and promote the child's growth. Considerate husbands also try to make her comfortable and satisfy her craving for special foods. As her pregnancy advances, she should stay at home to avoid contact with the "bad paths" of malevolent persons who might harm the child. This applies especially to the first child.

For her first child, she is taken to her parents' home at the beginning of the seventh month. On her arrival a small rite is performed. All her ornaments are removed, her eyebrows and forehead are shaved, a mixture of red ochre and butter fat is smeared on her head, face and torso, and a sheepskin similarly besmeared is tied acros her breasts to hide her bigness and keep the child warm. A sheep may be killed for her, its gall sprinkled

[1] Sekese, op. cit. pp. 36-41, who describes Ntili's successes.   [2] See Glossary.

at the back of the hut, and its *mohlehlo* or gallbladder[1] fastened round her neck. She may also wear a necklace of ostrich eggshells, threaded with her husband's clan beads, together with pumpkin seeds and a wildcat's claw[2] or tail-tip. This rite should bring luck and strength and marks the beginning of her seclusion. From now on she may not cut her hair (though Sekese says this taboo starts with the cessation of her menses), and may only be visited by women or by her maternal male relatives. According to Sekese,[3] she goes back to her husband after this rite and returns to her parents in the eighth month (*motlahali*), but so far as my information goes, she stays with her parents all the time. An obscure taboo, possibly connected with the widespread fear of sorcery, is that no one should walk behind her. These rites and taboos are only partially observed, although most women still go to their parents' home for their first child and are tenderly cared for.

As her time approaches, she is given medicines to "turn" the child and ensure an easy delivery. She is attended by her mother and by other old women of the village "of good reputation and conduct". If complications occur, she is given special medicines; if these fail, her midwives try manipulation. In extreme cases, a male doctor may be allowed to treat her.

It is a popular European belief that African women give birth easily. Statistics are unobtainable, but there is some medical evidence to show that Basuto women are not all so fortunate and the existence of these precautions indicates that the Basuto are well aware of the dangers of childbirth. Sekese[4] gives as reasons for women going home for their first child, the heaviness of their ordeal and their need for the best possible care and attention at this dangerous period.

Figures with regard to abortions and stillbirths are unobtainable as women do not readily speak of these even if they remember them. Abortifacients are known and used, but it is impossible to say to what extent. In cases of miscarriage or abortion, the foetus is buried in a broken potsherd in the ash-heap outside the hut, and the mother should undergo a brief purification ceremony.

As soon as the child is born, the umbilical cord is severed. About six inches of the cord is left attached to the child and this is heavily larded and gently tied against the child's body. The afterbirth is buried within the courtyard (*lelapa*) to prevent strangers hurting the child or the mother by walking over it. The child is washed with water and sometimes with a special lotion, and is rubbed with ointment. The mother

[1] *Mohlehlo* and gall are commonly used on ritual occasions connected with birth, marriage and death, but the people cannot explain why.

[2] The wildcat tail is associated by the Tlokoa with their totem. The pumpkin seeds are associated with birth and new life and are used in mortuary rites, described later, for the life hereafter.

[3] op. cit. p. 10.

[4] Ibid., p. 11.

CONCEPTION, BIRTH AND CHILDHOOD

(*motsoetse*) is also washed and particular attention is paid to her breasts and nipples. The breasts are milked a little as the child should not suck the first milk or colostrom (*lebese la litlobo*) though nobody knows why.

In the old days, the birth of a boy was announced by beating the father with a stick, and that of a girl, by drenching him with water. These acts are symbolical, for manhood is commonly represented by a stick (or knife) and womanhood by water. This symbolism also appears in the language of the initiation schools, in poetic innuendoes and in the taboo observed by women against stepping over a man's walking-stick or riding-whip. This would appear to be partly phallic and partly representative of the principal social functions of primitive men and women—fighting and drawing water.[1] Mofolo suggests that the water is a reminder of the lake at Ntsuanatsatsi.[2] Nowadays, news of the birth of the child is conveyed verbally or by letter.

The mother and child are confined to their hut until the child's navel string dries and falls off and are ministered to by her mother, sisters and other women of the village. When they are allowed to go out into the courtyard, a small feast may be held as a "thank-offering" to the ancestor spirits or to God, and to reward the midwives for their services. A sheep is provided by the mother's father and, in the old days, its gall was poured over the child and the bladder tied round its neck; the meat is given to the midwives and shared by visitors.[3] The mother now washes off her red ochre and cuts her hair and thereafter may be visited by other women and close kinsmen. Her seclusion is marked by a reed thrust into the roof of the hut; this symbolizes the birth by reference to the reed bed at Ntsuanatsatsi and at the same time warns men to keep away. Among the Tlokoa a single reed is sometimes used to indicate a girl, and two a boy, but among other clans no differentiation is made. The Phuthi stretch a grass rope outside the hut when she is "not at home". Segoete[4] describes other variations but does not say whether they are clan differences or not. Sekese[5] mentions that her fire is not allowed to go out, nor may the ashes be thrown away.

During this period, the *motsoetse*[6] is under the complete control of her parents who feed her, nurse her and provide for her medical attention.

[1] Segoete, p. 109. Segoete also says that the birth may be announced by the *melilietsa* (trilling shout) of the women, and the phrase "*Ho hlaba le pele*" if it is a boy, and "*Ha le tlala le mariba*" if it is a girl. The first of these phrases refers to the "spear"—the future weapon and symbol of status of the boy, and has possibly the same phallic symbolism as before; the second refers to the marriageability of the girl—"May the kraal be filled unto its utmost corners".

[2] Mofolo, 1931.

[3] For other details, see Sekese, p. 10.

[4] Segoete, p. 110.

[5] Sekese, op. cit., p. 10.

[6] This Sesuto term, *motsoetse*, will often be used as it has no simple English synonym. It means a woman who has recently given birth, is still nursing her child, is sexually continent and therefore ritually pure. It ceases to be applied after about six months.

This practice is so strict that even if she should become ill or have a difficult labour, her husband is not informed until she recovers or her illness becomes serious. Only in extreme cases is he permitted to call a doctor. This does not apply to subsequent births nor to occasions when the mother remains at her husband's home.

The period of seclusion lasts two or three months for the first child and less for subsequent children. At first the *motsoetse* may not receive visitors from other villages or go far from her hut, especially if she has to cross water or much-frequented footpaths. These restrictions are insisted upon, partly to allow her to give undivided attention to the child and partly to avoid contact with a dangerous medicine called *seteipi*, used by malevolent people, chiefly men. The child can be harmed by passing near where the *seteipi* has been dropped or by crossing a path taken by someone carrying this medicine. If the child has to go out before it has "set", it can be protected by a special medicine such as *mothaleho* or *mohato*, which is smeared on the fontanelle or the nape of the neck, and from ear to ear.

The mother's return home was formerly the occasion for ritual exchanges of cattle between her family and her husband's, which have now ceased. To-day she is simply accompanied by the people of her own village and welcomed by her husband who may kill a sheep in her honour. If he does so she should be given a piece of its intestines as *koae* to symbolize her rejoining the family in the same way as when she was welcomed as a bride, and to remove the taboo which previously forbade her eating that delicacy lest she should have difficulty in giving birth. The child may be treated with the gall in the usual ritual manner. From now on she resumes her full domestic life except that sexual intercourse is limited to *coitus interruptus*, until the child is weaned.

Socially the birth of the first child, the *ngoana oa matsibolo*, is the most important and is hedged about with strict rites and taboos which are relaxed for the birth of subsequent children. For these, the woman usually remains at her husband's home and is looked after by his people, unless there is no one there to look after her (as sometimes happens in remote Highland villages), or if a feast is bringing many people to the village which might lead to her neglect or increase the dangers of sorcery, or if she should have some ominous dream and be advised by her doctor to go to her parents. Though the husband is expected to provide a sheep to welcome (*ananela*) each birth and to thank the midwives for their help, he seldom does so after the first or second child and public interest in these events also lessens.

The birth of her first child also changes the mother's status. As childbearing is regarded as the main function of women, its fulfilment gives her greater standing in the community. Moreover, she is considered to have completed her family's side of the marriage contract, and the cattle (*maoto*) which had been held over from her *bohali* should now be paid. She has now given her husband cause to be proud of her, which is even more important from her point of view. The ideal is for her to have a son as her first-born, and thereafter produce daughters and sons alternately every two or three years, but no one worries much about this provided "her hips are soft" and she is fruitful.

As the first few months of a child's life are regarded as critical, it is protected in various ways. Almost immediately after birth, before being suckled, it is given a little porridge made of uncooked kaffir-corn (*mabele*). Some people say this is done to introduce it to what was traditionally its staple diet, while others maintain that it is a test of the child's humanity, for if it did not eat it would be a monster, probably the child of a familiar (*thokolosi*). This used to be an important rite but is now seldom observed. Segoete[1] says that the child is also scarified (*phatsa*).

When the child is brought out of the hut for the first time, it is shaved. Pieces of the hair are pressed into its hand lest it should "cry a lot, become moody and not recognize its mother". A small tuft of hair is left to which beads are threaded. It is also given anklets and wristlets made of similar beads and any necklace or charms worn by its mother during her pregnancy. Many clans and even families within clans have their own colours and types of beads, and some have particular ways of arranging them, e.g. the Ba-Lefe (the Tlokoa chief's lineage) have large black beads which should be strung in threes, the Taung have light blue beads and the Ba-Tsotetsi have red and white.

The child may be given a charm for good luck. Different charms are used according to personal tastes—some use the wildcat's foot, others special roots, others again small goats' horns filled with medicine. Segoete[2] says that grass rings (*mathapo*) are sometimes woven round its neck to help the fontanelle to close properly, but among the Tlokoa similar rings, called *lioti* or *liokhe*, are used simply for ornament. All these decorations and medicines should be provided by the maternal uncle or maternal grandparents.

At the first good rains after its seclusion, the child is stripped and placed naked in the *lelapa* until it begins to cry. Then everyone laughs and cries out 'Thief! Thief!' (*sholu ke leo*), and the mother rescues it. Until this rite has been observed, the child should not go out of doors when rain threatens, lest rain falling on its head should soften and deform it or, according to Sekese,[3] teach it to steal. This rite is also explained as an introduction to rain, the life-giver.[4] Among the Tlokoa, the father should cut his baby son's nails lest he grow up a coward. These rites are dying out, as are others recorded by Segoete[5].

In the case of wealthy and important families, a virgin boy or youth may be chosen for his outstanding character to look after the child. In the case of a chief's son, this boy eventually becomes his bodyguard or

---

[1] Segoete, p. 111. [2] ibid. p. 112. [3] op. cit. p. 12.
[4] See Hunter, 1936, for a very similar rite. [5] Segoete, pp. 113-15.

personal attendant. The child may also be fed with milk from a "clean" cow, one that has not been covered since calving.

I discovered no special customs relating to abnormalities, such as twins, children who teethed in an unusual manner or boys born without a foreskin (believed to be caused by its parents' eating the kidneys of a sheep), with the exception of "*ntja*" children described below.

The child is usually named by its father or grandfather, though sometimes a friend of the family or an eminent personage may do so. Names are seldom chosen at random and usually recall a grandfather or other important relation, or commemorate an important or unusual event or personage. An elder child is often called by its mother's marriage name.

The best examples of the first type are to be found in the chiefs' families. For instance, the names Letsie, Seeiso, Bereng, Masupha and Molapo recur frequently in the Moshesh family and eminent administrators such as Griffith and Lagden have been commemorated in the names of some of Moshesh's leading descendants. Of topical names there are no end, and the following chosen from Malingoaneng illustrate their variety. Join (father "joined" the mine recruits), Jubilee (named after the Diamond Jubilee of 1897 or the Silver Jubilee of 1935), *Borikhoe* ("trousers"—so called after his mother's marriage name Maborikhoe, given her because her husband was the first to be married in a pair of breeches instead of wearing the traditional loincloth), *Boteng* and *Ha-bo-eo* ("there is some" and "there is none"—Leligoana visited their mothers at the time of their birth—one had beer to offer him, the other none!), *Sehloho* ("cruelty"—its mother died in childbirth), *Tsebetsabaloi* ("sorcerer's ears"—at his birth a mysterious incident occurred), *Mosuoe* ("the circumciser"—in commemoration of the first initiation held by the Tlokoa in their new home), *Nyooko* ("gall"—born during a drought: the rain doctor tabooed the ordinary word for water (*metse*) until rain should fall, saying that the word "*nyooko*" should be used instead).

Although European words such as Join and Jubilee and surnames such as those quoted above are used as birth names, ordinary European Christian names are rarely so used. As a rule such names are given only to Christian Basuto on conversion or at baptism and to pupils in school, partly for convenience, partly because it is the smart and proper thing to do and partly to mark alteration in status. They are also often adopted when taking up European employment for much the same reason as well as to avoid the derogatory modes of address so often used by Europeans, such as "Sixpence" or "Jim". A few of these Christian names stick because they are unusual or attractive, such as my assistant's school name, Phineas. Some people acquire nicknames which are sometimes so apt or pleasing that they supersede their other names.

There are two cases in which special names are given to children. The first is after a stillborn child or the death of a child before weaning. The death of these children is believed to be due to sorcery, so that apart

PLATE I

Photo: L. Lewis

(a) General view near Matsieng

(b) View from the top of Thaba Bosigo

PLATE II

(a) Young girl acting as nurse to baby brother

(b) Mother and Child

Photo: L. Lewis

from the usual anti-sorcery precautions, an attempt is made to safeguard the next child born by making a show of neglecting it in the hope of lulling the sorcerer's vigilance. It is kept dirty and unkempt, its head is incompletely shaved, leaving a small tuft of hair (*hlotho*) at the back, which is not removed until initiation, and, as a final mark of indifference, it is given an unpleasant name, such as *Ntja* (dog), *Moselantja* (dog's tail), *Tsoene* (monkey), *Makhokolotsa* (rubbish) or *Masepa* (human excrement).

The second case is where a boy is born after a succession of girls, particularly where previous male children have died young. Here in addition to being treated in the same way as *ntja* children, it is dressed in a girl's *thethana* and is given a girl's name (usually unpleasant) such as *Phepheng* (scorpion).[1] As a further safeguard it is separated from its mother earlier than usual and sent to her home to be out of harm's way.

Twins are usually called by the same name, the younger twin's having the suffix *nyana*—little, e.g. Sebili, Sebilinyana. In one instance the father with wry humour gave his twins the names of his two stepmothers.

Boys are not expected to wear clothes until they begin to grow up. Apart from ceremonial and other festive occasions, when they are dressed up by having two small bead triangles or a bead belt tied round the waist, they go naked. After the age of about seven they are encouraged to observe the decencies and to wear a loincloth (*tseha*). This consists of any old rag. Later, as they become more self-conscious, they choose better material and take greater care to cover themselves. Eventually they may be given, or make for themselves, a well-cut sheep or calfskin loincloth. European influence, through the schools and other institutions, encourages the wearing of shorts or trousers, either alone or with the addition of shirts, jerseys, jackets and other articles of European dress.

Girls, on the other hand, wear a fibre skirt (*thethana*) as soon as they begin to crawl. From a very early age (about one), they are taught to conduct themselves modestly and not to expose their persons. An infant's *thethana* has fringes about two inches long and these are lengthened as the child grows up. In the old days, they used to wear no other clothing until initiation, after which they wore the cutaway *mose oa khomo* (cowhide skirt) over the *thethana*. Nowadays, they are taking to wearing short skirts and petticoats of European-made cloth with knickers instead of the *thethana*, and as they grow older, blouses or frocks.

Boys and girls are given their own blankets which they wear for show, warmth or shelter. The blanket is worn by the Basuto on practically every occasion and is regarded as the traditional or national dress.

For the first year, an infant's staple food is its mother's milk and for

[1] Sekese, p. 42. He also writes that where the mother was treated, her doctor's mother's name may be used.

the first few months this is about the only food it gets. If the mother is too weak to feed it, it is nourished on cow's milk, conveyed through a European-made baby's bottle: it is never given to a foster mother or wet nurse if its mother is alive, though if she dies, her husband's mother may suckle it if she can.

As the child gets older, it is introduced to other foods, which at first merely supplement breast-feeding and then replace it. The first of these foods is liquid porridge, a palatable and nourishing dish made from either maize or *mabele*. Other recognized foods are milk, tea and thin unfermented porridge, *lesheleshele*. They are fed to the child by means of a spoon or by cupping the hand round its mouth. It is given solid foods "when it is old enough", though this is never clearly defined and careless young nursegirls often feed the child, when very young, with scraps of whatever they themselves happen to be eating, e.g. maize, bread or meat. In spite of their sometimes pre-chewing this food, it often produces serious indigestion and other tummy trouble. By the age of a little over one, the child is usually given all the foods consumed by adults except fermented foods.

After the first year, the child comes to depend less and less on suckling for his main food, although he derives a great deal of emotional satisfaction therefrom. He goes to his mother frequently, whether hungry or not; a child of nearly two would go eight times to his mother in the hour, even though given scraps of food in between whiles—and will suck with obvious enjoyment, as he nuzzles up to his mother and buries his face in her bosom, squeezes and strokes her breasts, and looks up at her every now and again, smiling and roguish. It is also noticeable how quickly and readily he goes to her when frightened or scolded, and how much more easily suckling soothes him than any other sort of petting and cossetting. Consequently weaning, when it comes, probably creates a break of emotional rather than nutritional significance.

Weaning usually takes place at the age of two, though the age may vary from one to three years. The child is now old enough to fend for himself and his mother should resume her full domestic routine without constant interruption. She should also renew her full sexual life, not only for her husband's sexual gratification but also to produce another child. The latter is generally regarded as the most important factor in favour of weaning, but women are not always as convinced and pleased by it as they are expected to be and some try to postpone weaning for as long as possible as they like suckling their children and do not regard childbearing as an unmixed pleasure.

The child is prepared for weaning by his neighbours' mocking him when he runs to his mother to suck, telling him he is not a man but a good-for-nothing, making the usual expressions of disgust and trying to pull him away from her. At first he thinks this is a new game (especially when a reluctant mother, resenting this interference, encourages him),

CONCEPTION, BIRTH AND CHILDHOOD

but eventually he realizes that he is doing something wrong. His mother too will finally try to prevent him from coming to her, by distracting his attention, refusing to uncover her breasts or telling him not to bother her. This process is usually concluded, especially if weaning has to be ended abruptly owing to premature pregnancy, by positive action, such as the mother tying a cloth round her breasts or rubbing bitter tobacco or aloe juice on her nipples. Alternatively, the child may be taken to his grandparents till he has "forgotten" his mother. Unfortunately, I have insufficient data to say whether there is any real difference in the attitude of male and female children towards suckling and weaning: most of the children I watched happened to be boys.

The Basuto do not attach much psychological importance to weaning and say that, though the child always cries, he soon forgets and settles down happily. Nevertheless, weaning drastically changes the relationship between mother and child. Previously they were very close, the mother being extremely patient and tender and the child affectionate and readily going to her at any time; but now she tends to snap at him and treat him harshly instead of cuddling and coaxing him, and the child tends to stay more with his playmates and nurses.

At first, the child remains in the almost exclusive care of his mother. Later, when he begins to crawl, his horizon gradually widens; he plays with the small objects around him, such as sticks, stones, bits of cloth and domestic pets. Gradually he gains the attention of his brothers and sisters who tease him and play with him and encourage his attempts to stand and walk. His range of activities and interests increases, he follows his mother about the house and courtyard, chases venturesome dogs and fowls with a reed or whip and imitates the older children's games. He is now frequently left in the charge of a small nurse—an elder sister or a cousin—and accompanies her on her jaunts with other young nurses, and meets and plays with the other village children.

Boys do not bother much about sex differentiation and for years continue to play with girls, older or younger than themselves. Most of their games are aimless and desultory and consist chiefly of roaming about, playing hide and seek, digging on ash-heaps, making slides or watching the activities of their elders. At the age of about four or five, they begin to imitate adult occupations. They make collections of knuckle bones to represent herds, the larger bones representing bulls, others oxen, cows and calves, and with these they imitate cattle herding, or they challenge one another to fights. These collections are usually made only from animals killed by their own household—consequently the chiefs' sons, as befits their position, have the largest herds. They also imitate women's tasks, such as grinding and cooking. They take great interest in the ceremonies held in the village, and afterwards imitate the more dramatic incidents; for instance, after the boys' initiation, youngsters accompanied by young girls imitate the public ceremonial they have seen, repeat the *mangae* choruses and praise-songs they have heard and even invent their own. As they grow older, they spend more of their time at the kraal, watching the cows being milked or helping the older herd-boys chase the calves out of their kraal before milking, and occasionally they may go out with the junior herds to graze the calves and donkeys.

Formerly, from the age of about eleven or twelve until manhood, boys and youths formed a group separate from the rest of the community, but to-day, with the disappearance of many of their activities, their separation is less marked. They used to spend the day with their age-mates, herding cattle or other stock, milking the cows and attending to the stock in the kraal. In the evenings and mornings they would go to the *khotla*, or public meeting-place, where they had their meals, played and talked among themselves or listened to the story-telling and gossip of their elders. At night, they slept together in the bachelor's hut (*takaneng*). The younger boys might occasionally sneak home to be cossetted and petted by their mothers and given titbits of food. To-day much of this discipline has been relaxed. Boys are not forced to go herding and many are allowed to go to school, where they freely meet with girls and children of other villages. Nor have they to spend the rest of their time at the *khotla* or kraal but may stay at home, visit their friends or idle in the village. They may eat and sleep at home until they approach puberty when they should sleep with other lads in their own spare hut or kitchen or at the bachelors' hut.

Herding was and still is the most important activity for boys. In all large villages there are still two herd-boy groups. The younger boys are deputed to look after the calves and donkeys and the older group herd the cattle. This group consists mostly of initiates or young unmarried men. Younger boys are occasionally honoured and immensely delighted by an invitation to join them for a day or two.

Mofolo gives a graphic account of herding as it used to be: "Herding in Basutoland long ago was bad and painful, so that we may be glad we were born in these times of light. Light-hearted and careless young men used to herd, and fights took place every day. The cattle of the principal herd boy ('*mampoli*) would feed in the pleasant part of the country, in the largest pasture where there was much grass. They grazed long grass alone. At the drinking place the cattle of the principal herd boy were the first to drink when the water was still clean. Above all that, the principal herd boy would bully the others. The boys had to share everything with him when herding, whether bread or meat. He that did not share went herding knowing well that he would get the stick. If the principal herd boy smoked tobacco he forced the boys to get tobacco for him or to steal it from their fathers and bring it to him. If they did not there was more stick."[1]

[1] Mofolo, 1931, pp. 15-16.

In many parts of the country the herd-boys are younger than they used to be as many youths refuse to herd, preferring to go to school, work on the mines or loaf at home. The *'mampoli's* position is, therefore, less important than before and his duties less onerous. The herd-boys are left to amuse themselves while the cattle graze under their very tolerant supervision. They roam the country looking for edible plants, steal and roast potatoes, snare birds, hunt rats and mice, fish, ride donkeys and calves, indulge in short-lived single-stick fights, practise throwing stones at targets (at which they often attain outstanding proficiency), swim in the river pools and clamber up and down krantzes. Some of them play various musical instruments and vie with one another in their rendering of traditional tunes such as "*mamokonyone*" (mother of the little hard excrement) or "*matsikeletsane*" played on the *lesiba*. They also play tunes on a pipe made of a reed stem, and imitate a Jew's harp by manipulating their cheeks. They have a number of "intellectual" games, tell one another jokes and puns and ask one another riddles and conundrums. They coin words and phrases and concoct what they like to call a "secret language" with which to amuse themselves and sometimes to puzzle and outwit adults.

The boys' group is free and easy and is not bound by the conventions and standards of their elders. This is particularly noticeable in the sphere of their personal relationships. Most of the boys are related, but kinship as such does not count for much, and they tend to set more store on character and such traits as friendliness, intelligence, physical strength and prowess.

In contrast to the boys', girls' activities and upbringing are comparatively uniform and have changed little from the old days. Now, as then, they are closely identified with adult life. Girls in early childhood have much the same activities as boys with whom they play and many of whose pastimes they share. They also have their own separate activities and their own special games; they play with dolls of rags and straw and play "house-house" in little pebble-and-mud huts; but they are drawn into adult life and take part in adult activities at a much earlier age and to a greater extent than boys do. At first they act as nursemaids to the younger members of the family and spend a lot of time carrying these children about pick-a-back, feeding them and playing with them. Then at about six, partly as an amusement but with ever-growing seriousness, they learn to sweep out the hut, collect spinach from the fields or fetch water from the spring. At a later age they make the fire, go out into the veld for wood, help their mothers or elder sisters smear the hut, gradually acquire a knowledge of cooking, and occasionally may even be taught the complex process of brewing beer. By the time they reach puberty, they are doing the same kind of work in the house as their mothers and are almost as efficient.

In their spare time, they amuse themselves in a variety of ways. In slack periods they accompany one another or go with their mothers or other adult female relations to the local store, visiting friends en route, or they spend the afternoon in a nearby river, bathing, washing their clothes, gossiping, playing games or, particularly when the women are away in the lands, dancing and singing at home.

In all their activities, they pay little attention to age distinctions, and though the younger girls tend to play by themselves, practically all of the girls in the village between the ages of about twelve and eighteen join together on occasion. Initiation makes very little difference to them from this point of view, and there is practically no separation between the initiated and the uninitiated. Nevertheless, they are far less gregarious than boys. They do many of their tasks in company, but except on the above occasions they prefer to play and work with only one or two friends. They are less free and easy than boys and more conservative; they place far more weight on social status and relationship than boys do, choosing their friends mainly from within their immediate family circle, and usually from among their age-mates in neighbouring huts who are automatically close kin. They are in far closer contact with adult life through their occupations and their connexion with older women and they tend to accept adult values and conform to set standards at an early age.

The only change that has occurred in their routine as a result of European contact is the addition of further interests through the school and church. But this does not interfere with their ordinary occupations and merely adds to their activities, as they do their normal household work before and after school and when they leave school carry on with their usual domestic routine.

In their early youth, boys seem less sex-conscious than girls and people pay less attention to their sex. They dress with less care and covering than girls and even when they wear a loincloth or a pair of shorts for special occasions, they take them off as soon as they can for they are not abashed by their nudity and no one draws attention to it. Similarly, in early youth no notice is taken of a boy playing with his penis; this they do quite openly and unself-consciously. They also play a game of "cows", in which one boy chases, rounds up and rides another one, who runs on all fours, and then having "kraaled" him, milks him by pulling his penis as though it were a teat. This game is played by children from one and a half years old to anything up to about ten, and is rarely interrupted by adults. Some mothers try to promote the development of his sex organs by fondling the child's penis and encouraging him to do so himself, though others disapprove of this, saying it makes the child too interested in sex.

Girls are brought up much more strictly. From a very early age they are taught to sit modestly and decently, and a girl who "flops" down and exposes her person or who is careless about arranging her *thethana* or skirts is roughly scolded by any woman or old man who may have noticed her. Girls are also taught at a much earlier age than boys to micturate outside the hut and away from people. They take much more care over their appearance, and are so modest that for a girl to scratch or expose her person in public or display any interest in her sexual organs is most unusual. Ordinarily they do not take any obvious notice of the sexual organs of the boys playing around them, but a small girl of about five or six got exceedingly embarrassed when a naked boy of about two reversed up to her on all fours and asked her to "milk" him: their parents in the hut took no notice of the incident.

Ordinarily, girls tend to play less readily with boys than with other girls unless the boys are younger and other girls are present. Thus boys of seven and eight often join in the activities of girls older and younger than themselves, and boys as old as twelve to fourteen may watch girls singing and dancing, or join their evening gossip circle, whereas girls would never do this with boys unless they outnumbered them or the boys were considerably younger. Similarly, girls never infringe the divisions of labour based on sex. They do not, for instance, go herding with boys (though where boys are lacking they may look after small stock), or play in or go near the court or kraal except on special occasions; young boys on the other hand may go with girls to fetch water or collect firewood or spinach. Most games may be played in mixed groups, though a few boys' games such as leapfrog and *tsipo* are regarded as too immodest to be played by girls. They also dance together in dances such as the *motjeko*, and in others, like the *mohobelo*, the girls clap and sing for the men. Boys do not, however, take any part in the girls' *mokhibo* dance.[1]

According to all reports, relations between boys and girls used to be entirely innocent. Premarital intercourse, even in the restricted form of *ukumetsha* practised by the Zulus, was and still is forbidden. So pure were the youths and maidens of old, it is said, that they might even bathe naked together and yet remain chaste. It is difficult to say how true these reports really are, and one is tempted to discount them against the familiar "things-are-not-what-they-were-when-I-was-a-child" attitude of older people. But there is no reason to suppose, as is so often done in South Africa, that Africans are "naturally" immoral and promiscuous and that therefore such chastity was improbable if not impossible. On the contrary, various customs, particularly those concerned with marriage, described in Chapter V, clearly indicate that formerly the Basuto expected, and to some extent succeeded in obtaining, strict continence from their children. Unfortunately Casalis, who was in an excellent position to do so, does not comment on this aspect of Sesuto life. But whatever it was, the fact that the Basuto claim that

---

[1] These dances are described in Chapter VI.

former generations were chaste indicates their dissatisfaction with the present-day sexual laxity.

The general attitude still is that boys and girls, and unmarried young men and especially women, should be chaste, and this is still strong enough to cause considerable individual variation. Many do keep chaste and a doctor of many years' gynaecological experience considers that an appreciable proportion of unmarried girls are virgins. On the other hand, many Basuto allege and deplore that nearly everyone has premarital love affairs: there is good evidence that some children's sexual experience begins even before puberty. Actually, however, provided that lovers conduct themselves discreetly and the girl avoids pregnancy and is not promiscuous, no one worries much about their affairs. Indeed, they are half expected and a girl who had no lover would be regarded as unnatural and suspected of consorting with a familiar.

CHAPTER IV

EDUCATION

THE term "education" is used here in its widest sense to mean the process by which the child is trained to take its place in society. This process operates throughout its life, is continuous and incessant, and consists of innumerable details of environment, physical and human, which influence its behaviour. This is a vast and technical subject, and having had neither the training nor the time necessary for a complete study, I cannot hope to do it justice; but it is one which has been so much neglected in anthropology that I feel emboldened to describe the more obvious principles and techniques by which the Basuto train their children.

Informal Education
For the first few months the child is scarcely controlled at all and has his own way almost entirely. Whenever he cries, as he does frequently, his mother immediately responds. She takes him, wherever it may be and whatever she may be doing, and gives him her breast. If his attention is caught by something, he may drop her breast, and later when he wants it again, fail to find it and start to whimper; she again immediately responds by thrusting the nipple into his mouth and so quietens him once more. If he is not soothed in this way, as may happen when he is tired, she rocks him in her arms or on her back and sings him a lullaby until he drops asleep. But suckling is so favoured a sedative, that she will have recourse to it again and again until the infant splutters or chokes and only then will she try something else. Sometimes she may be so anxious to get on with her work that she tries to suckle the child at the same time. This is rarely successful for he is not comfortable and so continues to cry; rather than smack him or leave a nurse to wrestle with him, she then drops her work altogether and waits until the child is completely satisfied and soothed. Her patience and forbearance are astounding.

Patient though it may be, the treatment is completely negative and the mother makes no systematic attempt to provide for the child's wants or to discipline his behaviour. With regard to sleeping, for instance, she leaves him to adapt himself to his surroundings, and makes no effort to set aside definite periods for rest. She may occasionally leave him by himself in a hut to go to sleep, but generally she expects him to sleep where and when he can. When she is working she may put him down in the shade but, if this is not convenient, she carries him on her back and she would never dream of stopping work for his sake, provided he does not cry. She takes him wherever she goes, visiting, dancing or whatever she may be doing and she expects him to adapt himself to these circumstances; if he cries, she will soothe him by suckling. This somewhat drastic treatment does, however, achieve its object and, either through being inured to noise and movement or through utter exhaustion, he manages to sleep through the noisiest beer drink and his mother's most energetic dancing.

The position is similar as regards feeding. Meal-times are quite irregular and the child is fed only when he cries or asks for food. Some women try to observe midday as a regular feeding time, but they soon forget and are only reminded later by the infant's crying.

This casual and passive treatment, which consists almost entirely of responding to the child's demands rather than regulating, controlling or anticipating them, is typical of this period of his education, and is aptly summarized by the proverb—"the child that does not cry dies in the cradle". The Basuto do not try to train their babies, as they assume that they have insufficient intelligence at that age to respond. They also consider that the child himself is really the best judge of when he needs attention, and that he will not hesitate to use the weapon nature has provided—crying—to get such attention. If he does not cry, one may safely assume that all is well.

As soon as the child begins to have some "sense", at about nine months or a year, his cries and demands meet with varied responses. His mother may still suckle him, but if this interferes with what she is doing, she may try to soothe the child by petting him. She may also try to divert his attention from whatever is upsetting him by giving him food or a toy, such as the top of a tin or mealie grains, or if he is able to walk, she may ask him to take food or a message to his father or grandmother in another hut. Finally, if these devices fail, she may again resort to suckling. His young nurses also try to soothe him in similar ways, even to the extent of putting him to their own undeveloped breasts.

A remarkable feature of this system of education is the almost complete absence of harshness at this period. People very seldom shout at the child, frighten him, threaten him with punishment, beat him, try to intimidate him or force him to conform to their wishes. This forbearance endures under the severest provocation: for instance, on one occasion a child screamed for over a quarter of an hour and yet neither its nurse nor its aunt uttered a single cross word or relaxed their gentle efforts to soothe it. This forbearance is expected not only of the mother and other immediate kinsmen, but of everyone.

Another method of controlling the child is that of deflection. If he goes near the fire where he runs the risk of burning or hurting himself or if he goes too near the pots at the back of the hut where he might break something, he is seldom shouted at but is gently drawn away by having his attention attracted to something else, or, if the situation calls for rapid action, he is snatched away as though it were a game. Similarly, if he plays with a dangerous object such as a knife, axe or sickle, his attention is diverted to something else and the object then quickly hidden. Rarely is the object snatched away when the child's attention is fixed on it, or the child told "Don't touch it".

Little effort is made to teach the child to conform to the traditional standards of behaviour until he is weaned, for until then he is not regarded as "established or set" (*tiile*). Moreover, as shown earlier, this event completely changes the relationship of the child with his mother and so opens the way to the use of force as well as reason. The child is now expected to be old enough to understand and therefore to obey his parents' orders and so is treated with far less consideration and coaxing than before. His usual efforts to attract attention and secure satisfaction of his wants now meet with quite different responses. When he cries or makes a nuisance of himself, he is shouted at and told to be quiet, is threatened with a thrashing or is left alone; if he is hungry, he is told to wait until someone is free to come and feed him.

Apart from this, the child is left very much to his own devices and is scarcely interfered with. His faculty for imitation, guided and stimulated by his parents, is relied on to teach him to be a good Mosuto. It is in this way that he learns practically all the technical skills and forms of behaviour required. Learning to speak is an interesting example of this process. People show little tendency to talk down to the child or use baby talk, and usually speak to him in ordinary straightforward language; nor do they restrain their talk in his presence. Consequently, he soon learns to speak Sesuto correctly and fairly fluently. Much of his learning is acquired by subconscious absorption. But he soon learns much by conscious observation and repetition, and one may often hear a child repeating words just spoken, that have attracted his attention. On such occasions, if his repetition is faulty, someone, usually his mother or father, repeats the phrase and by maintaining his interest, not by exercising authority, tries to get him to speak correctly. If he tires of the lesson, he is left to himself again. Not till later, when he is older and has a better grasp of the language, are his mistakes pointed out. Knowledge of kinship terms is similarly acquired. The child hears cousins calling his mother "aunt", "*mangoane*" or "*rakhali*" and may address her in the same way: at first nothing is done about this, but later spasmodic attempts are made to correct it, either by telling the child what the right terms are or by the person addressed not answering until called by the correct term. Then, too, people often ask the child who a person coming into the hut is, and applaud him if he answers correctly, or laugh good-naturedly if he fails and say "No, no, it is your father", or whatever the relationship is.

The same unobtrusive help and encouragement, rather than direct instruction, are found in many other cases. Thus, in dancing the child learns the various steps by imitating others and is only occasionally shown by a friend how to do a particular movement. Similarly, girls learn to cook and grind grain and boys to milk or plough by watching others, being helped occasionally by someone showing them the knack, e.g. giving a slight flick with the wrists in grinding grain, or squeezing the teat properly in milking. In the more difficult activities such as brewing beer or weaving certain types of baskets, where instruction is required, the child's training is postponed till he is at least ten or twelve, by which time he will have intelligence enough to grasp what he is taught. At this age, he is taught definite rules of behaviour and is told to respect his elders, obey his parents, herd well, look after the babies properly, honour the chief, obey the law and so on. Many of these injunctions are quoted as maxims and precepts, such as "elders are respected". Others again may be impressed upon the children in the form of proverbs: "the wronged do not forget, though the injurer may"; "the cow is helped which helps itself"; "the lie which saves is good"; and "lies do not make one wealthy". Little use is made of fairy tales and stories as a means of instruction, as they are regarded as forms of entertainment.

These injunctions are backed by various sanctions. They may roughly be divided into two main categories—appeal to the child's self-esteem, and compulsion by force or fear. Like the others, neither of these sanctions ends with childhood, and most of them are themselves independent moulders of the child's behaviour. The first is used to encourage children to emulate their more skilled companions and to aim at greater expertness. Thus mothers clap and sing for their children to encourage them to dance. Again a young boy aged about three may be pacified and stopped from crying by saying "Hela, chiefs don't cry" or stimulated by a remark such as "What! a great bull like you, afraid?" It is noteworthy that little attempt is made to buy conformity and children are seldom offered rewards for good behaviour or obedience.

The second sanction, that of force, or threat of force, is only used after the child has been weaned. Rough words are often used and children are frequently threatened "*ke tla u 'nata*" (I will smack you), but such threats are seldom carried out, and if they are, the child may be slapped with the hand or beaten with a light twig or switch. Boys may be beaten up to any age but girls should not be touched after the age of five or six. Older boys may be threatened with a sjambok for some serious offence, but this threat rarely materializes and, though they may provoke their elders to torrents of wrathful abuse, they are seldom chastised. It is indeed noticeable how often children flatly disobey their parents and go quite unpunished, their parents' reaction merely being to ignore them, shrug their shoulders and grumble that they do not know what children are coming to. Adults other than senior kinsmen often have so little notice taken of them that they do not readily ask children to do anything for them.

EDUCATION

In the old days, by all accounts, children were treated more severely and corporal punishment was readily used. Even strangers could with impunity beat a child for impertinence, disrespect or other misdemeanours and passers-by were quite within their rights in flogging herd-boys whom they happened to find letting stock graze in the lands. But nowadays such severity is rare, and parents resent any interference with their children, whatever the cause may be. Schools and the initiation lodge are the only exception to this. At the latter, boys are frequently and severely flogged. In the former, the teacher is allowed to punish his pupils by beating them on the hand with a ruler or switch, but not about the body. Some parents resent this prerogative, but others, particularly those who deplore what they call the present insubordination of the young, welcome it and even try to get the teacher to punish their children for domestic offences.

Children are often threatened with supernatural or future punishment. For instance, a child is told it will turn into a monkey if it does not stop crying, or if it sits with its back to the fire. There are also taboos (breach of which will provoke some misfortune, such as impotence, sterility, or hail) on the consumption by children of delicacies which the old people like, such as kidneys, parts of the liver and marrow bones, and also on the playing of games, such as knucklebones, skipping and (among the Phuthi) *tsipo* near the village, where they may become a nuisance. Again, girls are told that if they dally on the wayside when fetching water, it will rain on their wedding day, or if they give a man water to drink from their water-pot on their return from the spring, their *bohali* (marriage) cattle will all be bulls or their children all males; similarly, herd-boys are told not to sleep in the veld lest they be choked by a goblin or a snake get inside their pockets or creep into their ears.

Children are also sometimes threatened with bogeys. They are discouraged from wandering away from the courtyard when their mother is busy or from making a nuisance of themselves in other ways by the threat: "the wolves[1] will take you" or "*thokolosi* will eat you". The chief may also be held up as a bogey in this way and it is possible that the police and Europeans are too.

Ridicule is a favourite weapon, and varies from a gentle chaffing to scorn. Sexual matters particularly lend themselves to this sort of discipline. Boys of about six or seven are encouraged to wear a loincloth by sarcastic references to the "peculiar conformation" of their genitals, and older boys are encouraged to leave their parents' hut and to sleep in the kitchen or at the bachelors' hut by veiled innuendos and even open suggestions of sexual perversion. Again boys refusing to go out to herd are jeered at by their companions: "Oho, you've eaten food with initiation girls", and girls are taunted for inefficient housework. In

---

[1] "Wolves" of the initiation school.

adult life the courts often try by sarcasm and derision to shame offenders into mending their ways.

Basuto children are strangely passive and this may be accounted for by the foregoing methods of education as well as by malnutrition, lack of sleep, the simplicity of their life and the lack of external stimuli. When a stranger comes to the village, they will approach him cautiously and then sit looking at him without stirring for a long time. Similarly, at ceremonies they sit stock still for an hour or more; they are interested in the proceedings but give one the impression by their slow movements and rather vacant expressions that their immobility is due not so much to self-control or deep absorption in the proceedings, as to sheer placidity and lassitude. Moreover, in their own games and activities, they show little enterprise and seldom go "exploring" or play games where daring and ingenuity are required; they never play practical jokes on their elders, or even on one another, and an independent, rebellious or "naughty" child is rare.

Formal Education

Initiation. The significance of initiation lies primarily in its function as a "rite de passage", marking and effecting the transition from adolescence to adulthood. It used also to be an important educational institution, but it is now becoming rare, except among the Tlokoa.

When the son of a chief or an important headman is about fifteen or sixteen, the question of his initiation is discussed, and if the prospects of the coming season are good, an approximate date is fixed for the following year. Preparations are then begun and adequate grain supplies accumulated. Among some clans, e.g. the Phuthi and probably[1] others, a special field is set aside and cultivated by tribal labour and its produce is earmarked for the school and for the beer used in various ceremonies. The chief's followers also make arrangements for their sons to be initiated with his. Important headmen may, with the chief's permission, hold their own initiation schools concurrently with, or subsequently to, his and these are attended by the sons of their friends and followers. This is one way in which difficulties over clan seniority are avoided. These schools or lodges never include more than sixty boys; the Tlokoa chiefs' lodges nowadays do not have more than about fifty boys and other lodges are smaller.

For several years beforehand boys are taught to regard initiation as an inevitable part of their upbringing and one they should look forward to. Until they have been initiated, they cannot marry, nor take part in various social activities and tribal affairs. As the time for their initiation approaches, they are told exciting stories of life at the lodge, which do not, however, reveal any of its secrets, and are promised that they will see their chief flying in the sky and be taught to bore their way through

[1] Sekese, op. cit. p. 16.

mountains. They are excited by the school's air of mystery and the prospect of being allowed to share the secret initiation language and to meet the "wolves" they have seen shuffling past the village during a previous initiation. In spite of these inducements, however, many are scared and stronger pressure has to be brought to bear upon them. They are then addressed in derogatory terms, and called "boy" (*leqai, moshemane*), "dog", "brother-in-law of a pole-cat". They are told that all uninitiated boys have horrible long monkey tails, visible only to initiates, which can only be removed at the school, and that they will never be free of lice until the small hole in their heads is stopped up at initiation. When they enter a hut all the men and women present draw back with exclamations of disgust and tell them to get out—and a friend later confidentially explains that they stink vilely in the nostrils of all initiates. If these devices fail and they are still unwilling, they will finally be forced into initiation by intimidation and flogging.[1]

The prospective initiates meet at the chief's village during the winter. A small feast is held at which the boys, together with all the nubile girls of the village, have their ears pierced. No one can explain why this is done nor why the girls are involved. The operation, which the children are expected to endure stoically, is performed quickly and skilfully with a needle, and the hole kept open by a thick piece of grass. This rite appears to be confined to the Tlokoa.

The next year, three or four months before the school is due to start, the boys visit their maternal uncles, and are given a small feast and *ntja* children have the tuft of hair (*sehlotho*) shaved off. The boys then meet at the chief's[2] village and are scarified by the official doctor in order of seniority. Next day they get up early and "run away" into the veld where they are later followed by the young men of the neighbourhood. After staying there for a time, which varies among different clans from a few hours to some days, the boys return to the chief's village and then to their own homes. Thereafter they meet daily, go out with the cattle and return home at night. This is a period of preparation during which they gather firewood, collect and dry a certain root (*tsoane*) to be used as tinder[3] at the lodge, weave grass ropes for their

---

[1] The need for bolstering the traditional "inducements", especially nowadays, when the opposition of schools, Chistianity and the principal chiefs has stengthened boys' fear and reluctance to face initiation, is clearly shown by the case of my young helper Borikhoe. As a lad of about twelve, he was wildly excited by the "wolves", the lure of the lodge and the excitement of its ceremonies, and he longed for the day when he would be old enough to go. But four or five years later, when his turn came, he was enjoying school and was so much afraid of being expelled if he went to the initiation lodge that he ran away from home and had to be forcibly brought back and pushed into the lodge.

[2] For convenience the word "chief" is used here to designate the organizer of the school.

[3] The tinder is lighted by a spark struck from a stone with a piece of metal. Another method of making fire by boring soft wood such as willow with a hard one (*Kolitsane unid*) is known but rarely used as being too slow.

huts and learn a number of secret songs. Any mistakes they may make are liberally punished by flogging.

The initiation lodge (*mophato*) is opened by a series of rites and feasts lasting three days. This is an exciting and lavishly celebrated ceremony, for which vast quantities of beer and meat are provided. The boys' parents and maternal uncles are expected to bring and exchange with one another from three to six huge pots of beer and an ox or sheep, part of which is consumed here and the rest taken home. The chief's village provides additional beer for the guests. This feast is as near an orgy as the Basuto ever get and fighting sometimes takes place. Strictly speaking, whatever offences or breaches of the peace occur on this occasion or at the lodge are not cognizable by the ordinary courts of law, but have to be dealt with by the men at the lodge. Nowadays, in their efforts to destroy initiation, some chiefs try to have such matters brought to their courts.

Towards sunset the boys, led by the young men, return from the veld bringing with them a black bull. The spectators become wildly excited, dance the ceremonial *mokorotlo* dance[1] and sing special initiation songs, some of which are obscene and exceedingly graphic. The boys are jostled into the *khotla* and once more doctored to give them courage and strength and to protect them from sorcery. While this is going on, the bull is killed, its right foreleg and shoulder are quickly skinned, roughly roasted,[2] cut into chunks and smeared with medicines. The most renowned warrior present then "feeds" the boys. Spearing a piece of meat with a double-pronged spear, he holds it over his shoulder and jerks it about, while the initiate kneels and, with his hands behind his back, tries to seize it with his teeth. When he catches it, he retires to eat it at the back of the *khotla* while the next initiate goes forward for his. When they have all been "fed", the rest of this ritual meat is eaten by the men or taken by the doctor. The boys then retire to a little hut outside the *khotla*, leaving the men to drink and feast, sing initiation songs, chant the chief's praises and dance the *mokorotlo*.

In all the important incidents, such as those just mentioned, as well as others described below, the boys follow one another in regular order, according to their genealogical and clan seniority. Among the Tlokoa, the chief's sons (*Ba-Lefe*) are always preceded by a *Tebele* of the Sekhosana clan and the Ba-Tsotsetsi are preceded by a *Tebele* of the Lekhomalo clan. This is done so that the *Letebele* may shield his seniors from harm and draw upon himself the sorcery of their enemies.

At about midnight the boys slip away from the village and go to a secluded spot near the chosen site of their lodge, where they are joined later by the men. At the first glimmer of dawn the men divide into two groups, some remaining with the boys and the others accompanying

[1] This dance is described in Chapter VI.
[2] Sometimes this is quite raw and is cut from the bull while still living.

PLATE III

(a) Mother making porridge with baby on her back

(b) Children round hearth

PLATE IV

Boys' initiation

Boys' initiation

EDUCATION

the *mosuoe* (circumciser) and the chief. One by one, the boys are taken from the first group to the second. There each boy has his loincloth cut away and is led before the *mosuoe* and sharply told "Look up and greet your chief". As he does so the *mosuoe* grabs the foreskin and, with a deft slash, cuts it away. It is usually done so quickly that it is over before the boy knows what is happening. If this ruse should fail, the boy is held firmly while the *mosuoe* circumcises him at leisure, his cries being drowned by the hullaballoo raised by the onlookers. Occasionally a boy has the courage and self-control to tell the men to let him be, and then undergoes the operation alone. Such courage is greatly admired, but it is not expected and those who flinch are not dishonoured.

When they have all been circumcised, they are left in the veld in the charge of a few young men, their foreskins being collected, burnt and buried. Some hours later a large bowl of medicine, consisting of roasted butterfat mixed with a powerful narcotic made of *leshoma* bulb, is brought to them. Each eats a handful and within a few minutes falls into a profound stupor, which lasts a day or more and effectively deadens all pain. The wounds are sometimes sterilized with brandy, or protected with the cool, smooth *leshoma* leaf. The operation is usually skilfully performed and cases of mutilation are said to be rare.

When the circumcision is over, the men build the huts which are to be the boys' home on a site that has been doctored in the same way as a village site. As soon as the huts are finished, they, too, are doctored. On this doctoring (*moupello*) the health and success of the lodge depends. Misfortunes, such as the desertion of an initiate, accidents and deaths are attributed to the use of inferior medicines. That same evening the boys are taken to the lodge.

The composition of the *mophato* varies among the different clans. Among the Tlokoa each boy is attended by a companion (an elder brother or cousin) called a *mobineli* (literally, the one who sings for him), whose duty it is to look after him and see that he comes to no harm, to teach him secret initiation songs, and help him to compose his own praise-song. In the old days, these companions were carefully chosen for courage and integrity, but now little attention is paid to such qualities. All the companions are expected to sleep at the lodge, to abstain from sexual intercourse, or, at any rate, not to commit adultery. They must also observe certain taboos, such as that they may not shave and may not carry their sticks about the village but should keep them at the back of the *khotla*. The *mosuoe's* official functions end with the circumcision.

Among the Phuthi (and judging from Ramseyer's[1] account, other clans as well), the boys are not accompanied by individual mentors but have two or three men for the whole school. They are known as *mosuoe*, though only one of them does the circumcision. They are usually much

[1] Ramseyer, 1928.

older men than the companions (*babineli*) of the Tlokoa and one of them, at least, should be an authority on tribal lore and custom. After a month or two they return to the village, leaving the senior initiate in charge, and only occasionally revisit the lodge. Phuthi lodges are also smaller than those of the Tlokoa, and consist of only about sixteen boys.

Every morning at sunrise the boys go to the river to wash their wounds. Those who shrink from cleaning themselves properly are held by the *babineli* while the wound is forcibly washed and any pus and dirt are scraped away by means of a stick. During this painful operation everyone sings and shouts vociferously to drown the boy's cries. After this, they go back to the lodge for breakfast. The Tlokoa cook this for themselves at the lodge from meal co-operatively ground at the village by their womenfolk. The work involved in feeding the lodge is enormous; in the case of a Tlokoa chief's lodge over 700 lbs. of meal were ground each week. All the implements used are traditional, even down to the bags in which the meal is carried to the lodge, European handmills and sacks being taboo though iron cooking-pots are permitted. Among the Phuthi, for the first month or so the food is prepared at home by a *motsoetse* or other ritually pure woman and taken in a huge bowl to a concealed place near the lodge where it is collected by the *mosuoe*. After this period the boys do their own cooking. The food should always be eaten as hot and as quickly as possible.

During the day the boys go out into the veld, dressed in cloaks of roughly tanned cowhide, and they may wear loincloths when their wounds are healed. Formerly they used to go on long marches through the mountains, to test their powers of endurance and to teach them the local topography from a military point of view; they were also taught various military manoeuvres, how to throw spears and how to parry them. To stimulate their courage and resourcefulness, they were encouraged to forage and steal from the neighbourhood, even to the point of robbing strangers who crossed their path. Since they were of military age these exercises stood them in good stead as is shown by the feat of the young Letsie who, while still at the lodge, warded off Sekonyela's attack on Thaba Bosiu during Moshesh's absence. To-day this aspect of initiation has inevitably died out though no non-initiate will dare approach a lodge, and herd-boys fear to collect stock which has strayed on the hillsides opposite the lodge. The most onerous of the boys' tasks nowadays is the daily collection of firewood and an occasional excursion into the mountains to visit a neighbouring *mophato*. Apart from this, their main occupation is the learning of the secret songs and language, and the composition of their praise-songs.

They return to the lodge towards evening and retire to their huts while food is being prepared. After supper, they sing again and then are sent back to their huts. Twice or three times a week they are flogged and have to run the gauntlet of all the *babineli* and visitors drawn up in two lines. They are beaten with specially plaited grass switches. This is repeated whenever they are visited by the chief and whenever one of their number has misbehaved during the day. They may also be beaten individually for outstanding churlishness and slovenliness, for mistakes in singing or for failure to observe the correct ritual when they enter or leave the lodge.

Occasionally they are given talks by the leading *babineli* on tribal history, correct forms of behaviour and morality. The virtues stressed are chastity, honesty, reliability, courage, humility, and respect for elders and the chief; these lessons are sometimes pushed home by punishment meted out at the school to adults who have committed some offence at home and who are flogged out of sight but within earshot of the boys. The only sexual instruction given consists of exhortations to avoid adultery. "Smut" and lewdness are not encouraged.

At night their rest is continually disturbed and they are frequently awakened and made to rehearse their songs. Apart from this, their sleep is not profound for, in order to make them tough, they are allowed only one skin blanket each, even during extremely cold and snowy weather.

The existence of the lodge affects life in the village as well. One of its strictest rules is that all who have previously been initiated should visit the lodge from time to time. Distinguished visitors, such as the chief, talk to the boys and look at their wounds, but others just sit about, talk to the *babineli* and join in the songs. Men afraid of visiting the lodge are jeered at for their cowardice and treated with marked disrespect by women; and their wives may refuse to sleep with them. On the other hand, notorious thieves are disgraced by not being allowed near the lodge. To-day these aspects of the lodge have changed—the morals of its visitors are less closely scrutinized and compulsory visits are no longer insisted on.

A point which, I believe, is peculiar to the Tlokoa is the institution of the "wolves" (*liphiri*). The "wolves" are the *babineli* dressed up in a flowing grass costume, with a longish tail, of a yellow straw colour woven at the lodge, and looking, at a distance, glossily soft. They move with a smooth shuffling movement, stop every ten yards or so, look round, jump and shake themselves, letting their costumes glisten and ripple in the sun. Dressed in this way, they occasionally "visit" the chief by suddenly appearing in broad daylight near the village, circling round it once or twice and then disappearing over the hill. Their movements are followed with intense interest by everyone, the men looking on from the *khotla*, the women clustering at the doors of their huts and the children peeping fearfully from behind their skirts. What relation these "wolves" have to the esoteric life of the lodge I do not know. They nevertheless have an appreciable educational influence on the people. Apart from being held up as bogeys to children, they are used to threaten and punish adults who misbehave during the life of the *mophato*. For instance, at Malingoaneng they tore down the *setloana* of a dissolute widow and cast it out of the village; this public reproof and perhaps the fear of more serious punishment was more than she could bear and a few days later she fled from the village and was seen no more.

Initiation usually lasts about three months and, though it should not end before the boys' wounds heal, it may last longer if food is available. Sekese records that the old lodges used to last six or eight months, and this was also true of the Phuthi.

The final day of the lodge is arbitrarily fixed for a convenient Friday or Saturday, when the people are likely to be free. As the date draws near, the chief prepares for the feast, which falls almost entirely on his shoulders. Wives and mothers of the *babineli* and the boys prepare their dress. This consists of loincloths and bands of beadwork; the loincloths are cut out of sheep skin and brayed till they are soft and smooth, the boys' being white and plain and those of the *babineli* coloured and decorated with brass rings, mirrors and other sparkling objects. At the lodge great efforts are made to perfect the songs and choruses and the boys may be heard practising for long hours in some secluded kloof.

On the last night the boys are allowed to sleep undisturbed until early dawn. Then they are suddenly awakened and told to hurry out of their huts. They rush for the doors, only to find them blocked; the brighter lads then hastily hack their way through the grass walls, being greeted with shouts of approval as they emerge, while their duller-witted companions are beaten for their lack of imagination. This incident, generally explained as teaching them to "bore their way through a mountain" seems to symbolize their return to normal life. As they will not eat again for some thirty hours, the boys are given a more substantial meal than usual and allowed to eat quietly and in peace.

The *babineli* now clean up the lodge, smash all the clay pots and take back to the village their iron cooking-pots and blankets. Formerly these also would have been destroyed, but nowadays they are too precious to be wasted. Even the boys' skin cloaks are now taken back and given to the younger boys of the village. At the village, the *babineli* shave and trim their hair, put on their new loincloths, and decorate themselves with beads and other finery. About midday they are formally sent back to the lodge by the chief, and they sing, dance and weave their way back and forth (*ho etsa monyakoe*) across the veld until they disappear over the edge of a hill and rejoin the lodge. The boys wash and then smear themselves from head to foot with a mixture of red ochre and butterfat, and are given new loincloths and two clubs. Most of this red ochre is ordinary "Venetian Red" bought from the stores, but to make it "genuine" and to provide a symbolical link with the tribal past, ochre, brought from Bopeli,[1] is added. Certain of the

[1] Bopeli is part of the Northern Transvaal and is believed to be one of the ancestral homes of the Tlokoa.

EDUCATION

chief's medicines are added to the mixture to secure the loyalty of the boys, strengthen their allegiance to the tribe and chief, and (in the old days) unite them to their fellow-warriors.

In the afternoon, the chief, accompanied by the official doctor, goes down to inspect the boys. When everything is ready, he gives the word for them to leave and then sets fire to the lodge. Practically everything is burnt but the small boys of the village who rush down there first thing next morning usually manage to find such odds and ends as spearheads or a bit of the "wolves'" clothing which they treasure for long afterwards. Meanwhile everyone in the village is agog with excitement, and as soon as the smoke from the *mophato* is seen, the women break into cries of joy, and dance and sing, redoubling their efforts when the boys appear. The latter advance quickly on the flank of the *babineli*, and when they are within a couple of hundred yards of the village, suddenly rush to the cattle kraal, leap over the walls, shouting and waving their sticks, while the men cheer and fire their rifles.

Once in the kraal, they huddle together in a corner while the women and children press forward to look at them and comment excitedly on their appearance. Then the men join them and distribute new blankets, provided by their parents, maternal uncles or, in the case of orphans, by the chief. The women then disperse, fires are lit in the kraal and the men sing their war songs and the chief's praises and dance the *mokorotlo*. They spend the whole night in the kraal, however bad the weather, the men gathered round the fires, the boys shivering in the darkness beyond.

At dawn a pot of unstrained beer is brought from the chief's hut and taken to the kraal. War medicine is mixed with the beer and "sealed" with a red-hot hammer-head, which has been heated all night under the older men's fire. One by one the boys go forward, kneel in front of the pot, take a mouthful of beer, follow the chief *mobineli* and line up against the far wall. Then as the sun rises over the horizon, they squirt out the beer, "pierce the sun" and so greet the dawn of their new life. They then drink[1] a little of the medicated beer, which "strengthens" their fearlessness and the warrior spirit with which they have been inculcated. After this they go out to the veld with the cattle, ease themselves after their long vigil and collect small bunches of firewood. They again smear themselves with the same red ochre mixture as before or with their own family ochre and medicines; members of certain clans, such as the Koena, also anoint their heads with antimony. They return to the village with the cattle at about eleven o'clock and take their places at the back of the *khotla* where everyone has assembled —men, old women and children inside, women and girls outside. The chief *mobineli* chants the chief's praises and does a few steps of the *mokorotlo*. The boys then follow; each stands up in turn, removes his blanket, and with his sticks in his left hand and his right on the muzzle

[1] Some doctors do not allow this, saying their medicines will make the boys drunk.

of a gun, recites his praise-songs (*lithoko*). The most talented are allowed to sing *mangae*, which are *lithoko* with a chorus whose refrain is taken up by the *babineli* and the rest of the boys.

The onlookers follow these songs and choruses with keen interest and applaud at the end of each. Many of them are witty, some salacious and a few beautiful and moving. At the end of a good recital people may be seen wiping tears from their eyes and, as often as not, the parents and friends of the boy concerned, overcome with pride and emotion, weep unashamedly.

When the last one has finished, the men break out into desultory singing, and a few dance the *mokorotlo*. Formerly warriors who had killed a man in battle would chant their own *lithoko* and dance a ferocious war dance in a circle cleared for them, bringing it to a climax by stabbing the ground fiercely, once for each victim, while the crowd murmured a deep-throated "Ha. . . . Hu. . . ." Men who had wounded a man or killed a wounded enemy had to hesitate before striking the ground. The wives of these blooded warriors were entitled to cover one side of their faces with white clay and make a white circle round the mouth.

Water and fresh cattle dung (*bolokoe*) are now brought to the *khotla* and the boys have their heads and eyebrows shaved by a *motsoetse* after which they wash their hands with the dung. When they have eaten, they go back to the veld with the cattle, while feasting goes on in the village. In the afternoon, those of the boys who live at some distance from the village go home with their people, and are welcomed with a small feast and the killing of a sheep.

In the evening the boys who have stayed behind return to the *khotla*. They repeat their songs and choruses, again being listened to by the villagers, and are then given food. They sleep in the *khotla*, but are allowed to warm themselves at the fire, which has to burn all night; if it rains or snows, they are allowed to sleep indoors. For the next four or five days they repeat this ritual, sing their songs morning and evening to an ever-dwindling audience, go into the veld with the cattle and return to sleep in the *khotla*. They are now no longer beaten and bullied at every turn, but may sleep as long as they like in the veld, may talk freely to one another and may even look about them when in the *khotla*. On the fifth evening, after they have sung their praises, they "plant their sticks in their home" and so bring their initiation to an end.

Initiation does not produce any immediate change in the boys' life, but it marks the beginning of a change. They now have, as a result of their experience, the indefinable quality of status—they are no longer "boys" (*bashemane*) but "men" (*banna*). They have to behave themselves with more dignity and poise than before and tend to gravitate to adult society. In the old days they were expected to stay with the chief and act as his servants and bodyguard and look after the *khotla*.[1] Nowa-

[1] See also Ellenberger and MacGregor, p. 283.

EDUCATION

days they have no such functions and are free to do what they like. Some spend their time loafing, others return to their herding or go to school and others turn their attention to the *khotla* and interest themselves in tribal affairs.

The principal aspects of the institution may be briefly summarized. In a general way, initiation completed the education of the child and prepared him for adult status. More specifically it taught boys to be warriors, and trained them in such virtues as bravery, obedience and honesty, their training being strengthened by medicines. Sex was not an important aspect and here initiation functioned not as an immediate introduction and stimulus to erotic experience, but only as an essential but indirect prelude to marriage. Initiation also provided social interest and entertainment and helped to keep alive old Sesuto songs and dances. It may sometimes have been instrumental in forging new social bonds[1] linking the initiates together.

In historical times it does not appear to have been an event of significance to the tribe as a whole. The chief organized the school primarily for his own family—his sons, his brothers' sons, the sons of his near relations and immediate followers—and not for the whole tribe. Influential headmen were allowed to have separate initiation schools for their own sons. The chief's lodge is the largest and excites most interest; its opening and closing ceremonies are the outstanding social events in the district and probably have some political value by emphasizing his wealth and importance.

A hundred years ago, initiation was probably the most important ceremonial institution of the Basuto, but to-day it is rapidly breaking down. Even among the Tlokoa, where old Lelingoana strenuously maintained it, it is beginning to decay and in 1935 the first revolt by the younger generation occurred—the youth in question, by the irony of fate, being one of the old chief's own sons. Elsewhere in Basutoland it is almost dead and it is only in the foothills that it is still occasionally held. Its decay is due mainly to missionary influence and to the inevitable change in Basuto ideas as a result of European contact. Initiation was one of the first things the missionaries attacked[2] and it is one of the few institutions that they are united in denouncing. It was early admitted that it had its good points—Casalis,[3] for instance, wrote: "There are traces of a real initiation to the good behaviour and duties of life," but these were regarded as a poor price to pay for the demoralization of the initiate and the "veritable moral infanticide" for which Dieterlen[4] claimed it was responsible. It was also regarded as a stumbling-block to the civilization and conversion of the people and as responsible for the "general degradation" of the Basuto. Holding such views the missionaries lost no time in attacking the institution, and though they

[1] Ellenberger and MacGregor, p. 283. [2] Ibid., pp. 285-7.
[3] Casalis, 1861, p. 326. [4] Dieterlen, 1912, p. 153.

could not get Moshesh to forbid it, they managed to secure his promise, about 1846, that his children and grandchildren should not be initiated. As a result, there grew up a number of powerful chiefs, such as Majara, Nehemiah and other sons of Moshesh[1] who were not initiated and who, therefore, could not hold their own initiation schools nor visit or take an interest in those held in their districts.[2] Some of them then merely neglected the institution whereas others actively opposed it, either by forbidding it in their districts or by protecting youths who ran away from it. This official opposition still continues and Seeiso, for instance, sheltered Lelingoana's son who ran away from his initiation and sought protection. The defection of these chiefs destroyed one of the most important objects of initiation, namely, the periodic renewal of tribal and political loyalty, and so caused many who supported it on general grounds to lose interest.

The missions forbade their adherents to initiate their children and refused to re-admit to their schools pupils who had run away to go to the lodge. This caused and still causes bitter feelings among the people, for they consider that as the schools are supported from public funds, they should not be closed to those who adhere to tribal customs which happen to be contrary to mission doctrine. The missionaries justify their action by saying that initiation "automatically excludes all other types of education".[3] This is an unjustifiable generalization; many initiates may be found who have managed to attend school, either by going there for the first time after their initiation or by changing to the school of another denomination; and these are just as bright as uninitiated children. As, however, initiation has now lost its old importance so far as the mass of the people are concerned, this particular point is no longer one of the burning questions of the day and so need be pursued no further.

Many Basuto have accepted the opinion that initiation is retrograde if not definitely immoral and now oppose it as strongly as any missionary. Others are indifferent and, since the social stigma of being uninitiated has largely lost its sting, they see neither harm nor profit in initiation and let their children please themselves. The only people who still support the institution are the old conservatives who are attached to their traditions and customs, or admire the virtues it inculcates.

Since it has lost its old significance, several initiation secrets have been allowed to leak out, notably that of circumcision. Initiation has always been associated with virility and this association has now been transferred to the physical act of circumcision. Consequently, some girls refuse to have connexion with an uncircumcised man so that nowadays many men go to the local doctor, native or European, to be circum-

[1] Jacottet, 1912.
[2] See Report, *Native Laws and Customs*, especially Letsie I., in evidence.
[3] Dieterlen, op. cit., p. 154.

cised. A few fathers take their young sons to the doctor for the same purpose.

Girls' Initiation

Lack of space forbids a detailed description of girls' initiation. It is the same, in essentials, as that of boys. It has its own ritual and ceremony, much of which is forbidden to men and uninitiated females, and its own secret songs and practices. Initiates, aged between fifteen and twenty, live together in a lodge in groups of about ten, or in a special hut in the village under the supervision of some important women, and are taught their future womanly duties and the general virtues of humility, obedience and respect. They may also receive a certain amount of sex instruction and undergo some physical operation, the hymen perhaps being broken either by the insertion of a horn or of a woman's finger, but I was unable to obtain reliable details of this. They are treated with medicines in much the same way as the boys; the women enjoy the same type of licence at the opening ceremony as the men do at the boys' initiation and many men are actually dreadfully shocked at the lewdness shown on this occasion by women who at all other times are models of propriety. The celebrations at the girls' initiation ceremonies are regarded as being primarily feminine affairs just as those of the boys' are men's feasts. The girls' lodge also has its own "animal", but it functions only during certain ceremonies. Other details of the institutions differ, one of the most interesting being that uninitiated girls are allowed to visit initiates at their lodge at certain times, to share their food and play their *morupa* drum and may even be told some of their secrets. The girls' initiation is less strenuous physically as it takes place in summer rather than in winter and the girls are not exposed to the same hardships as the boys. The lodge is situated in or near its sponsor's village and not away in the veld.

The functions of the girls' initiation are much the same as those of the boys'. It is a typical aggregation rite bringing them into the adult world. It is also regarded as a desirable, if not essential, preliminary to marriage and it is vaguely believed to encourage fertility. Consequently, a woman found to be uninitiated is sometimes sent by her husband to be initiated.

Girls' initiation is still fairly common and *bale*[1] girls may still be seen in all parts of Basutoland, even in sophisticated areas such as those round the capital at Maseru. The missions dislike girls' initiation for the same reason as boys', but have not opposed it as actively for it is not so rough and exhausting and lacks the more dramatic and pagan features. It has also been kept alive more readily because it is largely a domestic and feminine affair and women, being more conservative than men and jealous of their old traditions and of the secrets of the lodge, have pre-

[1] Initiates are daubed with white clay at one stage of their initiation.

served it. As it has little to do with tribal loyalties to the chief, the indifference of the chiefs has not greatly affected it.

The School

The school and initiation lodge are both educational institutions that aim at teaching the child by means of an organized routine. They differ in that the *mophato* intimately affects the child for a short period and achieves its object by its intensity and drama, whereas the school is continuous and humdrum and conditions the child slowly over a period of years. Furthermore, although the *mophato* comes to the fore only for brief and exciting periods, it exercises a continual influence over the community, whereas the school makes little direct impression on the public which it influences indirectly through its effect on the individual. The *mophato*, as an integral part of Sesuto culture, has become outmoded, whereas the school which was extraneous and alien is coming to be an accepted part of modern Basuto life.

The first schools were established over a century ago at central mission stations, and as teachers and evangelists were trained, new ones were opened farther afield. The missionaries were men of foresight and enterprise to whom the people responded with enthusiasm, and it was not long before schools were established everywhere throughout the territory, even in remote valleys in the heart of the mountains. To-day there are over 800 primary and 9 secondary mission schools belonging to the French Protestant, English and Roman Catholic missions. In addition, there are eleven other small missions which maintain a few schools, five Government schools, and a few private schools. All recognized schools are financed in part by the missions themselves and in part from Government grants-in-aid, which were first started in 1871, when the territory was annexed to the Cape. The number of children in the primary schools in 1947 was 28,882 boys and 50,713 girls, and in the secondary schools 2,342 boys and 2,500 girls. The secondary schools include two technical and six teacher-training schools. One of the three non-professional schools is a High School with classes up to and including matriculation. A small but unknown number of Basuto children go to school in the Union and a handful go on for university and higher education to the South African Native College, Fort Hare, the University of the Witwatersrand and to English universities.[1] About 75 per cent of the children of school age attend school, which is one of the highest percentages in Colonial Africa.

The elementary schools are very simply built and consist of one or more huts, similar to ordinary rectangular dwelling-huts, only larger. They are equipped with a few blackboards, perhaps a table and a cupboard, and sometimes benches made of wood or plaster. Their average

---

[1] The Roman Catholic Mission established a university college (Pius XII Catholic University College) at Roma in 1948.

EDUCATION

size is a little over 100 pupils, the largest being just over 300 and the smallest 20. Most of them are day schools. Intermediate schools are more elaborate institutions and are better built; as they cater for a wide area, dormitories and boarding facilities are sometimes provided for those children who cannot live with friends or relations near at hand.

Four terms are kept, the school year beginning in early February or late January and closing towards the end of November. Arrangements are made, if possible, for school holidays to coincide with the peak periods of the agricultural seasons, when the demand for the children's assistance is greatest. School usually opens between 8 and 9 a.m. in the summer and later in the winter. The day starts with prayers, followed by drill and physical exercises. In fine weather classes may be held outside, but at other times the children have to crowd into the schoolroom, two or three classes often being held in the same hut. Frequently, older children from the local village take their infant brothers and sisters to school, leaving them to play about by themselves while they do their lessons.

After a couple of hours, a break is allowed. The local children dash home for food, and in summer, when the cattle return from the morning grazing, the boys go off to help with the milking. School then continues till about 2 p.m. Thereafter, the boys join their companions who have not been to school, and go herding in the veld, and the girls go on with their usual duties. Homework, if any, is done either that same afternoon, or early next morning, while they sit sunning themselves at home.

Apart from this regular routine, several other activities may go on at school. In some, the boys may learn gardening, in others the girls may be taught sewing and knitting. They also play various games, and some schools are keen on singing. Sometimes, an interested headman may invite two or three schools to a competition held at his village, and provide a small feast for the competitors and audience. Organized sports, such as hockey, football and athletics, have been introduced, inter-school matches are played and an annual nation-wide competition is held.

At the end of two or three years at school, pupils are usually able to do simple sums in arithmetic, write in a large and somewhat unformed hand and read simple literature. Their knowledge of English is rudimentary, and of little practical use save to those who later go to European centres, but it gives the possessor some pride in himself and kudos among his friends. For this reason many teachers try to teach English, even when it is not supposed to be included in the curriculum, or else spend on it more than the scheduled time. "Morals" and Religion are taught as subjects. The former consists of precepts and improving stories about honesty, purity, self-sacrifice and thrift, and the latter of Bible stories and elementary doctrinal facts. It is exceedingly difficult to say what effect they have on the children. Arts and crafts find little place in the curriculum except in a few schools where girls are taught the elements of housewifery and needlework and the boys gardening. The importance of these subjects is now being recognized and gradually more time is being set aside for teaching them.

The people are on the whole keen on their schools and on education, even to the point of paying a special education levy of three shillings, first introduced in 1927.[1] They are imbued with a desire to advance, and though they have only a vague idea of what they mean by "progress" (*tsoelopele*), they have a firm belief that it will only be achieved through education. They also feel that the school, like initiation in the old days, is something everyone ought to go through—that some education is an essential part of one's social equipment. They recognize its practical value, as a help in coping with modern conditions, and it is noteworthy that many schools were started specifically in order to teach practical techniques, such as arithmetic or writing, and in the mountains several schools were started solely to teach boys how to read scales and calculate wool prices. Girls who have had some education are considered more eligible for matrimony than the uneducated, but this must not be taken too far; highly educated girls are the object of awed and envious admiration but are considered too advanced for the ordinary male to control or be happy with.

For these reasons, people are prepared to make some effort to send their children to school and to do without their services for a time. But, on the whole, they consider that a little goes a long way and that to give their children more than two or three years' schooling is, at best, a waste of time, and, at worst, an unsettling influence which may make them "cheeky", dissatisfied and spoilt. They also fear that more education will cause children to despise their less educated parents and elders and look down on Basuto traditions. Nevertheless, there is a small minority who set a high value on education, either because they are not as well educated as they would like to be or because they see the potential economic and social advantages of education; they long for their children to be better educated and make considerable sacrifices to achieve this end.

This qualified parental enthusiasm for education is shared by the children. They enjoy going to school, they like acquiring new forms of knowledge, languages and ideas, and welcome the companionship and activities they find at school. But they do not want to spend too much time there. Girls are more enthusiastic than boys at first for they find that school makes a welcome break from their domestic routine and they learn there valuable domestic techniques; but they learn all they want in the elementary classes and then prefer to go back to their ordinary life. But boys with ambition see that education is the best way

[1] In 1946 this special levy was absorbed into the general tax.

to prosperity and social success and make great efforts to pass on to the higher grades. It is for these reasons that girls greatly outnumber boys in the elementary schools, whereas the reverse is the case in the secondary schools.[1]

[1] This cursory account of education in Basutoland has not done justice to what is probably the best, deepest and most potent form of European influence. I realize and regret that this is so. My reason for being so brief is that my experience was limited mainly to the Tlokoa, where education of the modern type had penetrated very little and very recently, and had not yet made its influence felt; I could only guess at what was happening elsewhere. I could have analysed the general situation statistically and given tables showing standards of achievement, teachers' qualifications and monies spent, but as this is adequately done in the official Annual Reports and in 1945 was the subject of an enquiry by a special Commission (Report of the Commission on Education in Basutoland, 1946, chairman, Sir Fred Clarke) it seemed better that I should simply refer the interested reader to the original sources.

CHAPTER V

MARRIAGE

SINGLE blessedness is looked on as something abnormal and even a little sinister and marriage is regarded as right and proper for all adults. The latter state is usually achieved and very few bachelors and practically no old maids are to be found. Most men marry at about the age of twenty-three to twenty-six. Some, particularly the sons of the well-to-do who can afford to set up an independent establishment without delay, marry earlier; others marry later on account of poverty, or because they are interested in their work, such as teaching, and do not want to be distracted by matrimony, or else because they prefer the freedom and the pleasures of single life to the settled and responsible joys of marriage.

Women usually get married after initiation or on leaving school, between the ages of eighteen and twenty-four. Some are married almost immediately but the less fortunate may have to wait several years, though seldom longer, unless they are mentally or physically deformed. Nowadays the few who fail to get married, or whose married life is unsatisfactory, find refuge in Union urban areas, where the shortage of women guarantees them some male attention.

Marriage used to be, and to some extent still is, approached from the family standpoint. This applies especially to the wealthy and important families, particularly chiefs, and to principal wives of the senior son or sons, who are more concerned with the family's interests and traditions than are the junior sons or subordinate wives.

In choosing a wife for the senior son, the family is influenced by two considerations—the girl's suitability and her family standing. She should be respectable, chaste, modest, hard-working and good tempered: the sort of girl who will make a steady wife and a good mother. Her family should have a reputation for honesty, friendliness and respectability, and should be of at least approximately equal social and economic standing to theirs. Ordinarily there is a fairly wide choice for the Basuto are not particularly snobbish; but the chiefs and other leading families attach great importance to this point, and so limit their range of choice. In the extreme case of the Paramount Chief's house, which considers itself first in the land, there is no alternative but intermarriage. As the Basuto are patrilineal and as marriage between brother and sister is forbidden, the closest and most senior relative that one can marry is one's father's brother's daughter, and many important chiefs actually do choose their senior wives from among these cousins.[1] This type of union is further encouraged by the desire to retain the marriage cattle within the family, which is expressed in the couplet:

| *Ngoana rangoane 'nyalle* | Cousin,[2] marry me |
| *likhomo li boele sakeng.* | that the cattle return to the kraal. |

Second preference goes to marriage between cross-cousins. Custom dictates that one's relationship with one's maternal uncle and his family should be particularly friendly. Marriage with his daughter is in keeping with this injunction and strengthens it. Relationship with one's paternal aunt is not quite so cordial, but it is just as warm with her children and, for the same reasons as before, marriage with her daughter is desirable. In fact it is exactly the same type of marriage as the preceding one from the woman's viewpoint, for she marries her mother's brother's son. The next best match is with one's mother's sister's daughter. Intermarriage is opposed nowadays by some moderns who say that it is bad genetically,[3] "*U tla tsoala lihole*" (you will beget abnormal children).

Interest in this question of preferential marriages is strongest among the "best" families, such as the chiefs' and other leading families. They take a greater pride in their ancestry and family connections than humbler families and pay more attention to the old customary injunctions. Moreover, they are better able to indulge this traditionalism as they are usually wealthy and, being able to afford second wives, can marry their first according to prescription and others as their fancy pleases. Poorer people who can only afford to marry one wife prefer to take the girl they like rather than the one they ought to like.[4]

As soon as the family is agreed on its choice, the boy's father gets into touch with the girl's parents. If he has not already done so, he first makes informal overtures to sound their feelings and to give them time to discuss the matter with their family. Then, if they appear favourably disposed, he formally asks them for "a calabash of water", through an intermediary, who is usually a close friend.

Once the parents have consented, the prospective bridegroom, accompanied by two or three companions, pays the girl a formal visit. If she is agreeable to the match, she gives him a scarf (*moqhaka*) as a token of her acceptance. She should then offer them food, but this they should decline, lest it be said that, instead of being impelled by love, they came driven by hunger.

[1] The Paramount Chief Griffith, for instance, married as his first four wives daughters of his father's half-brother; his son Seeiso married their brother's daughter, who was thus both his mother's brother's daughter and his father's father's half-brother's son's daughter, who is classificatorily equal to his father's brother's daughter.

[2] Literally "my father's younger brother's child".

[3] For further brief discussion on this point see Appendix III.

[4] The question of kinship and preferential marriages is dealt with more fully in Appendix III.

Although the couple concerned usually have an inkling that something matrimonial is afoot, this is sometimes the first indication given to either of them of the projected marriage and, very occasionally, it may be the first time they have seen one another. They are always supposed to approve of the choice made for them. Normally they do so, for the choice is often well made and they usually approach the matter rationally and unromantically. But if either of them dislikes it, the proposal will probably be dropped, for their parents have no desire to spoil their lives and increase the risks of an unhappy marriage. Moreover, there is always the danger that insistence will encourage the girl to elope with someone else. Many people say that this lenience is a modern phenomenon and that formerly the couple had to go through with the marriage whether they liked it or not. They also say that these arranged marriages, even if forced, were usually successful, as the parents, though primarily concerned with the social and family aspect of the match, would try to choose compatible and congenial spouses for their children, being interested in their happiness and knowing that satisfactory "in-law" relationships depended on the success of the marriage.

If a youth wanted to get married and thought his parents were delaying unduly, he could send them a message to that effect through his mother's brother, or could discuss the matter with his mother. It was not "done" in the old days for him to broach it directly with his father. Nowadays this formality has largely been dispensed with, although a young man may still approach his father through an intermediary. The old convention of "kicking the little dish" (*ho raha moritsoana*)[1] has been completely abandoned.

Infant betrothal is said to have occurred occasionally in the old days.[2] Friends might promise one another their children in marriage and, instead of giving the full *bohali* cattle for his wife, a man might sometimes pledge his sister or daughter in marriage to one of her kinsmen. In these cases, one or two cattle, called *tebeletso* (expectation) were exchanged as a pledge of good faith.

Nowadays there are several departures from the "correct" procedure outlined above. The most common is that the boy, instead of waiting for his father to choose his bride, takes the initiative himself. As one informant put it, "When a man meets a girl who pleases him, he tells his father. If his father does not like her, the boy will leave her and look for another; but if his father approves he is told to go and woo her. He then courts the girl and asks her to marry him. When she accepts, his father goes to her father and tells him about their children's love for

---

[1] Sekese, op. cit., p. 1. The young man would go to the kraal early in the morning and prevent the cows being milked by letting their calves go to them. Alternatively, he sulked at the kraal and refused to eat when food was brought out to the *khotla*.

[2] Ibid., p. 2.

one another and asks him to agree to their marriage. They talk and, when the girl's father has consulted his daughter and his kinsmen, he agrees. The man's father will send some cattle to his *mokhotsi* and then they will talk further about the day for the feast". This terse account stresses the two main points of an acceptable modern version of the old procedure, namely, the freedom of choice allowed to the young people, and the negotiations between the parents.

A less acceptable variation which occurs in more than a quarter of the marriages made to-day is elopement (*chobeliso*). In these cases, the boy seizes the girl, usually when she is in the fields or visiting friends, and takes her to his home. Even though the elopement may have been instigated or connived at by her people and agreed to by the girl herself, she usually makes a show of resisting, either as an affectation of modesty or because she really is frightened when it comes to the point. Her lover does not harm her or have intercourse with her but leaves her with his mother, who breaks the news to his father. The latter then immediately informs the girl's parents, asks for her in marriage and, if they are agreeable to the match, as is usually the case, he arranges to give them some six head of cattle as an earnest of good faith and a first instalment of the full number of *bohali* cattle.

The motives for eloping are numerous and complex. In some cases where their parents are being "difficult" and will not agree to the marriage or are delaying the wedding through tedious discussion over the cattle or some other detail, the couple elope to compel them to act. In other cases, they elope to avoid a marriage with someone they do not love, or to hasten their marriage, perhaps already agreed upon, in order to cover up the girl's pregnancy. It is also considered a "sporting" thing to do and many couples elope even though their marriage has been agreed to and preparations for its celebration are well advanced. Some even elope after marriage, if the bride's people delay unduly in taking her to her husband's home. Occasionally, however, and this is the most serious type of *chobeliso*, a man may abduct a girl against her will in order to compel her to marry him, and then if she resists he often treats her brutally and may even force her to have connexion with him.

In its milder forms *chobeliso* has come to be a common if unacknowledged social practice, followed by many though deplored by some. As shown above, the term is a blanket one which covers a multitude of sins. Some of them are innocuous and others are reprehensible, but the churches take a serious view of almost every case and punish their offending adherents. The practice is also deprecated by the "better" families on account of the scandalmongering it provokes and the gossipy articles with a moralizing tone, which appear in the newspapers. Others are not greatly disturbed about it. They recognize that in most cases it it is only a harmless escapade and they point out that where children flout their parents' authority there is often good cause for doing so. Their attitude changes, however, when they themselves happen to be the parents concerned, and they then regard it as ill-mannered and rather scandalous behaviour which places them in a humiliating position. The girl's parents often get extremely angry about it but, provided she has been decently treated, they soon calm down and either leave her with her lover, or take her home pending the satisfactory conclusion of the marriage discussions.

The practical and unsentimental point of view held by many Basuto towards marriage was described by Dieterlen in 1912: "One marries her in order that she may abundantly accomplish the functions of maternity rather than to find happiness with her or to give her any. Marriage is for her largely made up of chores and duties, and she enters into it without illusions or emotion. She therefore is not greatly disappointed by it and she can gradually derive from it all the affection and contentedness that life together can produce."[1] This placid, uncomplaining and unromantic attitude towards marriage still persists, although the changing emphasis from arranged to love matches is giving greater weight to the personal feelings of the couple concerned.

Normally the wedding is held shortly after the marriage has been arranged. Until this has been celebrated, the couple are not supposed to have sexual intercourse with one another or to live together. If they cannot afford the expenses entailed, many families agree to postpone the wedding to some future date and let the couple begin their married life at once. In such cases, the girl's people provide her with a small trousseau and send her to her husband's home, where she is welcomed and received into the family in the same way as if the wedding had been held. At the same time, the husband's people usually hand over six to ten cattle as an instalment of the marriage cattle (*bohali*).

The wedding deserves to be described in some detail as it is sociologically important and is also one of the few occasions enriched by ceremonial and ritual.

Preparations for the wedding are made by both families; the man's family has to collect the *bohali* cattle, while the girl's people prepare the marriage feast. The boy's father is helped by his own father and to a limited extent by his brothers, paternal uncles and his wife's brother (the boy's maternal uncle) as well as by any married sons. The girl's family is helped by a wider group of people, which extends beyond the kinsmen mentioned above to include all co-villagers and many friends and followers. The contributions of the latter are small and vary from threepenny-pieces to baskets of bread and a few pots of beer.

Early on the morning of the wedding day the groom's father, accompanied by all his male relatives and friends, drives the *bohali* cattle towards the bride's village. As they leave the kraal, the cattle are counted

[1] Dieterlen, 1912, p. 49.

MARRIAGE

by the groom's young unmarried sister or other female relative, who taps them with a stick (*lere*) as they pass her. Towards midday two beasts (*selelekela*) are detached from the herd on the outskirts of the bride's village and vigorously driven to the kraal by the young men, while the rest of the party remains behind. The bride's womenfolk try to prevent them by shouting and banging tins or drums, but they give up laughingly as soon as they are beaten and welcome the rest of the cattle with trilling cries and shouts of "May the kraal be filled, even to the uttermost corners". This initial show of hostility is said to represent the women's unwillingness to lose their daughter and the superstitious say that if they succeeded in keeping the *selelekela* cattle out, it would be a bad omen and the marriage should be abandoned.

The groom's people then enter the village, dancing the *mokorotlo* and, without being greeted, go to the *khotla* where they are served with beer, called *ba lere* and *ba selelekela* in reference to the stick that counted the cattle and the two beasts that led them in. The bride's people go to the kraal and count the cattle. If all appears well, they now greet their guests, addressing them as "relatives-in-law" (*baeng*). After chatting together for a few minutes, they withdraw and formal discussions then take place through special intermediaries. The most important matters concern the *bohali* cattle, which are rarely entirely satisfactory—they may be younger than was expected or in poor condition, a horse may have been substituted or the numbers may be short. The groom's father does his best to account for these defects; the horse has been substituted for two cattle that died suddenly or had to be sold; cattle were promised by relatives but could not be collected in time and will be sent later; a cow has just calved and will be brought as soon as possible; additional cattle will shortly be forthcoming from a daughter's marriage; and so it goes on. Sometimes the groom's father has certain requests to make: that some of the cows be allowed to return "to make milk for the new household" or until their calves have been weaned; and even if these requests have been previously agreed to, they have again to be discussed and formal assent given.

While these negotiations are proceeding, there is a fairly tense atmosphere in the village; various minor activities are forbidden and taboos are observed for fear of prolonging them, or spoiling the marriage (for instance, the bride and her companions should sit with their legs straight out instead of folded under them in the usual way). As soon as agreement is reached, the bride's father sends word to his wife, "The marriage is concluded", and everyone relaxes. Food is brought to the court, including a pot of beer called *ba mokhele*, and both parties meet again and chat pleasantly while the cattle are taken out to graze.

An archaic custom rarely observed nowadays is for the groom's sister to carry the *lere* to the bride's village and to kneel in the mother's courtyard, holding the stick upright, until the marriage negotiations are settled. The bride's people will later return the stick to the groom, accompanying it with pots of beer and celebrating its return with a small beer drink. This should take place before the bride joins her husband.

After a while the cry is heard, "There is the *mokhele*", and a youth dashes out of the bride's mother's courtyard carrying a stick ornamented with ostrich feathers, ribbons and bunting. He runs towards the open country and is immediately pursued by the groom's companions and headed off towards the bride's people's cattle, which are rounded up and kraaled. Everyone now congregates round the kraal while representatives sing the parents' praises. The bride's father then selects two of his best oxen, "fat and unblemished", and directs his representative to present them to the groom's father. The latter acknowledges them and, amid general rejoicing, directs his representative to kill one of them, called *mafura* (fat), and to give the other to the groom's maternal uncle who, if he is in a generous mood, may also have it slaughtered. The girl's father should give (*hlabisa*) one beast for every ten *bohali* cattle given by the groom's father. If he cannot do so at the wedding, he must at least provide a sheep for the feast. When later he is able to give these cattle—and this may not be for several years—he should hand them over with some formality and invite his in-laws to a small celebration.

The girl's people skin the left side of the beast and the boy's the right; all work fast, for it is said that the side to finish first will dominate their future relations. The animal is then cut up and divided according to a complicated set of rules. Finally the gall is poured over the groom's hands, usually by his father, and the bladder is tied round his right wrist. From the legal point of view this is the culmination of the ceremony. Up to this point the marriage could have been broken off and the return of the cattle demanded. The gall bladder is the "ring" which binds the couple together.[1] Many modern couples substitute a proper wedding ring which is placed, in European fashion, on the third finger of the bride's left hand.

In the evening the groom and his companions repair to a hut where they are later joined by the bride and her companions. The girls first sit very demurely covering their faces with their blankets. The boys try to unveil them and the ensuing scuffle helps to break the ice. The girls then pinch, slap and tease the boys, while the latter joke and flirt with them. When food is brought, they try to make one another eat, but without success. The bride and groom are supposed to sit sedately together all through this jollity until well into the evening. Ellenberger and MacGregor write that they all spend the night feasting, philandering and doing "other things which cannot be described".[2] This suggests that the revellers have sexual orgies, but I doubt if this was ever the

[1] See also Ellenberger and MacGregor, pp. 275-6. [2] Ibid., p. 276.

case, as they are continually watched by two chaperons chosen by the bride's mother. Moreover, sexual indulgence on this occasion would be a gross breach of in-law behaviour and etiquette.

When morning comes, beer and other refreshments are brought to them, including the meat of a sheep specially killed for the occasion. When they have eaten, they are allowed to go to sleep and their vigil ends. They spend the day together and in the evening, after the groom's mother and her companions have finished their ceremonial visit, the party ends. The groom and his companions return home[1] and leave the bride behind.

Little significance is now attached to this vigil, and it seems to have been designed for the days when marriages were arranged between people who might not have known one another previously and to have served to help them get over their shyness and embarrassment. Now that many marriages are love matches and the couple may even have lived together before the wedding, it has become pointless and tedious, and so many spend the night eating, singing and dancing with their friends.

That same evening the groom's father meets the bride's parents and friends in another hut. The two groups sit facing one another and exchange amiable banter about the marriage. From all accounts they seem to enjoy this strange form of teasing, although they cannot explain its why or wherefore. Later a special pot of beer is brought in and this brings the raillery to an end. The beer is placed exactly between the two groups and meticulously shared out, an unusual feature being that each group has its own server. The party then becomes festive and goes on until the people tire and fall asleep. Next morning, soon after sunrise, a last pot of beer is brought, called the "beer of the walking-sticks", and thereafter the groom's father and friends take their leave.

It is now the women's turn. The groom's mother and womenfolk, who have remained in their own village all this time, now visit their new in-laws (*ba ea motabezong*).[2] The union of the two families is symbolized by the sharing of the intestines (*mala*) of the beast killed the previous day to celebrate the wedding. Before and after eating this meat, the groom's mother and kinswomen wash with soap and water supplied by the bride's mother, thus emphasizing the ritual. The intestines of an animal are closely associated with womanhood and figure in other rites concerned with marriage and childbirth. After this, the visitors, who have hitherto remained outside, are invited into the mother's *lelapa* where they are entertained with meat, bread, beer and other good

---

[1] Several other minor customs are occasionally found. Some are mentioned by Sekese, op. cit., p. 6.
[2] This word *motabezong* does not appear in the Dictionary, 6th ed. It may be a Tlokoa word. I have spelt it phonetically, as it sounded to my ear, although "z" is not usually recognized in Sesuto orthography.

things. They return home that same afternoon and before leaving ask that the bride may soon be sent to them.

These rites and practices are still celebrated by the upper class Tlokoa and possibly by a few other conservative Basuto, but many details, especially the symbolical features such as driving the *seleleka* cattle and chasing the *mokhele*, have been abandoned. Some of the older generation regret the change, but the younger people either affect to scorn the old customs or genuinely find more satisfaction and meaning in the new additions which are now fairly common except among the Tlokoa.

Many modern weddings now revolve round a religious ceremony held in the church to which the bride belongs. The groom and his friends, and sometimes his parents and their friends, go to the bride's village. When she is ready, he takes her on his arm and leads a solemn procession of groomsmen and bridesmaids, who follow in pairs behind them. They are often preceded by one or two young men and women who weave to and fro blowing whistles or some musical instrument such as a mouth-organ. The bride should look sad and weep at the thought of leaving her home. She is always dressed in a white wedding dress and carries a white bouquet and a white sunshade, as symbols of purity. She may not be a virgin, but unless this has been publicized by pregnancy or some scandal, the fiction of virginity is maintained, the truth being "a secret known only to God". The bridesmaids and her other companions should wear gay dresses in white and pastel shades. The groom and his companions wear smart European dress and he should have a white button-hole. This and the bouquet are usually made of artificial flowers, purchased at the local store. When they reach the church, they all take their places and follow the form of service observed by that particular denomination. Their union is symbolized by the groom's placing a wedding ring on the third finger of his bride's left hand. After the service, the couple and the wedding party return to her home in the same manner as they came, accompanied by fellow-villagers and other friends. Sometimes, if her home is some distance from the church, the couple and some of their attendants (especially the best man and bridesmaids) travel in motor cars decorated with ribbons. On their arrival, the guests are served with meat and drink, and the feast continues as long as supplies hold out. The couple, together with their close companions, the groomsmen and bridesmaids, sit apart at a special table, where they behave with decorum and restraint. Normally the groom returns to his home the following day —sometimes even the same evening if unwilling to face the all night vigil or celebration—and his bride follows later according to tradition. If, however, their homes are far apart, he may stay on for several days and then take her with him when he goes. In such cases, he should not sleep with his bride as it is unseemly for him to have sexual relations while he is in his mother-in-law's vicinity.

An alternative is civil marriage held in the magistrate's or District Commissioner's court. This is a simple ceremony following the statutory provisions of the law which takes the place of the religious ceremony described above.

Couples already married in court or by Sesuto custom, who wish to have their marriage confirmed by the Church, undergo a very simple religious ceremony. This usually follows some other church function, such as a Sunday service, and may be shared by several couples in a similar position. At the end of the main service, they stand up together, while a few short prayers are said and the essentials of the marriage service repeated. The couple's hands are joined in marriage and the ring is placed on the bride's finger. In the afternoon or evening, they give a small party at their own home attended by their close relatives and friends.

In all cases of civil or Christian marriage negotiations over *bohali* cattle take place on much the same lines as those previously described and the cattle are delivered to the bride's people before the wedding takes place. The onus of providing the wedding feast falls on the bride's parents, as in the case of the traditional wedding. The only exceptions occur in the case of strict French Protestants, whose church has forbidden its members to exchange *bohali* cattle. When this ban is observed, the groom and his parents contribute substantially in cash and in kind towards the expenses of the wedding and pay all or part of the cost both of the feast and of the bride's wedding dress. Her people still furnish her trousseau and household equipment. Some members of this Church either disregard the ban and drive the *bohali* cattle to the bride's people after nightfall—hence their nickname, "Christians of the Twilight"—or circumvent it by paying them cash to enable them to buy cattle.

Normally the number of *bohali* cattle is more or less fixed. The Tlokoa have fixed it at twenty cattle, plus the "driver" (*moqhoba*) which is an ox, and the "loincloth" (*setsiba*), which is a parcel of ten sheep and goats. In the case of a chief's family, only goats should be given. Among other Basuto the number has risen to twenty-five cattle and includes, besides the "driver" and "loincloth", a horse called the "shepherd" (*molisana*).[1] For chiefs' daughters, the number may be increased up to fifty. These amounts are higher than they used to be. In the early days[2] two or three beasts were enough, although Casalis says the rate was twenty-five to thirty.[3] In 1872[4] ten to fifteen sufficed, and in 1912[5] the recognized number varied from fifteen to twenty. The term "cattle" covers any sort of beast, young or old, male or female: if the recipient is agreeable, horses, sheep or goats may be substituted for one or more

---

[1] According to Sekese, op. cit., p. 5, this is a comparatively recent addition.
[2] Arbousset, *Voyage d'Exploration*, 1932.   [3] Casalis, op. cit., p. 229.
[4] Commission Evidence, 1873.   [5] Ellenberger and MacGregor, p. 272.

of the cattle at normal rates. To give the full number at once is a praiseworthy act as it indicates wealth, brings the giver prestige, honours the bride and her family and avoids any bickering and ill-feeling; owing to the present uneven distribution of wealth and slow rate of saving, very few can afford to do so. The usual practice is for an initial instalment of six to ten cattle to be given at the wedding, or when the girl is sent to her husband prior to the wedding, and for the rest to be made up later in dribs and drabs. It often takes years to produce the full number and the debt may be handed on from father to son; sometimes it is never liquidated. Some people deliberately withhold a few cattle (*maoto*—feet) as insurance against the bride's proving to be barren or dying without issue, for in this event they are not obliged to complete the number of cattle unless her parents provide another wife.

The cattle are distributed according to definite rules. One of the two *selelekela* cattle, called *seholoholo*, (the loins) goes to the bride's father and the other, called *letsoele* (the breast), to her mother or younger brother. The father should get the "loincloth" (*setsiba*). Among the Tlokoa, the girl's maternal uncle is entitled to some of the cattle if she is the first, third or fifth daughter of his "linked" sister, provided he has fulfilled his obligations at her initiation and wedding. Theoretically he may take as many as he likes, which are called *litsoa*, but he is not expected to take more than six. The rest of the cattle belong to the household. An ox called the *moqhoba* (the driver) may be given either to the women who accompany the bride to her husband's home or to the bride's mother as the "cow of her womb". This may be a clan difference.

The social value of *bohali* cattle (*lobola*, as they are usually called in anthropological literature, after the Zulu term) has been so exhaustively discussed elsewhere that there is no need to go into the subject in detail here. As, however, some missions[1] still actively oppose it, whereas most Basuto tenaciously adhere to it, the reasons for these conflicting attitudes may be briefly examined.

From the very first, the French mission has objected to the custom and has forbidden its adherents to observe it. The main objection[2] is that the woman is sold to her husband, and that not only is this derogatory to the dignity of women, but is also the cause of their inferior status. It has been frequently pointed out that this view is based on a misunderstanding of native ideas and of the true function of the cattle. The Basuto have themselves always objected[3] to their custom being called a sale. They point out that there is no pricing of the woman, no

---

[1] See also Dieterlen and Kohler, 1912, p. 468.
[2] The missions' case was fully stated in correspondence with the first Governor's Agent in 1872, and is published in the *Report on Native Laws and Customs*, 1873. See also Ellenberger and MacGregor, pp. 272-5.
[3] Casalis, op. cit., p. 229.

selling to the highest bidder; that she cannot be given or sold by her husband to another man, and that she is treated quite differently from a commodity that is bought and sold; that, in short, she is "married".

In spite of opposition, the custom is still strongly entrenched. One reason for this is that the French mission was alone in its opposition. Indeed the Roman Catholics once made valuable propaganda at a national *pitso* by publicly proclaiming their support of it. Another reason is that the mission's own Basuto priests are reluctant to enforce its prohibition and willingly turn a blind eye on unobtrusive exchanges of cattle; they also permit the exchange of *bohali* cattle when their adherents marry people of another faith.

The Basuto offer many reasons for retaining the custom. They point out that the cattle strengthen the bond of marriage between the two families and make the couple, especially the woman, realize that marriage is a serious contract which cannot lightly be set aside without bringing disgrace to the family; they admit, however, that women married without cattle are probably no less or no more reluctant to abandon their husbands than those married with cattle. They further claim that the cattle compensate the woman's parents for the cost of her upbringing and the loss of domestic services, whereas men are not lost on marriage and continue to serve their parents. To some extent, they also compensate the bride's people for the cost of the wedding feast, clothes, transport and trousseau.[1] Quite apart from these rationalizations, the ordinary Mosuto clings to the custom "because it is the custom" and because without it marriage is not marriage, and women do not feel "married".

After the wedding the bride usually remains at home for about a month. This period is devoted to preparing her trousseau and collecting her household equipment. Her whole wardrobe has to be refurnished, for she now wears full-length skirts in place of the short skirts worn by unmarried girls. Formerly her trousseau consisted of new skin aprons, mantles and cloaks, but nowadays it includes blouses of various materials, print and calico skirts, petticoats and woollen blankets. Her domestic equipment should consist of pots and cooking utensils, brooms, sleeping mats, blankets, cutlery, spoons, forks, beer strainers and flour mats. Some of this should be provided by her maternal uncle,[2] with whom she should go and stay for a few weeks, and the rest by her family, helped in a small way by neighbours and friends.

The following details illustrate the type of trousseau provided by "middling" prosperous parents, and the trouble taken to collect the various articles. The girl's father bought 5 mats at a store three days' ride away; 2 blankets in Natal four days' ride away and 2 blankets at a local store; 2 skirts in Natal and 3 at the local store; material for skirts, 3 *doeks*, 2 blouses, 1 pair of shoes, 1 pair of stockings, 1 broom, 2 water-

---

[1] See also Dieterlen and Kohler, 1912, p. 468.   [2] Sekese, p. 3.

pots, 2 drinking-pots, 5 large and 4 small billy-cans and 2 enamel cans, all from Natal. Friends gave 8 billy-cans, 1s. 6d. in cash, 1 beer strainer and 5 brooms, and relations gave *doeks*, skirts and other small presents in cash or kind.

When everything is ready, her parents exhort her to conduct herself properly. As Sekese[1] graphically puts it, "She must obey her in-laws, she must obey them in everything just as she obeyed her own parents; she must indeed respect all her husband's people; she must please them by feeding them properly and she must love them. She should give cause neither to her parents-in-law nor to her husband to hear anything shameful about her behaviour; she must always remember that she has been married with cattle. She should try by every means she can think of to please her husband and his parents, and she should love them as if they were her own. She should work industriously. She must give her husband food at the proper time and she must not be gluttonous; she must feed her husband's brothers as though they were her own. She must keep the hut clean and always make her husband glad." "And now go, my child. A girl child dies amongst strangers and is buried according to the rites of her husband's people. Oh, my child, do not bring disgrace upon us in the villages of strangers, so they should say, 'Who is her father? Who is her mother?'"

After this she sets out for her husband's village, accompanied by two or more kinswomen and friends. In the old days, on nearing the village, they used to wait by the side of the path to be met by young men from the husband's village, and would only consent to continue their journey when offered small gifts of money and trifling objects, such as a blanket pin. Every few hundred yards they would stop again and have to be coaxed on in the same way. This is a custom on which informants love to expatiate and which appears to have been general, except among the Tlokoa, but has now died out altogether. On their arrival they go straight to her mother-in-law's and are welcomed by the local women; her companions chat cheerfully with their hosts, but the girl herself should sit quietly by herself with her face buried in her blanket. Next morning they should rise early and prepare breakfast for her mother-in-law. Her father-in-law kills a sheep for them and gives her a piece of the intestines as a symbol of her acceptance into the family. This is called *koae* (tobacco). Until this has been done, she may not eat anything nor start her marital life. She is received with a similar rite in the case of elopement, should the boy's father be prepared to ask for her in marriage, and also if she comes to live with her husband before the wedding.

Formerly her companions used to stay on for two or three days to help her with her household work and ease her into her new surroundings. Before leaving, they might tell her how to behave with her hus-

[1] op. cit., p. 9.

band. Nowadays this formality is seldom observed and they usually return home at once or the day after they arrive.

The bride used to live with her mother-in-law for a few days until she signified her willingness to begin married life by placing a pot of water or beer[1] in her husband's hut one evening. If she delayed too long, her mother-in-law might tell her that it was time they lived together, and show her their hut.[2] She was entitled to resist her husband's advances, if she could, the first night—an unusual right which may be explained as yet another means of gradually introducing her to her new life. The outcome of their struggle aroused mild interest. If her husband was successful, she prepared the usual thick porridge for his breakfast and took it to him in the normal way to the *khotla*, where he speared it with a stick as a sign of his victory. But if she worsted him, she merely boiled him some maize (*likhobe*), the poorest of dishes, and sent it out to the *khotla*, much to the chagrin of her husband and the amusement of his fellows. Later, one of his friends would take him aside and enlighten him on matters of sex as his failure was probably due to sexual ignorance; many Basuto insist that this sort of thing actually did happen and that some men were so innocent that they quietly lay beside their brides, not knowing there was anything else to do.

The question of the bride's chastity also used to be a matter of interest. The morning after the consummation of the marriage, the groom's mother would take to his father bread shaped in the form of a horn. If the girl was a virgin, he would break it and eat it; if not, he threw it to the dogs. Alternatively, the husband might sit alone by himself instead of joining the men at the court or else come to the court with a hole cut in the corner of his blanket. There were no reprisals except that the blanket might be sent to her parents in silent reproach, and she would be treated with diminished respect and consideration. There was, however, no question of returning any *bohali* cattle. The question of chastity was determined by her response to the act of sex. If she was hard, tight and awkward, this was held to show that she was a virgin, or at any rate unused to sexual intercourse; whereas if she was soft and easy, she was presumed to have had intercourse recently or to indulge in it frequently. As the people were not so much concerned with strict virginity as with chastity, or the opposite of profligacy, this test was more reasonable and effective than at first sight appears. Rupture of the hymen was not a criterion, probably because it had already been damaged during initiation. Sometimes the old women inspected the girl and ascertained her chastity by the absence of bruising or distension of the vulva. Nowadays, the couple usually sleep together immediately after the *koae* rite. This rite is still strictly observed, but many of the other observances have been abandoned, especially those concerned with the sexual consummation of the marriage.

[1] Ellenberger and MacGregor, p. 227.   [2] For various minor customs, see Sekese, p. 8.

The couple does not immediately form a new household group and the bride continues to live with her husband's parents, cook for them, help with their domestic chores and work in their fields. At the beginning of the first season after their marriage, the couple should be given fields of their own, which they should work themselves (though still helping their parents) and whose produce they should retain. At the same time, the husband should apply to their headman, through his father, for a building site and should build his own hut. This should be ready by harvest time, and they should move into it before they reap their first crop, although if, as often happens, the woman is expecting her first baby, they may put off doing so until after the child is born. Formerly, among the Tlokoa, the first meal they had in their new home was prepared by the local girls and consisted of *likhobe*. This poor dish expressed humility and therefore promised success and prosperity for the future.

Before settling down for good, the girl formerly had the right to visit her family and could leave quite suddenly. The only warning she might give was to smash her water-pot at the spring. After a short stay at home, she returned with two companions, bringing three pots of beer; one to compensate for the destroyed water-pot and the other two for her absence. After this, she should leave the village only with her husband's consent. This convention of breaking a water-pot is still observed. Women also break their water-pots in this way when they run home without waiting or wanting to tell their husbands, as when they are discontented and unhappy or on bad terms with their husbands. This public act should bring the matter to a head, as the husband or his father should follow her and discuss the trouble with her people.

The woman is given a new name, invariably prefixed with *'ma* (mother of). Sometimes her first child, if of the appropriate sex, is given the same name; at other times she is later called after her children—"mother of So-and-so".

Marriage gives both men and women a new status in society and also new rights and privileges. Moreover, it involves the couple and their families in a new relationship. Between the bride and her husband's people there are numerous taboos and types of enjoined behaviour. Thus she must respect and avoid (*hlonepha*) the personal name of her father-in-law or of other kinsmen in that class and must call him by a special name. Should she inadvertently slip, she should immediately spit, to drive away evil arising from this disrespect. Among the Koena and Phuthi, this taboo scarcely extends beyond the father-in-law and his brothers, whereas among the Kholokoe[1] and Tlokoa it covers more distant relatives as well as any words occcurring in the names of these relatives. This avoidance is usually achieved by replacing the tabooed name by one of his children's names with the prefix *Ra* (father of).

[1] Sekese, p. 15.

For instance, Lelingoana's daughters-in-law would call him Ramponeng, Mponeng being his senior daughter; if they talked about a circumcised boy (*lelingoana*) they would have to use a word such as *lekau* which means a "young man". A daughter-in-law should always be decorous and modest in the presence of her father-in-law. She should keep her body covered and should not suckle her baby or dance the *mokhibo* in his presence. Nor should she remain in a room alone with him, sit near him, eat out of the same pot, shake hands with him or in any way touch him. She may cook for him and even spread his sleeping mats, but she should not wash his clothes nor touch his intimate property, such as saddle or gun. These rules are strictly observed early in marriage, but are gradually relaxed as time goes on.

Her husband's elder brother falls into the same category as her father-in-law and her behaviour to him is much the same. Nevertheless, it occasionally happens that on her husband's death he cohabits with her. This so completely changes their previous father-daughter relationship that it is regarded by some as akin to incest, and the thought of it so shocks them that they say it never happens.

With her husband's younger brother a woman is free and easy. Sex relations between them during her husband's lifetime are less seriously regarded than other forms of adultery, provided that they are discreet. On the husband's death he should cohabit with her and look after her.

With her husband's female relations she behaves in much the same way as with her own relations of the same type, only with greater punctiliousness. She is primarily under the control of her mother-in-law whom she calls "mother". She is friendly with her husband's sisters, but must treat them courteously and obediently when, as married women, they come home on a visit.

A woman's relations with her husband's other wives depend on her position. As senior wife she is entitled to the respect and obedience of her juniors. When she gets on in life, her husband's new wife should live in her household as a sort of daughter-in-law for a year or so until she is given her own establishment; when the senior wife is old, a junior wife may live in her household to help and look after her—*ho mo alela lipate* (to spread her sleeping mats). Junior co-wives are more or less equal among themselves in so far as their personal relationship goes, except that the more senior is always a little superior and, together with her children, takes precedence according to the order of their marriage. Wives are supposed to be friendly and to co-operate in ordinary domestic matters, but often become exceedingly jealous of, and bitter towards, one another.

A man's relationship with his in-laws is not as complicated or as important as his wife's, mainly because he does not often come into contact with them. He is on rather formal terms with them and between him and his mother-in-law, much the same type of "avoidance" behaviour exists as between a man and his daughter-in-law; these taboos again being strictly observed by the Tlokoa, Phuthi and others.[1] He is expected to visit his parents-in-law from time to time. On such occasions, he is received with great deference and politeness, is served with the best food and given a chair to sit on, even in the presence of the local chief's sons. But as this relationship is irksome, these visits should be short and infrequent. Similarly, the mother-in-law should visit the couple occasionally and not for longer than two days or so, unless she has come to nurse her daughter or grandchildren in an illness; she should never scold her daughter in her son-in-law's presence or hearing. He is free and easy, even intimate, with his wife's sisters and in the event of her dying he should marry her younger sister in her place. Relations with his brothers-in-law should be friendly and pleasant, though formal. Relations between the parents of the couple are expected to be friendly and easy. It is significant that in-law kinship terms, such as *soare* (brother-in-law) and *mokhotsi* (used between the couple's parents), are frequently used by unconnected people purely as terms of friendship.

Relationships between a man and his wife are of two main kinds, personal and domestic. Husband and wife are supposed to be loyal and affectionate, and the woman is expected to honour and obey her spouse. As most men are away at the mines frequently and for long periods, it is difficult for the more personal aspects of this relationship to be realized and there seems to be little affection, companionship or trust between them. The happiest marriages I knew at Malingoaneng were those of men whose work kept them at home. Nevertheless, husbands are usually peaceable and seldom quarrel or beat their wives, except after beer drinks and when they suspect infidelity.

Husbands and wives have numerous specific duties towards each other. The wife should sleep with her husband whenever he wants her, and he should do the same—but as he is a man and there are many women available and anxious for attention, his desires tend to be more fully satisfied than hers. A polygynist should distribute his favours equally, but here again the rule is often honoured in the breach, and he usually pays most attention to a favourite junior wife, probably his most recent acquisition. The husband should also respect his wife's sexual taboos, such as those after the birth of a child. Menstrual periods are not taboo, but are usually respected for aesthetic reasons. As one of the objects of marriage is the production of children, the husband and wife should satisfy one another's sexual needs properly and, for reasons given earlier, they should remain faithful and eschew adultery. When jointly given medicines to promote conception, both should play their parts as prescribed by their doctor.

The care and early upbringing of their children is principally the woman's task. She is also responsible for carrying out the ordinary

[1] Sekese, p. 15.

domestic tasks, such as keeping the hut clean and neat, preparing, cooking and serving food, and fetching water and wood. She also has to carry out various agricultural tasks, such as weeding and harvesting, and, generally, to look after her husband and attend to his wants. This does not mean that she has to do all these things herself, but if she has helpers and servants, she has to supervise them. Her husband must supply her with clothes, keep their hut in good repair and build a new one when necessary. He should see that their lands are ploughed and should also help with the harvesting. If they have stock, he is responsible for looking after it.

In the management of their household and the disposal of their property they should consult together and respect each other's views. In most matters, especially those relating to stock and to the family property, the husband's view predominates, but in matters relating to her daughters or young children the woman's views are given the greatest consideration. If the husband's attitude and orders are harsh and unreasonable, she may complain to his mother directly or through her parents and, in extreme cases, may run away to her own people.

In spite of the fact that it has been dubbed marriage "according to Thembu fashion", polygyny has been practised for hundreds of years. To-day it is still common in spite of a century of missionary effort to stamp it out. In 1936[1] there were about 8,000 polygynists in the country, of whom one had ten wives, twenty-one between ten and five wives, and 6,287 only two. The Tlokoa have always been moderate; Lelingoana had only eight wives at a time, and no one else in his time had more than seven; to-day (1946) his son Mosuoe has four, and there are only six others who have as many or more.

Polygyny has been attacked by many as pandering to man's grosser nature and has been regarded as a reason for the "backwardness" of the Basuto.[2] But there is much to be said in its favour. Moderate polygyny as found in Basutoland is not an unreasonable institution. It satisfies a man's sexual appetite, flatters his social vanity and fulfills a most useful function in providing every woman[3] with a husband and a home.[4] It may sometimes lead to domestic strife and bitterness, but I doubt whether it does as much harm to family life as is generally supposed and it certainly does less harm than the exodus of the men to the mines, which is not as resolutely opposed by these critics. Polygyny is regarded as an enviable condition and those who can afford it are quite

[1] Basutoland Census, 1936, p. 19. Figures exclude absentees.

[2] Casalis, 1861, pp. 268-90; Dieterlen, 1923, pp. 43, 50-3; and Commission on Native Laws and Customs, 1893.

[3] According to the census in 1936 there were 343,237 females to 317,309 males giving an excess of females of about 9 per cent. In view of the difference in marriage ages of men and women (i.e. about 26 and 18 respectively) the surplus of marriageable women may actually be higher.

[4] See also Dieterlen, 1912, p. 43.

prepared to risk being plagued by the "intrigues and malice"[1] of several wives. I find it difficult to believe that Casalis was not misled in believing that "monogamists are generally esteemed and pass among their fellow-men for models of virtue".[2] That certainly is not the case to-day, at least among heathen Basuto. The churches have unanimously outlawed polygyny, but it is noticeable that many chiefs and other wealthy men are prepared to be excommunicated for its sake. Others again, having had their day, are prepared to put aside their many wives and be accepted into the Church. All in all I would say that it used to be universally approved and no one had any moral scruple about practising it, when he could afford to; nowadays many believe it is "heathen", backward and wrong and look on monogamy as Christian and a mark of "progress" but, nevertheless, have a sneaking feeling that it would be rather pleasant to be a polygynist.

The traditional polygyny that is still practised by the Basutos must, however, be distinguished from the unbridled licence indulged in by some Koena chiefs during the nineteenth century and until recently. In those days many of the chiefs used to have wives whom they numbered by the score. Accurate figures of Moshesh's or Letsie's wives are unobtainable, but estimates range from thirty to a hundred;[3] Lerotholi had about sixty, and other chiefs had as many. Jonathan, who died a few years ago, was reputed to have at least eighty. This excessive polygyny was introduced, according to Arbousset,[4] by Mohlomi for political purposes and used by him and his successors as a method of attracting and securing the loyalty of their followers, for they encouraged their wives, other than their senior and favourite ones, to provide the *khotla* with food and to look after,[5] and perhaps form more or less permanent attachments with, their poorer followers. Later chiefs maintained this system and though its political importance declined with British protection, it was maintained as a sign of wealth and status, as well as a means to sexual satisfaction. Motsoene, for instance, the most notorious of them all, is said to have sent his men with full *bohali* cattle to the parents of any girl his lusting fancy lighted on. When he had sated his desires, he had nothing further to do with her—and yet, so it is alleged, he kept her jealously guarded from the world, behind a wire fence under the supervision of an eunuch! Most other chiefs had the same selfish attitude, though a few are said not to have objected to their secretaries and other court officials philandering with their most junior wives. This morbid aberration has now come to an end and recent chiefs have been more moderate owing to various factors,

---

[1] Casalis, op. cit., p. 234.   [2] Ibid.
[3] Casalis says Moshesh had thirty to forty, op. cit, p. 213; whereas Ellenberger says he had from sixty to eighty and that Letsie I must have had from eighty to one hundred. *Livre d'Or*, p. 676.
[4] Arbousset, 1932.   [5] Casalis, *Souvenirs*, p. 269.

such as mission influence, and the opportunities provided by the European economic system for spending their wealth in other ways. The last two Paramount Chiefs, Griffith and Seeiso, had fourteen and eleven wives respectively, excluding concubines and the widows of their predecessors, some of whom they lived with.

Normally, the first wife to be married is the senior wife[1] and she is officially designated the *mofumahali*. She is the mother of the heir and, as a tribute to her position in the tribe, the chief's senior wife may be called *'ma-batho* (mother of the people). Her household is sometimes known as "the big house", and it is there that her husband is supposed to keep his weapons, riding equipment, medicines and family heirlooms such as old shields, battle-axes and ornaments. In effect, her hut is his principal dwelling place, although he may have another hut for occasional private use. The second wife is sometimes referred to as "of the horn" and other wives as "the heels" (*lirethe*). The latter have been referred to as "concubines".[2] This is an ambiguous term, defined by the Oxford English Dictionary as either "a woman who cohabits with a man, not being his wife" or "among polygamous peoples, a secondary wife". Used in the second sense the term is applicable, although it carries a stigma that the Basuto would not recognize. The first sense is quite inappropriate for, from the strictly legal point of view, these women are full wives, although their social status is lower than that of the principal and second wives.

The ranking of co-wives is normally based on their sequence in marriage and the seniority of their children follows the same order. Two exceptions, apart from rare instances mentioned in Chapter XIII, are *'mala* and *seantlo* marriages described below. Both these are marriages of substitute wives, who take the status of the senior wife for whom they are substituting and, therefore, rank as senior to other wives married before them. In order to avoid later disputes over succession and inheritance, these marriages have to be contracted in the presence of witnesses, representing the husband's family and the chief of the district.

Junior households are not arranged in any regular pattern round the senior, although they are usually grouped round the back and on either side of the "big house", more or less in order of seniority, the second house being on the right and the third on the left. It is desirable that all the wives should live in the same village, but this ideal is not often achieved owing to conjugal jealousy (*lefufa*). This jealousy causes constant bickering and frequently leads to the illness of one of the wives, which is attributed to the sorcery and malice of a co-wife, and makes her removal to a separate village of her own advisable. There she can have her own set of medicines to counteract the witchcraft. The fact that she will have her own separate establishment doubtless also con-

---

[1] Further details are given in the chapter on Political Organization.
[2] Casalis, op. cit., p. 235.

tributes to her recovery. Lelingoana managed to control all his wives satisfactorily by the drastic method of sending them home whenever they quarrelled and leaving them there till they repented. But his son, Mosuoe, in common with at least five other Tlokoa polygynists, is less successful and his four wives are scattered through three different villages. Such failure is pitied rather than censured.

In spite of the growing tendency to regard marriage as a personal affair, the family aspect is still of importance. Although this is not explicitly formulated, marriage is a contract whereby the wife's people undertake to provide her husband with a woman capable of satisfying his ordinary physical needs and producing offspring to continue his name and lineage; the husband's people undertake to provide the necessary framework in which she can function. From these two sets of obligations flow the subsidiary duties and rights which have already been discussed. Theoretically the marriage contract can be broken only by the families concerned and not by the individual action of either husband or wife. Consequently, although the death of one of the spouses obviously destroys the personal aspect, it does not terminate the marriage but still leaves the two families and the survivor bound by various obligations.

These obligations differ according to circumstances. If the marriage has subsisted for many years, and especially if the woman has borne children, the wife's family are considered to have fulfilled their side of the contract. On her death, therefore, they are under no further obligation to her husband's people, apart from their "maternal uncle" relationship to her children. If, however, she dies childless soon after marriage, they should provide another wife to take her place. If they do so, they should be given a reduced number of *bohali* cattle (usually half) as well as any outstanding from the first marriage. If they refuse, they forfeit their right to the latter, but they do not have to return any if the full number have already been given—hence the precaution mentioned earlier of withholding a few. If the wife dies leaving young children, it is desirable that her younger sister should take her place because the latter's "blood will cry out for the children" and she can be expected to take better care of them than a stranger would. Full *bohali* is payable for her. Both these are *seantlo* marriages. Such marriages are only agreed to in the case of the senior wives of important people, and even then not always.[1] In both these *seantlo* marriages and in the '*mala*

[1] Chief Matlere Lerotholi's mother was a junior wife of Lerotholi, her position being somewhere in the tens. In 1949 he told me that she was married *seantlo* for her paternal aunt (*rakhali*) Taeli who was Lerotholi's fifth wife and died childless. If this is so, her children should rank as the latter's children and therefore be regarded as fairly senior. Unfortunately, I was unable to check this, but I feel this claim cannot be substantiated and is an interesting attempt to bolster up his genealogical status. He is a man of considerable political importance as the Paramount Chief's representative at Mokhotlong, but is regarded by many as rather an upstart owing to his comparatively lowly birth.

marriages described below, the substitute wife should be the other's younger sister, and failing that, her father's younger brother's daughter, her father's elder brother's daughter or her brother's daughter. Examples of all four relationships were found among the Tlokoa. Although the second type of *seantlo* marriage is contracted to provide a sympathetic stepmother for the children, the latter are actually often cared for by other relations, such as the paternal or maternal grandmother.

If the senior wife proves barren, she should encourage her husband to marry another to be her womb (*ho mo etsetsa mala*). The husband should then approach her people and ask for her younger sister or other close relative and they should accede to this request on the same conditions as with the first type of *seantlo*. The new wife will form part of the senior wife's household and, although she will have her own separate hut, she will work and cook for the senior wife, who will be regarded as the mother of her children.

When the husband dies his family is obliged to provide for the widow, look after her material needs and co-operate with her in the education and upbringing of her children; in addition, some close kinsman should consort with her (*kenela*) to raise up seed in her husband's name, unless she already has grown-up children who will be responsible for her maintenance, support and protection.

This *kenela* custom or levirate provides another of the many instances of conflicting attitudes which arise under conditions of change, as was clearly shown in the recent dispute between Bereng and the Regent Paramount Chief 'Mantsebo. One side asserted that the levirate was still an established custom and that in a polygynous society it was the life blood of the nation and the guarantee against widows and fatherless children sinking into poverty and depravity. The other side contended that it was fast disappearing, was no longer generally practised and that it perpetuated a degree of servitude entirely inconsistent with that stage of civilization to which the Basuto nation had advanced.[1] It is strongly opposed by missions as adultery.

When the levirate is observed the widow with her consort visits her former home, where her widow's weeds are discarded and a beast or sheep is slaughtered. The gall is sprinkled over their hands and the bladder tied to the man's wrist. Other variations are said to occur. Among the Tlokoa they sit back to back and the slaughtered animal's skin is placed over their heads for a moment to symbolize that in future they will share the same blanket. Among the Phuthi, the widow fetches water and places a sprig of a special plant in it. The two then wash with this water and afterwards eat together and exchange spoons as a sign of their union.

Under this system the widow's consort should be her husband's

[1] Lansdown, Judgment, 1943, p. 22.

younger brother and theoretically he should take over all the widows, but there are many exceptions. Occasionally (in three out of thirteen cases) the husband's elder brother becomes the consort because there are no younger brothers available, or because they are too young or sickly, or, in rare instances, because the elder is enamoured of the widow. This shocks some Basuto who regard it as a form of incest, since the husband's elder brother stands in the relation of father to her.

Formerly, some of the large-scale polygynists used to apportion their inferior wives and children to their principal sons. I have no details showing how this worked out or to what extent the sons really cohabited with their stepmothers or merely acted as their guardians. I found only one instance among the Tlokoa of a widow being officially *kenela*-ed by her stepson, but there were several cases where a widow lived with him from choice rather than duty. For example, one of Lelingoana's nephews (younger brother's son) lived with his (Lelingoana's) junior widow, the latter being her lover's classificatory grandmother. Similar instances occur among other Basuto, the most noteworthy being that of the late Paramount Chief Seeiso who cohabited with Agatha, his father's young widow. This was "an ordinary instance of the resumption and consummation of an interrupted love affair".[1]

A widow who already has children need not have sexual relations with her brother-in-law, although she remains under his general guardianship until her eldest son grows to manhood, and has to consult him in the administration of the household and family property. But if her husband dies childless and she is still young enough to bear children, she should cohabit fully with his younger brother or, if she strongly dislikes him, with some other close kinsman. Sexual relations with men outside the family occur, but are deplored, lest children begotten by them should succeed to the chieftainship or become head of the family and so introduce inferior blood into the main family stream. All posthumous children are regarded as belonging to the deceased and have exactly the same rights theoretically as if they had been born during his lifetime or begotten by him. In practice these rights are likely to be ignored or incompletely admitted, unless the widow was properly *kenela*-ed by her brother-in-law. Consequently, where the issues at stake are considerable, such as succession to an important chieftainship, the younger brother of the deceased may refuse to *kenela* his widow lest by so doing he should strengthen her children's claims at the expense of his own. For instance, Griffith accepted the Paramount Chieftainship in 1913 in succession to his brother Letsie, on the express condition that he did not *kenela* his widow. Similarly a widow who succeeds her husband as full chief or as regent is not provided with an official consort, lest he, being a close relation who fancies his own chances for the succession, should become jealous of her position and be tempted to do

[1] Lansdown, Judgment, 1943, p. 26.

her children harm for the sake of his own. Furthermore, his position as consort would give him authority over her which would be derogatory to her own position as chief.

On the other hand, a very junior wife is not officially *kenela*-ed as she is not important enough to warrant such formal consideration. Accordingly, she may take lovers at her own choice. Nevertheless, she must continue to live in her husband's village, her children are regarded as his and his relations should continue to look after her. These obligations are observed with a strictness that diminishes with decreasing status and are often entirely relaxed for the most junior wives. Moreover, as it is becoming increasingly difficult to make a living in Basutoland, many families find the burden of maintaining a widow too much for them and either neglect her or raise no objection to her leaving the village and leading her own life elsewhere.

I found among the Tlokoa thirteen widows who were officially consorting with their husbands' brothers. This clearly showed that the system still continues there. Sufficient evidence was produced during the Bereng-'Mantsebo case to satisfy the judge that the practice "had not fallen into total desuetude"[1] elsewhere. On the other hand, many examples were given in the same case to show that it is a "decadent system" and that many important widows had never been subjected to it. Similar cases could be cited from the Tlokoa. There is no doubt, therefore, that the custom, as well as the contractual family aspect of marriage of which it is a product, is breaking down.

The process has not yet reached the point where widows are freely permitted to remarry. Such a marriage would completely sever the original marriage bonds between the two families, and that is going too far. Indeed the Paramount Chief Griffith categorically declared in 1939 that Sesuto law actually forbade the remarriage of widows.[2] This overstates the position (I came across one case of remarriage dating back to about 1890 and two recent cases—one of which concerned a widow of Griffith's own son Seeiso, and I am certain that many others occur in the Lowlands); it does, however, reflect the conservative opinion of the older generation and of the courts, who are not yet prepared to acknowledge the logic of the present trends.

Marriage can occasionally be dissolved by divorce although, for the reasons just discussed, the Basuto oppose this. Ill-treatment, neglect, desertion and expulsion are all possible grounds for divorce. Ordinarily the families concerned are expected to settle difficulties arising from personal differences. If the wife neglects her husband, cooks badly for him or is slovenly and negligent, he may take the law into his own hands, berate her and, if that fails, beat her. If she persists, he should enlist the support of his mother and finally, if unsuccessful, he should send her home for her parents to deal with. On the other hand, if he

---

[1] Lansdown, Judgment, 1943, p. 26.   [2] Basutoland Council, Proceedings.

wilfully neglects her, or beats her unreasonably hard and often, she should complain to his parents, and in the last resort seek refuge with her own family. Her husband should follow her in due course, or send a representative, to ask her to return. His request is usually refused at first, in the hope of making him realize his loss and bringing him to his senses, and is only acceded to later after he has promised to treat her better. If he drives her away or refuses to come and ask for her return, or if she deserts him, her people should take the matter up with his family. Both sides should exert pressure on the guilty party to mend his or her ways and do all they can to reconcile the couple. If they fail or are themselves opposed to reconciliation, the matter may be taken to court. The courts are strongly opposed to divorce and will use all their influence to bring the parties together. Only in extreme cases will they order a divorce. One important court, that of Chief Bereng, did not grant a single divorce in the twelve years up to 1934. This is one of the few traditional attitudes which have been strengthened rather than weakened by mission influence.

The plea of desertion, when made by the wife, would only be considered if the husband had deserted her in favour of another woman living nearby. It would not normally be accepted if he had left the country and refused to return to her or support her, whether he was living with another woman or not. In such cases, though she is not free to remarry, her husband's family would condone her having a lover, especially if the latter were to give her presents of clothing from time to time. Her husband would have no right to complain of her infidelity, though he might refuse to recognize her children. The position is similar where the husband is "lost" and has not been heard of for many years. In both cases, her husband's younger brothers should look after her; they may even cohabit with her and, although this would be irregular and savours of theft (*ka ho utsoa*), it would be condoned.

Various witnesses before the Native Laws Commission in 1873 stated that adultery was recognized as grounds for divorce. This does not appear to be the case nowadays in so far as Sesuto law is concerned. The wife has no redress for single acts of adultery by her husband, but she can sue him for maintenance if his continued adultery with some woman causes him to neglect her. Where the wife is the guilty party, her husband may beat her, especially if she is caught *in flagrante delicto*, and may sue the co-respondent for damages. Marriage contracted according to European law in church or by a civil marriage officer may, however, be dissolved on grounds of adultery by European courts.

A special case in which divorce is granted by the native courts is where a polygynist becomes a Christian. When he is admitted as a church member he has to "put away" all except one of his wives. The missions take a broad-minded view of this and allow him to keep them in his village and look after them, provided he ceases to have sexual intercourse with them. His older wives, though profoundly hurt by this separation *a thoro*, usually accept it, as it does at least provide for their material wants and frees them to have lovers should they wish. Younger wives, on the other hand, who have more chance of being remarried, prefer to obtain a divorce and be free to remarry should the opportunity occur, thus returning to the more dignified status of a proper wife. This innovation, consequent on the introduction of Christianity and the practice of monogamy, is of long standing and goes back at least to 1843 when Moshesh, though never formally converted, granted "letters of divorce" to some of his own wives.[1]

Theoretically, divorce can be arranged privately by the consent of the two families concerned, but in practice this rarely happens as divorce raises contentious matters, such as disposal of the *bohali* cattle and custody of the children, which the families seldom agree on. Practically all cases of divorce are, therefore, referred to the native courts. The law on these matters may be briefly summarized as follows.[2] Unless he is seriously to blame, the husband may choose whether he will keep the children of the marriage or sue for the return of the cattle. If he keeps the children, even if there was only one child, he has no right to the cattle. If there were no children, he can claim the cattle; the number which will be given back to him depends on the respective responsibilities of the couple for the break up of the marriage and the length of time they have been married—the longer they have been married and the greater his fault, the fewer he will get. Occasionally they may agree to share the children and the cattle. Very young children will be allowed to remain with their mother until they are able to do without her and then they will have to go to their father. Those children who remain permanently with their mother become full members of her family and adopt her clan name and clan affiliation.

[1] Commission Report, 1873.
[2] See also the evidence of Sofonia Moshesh and others in the Native Laws Commission Report, which is true to-day. The evidence of Mr. Griffith, first British Agent, does not correctly describe the position as it appears to be to-day.

CHAPTER VI

SOCIAL ROUTINE AND ACTIVITIES

THE pattern of a Mosuto's day is simple and fairly uniform. It starts early. At sunrise, or soon afterwards, everyone gets up, dresses, folds his sleeping blankets and sallies out into the morning air. After greeting and chatting with their neighbours, the men go off in ones and twos to relieve themselves at the "place of the flat stones", usually a donga, wood or depression out of sight of the village. Women have their own place elsewhere. On their return they wash the head, hands and perhaps torso and when necessary shave, using ordinary soap, cold water and an old razor blade or piece of metal sharpened on a stone or the palm of the hand. They then sit about in the household courtyard (*lelapa*), or join their friends at the *khotla* or at the cattle kraal, where they bask in the sun, smoke and gossip until breakfast time.

Breakfast is a customary meal which everyone has, except a few who prefer to do without it and the very poor who cannot afford it. It usually consists of maize or kaffir-corn porridge or maize or wheat bread, with boiled or sour milk as a relish and very occasionally meat. In summer it may include mild cool drinks, made from maize or kaffir-corn and in winter those who can afford it have hot stewed tea. It is usually eaten about two hours after sun-up, if it consists of cold foods left over from supper or quickly prepared food such as porridge; but if bread or meat has to be cooked or meal to be ground, it is often considerably delayed. The family usually eats together, sitting in the main hut or, on sunny mornings, in the courtyard. When visitors are present the men eat by themselves, women and children having their food later. In the old days the men ate at the *khotla* where their wives brought their food.

The court is supposed to open at nine o'clock and those who have business there tend to drift towards it about this time. Formerly men spent most of their day there, but nowadays few do so except when they go there on business or to accompany a friend. For those who do not go to the court, there is little to do, when they are not ploughing, weeding or harvesting, save to lounge about in the village, chat with friends, visit cronies in a neighbouring village or do odd jobs, such as mending a roof, branding young stock, braying a skin, settling a debt, arranging for the loan of a beast or implement and generally pottering about. Except for the few in routine employment, such as clerks and teachers, lunch is not a regular meal, although about midday some may try to scrounge food or beer from their friends. In the afternoon, unless they have something special to do, they may go to the *khotla* (where official business will probably be finished for the day), and sleep, bask in the sun, gossip and play *marabaraba*[1] with others similarly at a loose end. During boys' initiation, they spend a lot of time at the lodge. Doctors, basket-makers and pedlars may occupy part of the day in pursuing their avocations and interests—digging for and preparing medicines, visiting or looking for patients, collecting grass, displaying their wares and prosecuting their business—but even they have a lot of spare time on their hands. The only people whose time is fully occupied are energetic chiefs, officials attached to an important court and those in regular employment, such as servants, shop assistants, clerks, teachers and policemen.

Towards evening the men drift homewards. *En route* they may drop into a friend's place for a chat or else pause at the cattle kraal to watch the cows being milked or listen to the news retailed by some visitor. At sundown they go to their huts and sit and talk with their womenfolk or guests and wait for their evening meal. Food is usually freshly prepared at night and is ready an hour or so after dark. It is very similar to that eaten at breakfast,[2] supplemented perhaps with a relish in the form of spinach or a mess of beans. The meal is eaten *en famille*, unless strangers happen to be present, slowly and sociably. At the end, the women wash up, while the men sit and talk. Except on clear moonlit evenings, when the young folk dance, there is little for people to do, and as it is dull and perhaps cold sitting in the dim and smoky light of a tiny paraffin lamp, they retire early to bed. Once in bed they may talk a little more or the grandmother may tell the children stories, but soon they all relapse into silence and sleep.

Most people sleep on the floor, using hard semi-tanned cattle skins and tanned goat and sheep skins as mattresses; but increasing numbers are taking to wooden or iron bedsteads and stuffed grass, horse-hair and inner spring mattresses. Adults wrap themselves up in a *kaross* or in ordinary woollen blankets, although the wealthier and more advanced use sheets as well, and children use sheep- or goat-skins or small blankets. Often for warmth's sake two or three people may share the same blankets. Formerly they used wooden blocks for pillows, but nowadays, if they cannot afford a feather or kapoc pillow, they make do with a roll of clothes or a small blanket. They usually sleep naked, though the more sophisticated use pyjamas and nightdresses and during her periods a woman should wear a petticoat. Formerly, they anointed themselves with fat mixed with red ochre as a cleanser, but nowadays this practice, particularly the use of red ochre, has died out except in the mountains.

The daily routine of women is more strenuous than that of men, and varies more with the seasons and with their social status. Their day begins in much the same way as the men's, only instead of sitting

[1] A game like draughts, played on a flat stone. [2] For details, see Ashton, 1939.

about waiting for breakfast, they have to prepare it. During the height of the weeding season, they get to the lands early and start work before sunrise, sometimes as early as three in the morning. They are also responsible for seeing that the hut is properly swept and aired before breakfast. In the afternoon they grind more grain and prepare food for the next meal, and do other odd jobs about the house, although where possible they leave this to their daughters. It takes from one to three hours to grind sufficient grain for the family's daily requirements, the time taken depending as much on the size of the family as on the expertness of the woman and the nature of the grain.

Apart from their domestic duties, agriculture takes up most of their time. Ploughing is men's work and the women are expected to take food out to them during the morning. Those women who have no men to plough for them have to do it themselves. In the summer and autumn the women are responsible for weeding and thereafter for harvesting. For the most part they work from about 9 o'clock in the morning till early afternoon, but at the height of the weeding and harvesting, they have to work from sunrise to sunset, and the older women are sometimes so exhausted at the end of the day that they drop off to sleep, even while eating. During slack periods they have other domestic tasks to do, such as smearing the huts (the floors are usually smeared once every month or two, and the walls once or twice a year), rebuilding the reed fence round the hut, cutting reeds or grass for thatching, and making or mending clothes. Saturday is washing day and among Christians Sunday is spent in going to church. Few women miss a chance of visiting their friends and of going to feasts and ceremonies.

Gossiping, eating, drinking and visiting are the main social activities. Of these "visiting" is the most important. There are several kinds of visits: sociable visits between friends and relations, and official visits to express condolence and to fulfil kinship obligations, as between a man and his parents-in-law. The initiative usually comes from the visitor rather than from the host. Etiquette insists that a guest be given food, and even on the most informal occasions, when a woman merely "drops in" on a friend on her way home from the fields, an effort should be made to give her something, be it only a few boiled mealies. When the visit is important and formal, it must be honoured by more elaborate hospitality. Indeed so imperative is this rule that visits should not be paid if there is any danger of the host's being embarrassed through lack of food. Consequently, ample notice should be given of an intended visit, so that adequate preparations can be made. If it is unwelcome, the prospective host will reply, "We have had a bad season, famine is killing us"—a polite way of saying, "We are not 'at home'."

The following extracts from my assistant's diary show the close association between hospitality or friendly reception and the provision of food. "M's daughters arrived at T's village (two and a half miles away) and

SOCIAL ROUTINE AND ACTIVITIES

met his sisters. After greetings, the former said, 'We are visiting here'. The latter then exclaimed, 'Why didn't you let us know, so that we could prepare you some food.' 'We are sorry—we had no one to send with a message.' 'Oh, well, that is all right, as you did not do it on purpose. We'll cook you some boiled maize or light porridge.' They did so and the girls stayed all day chatting."

"I went to R's where I found two youths sitting with a girl. They were quarrelling with her and beating her, saying she was having an affair with another youth and would not have anything to do with them. I scolded them and got very angry. They ran away. It was the saving of that girl. She then refreshed me, she gave me *mahleu* and bread. I ate and finished. I went to L's where I found two women. They were eating thick porridge; they were getting ready for a dance and had just washed themselves. There I found famine—I had nothing to eat. I left there and went home. On my way I passed the *khotla*, and also M's place. There I found him sitting outside with four men, they were weaving grass ropes to make the type of basket called *linti tsa motolo*. They weren't eating anything, they were just weaving."

On the occasion of formal visits a lot of fuss is made of the principal guest or guests. They are given the best seats and are waited on by their hosts, both men and women, and served with the most tasty morsels. Even if they are socially inferior to other people there, they are given precedence on these occasions. A son-in-law is always given priority, except when he has outstayed his welcome or when the chief is present. When the guests depart, their hosts should accompany them part of the way and if there is a river near the village, they should see them safely across. This applies even in the case of ordinary informal visits.

Apart from this, little etiquette is observed and the Sesuto code of manners is extremely simple. The guest of honour is always served first and, on very formal occasions, other guests do not eat or drink until he has finished. People usually eat out of the same dish and drink from the same pot, but on formal occasions they wait for the guest of honour to invite them to join in. Chiefs and other influential people are treated with greater deference and politeness than other guests. Beyond this, little differentiation is made, except in the case of the very poor and lowly, who may be treated roughly and kept in the background. Women are generally treated as inferior to men, although the wives and senior daughters of a chief are to some extent accorded the deference paid to him, When entering or leaving a hut, women should allow men to go first.

No particular etiquette is followed with regard to seating arrangements within the hut. Men and women usually, though not invariably, sit in separate groups, on either side of the hut, and important people are given chairs or boxes. People are allowed to sit on the raised bench at the back of the hut where pots are kept, but should not sit on the grinding stone unless it is covered. This understandable prohibition is sanctioned according to Dieterlen by the threat of lumbago.

People usually shake hands when meeting. When greeting women one takes the tips of the fingers of the right hand. A full handshake, though not quite correct is not improper, provided it is gentle and soft. Men shake hands firmly, but compared with the Britisher's wrist wringing, they do so very softly. They sometimes use a double handshake, the ordinary handshake followed by slipping the hand round the base of and clasping the other's thumb. This sounds clumsy, but is a most gracious gesture. Where the social difference is fairly great, people do not shake hands or, if they do, the juniors make a sort of curtsey at the same time. Inferiors should always doff their hats to their superiors. Occasionally a person may kiss another's hands as a sign of obeisance. Women kiss one another in greeting on the cheek or lips, and both men and women kiss their children and lovers.

People also greet one another verbally by saying, "*Lumela*"; to which the other replies, "*Ee—Lumela*," and they call one another by name or by kinship terms of respect or by the clan name. Important clan names, such as *Mokoena*, may also be used as courtesy titles to people whose clan affiliation is inferior or unknown. These salutations are followed by exhaustive inquiries as to each other's health and the health of members of their families. When they take their leave they say good-bye with a phrase "*Sala hantle*" or "*Sala ka khotso*" to which the reply is "*Tsamaea hantle*" ("Remain well" or "Remain in peace" and "Go well"). They have no casual form of adieu, though when leaving friends at night they may say, "Sleep well" or "Peace", or use the colloquial expression, "*Funane*". They are polite, friendly and forthcoming, and greet strangers as well as friends in this way. Travellers passing on the road, visitors to the courts and casual acquaintances meeting in the village all stop and greet one another and take a kindly inquisitive interest in each other's health, parentage and business, in where they have come from and whither they are going.

On arriving at a village a stranger should go straight to the court and greet the chief or headman, or send a message to him. If he has no friends there and wishes to stay the night, he will be allowed to sleep in the office or share a hut with the young bachelors; if he is a person of consequence, he will be fed at the chief's hut or be given a sheep for himself and his party, and a guest hut will be set aside for him. The Basuto pride themselves on their hospitality and, quoting the proverb, "The traveller is not chased away", boast that a person can go from one end of the country to the other and never want for food or shelter. Formerly this was not unfounded, but nowadays, with the increased coming and going of travellers of all sorts and the greater struggle for a living, the Basuto are not as forthcoming as they used to be, although they are still extremely hospitable. Consequently, those who have to travel a lot, such as transport riders and hawkers, usually take their own food and cooking utensils with them and make themselves as independent as possible. Chiefs' messengers, tax-collectors and others travelling on public business should be provided for by their chief, or receive some compensation when they return from their business, and messengers should also be entertained by the people to whom they are sent.

The most important social occasion is the feast. This is usually held in connexion with some ceremony and seldom just "for the sake of a party". The significance of the ceremony is, however, treated lightly, except on particularly picturesque occasions, such as those connected with initiation, and many of the guests do not arrive until the ceremony is over and the food is about to be distributed. The principal attraction is the prospect of getting food and, above all, beer, and the success of a feast is measured by the quantity and strength of the beer and the amount of meat available. From the host's point of view, its success also depends on the number of people present, so even uninvited guests are welcomed and entertained.

The organization of a feast is usually simple. Special guests go to their host's hut, while the rest divide into groups, roughly according to the villages or wards from which they come, men and women often being separate. The men move about freely, chatting with the local villagers and their friends, but the women sit quietly together, unless there is dancing or some other jollity. Bowls of food and pots of beer, tea and other beverages are then brought out and presented to each group and served out by its head. Large pieces of meat are divided between friends and beer served in small drinking pots is handed round from person to person. Each recipient takes a good drink fairly rapidly before passing the pot on to the next man. Women drink more slowly and with greater decorum. Certain feasts are regarded as either men's or women's affairs—boys' initiation the former and girls' initiation and the *motabezong* wedding rite the latter. On such occasions food is distributed only to men or women, as the case may be, and people of the opposite sex then have to depend on the generosity of friends for their refreshment.

Occasionally beer may flow like water and meat be had in plenty. At one Tlokoa feast I attended, over two hundred gallons of beer and twenty-five sheep were provided, as well as many baskets of bread, samp, porridge and other foods. Most feasts, however, are given on a modest scale and provide only about twenty to forty gallons of beer, the meat of one or two sheep, and proportionately less bread, tea and other foods. Although many gather in the hope of getting a good deal to eat and drink, the uninvited guest can seldom hope for more than a pint or two of beer and a small piece of meat. Sometimes they may not get even that—but then it is a "rotten party". Apart from this material aspect, people do enjoy feasts and ceremonies (the terms are synonymous in Sesuto) for purely social reasons; they enjoy meeting their friends under pleasurable conditions and they appreciate the opportunities offered for quiet lechery; they like the break in the monotony of their routine, the excitement of dressing in their best clothes and getting away for a little from the village and their ordinary surroundings. They talk about an important prospective feast or ceremony for weeks beforehand, and if they are going to participate actively in it, spend happy hours of preparation.

People's behaviour at feasts and other social gatherings is generally quiet and dignified. They talk a lot, usually topical trivialities, with a gusto which varies greatly with the occasion. On formal occasions they are restrained and sedate, but their behaviour varies considerably with the nature of the occasion. Thus the opening celebrations of boys' and girls' initiation allow wide licence to men and women, as the case may be, and the former particularly are liable to become quite unrestrained; weddings and witch doctor séances, described later, are jolly; funeral feasts are quiet, sometimes almost lugubrious. Feasts that are primarily family affairs, such as weddings, the return of the bride, or the various small rites described in the previous chapters, are more or less informal, depending on the importance of the occasion and the status of the host, and the guests may laugh, joke and enjoy themselves in a friendly and free (but not licentious) manner. Ordinary beer drinks, such as those held on Saturdays and Sundays or at the end of a *letsema* (agricultural work party), and occasionally at a "canteen" where beer is sold, are liable to become noisy, drunken and quarrelsome. On the whole, the people dislike any sort of strong emotional display or rough, undignified behaviour and are quick to rebuke a youngster for unmannerliness and to pacify anyone whose natural quick temper or over-indulgence threatens to provoke a scene. Sometimes before a feast begins the host may appeal to his guests not to spoil it by fighting, but such efforts are not always successful, and the prudent keep away or leave when it begins to get drunken.

The number of feasts held in any area varies considerably. Some, such as those connected with birth and death, are quite irregular—several may come together and then none for a long time; others, such as those connected with initiation, have their proper season and so are more regular and constant, although, as they are expensive and need large quantities of foodstuffs, they have to be postponed in bad years until a good harvest. This applies even to ceremonies connected with unavoidable events, such as death. In the five months I was with the Tlokoa there were six boys' and twelve girls' initiation ceremonies, at least six marriages of importance and several delayed funerary rites, all within a radius of a few miles of Malingoaneng.

To-day, wherever European influences have penetrated, many old ceremonies and their concomitant feasts have died out or are disappearing. The social loss is considerable although to some extent it is mitigated by the fact that even if the original ceremony disappears, or is reduced to the barest sketch, the occasion may still be honoured by some sort of festivity, and that in some cases, such as weddings and funerals, elements of European ritual have been added. Moreover, many Christian festivals as well as regular church services have become occasions for festivity. Thus parties are given to celebrate the baptism or confirmation of a child or an adult. Furthermore, apart from their religious significance, church services have much the same social value as feasts. They offer to both young and old an opportunity to deck themselves out in their finery, to meet friends, to flirt and to get away from domestic routine.

Apart from these feasts and ceremonies people often have small private beer drinks, usually over the week-end and in the slack season after the harvest. Beer brewed for sale may also be had at "canteens". Officially this is illegal, but nevertheless it occurs widely. Violent intoxicating beverages, such as Barbeton, Skokiaan and "Kill-me-quick", brewed in Union slums, where Basuto women have an unenviable reputation as Skokiaan Queens, are finding their way into the country, mainly in the villages near Government centres and chiefs' headquarters, where there is always a lot of coming and going of unattached men. Brandy and other forms of European alcoholic drinks have long been forbidden as the people appear to be unable to drink them in moderation. Chiefs and other leading personages may, however, acquire such liquor under permit, but show a lamentable lack of self-control. Such drinks are usually consumed neat or, in extreme cases, with a "chaser" of stout.

Other social pastimes are singing and dancing, usually as an accompaniment to ceremonies and to ordinary social activities. The most common dances are the *mokorotlo*, the *mohobelo* and the *mokhibo*, as well as special ones danced at initial rites of girls' initiation and at *maqekha* séances.[1] The *mokorotlo* is a slow and impressive dance which is performed only by men. It consists principally of rhythmic swinging backwards and forwards and regular slow stamping; the leader sings solo in a high-pitched voice and is followed by a deep throaty refrain sung by the rest of the group. Every now and then one of the men breaks rank to leap and prance in front of the chief, miming the thrust and parry of battle; the other men then stop singing and urge him on by shouts and cries of encouragement, calling him by his special dancing name. Sometimes he may recite his or the chief's praises or those of some doughty character of the past. When he has finished, he prances back to his place and the chanting and slow movement of the main

[1] *Maqeha* are a kind of diviner. They and their séances are described in Chapter XVI.

dance are resumed. Some of these dance names are vigorous and picturesque—Mosuoe was called "*sea ja, sea rora, sebata*" (it roars, it devours, the wild beast), a headman, *Chomporo*, and a local albino, *Offisiri* (police officer). The *mokorotlo* is danced mainly on important ceremonial occasions, such as big political meetings attended by the chief and his followers, or when the chief goes to the boys' initiation ceremony, or returns with his men from cultivating the tribal field (*tsimo ea lira*). In a simplified form, it is danced at large organized work parties (*letsema*) and, in the old days, at the beginning of wedding ceremonies.

The *mohobelo*, which formerly was a part of the *molutsoane* (rain ceremony), is now danced purely for recreation and amusement. It is a vigorous men's dance and requires a great deal of energy and endurance to be done well. Nowadays, it is danced generally in the evenings, when the local youths are moved to disport themselves, and to while away the time at some tedious ceremony. In 1949, I was lucky enough to attend a most pleasant party near Malingoaneng, to which dancing teams from several villages were invited, held to dispel the evil that still lingered from a lightning strike. For many years Chief Goliath at Mohale's Hoek had a finely disciplined team of dancers, with which he danced on social occasions, such as weddings, and also on official occasions such as a *pitso* (tribal or national gathering).

The *mokhibo* is a girls' dance. It has the unusual feature of being danced on the knees. The knees beat the ground as the body rises and falls, accompanied by a graceful lateral and upward sweep of the hands; a chorus of women stands behind the line of dancing girls, singing and clapping to keep time and mark the rhythm. The pace quickens, the dancers go faster and faster, till they bring the dance to a climax with a whoop, body erect (but still kneeling) and arms flung upwards fully extended. Well done, it is a graceful and attractive dance. It early evoked the indignation of the missionaries because of the opportunities it gave the girls to display their breasts and thighs and, through their opposition, it has now largely died out and is rarely found outside the remoter areas. The dances sometimes seen in the Lowlands purporting to be the *mokhibo* are a pathetic travesty of the original.

The only other dance commonly found is the *motjeko*. It has many varieties and the term covers all dances in which men and women take part. It consists of a jerky step, the dancers either dancing independently or holding hands, but not *corps à corps*. One variety is danced at the concluding feast of a girls' initiation; another is given at modern weddings by the groomsmen and bridesmaids who accompany the couple to the church, and later by the guests at the wedding feast. European types of ballroom dancing and jive are rapidly becoming popular. Children and girls perform a number of simple, light-hearted rhythmic movements to various tunes.

PLATE V

Girls' initiation: matron of honour in traditional dress bearing sleeping mat and water pot

Girls' initiation: girl initiate holding emblematic reed

PLATE VI

(a) Boys' initiation

(b) Girls' initiation: girl initiates returning from the spring, led by matron of honour carrying sleeping mat

Singing is an essential accompaniment to all these dances. In the *mohobelo* and *mokhibo*, a chorus composed of women and girls is drawn up behind the dancers and they sing and clap to keep time. The tunes of the songs are traditional, but the words are meaningless or consist of an impromptu commentary on local events or matters of topical interest. On some occasions, such as the girls' initiation, they are long thematic poems[1] sung as the women slowly rotate in a circle round the fire.

Songs are often sung as an accompaniment to action, whether dancing, hoeing, threshing or grinding grain, running or doing any other rhythmic movement; crooning lullabies are sung to soothe children. Praise-songs (*lithoko*) are chanted at initiation feasts and on other appropriate occasions. Occasionally singing competitions are held. Two or three people sing in turn, usually at a beer party, the audience applauding the best performance. Children and young people from neighbouring villages may also compete at occasional singing contests; and, if lucky, the winning team may be presented with a sheep by the headman of the village where the contest took place. *Mohobelo* and *mokhibo* parties and contests are also occasionally held.

A number of musical instruments are used but, with the exception of the *morupa* and the *lekoko*, these are all purely solo. The *morupa* is a small drum made of a clay pot, covered with a taut skin, and with a hole pierced at the bottom. It is only used at girls' initiation and is played by beating it with the hands. The *lekoko* or *sekupu*, which can scarcely be called an instrument, is an old, hard, rolled cow-skin, which is beaten with sticks and gives out a dull "thumping" sound. It is used almost entirely for *maqekha* séances. The term *sekupu* is also applied to a drum made by stretching a skin over both ends of a hollow agave block and beaten with a stick.[2] Other instruments are the *lesiba* and the *thomo*. The former consists of a stick, at the end of which two projections are inserted and linked with a horse-hair string, attached at one end to an opened quill. Queer, nostalgic sounds are produced by sucking the quill to vibrate the string.[3] The *thomo* is a bow, with a wire or horse-hair string, which may be tautened by means of a wire fastening in the middle. It usually has a resonator, either a calabash or an old paraffin tin, and is played by plucking the string or picking it with a stick. Both the *lesiba* and *thomo* are very popular with herd-boys; the *thomo* is also played by girls. Various instruments of European origin and

[1] The existence of these thematic songs, particularly those sung at the girls' initiation, was not mentioned by Dieterlen in his discussion on Sesuto poetry, *Livre d'Or*, pp. 118–22; so it is possible that they are peculiar to the Tlokoa.

[2] Ramseyer, communication. It is mostly used in ordinary schools to accompany physical training.

[3] A *lesiba* should never be used to strike man or beast: it may therefore be made from the *monkhoane* tree (p. 31), which, being a "royal" tree, should not be used for ordinary sticks, as they would kill whomsoever they struck. (Ramseyer, communication.)

manufacture have also been introduced into the country. Of these the most popular are mouth-organs and concertinas, which are used to keep up the flagging spirits of travellers on the march, and as an accompaniment to the various *motjeko* dances. Police whistles are popular as accompaniments to all dances other than the *mokorotlo*. A few people own portable gramophones on which they play European dance music and recordings of Bantu songs.

In the old days people hunted a lot, but as there are practically no wild animals left there is now little scope for this sport. Though they may be thrilled by the magnificent views offered them when they are dragged to the top of a peak by some restless European companion or during their escapades as herd-boys, the Basuto rarely climb their mountains for fun. Fighting and cattle-raiding used to be their major sports, but these are now denied them. Apart from herd-boys, few people ride for pleasure, except at race meetings. Racing is an old sport. Formerly special oxen were raced over arduous courses of many miles, but they have now been replaced by horses. Race meetings are held once or twice a year at most Government stations and occasionally chiefs organize small meetings of their own. A few chiefs own race-horses, worth comparatively large sums, which they race both in Basutoland and in the Union, but at most meetings, especially at the impromptu district meets, most of the horses are ordinary hacks. Betting is practically unknown, although occasionally friends challenge one another to a race and wager an ox or the horse itself on the result.

Many of the schools have introduced European games, such as soccer and basket ball, and in many parts of the country regular matches are arranged. Both sons of the late Paramount Chief Griffith were keen soccer players and encouraged the game. Athletics, such as running and jumping, have also been introduced but are little indulged in outside the schools. Cricket and tennis have been taken up by the more sophisticated, such as policemen, teachers, clerks and others living in the camps.

The only common "indoor" game is *marabaraba*. For some reason which I failed to ascertain, it is rarely played by the Tlokoa, but is widely enjoyed throughout the rest of Basutoland. It is played with black and white pieces or "cattle" on a "board" drawn on a flat stone. At trading stores, the *khotla* of old villages and other places where people gather, such "boards" are deeply grooved through years of use. The game is supposed to be played by two people, but onlookers readily take sides and shower good advice on the player they are backing. Draughts or "Chequers" is a game played by some of the more sophisticated Basuto such as teachers, chiefs and clerks. Cards and dicing are occasionally and surreptitiously indulged in by young bloods who have introduced these forms of gambling from the Union urban areas.

Another game was called *sekhopi*. A stick was stuck up in the ground and the players tried to knock it down with other sticks, from a distance of forty to fifty yards. The one who hit it first was the winner and was said to have struck his grandmother![1]

[1] Communication from Mr. D. Mochochoko.

CHAPTER VII

OLD AGE, DEATH AND RELIGIOUS BELIEFS

OLD age is as much a social state as youth and infancy. It is not ushered in by any *rite de passage*, but is imperceptibly entered by the slow accretion of years. The old are not treated with any particular veneration. It is accepted that age should bring with it wisdom, and for this reason grey hairs are entitled to respect. Provided they are not doddering and senile, the counsel of old people should be listened to with respect and their advice heeded. Correspondingly, they should set a high standard of behaviour; if they fail and their misconduct comes before the courts, they will be gravely censured.

At the same time old age brings its privileges, and the strictness with which various taboos and irksome forms of behaviour are enforced is relaxed. Old women need be less careful in their dress and circumspect in their speech and behaviour. They rid themselves of their blouses and vests with little compunction and may work in the fields naked from the waist up, whereas younger women would not dream of doing so. They may be outspoken and frank in ordinary speech, and may rail against their menfolk and those in authority to a surprisingly unrestrained degree. Having passed their climacteric, they may ignore various sex taboos and may freely go to the court on ceremonial occasions or enter the cattle kraal. They may also relax kinship formalities, particularly the various in-law avoidances, other than the ban on words connected with the names of their sons-in-law. Good manners and many food taboos reserve to them titbits such as marrow bones, eggs and soft meats, and in the old days—so it is said—they were the only people, other than imbeciles,[1] who were allowed to drink beer.

Occasionally old people are neglected and left destitute by their children or relatives, but on the whole the Basuto are kindly and considerate and give them the attention and consideration to which their years entitle them. Old characters, such as Lelingoana, inspire tremendous loyalty and affection.

This story is told of how death came to the world: "They say that in the days of old there was a chief; his son was called Leobu. The chief heard that his people were in distress. He called to his son who was named Leobu. But a servant of that chief was present; he heard when the chief was giving orders to his son. The chief said to his son Leobu: Go and tell my people that they shall die and rise again.

[1] And slaves. (Ramseyer, personal communication.)

"Leobu went. But the servant, whose name was Khatoane, went out quickly, quickly. When he came to the people of the chief, he said: It is said men shall die and not rise again. He went to the villages and the hamlets, telling the people that it was said, men shall die and not rise again. He went round all the villages and all the hamlets. Thus Khatoane.

"It was there that, afterwards, arrived the son of the chief, whose name was Leobu. He said: My father says that I must tell you that men shall die and rise again. They said: No! the first message is the first message; the one which comes afterwards is but mere talk. He said: No! I must tell you that the chief said that I must tell you: Men shall die and rise again.

"They refused, saying: No, we don't know you. They said: We have listened to Khatoane's message: he said that men shall die and not rise again; as for your message we do not believe it. The first message is the first message. That is where we stand; the first message is the first message, the one which comes afterwards is but mere talk.

"It is the end of the tale."[1]

So death, the ending of corporeal existence, is accepted as normal and inevitable. As the saying is: *lebitla ke mosima o sa tlaleng* (the grave is a pit which never fills).

The dying are treated in the same way as the sick. When it becomes obvious that a person is going to die, his relatives and friends are informed of his condition so that they may gather in the village or prepare themselves for the funeral. The actual moment of death is not heralded by ritual wailing or in any other particular way, though formerly it was "made known to the neighbours by piercing and lugubrious cries".[2] Those concerned simply react to the situation according to their own personal feelings. Women usually weep a little and even men do the same, but on the whole both sexes behave with restraint.

Death is formally announced verbally or by letter to the deceased's relations, friends and headman by his next of kin. It is customary for him to make this announcement by expressing his sympathy and condolences on the loss of their friend. For instance, in his letter of farewell to the retiring High Commissioner, Seeiso, who had just succeeded his father as Paramount Chief, wrote: "I also express my condolence to you on the death of my father, the Paramount Chief, who was your friend." Where the deceased was a person of note, his death should also be reported to the local chief and even to the Paramount Chief, and the announcement should be accompanied by a "consolatory" gift of cattle.[3] The size of the gift varies with the importance of the dead man.

---

[1] Jacottet, 1909, pp. 46–8.
[2] Ellenberger and MacGregor, p. 261.
[3] Mr. Ramseyer writes: "When Jobo, son of Mokhachane, died, his sons omitted to report his death with the consolatory gift of cattle. After this they lost their status and

On Lelingoana's death, four oxen were presented to the Paramount Chief.

To avoid frightening children, the death of close friends or kinsmen may be announced to them at night, by whispering in their ear: "So-and-so has run away and cannot be found." This delicacy of expression is also used in ordinary speech, and a person's death is usually reported as "So-and-so is missing" or "So-and-so has passed on". "Man is not an animal that one should bluntly say, 'He is dead.'" If the deceased is referred to by name, the prefix *mofu*—the "late"—should be used and this is fairly punctiliously observed.

Preparations for burial are begun at the earliest opportunity. According to tradition, the corpse is placed in a crouching position, knees drawn up to the chin and hands clasped in front, and it is tied with grass[1] ropes. If rigor mortis has already set in, the sinews have to be cut, so that the limbs can be bent. The body is washed, dressed, wrapped loosely in a black ox-hide, and lightly bound with another grass rope. Among moderns, the crouching position is regarded as disrespectful, so the body is laid out straight, with the hands folded across the chest, and clothed in European dress, including blanket, hat or *doek*, and laid in a wooden coffin if this can be afforded, or if not, in an old blanket or skin.

The work of laying out the body is done by close relatives of the deceased, excluding the immediate family, and should be supervised by a doctor. Ordinarily, the corpse is not ritually purified in any way, though among important families it is washed with a lotion prepared from various plants,[2] which cleanses the body and protects it from witchcraft. Those who tended the patient or handled the corpse in these or subsequent proceedings should be cleansed by washing with medicines[3] and the hut occupied by the corpse purified by fumigation,[4] otherwise the crops would be ruined. The doctor who attended the deceased should also wash himself with a lotion[5] and sprinkle all his medicines with froth before using them again.

Burial takes place as soon as possible after death, allowing time for friends and relations to attend the funeral. All of them should view the body to pay their last respects to the deceased. The body is kept in the principal hut of the household and is watched over day and night. If

---

were not shewn in the 1939 Schedule of Authorities (H. Cr's Notice No. 171 of 1939), and whenever they tried to protest, each successive Paramount Chief pretended amazement. 'What do you say? Your father is dead? We never heard, we do not know.' Nkhaulise, a descendant of Jobo, attributes his recent rehabilitation to the long overdue payment of the said 'consolatory' cattle."

[1] *Moli, molila* or *teele*.
[2] *Khashe, lokolo* (from Bopeli), *pheta* and *tsita-baloi* were used in one Tlokoa case.
[3] Such as *lefero* or *bolao*.
[4] *Sehalahala-se-se-putsoa*.
[5] *Bolao*.

OLD AGE, DEATH AND RELIGIOUS BELIEFS

the deceased is a man, three or four close adult male relatives sleep in the same hut, while others sleep in the courtyard outside or, if too cold or wet, in a neighbouring hut. In the case of women, the near kinswomen and co-villagers sleep in the hut, while male relatives sleep in the courtyard. This is done as a matter of sentiment—it would be cold and unfriendly to leave the body alone—and to prevent sorcerers molesting it. During the day one or more attendants should remain constantly with the body, and someone should support it when it is being viewed.

DIAGRAM: SITING OF GRAVES

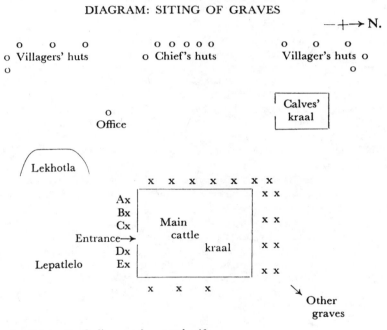

A = 'Matootse, Lelingoana's second wife.
B = Lelingoana.
C = Mokotjo, Lelingoana's senior grandson—senior son of Mosuoe, who is still alive.
D = Mamosuoe, Lelingoana's senior wife.
E = 'Masemai, Lelingoana's fourth wife (his third was still alive).

Graves A–E were all made under the kraal wall, which was pulled down each time to enable this to be done. Other wives, children and kinsmen of Lelingoana, together with the latter's wives and children, are buried under the three other walls and in the ground just beyond the wall. Other villagers are buried in a small graveyard, not demarcated, about one hundred yards from the kraal.

The dead should be buried at home. If a person dies elsewhere, his body should, if possible, be brought home immediately. The site of the grave is pointed out by the local headman. In the old days this used to be in the kraal, so that all trace of the grave would be quickly obliterated and enemies and sorcerers would be prevented from rifling it. This custom has now died out, although many still bury their dead under the kraal wall which is temporarily pulled down for the purpose. The graves of the senior members of the family are sited near the entrance to the kraal, those of their young children and other kinsmen just outside the kraal, and those of other villagers just outside the village. The diagrammatic sketch of the location of graves at Malingoaneng illustrates the position.

Where the custom of burying in or near the kraal is no longer followed, the graves are located together outside the village, sometimes in a cemetery enclosed or marked off, but more often just in the open veld. Many missions have consecrated cemeteries near the church where their adherents may be buried. Important chiefs of the Moshesh lineage are buried on the top of Thaba Bosiu unless for personal reasons they prefer, like the late Paramount Chief Griffith, to be buried at home or in a mission cemetery. Stillborn babies may be buried in the household ash-heap[1] or courtyard, or under the hut floor. Very young children may also be buried in either of the two latter places.

People who have been drowned or killed by lightning should be buried near the river. If this is not done, the river will be deprived of its victim and will seek others in his place. During the funeral service, the river is besought to be satisfied with the victim it has already taken, to leave the living in peace and to allow them to cross without fear. Similarly, with those struck by lightning, "because lightning and water are one", and unless they also are buried near the river it is feared that lightning will strike the village. Those who assist in the burial have to be purified with special vaccination and aspersion. The corpse is also sprinkled with medicine.

People killed in battle should be buried at home or at least where they lie, lest the enemy get hold of their remains for use as medicine. But for obvious reasons this is often impossible.

"Rona, banna, re pholo tsa matlaka
Re pholo tsa abeloa manong,
Tsa ho jeoa ke mahakajane thotheng."

"We, men, we are the oxen of the vultures,
We are cattle to be shared by the vultures,
To be devoured by carrion crows in the veld."

[1] Mr. Kennan records that in an infanticide case, the Basuto assessors were convinced that, because the body had been buried in a donga instead of placed in a clay pot in the ash-heap, the child had been born alive and subsequently suffocated.

OLD AGE, DEATH AND RELIGIOUS BELIEFS

The traditional grave, still used by some Tlokoa, is a small oval cave, hollowed out of the side of a pit. The cave is just large enough to admit the body in a crouching position, the actual size being accurately measured with a reed, which is subsequently left in the grave. Mokotjo was buried in this traditional way in 1936. The modern type of grave, which is now widely used, is a narrow trench, some six or seven feet deep and about two feet wide. Occasionally a mixture of the two is found, where a horizontal cavity is hollowed out of one side at the base of the trench, to form a "little room" for the corpse.

The grave is dug in the morning.[1] The first sod should be formally cut by the senior member of the family who is followed by other close male relatives in order of seniority, each merely digging out one or two sods or spadesful of earth. The number taking part in this rite depends largely on the importance of the family and the closeness of their kinship ties—for Mokotjo's grave about thirty people took part, whereas for a humble villager only two or three do so. After this, the local male villagers set to work in relays. Close relations of the deceased should be spared this, if possible, but as unimportant people will not have many people to help them, even the brothers and sons of the deceased may have to dig.[2]

The funeral should take place in the afternoon, after the sun has passed its meridian, and should be as near sundown as possible, although it must be completed by sunset. Occasionally, to avoid delaying an important ceremony which has been arranged in the neighbourhood, unimportant people may have to bury their dead in the morning.

Mortuary ritual is simple and straightforward. The corpse, borne by people chosen by the family head, usually close kinsmen, is carried out of the hut feet foremost and taken to the grave by the shortest route. Formerly it would not have been taken through the door of the *seotloana*, but through a gap made to the right of the door for men and to the left for women. This was done in the case of Letsie II, who was buried from Moshesh's hut at Thaba Bosiu,[3] and, so they told me, is also done with the Baphuthi. Among other Basuto[4] the body might be taken through

---

[1] Divergent customs recorded by M. Martin, which I find difficult to credit, are that the body is tied into a sitting position before death and then taken out of the hut so that the spirits can gain readier access to him; that the grave is dug after nightfall and the body placed at the entrance to the cattle kraal just before nightfall and left there till buried just before dawn. (M. Martin, *Basutoland*, pp. 89-91.) Although night burial might have occurred in time of war, it is almost inconceivable, in view of the belief in ghouls and witches, that the dying should have been treated in the way described or that the body should have been left unattended outside.

[2] Rule 30, *Laws of Lerotholi*, 1946, makes it a civic obligation on every male adult residing in a village to help in digging the grave, and empowers the chief, sub-chief or headman to order any adult male to help if there are no male adults in the village. Refusal to obey such order is punishable with a maximum fine of £3.

[3] Letter, T. B. Kennan. The reason given him was to prevent the deceased's spirit re-entering the hut and worrying the living. [4] Ellenberger and MacGregor, p. 262.

a hole pierced through the back of the hut. Nowadays it has become customary, even among the heathen, for a priest to be invited to say a few prayers before the body is taken out of the hut or courtyard.

On reaching the grave, the corpse is handed down to two or three men standing inside, and is then gently seated in the little cave or laid on the bottom. The Tlokoa place the body facing the north-east, towards their original home, whereas other Basuto, with the same object in mind, put it facing the east. If buried according to the European method, but without a coffin, the body is placed on its back, with the head resting on a pillow and turned in the proper direction. The grass ropes are then cut and left in the grave, and also the reed used as a measuring stick. Kaffir-corn, gourd and pumpkin seeds[1] are placed on or near the body with wisps of *mohloa* and *molile* grass, each plaited into a miniature platter. The deceased's snuff-box is also placed beside the body, with the words "There is your tobacco". Among the Tlokoa, a few beads, proper to the deceased's clan, are also buried with him. A man's milking pot and thong and a woman's stirring rod and porridge stick[2] used also to be placed in the grave, but this is no longer done. Bread and water may also be placed there in a clay pot.

At this point the local priest or evangelist may again be asked to say a few prayers. These he concludes by throwing into the grave a few handfuls of earth, with the words, "Dust unto dust, ashes to ashes". The mouth of the cave is then sealed with flagstones and the interstices carefully plugged with grass so that no earth should fall on and besmirch the body. One by one, roughly in order of seniority, men preceding women, the deceased's relatives and friends come forward and throw or shovel a little earth into the grave. When they have finished, the helpers take over, fill the grave and rebuild the kraal wall. Where the grave is outside the kraal, they may mark the head and foot with a couple of stones. Some later neatly square off and plaster the mound above the grave and a few erect a cross or inscribed tombstone.

When they have finished the men gather round and, at a word from the head of the family, spit on a pebble and toss it into the grave murmuring, "Sleep peacefully", "Go in Peace" (*U re roballe boroko— tsamaea ka khotso*). At small funerals, or where the traditional usages have been abandoned, women may join men for this last salute; otherwise they do it later by themselves.

On important occasions, the chief or his representative then makes a short speech, extols the virtues of the deceased and announces the period of mourning during which the courts will be closed and agricultural work will be forbidden. If the deceased was a headman or junior authority, the name of his successor may be announced. This concludes the

---

[1] These are said to be the original foods of the Basuto. Newly introduced ones such as maize or wheat should not be put in the grave.

[2] Ellenberger and MacGregor, p. 262.

funeral ceremony and the guests then return to the village for the funeral feast, or leave for their own homes. The deceased's close kinsmen should have their hair cropped.

At no time during the rite is there any organized wailing. The people are restrained, and usually there is little or no weeping except for understandable bursts of sobbing when the body is lowered into the grave and the earth is finally shovelled in. Women, throughout the day, are quiet, subdued and tend to sit about with their faces sunk in their blankets. The men chatter and joke, though less noisily than usual.

Graves are not regarded as sacred except in mission cemeteries. Formerly,[1] if a mother saw her child run over a grave, she would call it to her and light a small fire at its feet to purify it, but no one seems to observe this nowadays and people have no hesitation in walking over or sitting on a grave.

Whenever possible, a feast is provided for the friends and relatives who have come to the funeral. According to strict custom, a beast, called *mohoha*, pure black and of the same sex and approximately the age of the deceased is killed. If this cannot be afforded, a sheep or goat will do instead. The meat is cooked and distributed in the usual manner and no particular observances mark this as a special occasion. Beer should also be provided. Much of the food and drink may be consumed before the funeral actually takes place so that visitors can reach home before dark.

The *mohoha* is said to be the deceased's "companion" on his heavenly journey and, according to some, furnishes him with a blanket to cover his nakedness in the next world. A story of the origin of this custom which admirably reflects popular belief about it, runs like this: "A rich man died and was buried like other people. After a time his spirit returned and became a ghost, and went to his cattle and opened the kraal at night. However hard the people tried to keep them in, they always broke out. So they ran to a diviner. He went into his medicine hut and anointed himself with the foam of the medicines in the hut, and then he came out and said, 'Alas, alas, a great man has died, a rich, proud man. The gods have refused to allow him into their village, saying he was too proud and arrogant for them to let him in. And so his spirit has returned to his cattle for shelter.' So they appealed to him to advise them what to do. He retired to his medicine hut, and they remained outside, amazed at this unprecedented happening. Then he came out again to them and said, 'Do this. To-morrow, early in the morning, take his biggest ox, kill it and skin it quickly, and before you have finished skinning it take out the stomach and the second stomach and from the little pocket in the first (the "madman's dwelling" *ntlo ea*

[1] Casalis, 1861, p. 324.

lehlanya)[1] take the cud that has not been chewed. Then as the sun rises, sing his praises, spit on this cud and throw it on his grave.' They did so and the cattle were quiet for ever after. People say this beast attracts (*hohela*) the dead to the dead."

This rite is one of the very few which are still widely observed by Christians as well as non-Christians. It is done in order to "make the grave firm" and to pay one's last respects to the dead. For this latter reason the animal is called the deceased's table (*tafole*) at which they are eating for the last time. Owing to the expense involved, only the wealthy can observe both this rite and the later one described below. Most people, therefore, combine the two and hold the double rite when convenient, either immediately after the funeral or some months later. Some people, the Phuthi, for instance, mix some of the strainings of the beer with the chyme of the *mohoha* beast and leave it in a broken potsherd near the grave. Friends who wish to pay their last respects to the dead take a pinch of this, spit on it and spatter it on the grave, as above.

The Tlokoa chiefs have a peculiar observance of their own and slaughter two beasts, one for the feast and the other, *khomo ea khurumetso*, for a special rite. The second stomach (*khitsane*) of the latter beast is removed, cleaned and fitted over the deceased's head just before burial. This is called his "hat" or covering (*khurumetso*). The beast is so closely identified with the deceased that its meat may not be eaten by his relations and friends ("it would be like eating himself"), and should only be eaten by strangers and tribesmen of low caste, such as Tebele; members of the Sekhosana lineage, who are the chief's close personal servants and act as his bodyguard, are also debarred from eating it.

In the evening, after the visitors have departed, a doctor, chosen by the family head, unobtrusively sprinkles the grave and the soil round it with medicine. This is done to protect it from violation by ghouls and witches who might try by means of powerful medicines or by actually opening the grave to gain control of the dead man's spirit.

The next morning all the deceased's relations, except his widows and daughters, should have their heads shaved. The hair should be burned or buried in the ash-heap or in a marshy place near the river. If this is not done, sorcerers may get hold of it and through it do harm to the persons concerned; or birds may build it into their nests and so cause them to go mad. Everyone, including the local villagers, both men and women, should bathe and anoint themselves with medicines.[2] (This is not punctiliously observed; in one case which I was able to

---

[1] Madness was believed to be an affliction sent by the gods. A madman could be cured by being scarified with appropriate medicine, and then having this little pocket, sprinkled with medicines, fitted over his head. This organ was specially associated with the ancestors and was regarded as their meat which could only be eaten by old people. Casalis records (p. 309) that the Barolong actually regarded the mad with awe, believing them to be under the direct influence of the gods.

[2] *Selepe* and *mathethebane*.

check, only the women did so.) Relatives wear a sign of mourning (*thapo*), which consists of plaited *teele* grass or a strip of black cloth; widows thread a metal chain or link on to the *thapo*, and orphans a necklace of chipped ostrich shells, together with the chain or link.

If, as is usually the case, the deceased's hut is in constant use, the floor should immediately be smeared with fresh cow dung unmixed with soil. From the day of the death until the day after the funeral, members of the deceased's village, if a small close-knit one, and near relations, should not do any agricultural work except at a prearranged work party (*letsema*), nor such domestic chores as smearing[1] or repairing huts. For the death of chiefs or of chiefs' close kinsmen, such as sons or senior wives, this period of mourning may last as long as three weeks or a month. Normal domestic or village life is not interrupted in any other way and sexual intercourse is not forbidden although, for decency's sake, people are expected to abstain from the day of death until after the funeral. Widowers are not subjected to any particular restrictions and continue to lead a normal life, although they should behave soberly and quietly for a while. Widows and children and, to a limited extent, their close kinswomen, should not have sexual intercourse until they have been purified, and men sleeping with them are liable to *mashoe*, a venereal affliction, which can be prevented or cured only with difficulty and by the use of special and little-known medicines. They should also keep aloof from ordinary domestic activities for several days and should not cook or handle food, or work in the fields lest the crops should be damaged by hail or frost, or, if already mature, be reduced by "evaporation". They should wear sombre clothes and black *doeks*, and keep their heads unshaven and they should not administer medicines until purified.

As soon as convenient, but not less than a week or two after the funeral, the family head should carry out a small rite to purify his womenfolk. This rite is a quiet and undemonstrative family affair and, except among wealthy Tlokoa, is now rarely held. All the female members of the family gather at his village and a sheep is killed for each of those who are to be purified. They are shaved in the usual ritual fashion, the hair being moistened with the sheep's bile, and the gall bladder is strung round each woman's neck or wrist. The family head then presents each of them with a new outfit of clothes—a blanket, skirt, blouse and *doek*—and in return, takes their "impurity" i.e. their mourning clothes. These he gives to his sisters or to the old women of the village or anyone else he likes; although he could do so, it would be considered mean of him to keep them for his own wife and daughters. If for some reason, such as poverty, he cannot kill a sheep for the women he should purify them by anointing them with aloe juice instead of gall. (The

[1] No cow dung should be taken from the local cattle kraal until the *tea lejoe* ceremony is held.

bitter quality of these substances is suggestively symbolical.) In the afternoon women from neighbouring villages come to pay their respects to the bereaved and join in the small feast provided. When they return home, the family head is supposed to give each of his womenfolk a beast to take with her, but only the very rich can afford to do so.

Some time after the funeral—months or perhaps years later, if it cannot be afforded earlier—another purification ceremony is held. This is to "make the grave firm" (*ho tea lejoe*) and at the same time to "wash" the deceased's possessions and the objects used at the time of the funeral. On this occasion the male relations and the maternal uncle of the deceased gather in the village. A black beast, called *mohoha*, similar in age and appearance to the one previously killed, is slaughtered just before daybreak and disembowelled. The chyme from the second stomach (*qati* or *ntlo-ea-lehlanya*) is placed in a potsherd, and the stomach itself is thrown to the dogs or given to some poor old woman. Then, as the morning star rises and the first glimmer of dawn appears, all the men gather round the grave and, murmuring, "Sleep for us", "Send us *mabele*", bespatter the grave with chyme. Later, after the beast has been skinned and cut up, they reassemble in their senior's courtyard together with their wives and the women of the village. In order of seniority, each receives a strip of suet (*mohlehlo*) taken from the *mohoha* ox and ties it round his neck or wrist or pins it to his blanket. This is a "sacred" rite, so nothing modern may be used and the suet has to be cut with split reeds and not with a trade knife. It should be worn until it drops off, but some of the younger men rather self-consciously take it off after half an hour or so and throw it to the dogs.

The deceased's personal property is now collected together. Each article is smeared with chyme from the *mohoha* ox by a menial or a junior relative in the presence of the others, and those not required for daily use are laid away in a storeroom. The tools used in digging the grave, which should not have been used in the interval, should also be smeared. This smearing makes the articles "firm". Hitherto they are said to be weak and watery, as they have been mourning for their owner and if used they would have broken or become damaged. The floor of the hut, where the body lay, is also smeared with fresh cow dung mixed with chyme. A few days later the doctoring (*moupello*) of the huts should be renewed, lest the death should have affected its potency.

The deceased's personal belongings are distributed either immediately after this rite or during the following winter. This may only be done in winter for fear of provoking frosts, hailstorms or damage to crops. The dead man's maternal uncle or, if the latter is dead or unable to do so, the uncle's son carries out this task. On the appointed day, the uncle (or his son) accompanied by his relations is met on the outskirts of the village by some of the local villagers who kill the ox he has brought with him and carry the meat into the village. The deceased's goods are then brought out of the hut where they have been stored and are again smeared with chyme from the ox. The maternal uncle then picks out those articles that he is entitled to inherit, presents some of them to the father, sons or brothers of the dead man and keeps the rest. The remainder is given to the deceased's heir. A small feast is then held using the meat of the purification ox brought by the uncle and beer provided by the home villagers. At the end of this the uncle is given an ox to replace the one he brought and to transport his property. If this is not done, he may "lose his way", and his relationship with the family of the dead man may be embittered and the ancestors provoked to make trouble.

A woman's property should be distributed as soon as winter comes after the "firming of the grave", without further ceremonial. According to strict custom, her beer pots and other pottery should not be used until purified by a further small feast, when beer is brewed specially to "wash" them, or until they have been washed with the juice of the spotted mountain aloe.

These rites can only be fully observed by fairly wealthy people. Poorer people content themselves with a simpler purification. They may kill a sheep, and smear some of the chyme on their heads and/or eyebrows, and then shave their heads. In the evening the meat is eaten by close friends and kinsmen.

Another rite, also called "to wash the pots", is held some time, perhaps years, after a person's death. This is simply a beer feast held to honour the dead and is attended by his or her friends and relations. According to my assistant, who attended the feast held for Mokotjo, in addition to ordinary beer, two or three pots of unstrained beer (*mohlaba*) were kept overnight and drunk next morning by the older people. He did not say whether any special offering was made to the dead, but the use of this beer suggests that the feast has, or once had, some religious significance. It is held only for prominent members of important families.

This traditional series of mortuary rites is observed more or less completely only by a small section of the Tlokoa, principally the chiefs and other leading families. Even there, the rites are rapidly breaking down and losing their significance. For instance, at the purification rites after the death of Mokotjo (the chief's senior son), several of the leading participants were uncertain about various details, such as whether the goods should be purified before or after the mourners had received the *mohlehlo* strips, nor did they care very much one way or the other; when additional *mohlehlo* strips were needed they were surreptitiously cut with a knife instead of with the traditional but cumbersome split reed; and the proceedings generally were carried out in an atmosphere of casualness and indifference. Elsewhere the rites have been abandoned to a greater or less degree, or replaced wholly or in part by rites of European origin, such as church services.

Religious Beliefs

Basuto beliefs and doctrine regarding death and the after-life are far from being coherent, stable or uniform. Some of the old beliefs can still be found but, for the most part, they have been fused in varying degrees with Christian doctrines. The position is exceedingly complex and I cannot hope to do it justice in view of my limited experience; at best, I can merely give a general idea of the major tendencies and traits.

Man (*motho*) is believed to be composed of two elements: the corporeal body (*'mele*) or flesh (*nama*), and the incorporeal spirit (*moea*, which also means the wind) or shadow (*seriti*). The body can be perceived by the senses, and is subject to decay and destruction. The spirit is indestructible and immortal: it is normally imperceptible, but may occasionally be seen and heard by others in dreams and visions during a person's lifetime and after his death. It may also be seen in his lifetime as an emanation or second shadow, the most favourable time being at sunset when it separates itself from the body's ordinary shadow. It may occasionally be seen after death, glimpsed out of the corner of one's eye, but never seen clearly or directly.

During life the spirit resides in the body, some say in the heart[1] and others in the head, though the usual view is that it suffuses the whole body. It may leave the body of its own accord at night, and wander about at will. Dreams are the consciousness of these experiences. A witch is the only person who can deliberately make his spirit leave his body and can direct its activities. Ordinarily, the spirit is not subject to the ills and afflictions of the flesh, but it may occasionally get disordered as the result of sorcery or the action of departed spirits. These disorders affect the normal functioning of the body and cause hysteria and other mental aberrations, such as *bothekethek*.

The spirit is not regarded as a motor or vital force, which keeps the body going, and whose withdrawal would cause it to decay, but merely as a part of a person which sojourns in the body. When death occurs and the body ceases to function, the spirit departs from it. For a time it hovers near the body and even goes into the grave with it, and, according to orthodox doctrine, is not completely released from the body until the grave has been "made firm". Until this happens, it is vulnerable to sorcery. It could, for instance, be captured and turned into a ghost by cutting the dead person's tongue out or by driving a peg into his head. It therefore needs the protection of the vigil and the medicines mentioned above. When the final rites have been performed, the spirit rises to its feet (to help it to do this easily the body

[1] Casalis, 1861, p. 305.

PLATE VII

Photo: L. Lewis

(a) Women fetching water

Photo: L. Lewis

(b) Women winnowing at sunset

PLATE VIII

Photo: Constance Stuart

(a) A Mothepu belle

Photo: L. Lewis

(b) Clerk of the Court at his desk

OLD AGE, DEATH AND RELIGIOUS BELIEFS

should be buried in a crouching position) and proceeds on its way to Ntsuanatsatsi. Even now, it is still rather helpless and has to be correctly orientated for its journey; this is achieved by placing the body in the correct position, otherwise it may stray, fall into the hands of witches or wander aimlessly as a lost soul (*sethotsela*), plaguing its living relations until they set it on its proper path by sacrificing an animal.

From the grave the spirit goes to the ancient tribal home. Nobody is quite sure where this is, whether on earth at Ntsuanatsatsi or in the heavens, though everyone seems agreed that it is not in the bowels of the earth as their fathers believed.[1] But wherever it is, existence there is much the same as here. People live in villages, on the familiar pattern of home life, though it is doubtful whether they marry or beget children; they have the same sort of social organization under the leadership of their former chiefs. They also continue the same pursuits, and so they must take with them the wherewithal to establish their new crops, herds and homes; accordingly seeds and *mohloa* grass[2] must be placed in the grave so that their essence may be taken by the spirit.

The journey is uneventful, provided the spirit has been set on the right path. Some say that the spirit needs an introduction to gain admission to the heavenly home and they consider that the *mohoha* beast provides this and that until it has been killed the spirit will wander about and worry the survivors. Some also say that the *khomo ea khurumetso* is the Tlokoa chief's "pass" across a Stygian river which must first be crossed. No explanation was offered as to why only this clan requires such a pass, and I feel that this statement may possibly have been made on the spur of the moment to cover ignorance and satisfy importunate questioning. The idea of a Styx-like river is, however, fairly common, and it is often mentioned as one of the barriers on the road to heaven. Casalis records[3] that the Bapeli believed in such a river called Tlatlane, but he gives no details which would enable us to connect the two ideas.

The Basuto dread death. They feel terribly exposed and defenceless before disease, misfortune or sorcery, and are almost morbidly aware that death may be their lot at any time. They, therefore, treat the subject with some awe and delicacy—they think the hearty greeting of many Europeans, "What! not dead yet?" rather poor form—and prefer not to discuss it or talk about it. They consider that the dead should remain with the dead and so they do not try to establish contact with the departed or keep their memory alive; on the contrary they try to forget. This is the significance of their prayer to be left in peace and the reason for throwing earth into the grave at the funeral and be-

[1] Casalis, op. cit., p. 309.
[2] *Mohloa* grass symbolizes family and community life as it always grows where settlements are established.
[3] Casalis, op. cit., p. 310.

spattering it with chyme afterwards, as these acts symbolize the final severance[1] of all ties between them. This is also a reason why few people favour any memorial in the form of a tombstone, and why graves are not treated with awe and respect.

The living are actually afraid of the dead, and if they find themselves dreaming of their kinsmen and friends or brooding over their death, they resort to various rites to stop it. If the dead are only just glimpsed in a dream, it may not mean much more than that they are still interested in and fond of one; but if they appear looking cross or loving, it is serious and means either that they are angry with one for having neglected some obligation towards them or towards a living relative, or that they long for one to join them. In the first case, they can be propitiated by the sacrifice of a goat, or a libation of beer or by fulfilment of the shirked obligation, indicated by guilty conscience or by divination. In the second case, they may be "soothed" by observing or repeating the original graveside rite of spitting on a stone and throwing it on the grave, saying again, "Sleep peacefully for us". If this is not done, they will either bring trouble on one's household or cause one to become moody and listless, fall ill and die. This belief is still so firmly held by some that they will go to great lengths to propitiate the dead. In one case an old man of over eighty, who had been Lelingoana's doctor and companion, made a long and arduous journey from Natal to Malingoaneng simply to "soothe" the spirit of the old chief who had been appearing in his dreams.

In spite of the apprehension with which they are regarded individually, the spirits of the dead are not regarded as necessarily malevolent. On the contrary, the *balimo*[2] are expected to take an interest in their survivors' material well-being. They have some influence over the crops and can improve the harvest if they want to; they often send a bumper harvest (*lehlona*) after the death of a parent or a child to console the survivors. Their help is both sought and acknowledged at the end of each season by the gifts of *phabalimo*,[3] by occasional brewings of *joala ba leoa*[4] and by pouring a little *setoto*[5] into the fire when beer is brewed for important feasts.

In the old days,[6] each family was considered to be under the direct

[1] The *qati* from which the chyme is taken is the second stomach of a cow. Once the animal's fodder has reached there, it cannot be returned to the mouth. It is thus held to symbolize finality. The *mohlehlo* may also have had some similar significance, but no one could explain it.

[2] This term is usually and conveniently translated as "ancestor" spirits though it means simply the spirits of the departed, and may refer to childless adults and children of living people. It is collective and is never used in the singular to indicate a particular spirit.

[3] Described in Chapter VIII.

[4] Ibid.

[5] The unfermented porridge from which beer is made.

[6] Casalis, op. cit., p. 310-11.

influence and protection of its ancestors and the tribe as a whole under those of the ancestors of its chief. Thus the Basuto prayed to Monaheng and Motlomi, and the Bahurutsi and Barolong to Tobega and his wife Mampa. It was believed that the earlier gods were more powerful than the more recent ancestors so that many prayers began with the phrase "New gods pray for us to the gods of old". According to Dieterlen[1] during times of national calamity and danger, the principal chiefs of Basutoland used to meet at the graves of Moshesh and of other early chiefs at Thaba Bosiu to pray for their help; I am told that they still do so, particularly chiefs from Leribe and Berea, and that on such occasions a beast is sacrificed. So, too, Lelingoana prayed to his ancestors when he first arrived in the Highlands. Formerly the *molutsoane* and other rain ceremonies were addressed to the chief's ancestor spirits.

The sphere in which the help of the ancestor spirits is still sought is that of sickness. Formerly[2] all illness was attributed to them in the belief that they continually tried to compass the death of the living in order to secure their companionship; to-day only a few maladies, such as hysteria, insomnia and epilepsy, are ascribed to them. These can be cured by propitiating the spirits and restoring them to good humour, either by sacrificing an animal or by performing a duty which has been neglected. Maladies such as sterility, or indeed any disease, even though not directly caused by them, may be cured through their influence; in such cases, the correct approach and the appropriate remedy may be revealed by divination. Their help may be invoked directly by calling by name on individual ancestors. At the same time a sheep or goat should be shown to the patient, and then killed by being pierced with a needle behind the shoulder: the longer it takes to die, the surer will be the cure. The gall is poured over the patient and the gall bladder tied round his wrist or neck. Medicines also may sometimes be used to assist the cure. A few special cases, notably ulcers called *setsoa*, are curable only by the maternal ancestors who have to be approached through the patient's maternal uncle or his representative. The cure may be effected by the uncle's "laying on" of hands, by spitting on the sores or by washing the patient with the appropriate medicine or with the gall of a goat sacrificed for the occasion; at the same time, he should call on his ancestors by name and recite their praise-songs.

The ancestor spirits also reveal new medicines and new kinds of treatment. They may do this to any kind of doctor, but particularly to *mathuela*[3] whom they constantly guide and help.

Dieterlen mentions[4] that "as part of their domestic cult, some Basuto have a little niche at the back of their hut, where they store the gall bladders of sacrificed animals and keep overnight beer used on

[1] Dieterlen, 1912, p. 141.
[2] Casalis, op. cit., p. 311.
[3] See p. 286.
[4] Dieterlen, 1912, p. 139.

semi-religious occasions". The nearest approach to this that I have found was the practice of pouring some of the bile of sacrificial or ceremonial animals (such as the sheep killed to celebrate a birth) on the floor at the back of the hut.

The Tlokoa still believe strongly in the ancestor spirits, although some of them are turning to the belief in one Supreme Being, which has been widely accepted by other Basuto. The Tlokoa are probably also the only people who observe to any great extent the practices just described; elsewhere they have been modified by praying direct to God instead of appealing to the ancestor spirits.

When the early missionaries arrived, they found with joy that the Basuto had some idea of a Supreme Being which corresponded, albeit vaguely, with the Christian conception of God. The traditional Sesuto conception of God was of a very distant being, situated somewhere in the heavens, too remote and too aloof to pay much attention to man and his petty affairs, although prayers for his help were made in time of drought or sickness and by barren women. The latter carried a clay doll on their backs, in the same way as children are normally carried, and prayed, "Oh, Light, through this child grant me a child". Such prayers might also be accompanied by sacrifice of a sheep or goat.

The Supreme Being was known as *Molimo* (God), *Leseli* (Light), *Ra 'Moloki* (Protector, Father of our Saviour) or *Hlaa-hlaa-Macholo*, but except for the first two, these terms are not used in ordinary speech, and only occur in special witch-doctors' initiation rites.[1] The old Basuto had little idea of a *Dieu créateur*; "it never occurred to them that the earth and sky could be the work of an invisible being",[2] and they were not greatly concerned about this question. God was sometimes said to manifest Himself as lightning or as a thunderbolt, and when this struck a village a feast would be held in honour of the visit.[3] Whether or not the Basuto ever had a stronger and more definite faith, originating at some earlier date of greater enlightenment, which has since deteriorated[4] is, of course, impossible to say and the problem need not concern us here.

Nowadays, a fairly definite belief in God is widespread owing to missionary influence and teaching over the past hundred years. Practically everyone has some knowledge, no matter how garbled, of Christian doctrines, but the degree to which these doctrines have been accepted and the old ideas abandoned varies greatly, and to-day Sesuto

---
[1] These rites are described in Chapter. XVI
[2] Casalis, 1861, pp. 298-9.   [3] Dieterlen, 1912, pp. 142-3.
[4] Dieterlen, for instance, argues that there was one old group of Basuto who knew more than the present people do, and that they had a much fuller belief in God than have the pagan Basuto to-day. So, too, he regards "the few fragments" of their religion less as the first gropings after a God than as the vestigial and hsapeless debris of a religion which has known better days. Dieterlen, 1912, pp. 132, 137, 143. See also Casalis, 1861, pp. 298 and 310.

belief ranges from the complete orthodoxy of ministers and teachers of the gospel to the traditional paganism of the conservative Tlokoa. The beliefs of the majority of the Basuto fall somewhere between these extremes; so far as the Tlokoa are concerned, their beliefs follow very much the lines described below, though elsewhere they are more fully Christian and tinged with sectarian doctrine.[1] They widely believe that God was the founder of the world, and many people firmly believe the Old Testament account of the Creation. Many also believe that God is the prime causal agent in the world, the ultimate source of power and of good and bad fortune. From this, some have developed an extreme fatalism and have resigned themselves to His Will, as the ultimate arbiter of their affairs. Thus they say, "It will rain, if God wills," "The crops will be good or the sick recover, if He wills," or, "I shall have enough cattle to marry next year, if God wills." Many use these expressions casually or indifferently, as mere figures of speech, without meaning what they say, but others are sincere and, feeling that He will act as He considers best, apathetically wait to see what will happen and make little real effort to fend for themselves over and above the obvious necessary minimum.

Others believe that He takes a kindly interest in human affairs, though there is a tendency to regard Him as somewhat remote and detached, rather as a chief, who is interested at a distance in his people, than a fond parent. In all services held in church, school, and in private gatherings organized by teachers, evangelists and other converts, or at funerals and other occasions when a Christian leader is present, prayers and petitions, familiar to church-goers in our own society, are offered up: prayers for safety, for good crops, for rain, for health, for the guidance of those in authority, for protection, for the happiness of the married couple, for the consolation of the bereaved, for the godliness of the converted. National days of prayer for rain are occasionally appointed by the Paramount Chief in periods of acute drought. Prayer is also used in sickness and, on one occasion, the Protestant pastor at Malingoaneng cured a woman of alleged *botheketheke* by pouring holy water over her "in the name of the Father, the Son and the Holy Ghost". It is also used in trivial human affairs, as in the case of my assistant and his pagan friends who prayed for help in finding their strayed animals, saying, "God give us good fortune, especially in respect of our lost horses". It is impossible to say how genuine is the belief in God and in the efficacy of prayer. There are some scoffers; there are undoubtedly also wholehearted believers.

[1] Though the Tlokoa had had a French Protestant Mission among them for over forty years, and a Roman Catholic Mission just across the Orange River for some ten years, they remained so obstinately pagan in outlook that, in 1930, not a single authentic Motlokoa was a Christian, and the only Christians among them were immigrants from other parts of Basutoland. (See Ellenberger, 1930)

The shift in emphasis, due to Christian influence, from the *balimo* to *Molimo*, from the ancestor spirits to a single God, and the attribution to the latter of phenomena and powers (albeit greater) that were previously attributed to the former, are changing the Basutos' ideas about medicine and disease, and also opening up wider opportunities for prayer and other non-medical means of controlling their environment. For instance, the "Apostolic Church", founded by "Edward Motaung, the Lion",[1] accepts the Bible as a source of authority and as a guide to conduct, but at the same time he and his followers strongly adhere to all Sesuto custom, with one notable exception, namely the use of medicine. Instead of this, they rely entirely on prayer and they regard the use of any medicament as wrong and sinful. This sect also opposes the Roman Catholic practice of wearing medallions of the saints, quoting the Second Commandment in their support.

The old ideas of Ntsuanatsatsi and the tribes' spiritual home are also changing and are becoming mingled with ideas of Heaven and Hell. The result is confusion. Many people are not sure where the spirit goes on leaving the body: whether it goes to Ntsuanatsatsi as a sort of paradisal half-way house to Heaven or Hell, or direct to one or other of these places, depending on the conduct of the deceased and on his repentance, forgiveness and redemption. Nor can they explain in terms of Christian belief or any other coherent ideology the remnants of old beliefs and practices which still persist, such as the traditional orientation of the body to the east and the killing of the *mohoha* beast. If forced to recognize the inadequacies or contradictions of their present beliefs and practices, they merely shrug their shoulders and say, "Well, we don't know," and leave it at that.

It is difficult to say how religious beliefs affect conduct. The subject is a vast and intricate one, and I am not qualified to deal adequately with it; I can only offer some brief and superficial observations.

The old religion had little concern with conduct except as regards the observance of certain rites and kinship obligations, and its influence was retrospective rather than prospective: if a person wanted to shirk his obligations, he did so without thought of the gods, and they only affected his behaviour if later they showed their displeasure and induced him to make amends.

Christianity is a different matter and is deeply concerned with conduct. Its sanctions may be briefly if inadequately summarized as love

[1] All-night prayer meetings are held in the open away from the village, during which the congregation prays, sings hymns and chants litanies in an unintelligible gibberish. At one time, Edward's following among the Tlokoa was extensive, but now is exiguous. Edward managed to collect money to build a huge stone church for the "children of God" as he called his congregation. Before he could build it, he was hounded out of the district, and eventually out of Basutoland. The chiefs disliked his popularity and objected to the sexual orgies into which his prayer meetings degenerated.

OLD AGE, DEATH AND RELIGIOUS BELIEFS

of God and desire to please Him, hope of Heaven as a reward for good behaviour and fear of Hell and damnation as a punishment for sin. The first scarcely affects the Tlokoa, except isolated converts, for as yet their belief in God does not portray Him as a being to whom one should, or could, pay personal devotion; still less does it indicate Him as the personification or representation of the Ideal to be striven for for its own sake.

Heaven is vaguely thought of as a place somewhere in the skies, consisting of elaborate and magnificent shining buildings. The central one is a particularly imposing hall and here God presides, seated on a dais, beautifully dressed, crowned with a golden crown and wearing a large sombrero ("gentleman's hat", as one person put it), and surrounded by angels, radiantly arrayed, continuously singing His praises. Quite what the spirit will do when it reaches here is not certain, but it is commonly believed that it will be very happy and also do a great deal of singing.

Hell and hell-fire have caught the popular imagination to a greater extent. Here, again, the people are not quite sure where and what Hell is, but they are prepared to believe that such a place exists, a place "full of fire and boiling rocks", as some describe it, where sinners are thought to suffer damnably.

The missions and churches have their own rules for the conduct of their adherents, and some forbid the observance of traditional customs —dancing, beer-drinking, polygyny, marriage and funerary rites, brideprice, and medicine, divination and mediumship (*bokoma*). They also have their own sanctions: ministerial disapproval, punishment by fining, exaction of unpaid work for the church, imposition of various penances, and finally excommunication and expulsion. Their control of schools and hospitals also provides opportunities of exercising moral pressure.

CHAPTER VIII

AGRICULTURE

THE Basuto are not agriculturists by tradition and rather grudge the amount of time they have to spend on their lands. Time and economic necessity are slowly modifying this attitude and nowadays they reluctantly admit that "grain is the artery of life", or more prosaically that "the wealth of a Mosuto is the land". This has been forcibly brought home to Government and people by several recent reports,[1] the latest and most authoritative of which,[2] bluntly says, "Basutoland is purely an agricultural and pastoral country; the prospects of mineral development have been shown to be entirely limited to the remote possibility of discovering an abnormally rich diamond deposit. The future of Basutoland is then definitely wedded to agriculture and stock raising."

The geological structure of Basutoland is simple and consists of horizontal beds of Drakensberg volcanics and various types of sandstone. They are traversed by dykes and sills of fine-grained dolerite. "The line representing the base of the volcanics is one not only of geological, but human importance, and divides the country into two distinct areas, each with its own type of topography, soil, climate and production. There is a sandstone, or lowland Basutoland, and a volcanic, or upland Basutoland. The distinction is also made by the natives, who invariably use the word 'Lesotho', Basutoland, to denote the lowland area in the west, and refer to the volcanic uplands as the Malutis.

"The volcanic beds form a large proportion of the country. This area consists of a maturely dissected plateau, whose highest points exceed 11,000 feet in altitude. It is a region of long, steep, grassy slopes, often bearing a strong resemblance to the southern uplands of Scotland, or to parts of central Wales. The rock disintegrates into a black, fertile soil which is well watered, and produces excellent crops of wheat.

"Immediately below the volcanic beds comes the Cave Sandstone, underlain in turn by other sandstones, with subordinate shales. It is of a light creamy colour, and forms one of the most constant and prominent features of the country. Wherever it outcrops on a hillside, it gives rise to nearly vertical, or even overhanging cliffs, whose light colour stands out in sharp contrast with the grassy slopes above. Along its outcrop occur many caves, and rock shelters, formerly occupied by the Bushmen. The western lowland consists largely of lower beds, but is thickly dotted with prominent isolated hills, capped by out-liers of the Cave Sandstone. Such hills are flat topped, and are surrounded by

[1] Pim, 1935; Staples and Hudson, 1938.   [2] Stockley, 1949, p. 90.

steep cliffs, so that they are often accessible only by a few steep and broken paths.

"The scenery formed by the volcanic rocks differs greatly from that due to the sandstones. The former give rise to long, grassy slopes, whereas the sandstones form a series of terrace-like platforms, bounded by rocky escarpments. Again, whereas the areas of volcanic rocks are fairly well supplied with springs and brooks, as the result partly of a higher rainfall, partly of their comparative impermeability, the sandstone areas are frequently very deficient in surface water, and the springs are liable to fail in the dry season."[1]

The average rainfall of the country is about thirty inches, that of the Highland area, except in the valleys, being slightly higher owing to winter precipitation in the form of snow. Seventy per cent of the rain falls between November and March with moderate spring rains in September. Much of the precipitation takes place during short-lived storms except along the eastern border where drizzling rain is encountered. The run-off is rapid. Hailstorms are not infrequent and often do great damage. The range of temperatures is wide for both Highlands and Lowlands—in the Highlands they vary from a mean monthly maximum of 60° F. to a mean monthly minimum of 11° F., and in the Lowlands from 85.2° F. to 28° F. The cold in the higher mountain regions can be very severe.[2]

Formerly, only the Lowlands used to be cultivated, but nowadays much Highland pasturage is being turned into ploughland, up to about the 8,000 feet level. In both areas, the lands are mainly to be found in the valleys and on the lower and gentler slopes of the hills, but such is the dearth of land to-day that many families have ploughed the steeper slopes, thus destroying valuable pasturage and leaving them a prey to erosion. Efforts are being made by the Administration, through the chiefs, to prevent this practice.

The soil in Basutoland varies greatly. The Basuto recognize this and discriminate between different soils, both as regards their physical characteristics and their suitability for different crops. The heavy black soil, called *selokoe*, is described as a rich soil, producing a heavy crop in a wet season, but little in drought years as it dries out quickly, becoming sun-baked and difficult to work. A lighter reddish soil, *lehlohlojane*, is said to be not so productive in wet seasons, but it does not dry out so quickly and is easier to work; and a grey, sandy soil is criticized as being too light to produce good crops.

In the old days, the Basuto were able to make use of this elementary agronomic knowledge and could choose whether to have all their lands of one type or divide them between the available types of soil. They

---

[1] R. U. Sayce, 1924, pp. 7-9. See also Stockley, 1949; and Staples and Hudson, 1938.

[2] Sayce, p. 10 and Staples, pp. 6-9.

liked to have their kaffir-corn lands away from the rivers and reed beds, so as to minimize the ravages of birds and avoid the cold and marshy hollows which delayed the growth of the crop; for mealies they preferred low-lying lands which could be irrigated, and they liked to have a land on a sunny slope for late ploughing. Nowadays unoccupied land is so scarce that they can rarely pick and choose, and are only too thankful to have any land at all.

The Basuto grow several different crops. The most important are maize, kaffir-corn (*mabele*) and wheat. Minor crops are sweet cane, peas, beans, oats and barley. The extent to which any of them is grown varies considerably. Kaffir-corn, which is common in the Lowlands, is scarcely grown in the Highlands owing to the shortness of the season; on the other hand, wheat, beans, peas, barley and oats are grown more widely in the latter area.

Kaffir-corn is the traditional crop and its legendary origin is described in the following story: Originally kaffir-corn was called *moleso oa likhomo* (left to the cattle) and was believed to be a poisonous weed. A woman tried to murder her co-wife, who was great with child and the favourite of their husband, by feeding her on porridge made with the grains of this plant. Far from dying, the woman throve and in due course gave birth to a beautiful son. Her would-be murderess then confessed to what she had done and they all lived happily ever after on a diet of *mabele*.[1]

Maize and black beans have been known to the Basuto for many generations, although the Taung and Lihoya[2] are said not to have seen the former until they met the Tlokoa during the Lifaqane, early in the nineteenth century. Wheat, fruit-trees and other kinds of vegetables were introduced by the early missionaries.[3]

Different varieties of cereals, pumpkins, squashes and other crops are identified by name. Many people pay no attention to these differences and merely sow such seed as they have or may have bought or borrowed. Others try to grow a pure strain of one sort or another for definite reasons, and make good use of improved varieties introduced by the Government. For instance, yellow maize (*poone e khubelu* or *jalo*) may be grown in small quantities to be eaten as green mealies, but it is unpopular as a large-scale crop, as the ripe grain is said to be "fit only for horses" and "bites the stomach"; *teremane* (ninety days flint maize) is favoured if ploughing has been delayed because it matures very quickly; *borotho* (bread maize) is liked by old women because it is easy to grind. The following are some of the qualities attributed to three varieties of wheat: *teluntsu* is easy to grind, *mankale* makes a fine "white" bread and has a pleasant flavour, and *motanyatsane* is heavy and a prolific bearer, and so yields a good monetary return.

[1] Told me by a Mosuto. Also quoted by Jacottet, 1909, (pp. 54-6) and 1912.
[2] Ellenberger and MacGregor, p. 54.   [3] Casalis, 1930, pp. 241 and 278.

The Basuto are beginning to use European watches, calendars and chronology, although for the most part they are not greatly interested in the accurate measurement of time. They usually determine past periods by reference to notable events, such as a chief's reign, flood, famine, or war; they tell the time of year by reference to the month, literally the moon (*khoeli*) and the time of day, literally the sun (*letsatsi*), by pointing to the position of the sun in the heavens or using such terms as sunrise, sunset. The year itself, and the seasons and months, are largely agricultural conceptions, and referable to or associated with agricultural events. The term for "year" is *selemo*, a word derived from the concept of cultivating (*ho lema*); spring is *nako ea selemo* (the time of cultivation). Other seasons have their own non-agricultural names: *lehlabula* (summer), *lehoetla* (autumn) and *mariha* (winter), but various periods are often referred to in agricultural terms, such as, "when people weed" (about December), "the great weeding" (about January) and "at harvest time" (June–July). The year is divided into twelve months whose names in many cases are directly derived from agricultural phenomena.

In the old days the New Year started about August. The village *moupello* (doctoring) was renewed, everyone was "scarified" afresh, together with the leading animals of their herds, and fresh *kubetso* (fumigant) was burnt in the kraals. This anticipated the new agricultural season, the beginning of which was not heralded in any particular way except among the Tlokoa. Here the season was opened by the ploughing and planting of the *tsimo ea lira* by all the available tribesmen, under the chief's personal supervision. It was a festive occasion and the chief's wives and other women of his village, dressed in their brightest clothes, brought beer and food to the workers, who welcomed them with singing and dancing. When the work was done, they all returned to the chief's village where they danced the *mokorotlo*, sang the chief's praises and feasted on the meat and drink he set before them. Thereafter the season was declared open and the people might begin their own ploughing. No magical or religious significance appears to have been attached to this event and its principal meaning consisted, as the people themselves say, in its affirmation of tribal cohesion. The practice is continued in a half-hearted way even to-day.

The ploughing season varies with the type of crop. In the Lowlands, ploughing for wheat begins in April, for kaffir-corn in September and for maize in October, lasting until January if the season is late. In the Highlands, wheat ploughing begins in September and maize ploughing soon after; the season ends about January. The signal for spring ploughing is the advent of the early rains. Some anticipate this, if they can, choosing their time by reference to the calendar or "to atmospheric phenomena and the state of the vegetation",[1] as, for example, the budding of willow trees.

[1] See Casalis, 1861, p. 208.

Formerly the people tilled the ground with diamond-shaped hoes made of locally wrought iron. Ploughs were introduced by the first missionaries.[1] These new implements soon came to be regarded as such essential articles of domestic equipment that a girl could justifiably refuse to marry a man who did not possess one. Nowadays only the very poorest, or those whose lands are too steep and inaccessible, dig or hoe their fields instead of ploughing. Two types of plough are in common use: the single-furrow plough (*plou*) and the reversible hillside plough (*phetlo*). The latter is used mainly in the Highlands as it is lighter and handier for ploughing on a slope and, owing to its reversibility, saves the long and tedious turns which the span has otherwise to make. Its use is also officially encouraged as it tends to terrace the ground and so prevent surface soil erosion.

The technique of ploughing is simple. The span or ploughing team usually consists of from four to eight oxen depending on the weight of the plough and the wealth of the owner; occasionally only two oxen may be used. Poorer people make up the span with donkeys, horses or cows, and very occasionally an all-horse team may be found, which arouses considerable interest. The best trained and most intelligent oxen lead the span, the weakest are placed in the middle. The ideal, seldom realized, is for each animal to keep to its own place throughout the ploughing season and for the span to be properly matched. The full human team consists of a small boy as leader, a youth as driver and an experienced man as ploughman. Owing to the dearth of males, due to labour migration, the most varied combinations may be found. Sometimes there is no leader, at other times boys of twelve or thirteen may have to take the plough and girls and women often have to be inspanned as drivers or ploughmen. The effect of this absence of men is serious and an important contributory cause of the low standard of Basuto agriculture. A good driver can turn and keep his span straight merely by shouting at them, calling the animals by name and stimulating them by whirling the whip lash above their heads—but a bad driver tends to flog them over much and cause them to plunge about and plough unevenly.

For ploughing the fields are divided into long rectangular strips about fifteen yards wide, called *akere*. When a fixed plough is being used, the perimeter of each strip is ploughed first, the soil being turned inwards and the area gradually reduced until the whole has been ploughed. This method is systematic, but suffers from the disadvantage that as the strip narrows it becomes difficult to turn the oxen and.get them back on the right lines, with the result that the last few furrows are often badly ploughed. When a "hillside" plough is used, it is merely taken to and fro making parallel and adjacent furrows. The Basuto usually plough fairly deeply (from five to eight inches), but the furrows

[1] Dieterlen, 1912, p. 451.

are often widely spaced leaving ridges (*banke*) of unbroken soil in between. This fault is deplored by those who like to see a land ploughed closely and evenly but, according to some agricultural experts, it has the advantage of checking surface erosion on steep slopes. Many plough indiscriminately on the level or up and down hill, and this has facilitated soil erosion, which throughout the country has reached alarming proportions. Since 1935 the Government has conducted an active anti-erosion campaign and has established thousands of miles of contour terraces, training banks and grass strips. It had been feared that these protective measures would be destroyed by continued indiscriminate ploughing but, thanks to the Paramount Chief's orders,[1] and later the realization of the value of these measures, the old practice has been partially modified.

The time taken to plough a field varies from two to six days under ordinary conditions. Most fields are about two or three acres in extent. At the beginning of the season, when the ground is hard, the oxen weak from the winter, and the people lazy and confident that they still have plenty of time in hand, work begins a couple of hours after sunrise and continues with short intervals for about three hours. The oxen are then outspanned and given several hours' grazing and rest before doing another two or three hours' work. Later, as the season progresses and work gets behindhand, ploughing may start before sunrise and continue until the animals literally drop from exhaustion. A few people have spare spans of oxen and so can work extra time. No work is done on Sundays, during periods of mourning or the day after hail, unless a *letsema* has been prearranged. Mourning for the death of an important chief may last as long as a fortnight, and so may seriously curtail ploughing time if it falls in the ploughing season.

The members of the household themselves do their own agricultural work wherever possible, but as ploughs and other equipment are expensive, very few families can afford to be self-contained and independent. Consequently, most of them have to get together in groups of two or three and pool their resources of labour, oxen, ploughs and other equipment.

These groupings are of two kinds. One consists of rich men and poor men; the former supplying the material and the latter the labour. As the rich man is the dominant partner, he usually stipulates that most, if not all, of his lands shall be ploughed first, with the result that the poor man's lands are often ploughed too late in the season to produce

---

[1] Now codified in Sect. 4 (2) Order issued by the Paramount Chief under provisions of Sect. 8 (1) of the Native Administration Proclamation No. 61 of 1938:

"In areas where there are contour works ploughing shall be carried out by landholders on the contour parallel to the terraces or grass strips. Ploughing up and down the slopes between the contour works or ploughing into or over or at an angle to the contour works is prohibited. Where anti-erosion work has not yet been carried out, the land should be ploughed across the slopes."

a good crop and sometimes are not ploughed at all. The second group is formed of relations and friends, and their contributions are much the same in value though possibly different in kind. Their lands are usually ploughed in rotation, and one land belonging to each member of the group is ploughed before the other lands are ploughed. This system does ensure that each household has at least one land properly ploughed in good time, but it is cumbersome and, as few preparations are made until the weather is favourable, precious days and even weeks are wasted in haggling over individual contributions.

After marking out the field the worker broadcasts seed over the first two or three strips, ploughs it in and goes on to the next two or three strips, repeating the operation until the whole field is sown. This method is wasteful and much of the seed may be planted at too great a depth. The Basuto are now taking to the use of planters in ever-growing numbers as they learn their value from demonstration and experience.

Most fields are divided between two crops, such as wheat, peas or beans on one part, and maize or kaffir-corn on the other. The latter are usually mixed with pumpkins, squashes, gourds and sweet cane, whereas wheat, oats, peas and beans are planted alone.

When breaking new ground, a thorn (*sefeamaeba*) may be placed under the fore part of the plough. This is believed to prevent the share being broken by hidden rocks, or by roots or bulbs of plants, such as the *leshoma* or *senyarela*. Some people doctor their seed to encourage its germination and fertility by smearing a handful with medicine[1] and then mixing it with the rest of the seed. A little of the doctored seed is sometimes kept to be added to the next year's seed as there is an idea that this continuity is beneficial. Christians, particularly Roman Catholics, sometimes have their seed blessed by their priest.

The Highland areas are "blessed with rich fertile uniform soil derived from the disintegration of basaltic rocks and need no artificial fertilizers. The Lowlands have poor sandy soils lacking in lime, phosphates, potash and available nitrogen."[2] The people have no tradition of using manures and since they scrupulously collect every bit of dung for use as fuel, they prevent the fortuitous fertilization of their lands with the manure dropped by their grazing cattle. The use of fertilizers, particularly of manure and ash, improves yields more than any other single factor, as demonstration and test plots have shown.[3] As a result of years of exhortation, demonstration and, latterly, practical help through Government loans of scotch carts to transport ash and manure to the

---

[1] One such medicine is called *tlhong*, the hedgehog, after its chief ingredient.
[2] Stockley, op. cit., p. 91.
[3] Yields can be increased from 306 lb., 220 lb. and 182 lb. per acre respectively for maize, *mabele* and wheat, to 980 lb. (sometimes even 3,200 lb.), 512 lb. and 540 lb. per acre, mainly through the application of manure and ash. (Annual Reports of the Agricultural Department, 1945, 1946.)

fields, Basuto are gradually learning to fertilize their lands and also to grow leguminous crops as much for their fertilizing properties as for their direct economic value. At the same time, considerable official efforts are being made to encourage the planting of trees for use as fuel in the place of cow dung.

Here and there conditions are favourable for irrigation and, from the earliest days, some have irrigated their lands. A few rudimentary irrigation works may still be seen among the Tlokoa and at Bethel, near Phamong, where there is a magnificent water supply, an extensive irrigation system has been evolved. Owing to opposition from the chiefs and fear of legal complications, full advantage has not been taken of existing natural facilities.

A couple of months after sowing, the young plants should be established and should be sprouting their collateral leaves—"bringing forth children". They are then ready for weeding. Good agriculturists cultivate their fields by hoeing all round the plants, whether there are any weeds or not, and explain that they do so to prevent the ground getting hard and dry. The more conscientious actually pile a little earth round the stem of each plant to give it additional "strength". Most people also thin their crops so that the plants "should not crowd one another". But, in general, weeding is done erratically and carelessly and the general standard is poor. Wheat, peas and beans are not weeded because their growth is too dense.

Weeding is done mainly by the women and girls, occasionally helped by the men. In the Lowlands people complain[1] that owing to the spread of education the women are becoming reluctant to work in the fields. Men sometimes weed alone or help their wives, but usually they only do this sort of work when they take part in organized, co-operative work parties (*matsema*). At the beginning of the weeding season people work about five or six hours a day, but as the season progresses the tempo of the work increases and at the height of the season, they work from sunrise to sunset. It takes nearly a month for one person to weed a field alone, so that it is difficult to get every field weeded without *matsema*, and occasionally some have to be left untouched. A few wealthy people cultivate their lands once or twice a season with harrows which they own, hire or borrow.

Medicines are sometimes used to protect and promote the growth of the crops. The main battle is against pests, such as the cutworm. The medicine for this is mixed with layers of worms and of leaves culled from the injured plants, and burnt in a small fire in the windward corner so that the smoke may drift over the field. This treatment is said to be effective at a distance and to cure not only the field in which the fire was made but also other fields from which worms and leaves were collected and added to the fire. Several variations of this treat-

[1] Pim Report, p. 162.

ment occur. Later, just before the plants are ready to flower, another medicine, called '*meseletso*, may be burnt every evening and morning in the lands, to strengthen the crop. It is possible that the smoke from the fire in which the medicine is burnt really does benefit the crops by reducing the severity of frosts.

Birds, such as pigeons and finches, often do considerable damage to kaffir-corn and wheat crops, so as soon as the grain begins to form, children are sent to the fields to protect the crops. Perched on a mound of sods, or a platform of sticks, they scare the birds away by means of clay pellets flung with long whippy sticks, or by beating an empty petrol tin or by shouting. Their work lasts from January to April, but occasionally their parents, if keen on their education, may take over from them in the morning to free them for school. Sometimes they build themselves temporary shelters at the lands to save journeying to and from the village.

Scarecrows, consisting of old rags, tins and eagle's wings are occasionally used. Fields of short-stemmed varieties of maize are protected from crows by grass or horsehair ropes fastened along the outside. Certain medicines tied at the corners of the field are supposed to keep birds and even stray stock away. One prescription given me was "the root of the plant *bolilakhomo*, burnt with the young of grain-eating birds, such as finches, weavers and widow birds, and mixed with uncooked butterfat. The mixture is then rubbed on rags or sticks and hung round the field."

So far as I could ascertain, the Tlokoa are the only Basuto who still observe[1] any form of first-fruits ceremony, and even they have largely given it up. It is said that they should not eat their first-fruits until the chief has eaten his, unless they first make him a small offering of these fruits. Furthermore, the first-fruits should be eaten by the members of the family in order of seniority, starting with the senior son. These observances have no religious or magical significance and are followed, so it is said, to emphasize the importance of the chief and of primogeniture. They are vaguely sanctioned by the belief that offenders will be crippled "because they have eaten what they had no right to".

In the Lowlands wheat is reaped in November and December and in the Highlands from January onwards. The harvesting of other crops does not begin until after the first frosts, for it is not until then that ripe grain can easily be distinguished from the green and immature. Harvesting is done by picking the cobs of maize or by reaping the heads of wheat and kaffir-corn with knives or sickles. The heads are stacked in or near the field and the grain sorted. Unripe grain, called *talane*, cannot be stored as it rots, and so has to be eaten immediately. Maize which has slightly rotted, called *motamo*, is used for making a soft drink or light porridge (*mahleu* or *motoho*), but not bread, as in that form "it

[1] Casalis, p. 270.

smells horribly". Rusted kaffir-corn and wheat can be used for brewing, even though they turn the beer black. Other unripe or imperfect grain is used as horse- or cattle-feed.

When the whole field has been reaped the grain is threshed on a hard, clean circle, 15–20 feet in diameter. Kaffir-corn and maize are threshed with sticks or knobkerries, and wheat, peas and beans either by machines brought over from the Free State or by "treading out" by horses. Men usually thresh the kaffir-corn in one day at a *letsema*, whereas women thresh the maize either in small parties or alone. Sometimes the maize cobs are taken to the village and threshed there, as and when required. After threshing the grain is winnowed and transported in sacks or large skin bags to the village, where it is stored in wool bales or large grass baskets (*lisiu*). The latter hold from two to three thousand pounds of grain and are so closely woven that they remain watertight for two or three years. They are usually kept outside the hut, closed with a stone or cemented with cow dung or plaster, and may be protected from rodents by a prickly bush, called the "mouse blinder[1]".

Harvesting is a straightforward affair, but in the case of kaffir-corn one or two customs may be observed. A stone smeared with medicine may be placed underneath the unthreshed grain-stack to protect the grain from thieves and prevent it from "evaporating". Other charms may also be used, and I once came across a heap protected by a medallion of the Blessed Virgin Mary. "She looks after us, she will look after our food." As a further protection, the kaffir-corn stalks fringing the threshing floor are left standing until the rest of the crop has been threshed. If this were not done the crop would "evaporate".

The same precaution against "evaporation" pervades the process of threshing grain. As the grain is beaten out, it is swept into separate heaps which are immediately crowned with one or two heads. These heads which are called "shepherd" or "increase of food" (*katiso ea lijo*) are believed to protect it from sorcery or "evaporation". They may occasionally be smeared with medicine to give them strength and they remain in position until all the grain has been threshed and winnowed. They are then threshed together with heads of the stalks fringing the floor which have been left uncut. In the old days a special beer, *joala ba leoa*, made from this grain (*leoa*)[2] was ceremonially drunk by the family heads as a thank-offering to the ancestors. Among the Tlokoa this special beer is only made after a really bumper harvest; normal harvests are celebrated by an ordinary beer drink.

A handful of grain should be left on the threshing floor as a thank-offering called *phabalimo* (gift to the gods). The ancestor spirits are believed to come at night and eat the essence of the grain, the material

[1] Phillips, 1917, p. 76; also quoted by Laydevant, 1931, p. 222.

[2] In the *Sesuto-English Dictionary*, Mabille and Dieterlen, 1937, p. 188, this grain is said to be given to the parents-in-law.

shell being left for the birds and field mice. This rite is still punctiliously observed by the Tlokoa.

Other minor customs observed by the Tlokoa may be mentioned. When the women begin to winnow the grain, or pour it into bags to take to the village, they should face north-east, towards Ntsuanatsatsi "as it was there we used to live". When they take up their second basketful they should face their home. They should never empty the basket, but should always leave a few grains in it, which they should toss on to the heap of unwinnowed grain before taking another basketful. This observance, whose object seems to be to preserve the continuity of the agricultural cycle, is said to be strictly followed. Some Tlokoa also believe that the harvest should be completed before the Pleiades disappear (about July) as grain harvested after this date "evaporates". The names of this cluster of stars and of the star Achernar, *selemela-se-setsehali* and *selemela-se-setona* (the female and male *selemela*) suggest that they had some further traditional connection with agriculture, which is now forgotten.

Casalis records[1] two customs which I did not come across. Before the grain is taken from the threshing floor, the owners bring a new pot in which they boil some grain. When this is cooked, they throw a few handfuls on the heap, saying, "God, we thank you, and to-morrow give us bread again". Having said this, they eat the rest of the cooked grain and the harvest is now said to be pure. Furthermore, he writes that "impure" people (presumably menstruating women and people in mourning) should not come in close contact with new grain.[2]

As soon as the crops have been reaped and cleared from the fields, the lands are thrown open to grazing. This is done on the word of the local headman and thereafter the local stock may graze on the stalks and on the grass banks and patches in and around the lands.

The various agricultural tasks are usually done by the members of the household to whom the field belongs, and mostly by women, working alone or with their unmarried daughters or female relations and dependants. Sometimes for company's sake two or three women, co-wives or more often sisters-in-law (for example, wives of two brothers) may work together, doing each other's fields in turn. Girl helpers are rewarded with a basketful or two of grain or *talane*, which they can use to brew beer for sale. Kinsmen and friends of the young girls are invited to come and buy her brew and so provide her with a little pin money. This sort of brewing is discreetly called *kongkotia* and is distinguished from beer selling or canteens (*cantene*) conducted by adult or married women. Among the Tlokoa casual helpers are given small

---

[1] Casalis, 1861, pp. 314-15.
[2] Ramseyer (personal communication) says that children below the age of puberty are forbidden to eat new grain on the threshing field as they are still unfertile and so might sterilize the seed.

token gifts of grain (*moella*) to thank them for their assistance. Daily labourers are engaged by the wealthier families and are paid in cash or kind, e.g. a tinful of butterfat or a handful of tobacco per diem. Others are hired for the season, and are paid at the rate of a bag of grain or ten shillings for each field weeded or harvested. These paid labourers are usually people whose own crops have failed or whose ploughing equipment was insufficient to till their lands, or who have few or no lands of their own.

In all phases of agricultural work great use is made of organized, co-operative work-parties called *matsema*. These are gay, sociable affairs comprising from about ten to fifty participants of both sexes. Ordinary people invite their close friends and neighbours to help them, headmen and chiefs call on their followers as well. Uninvited guests are welcomed provided they do some work. These *matsema* are useful though not very efficient. They assemble in the morning about 9 o'clock and work, with frequent breaks for light refreshment, until about 3 or 4 o'clock in the afternoon, to the accompaniment of ceaseless chatter and singing. There are different songs for weeding, harvesting and threshing, the tunes being standardized throughout Basutoland, whereas the words are composed, *ex tempore*, by the leader. Occasionally praise-songs are sung and one of the workers executes a *pas seul*, accompanied by the applause of the men and the trilling cries (*lilietsa*) of the women. When the host thinks they have worked enough, they adjourn to his house where food and drink are provided and the party becomes purely social. These parties involve considerable preparation and expense as far as the provisions are concerned. The food at a small party might consist of one gallon of porridge, three gallons of *mahleu*, seven gallons of beer, and three large balls of bread for a party of eight invited guests, which means about three days' preparation plus a little cash outlay. They are worth it to those who can afford it, for they turn days of backbreaking tedium into a brief and merry entertainment. Chiefs and other important authorities have the right to call their subjects to so-called *matsema* to work in their fields, on pain of being fined ten shillings. Such work is supposed to be confined to the chief's public fields (*lira*) and not extended to his wives' private fields,[1] but this is a distinction which is not always observed. Traditionally, too, the chief has a moral obligation to reward the workers with food and drink, but very few observe it, with the result that compulsory *matsema* are reluctantly and grumblingly attended.

An essential element of agricultural technique is the use of medicines for various purposes. Some of these have already been mentioned, but

[1] "Rules", No. 12. A proposal, put forward in 1949 by several District Councils, that this obligation to work for the chief should be commuted by payment of one shilling per annum, which would be given to the chief to pay for hired labourers was implemented in 1950 (Marwick MS.).

others, mainly those concerned with the control of weather, remain to be described. Foremost among these are the rain-making rites. Formerly, prominent chiefs had a permanent rain-maker attached to their court, whose duty it was to perform the appropriate rites when required. This functionary has been discarded and it is now left to the chief to engage an appropriate doctor when necessary. The details of the medicine used and the ritual followed are very secret, but the principal feature is that a number of herbs are mixed together in a pot, salt- or seawater added, and the mixture churned into a froth—whence the expression used for rain-making "to churn for rain". The rite is carried out in the strictest privacy. Many people are very sceptical about the claims of rain-makers, but belief in the possibility of making rain is by no means dead and professional rain-makers may still be found. To claim to be able to make rain has recently been declared a criminal offence. punishable by fining and/or imprisonment.[1]

Should the doctors fail to produce rain, recourse was had in the old days to two public rites. The more important was the men's, called *molutsoane*. On a day appointed, all the young men of the tribe went in parties up the river flowing past the chief's village and its principal tributaries and killed every animal (other than domestic animals) they came across; they disembowelled them and threw the stomachs into the watercourse. When they reached the source of these streams, they turned back, reassembled outside the village and danced their way to the chief's court. The clouds should then come up and the rain pour in torrents, as one old Mosuto said, "just as the sweat streamed down the young men's backs".

The other rite was performed by women and also involved considerable physical effort. Starting from their chief's village, the young women went to the hut of a neighbouring chief and there forcibly seized his principal wife's porridge stick, an exceedingly personal piece of property. Then they battled their way out of the village and sent the stick to their own chief's wife by means of relays. Finally they all reassembled at their village and danced the *mokhibo* dance until evening. The women's rite has been neglected for many years,[2] and I never found anyone who had actually witnessed it. The *molutsoane* was held by the Phuthi as recently as 1910, by the Tlokoa about 1920 and in the Quthing area about 1926. It is highly improbable that it will be repeated, for, apart from the dearth of wild animals, few people now believe in it, in spite of the fact that it used to be considered quite infallible.

The people are now turning to the churches for help and, in bad

[1] Proclamation No. 44 of 1948.
[2] Ramseyer (personal communication) says that rain which fell in Sept. 1949 was said to be due to the performance of this rite at two different places (Masianokeng and 'Manstebo's at Qeme).

years, special services to pray for rain are held. Not everyone has yet adopted the new faith. In 1936 the Tlokoa ignored a general order from the Paramount Chief, setting aside a particular Sunday for prayers for rain, and professed that they were not surprised that nothing came of it for "had not their own doctors failed to open the heavens?"

Attempts are made to control other natural phenomena, such as hail and lightning, which frequently do considerable damage. Districts are protected by stones, smeared with medicines, placed on the tops of surrounding mountains in the quarter from which the storms usually come. Individual fields, villages and huts are similarly protected by long poles, medicated *mofifi* sticks, or cairns of medicated stones. Storms may also be warded off by waving a medicated *mofifi* stick or doctored spear towards the storm. Dieterlen[1] also records the use of whistles made of vultures' bones as a means of dissipating hailstorms. These protective measures are still extensively practised.

There are also numerous taboos which have to be observed lest the crops meet with disaster from hail or frost. Children may not play knucklebones in the village, firewood should not be brought home at midday, people taking refreshment in the fields should do so sitting down. For the same reason, no work except that of prearranged *matsema* should be done on the day after a death or a hailstorm, a corpse should not be carried through the fields to burial during the day and the deceased's goods should only be distributed in the winter. The last three observances are still firmly adhered to, but the others are not taken seriously.

[1] Dieterlen, 1912, p. 101.

CHAPTER IX

ANIMAL HUSBANDRY

BASUTO cattle were probably originally descended from the African Zebu, but now through extensive intermixture with other types, this old strain has been almost completely submerged, though not entirely forgotten. The hump-backed cattle, still to be found in their herds and called *mekharane*, are said to be throw-backs to this original strain and herd-boys in their little clay models of cattle portray the characteristic hump and long horns. The present-day cattle are for the most part small and sturdy. Their colour is extremely varied, and their horns are of all sizes and shapes. Oxen are used mainly for draught purposes, cows for milking. They are also used for meat and they figure in every important ceremonial occasion.

Horses were unknown until introduced by Europeans. One of the first horses ever owned by a Mosuto was presented to Moshesh by the Phuthi chief, Moroosi, having been stolen from a farmer in the Cape Colony. Since then the country's stock of horses has been entirely built up from animals bought or stolen from European farmers along the borders. Many varieties were thus imported, and as a result of their intermixture and the rigorous climatic conditions of the country, there was eventually produced the famous Basuto pony, hardy, fast and surefooted.[1] The tremendous demand for these ponies as remounts during the Boer War drained the country of its best horses,[2] and for a time the breed deteriorated. Latterly, it has improved again through Government importation of good stallions from the Union of South Africa and from Nigeria.

Donkeys and mules have been more recently introduced, having mostly been imported since about 1921. They are used mainly for transport and are fairly popular because they are cheap and exceedingly hardy. Recently Catalonian Jacks have been introduced by the Administration to encourage mule-breeding of a good standard.

The original types of sheep (*kalpense*) and goats (*mabereise*) were tough, scraggy, multi-coloured and had "a fleece more like hair than wool".[3] These characteristics have now been almost completely submerged through the introduction of merino sheep (*faralane* and *malangwool*) and angora goats. These are valued for their wool and mohair and are a source of meat and, to a lesser extent, milk; their fat is used to make

---

[1] For an interesting and full account of the Basuto pony, see Thornton, R. W., *History of the Basuto Pony*, 1938.
[2] In 1901, 15,684 horses valued at £262,992 were exported.
[3] Dieterlen, 1912, p. 88.

ANIMAL HUSBANDRY

soap and ointment. They are also used extensively on ceremonial occasions and in certain religious rites, sheep ordinarily being used for celebrations and black sheep and goats in cases of sickness and sorcery.

Other domestic animals are pigs, cats, dogs and poultry, the first two having been introduced from Europe. Pigs are much prized for their meat and fat, although, owing to their dirty scavenging habits, some people refuse to eat them. Except for a few hunters, the people pay little attention to their dogs—they like to have them about as watch dogs, but leave them to fend for themselves. Many people keep chickens for food; very few keep ducks owing to the lack of water or turkeys because of the difficulty of breeding them.

Cattle are grazed by themselves and are always taken to the best pastures. Though they may be kraaled separately at night, the different herds of the village usually graze together and often join up with the herds of neighbouring villages. Calves, donkeys and sometimes horses are herded together on inferior veld near the village. Horses are usually tethered by themselves on the grass strips between the nearby lands. Sheep and goats are tended by a shepherd especially detailed for this duty and are usually taken to the most distant pastures.

The routine of herding is simple. An hour or two after sunrise the cows are milked. Then after the calves have been separated from their mothers—an energetic operation which involves much shouting and excitement—the cattle are taken to the pastures. When they reach the spot selected for the day's grazing, they are left in charge of the younger herd-boys, while the elder boys amuse themselves. At midday they are taken to water and towards sunset they wander home, being led at a leisurely pace by the bull or some prominent ox, while some of the herd-boys go on ahead playing the *lesiba* and the rest bring up the rear. When they arrive at the village, the cows are milked. Then, as the sun sets, the calves are again separated and the cattle shut up in the kraal for the night. At the height of summer, this routine is changed. The cattle are taken to the pastures before dawn and the cows are brought to the village at midday for milking. At about 2 o'clock (these times are judged by the sun and are amazingly regular) they go to graze again and finally return in the evening at the usual time. This custom (*ho ea lephola*), which is followed only when there is plenty of grazing, is observed for the obscure reason, on which I was unable to get adequate light, that cattle should not lie down in the veld and must, therefore, return to the village to chew the cud.

At milking time the cattle stand in front of the kraal, while the calves are shut in a small kraal of their own. When the milkers are ready, they call out the name[1] of a calf. A boy at the calves' kraal repeats the name

---

[1] Cattle, horses, dogs and occasionally outstanding specimens of sheep and goats are given names. Oxen are almost invariably given European names or names of European (Afrikaans) derivation, such as Blackfoot, Terrier, Joubert, Bantome,

and drives the calf out. It is then allowed to suck for a few moments to start the milk flowing, after which it is driven away. The milker ties the cow's hind legs with a thong and milks from the left side holding the pail between his knees. When milking is finished, the calf is allowed to go back to its mother where it may have to compete with the younger herd-boys who love drinking from the cow, milking directly into their mouths. Milk production varies considerably. Most cows give from two to three quarts at a time; at the height of the summer the best may give two gallons, but in winter and early spring production drops to nil.

Only those cows are milked which are suckling a calf. It is said that they dry up if they have no calf and that even if they have a calf they hold the milk back unless the calf draws it off. Consequently, should a calf die, either its predecessor is allowed to continue to suck in spite of its age and length of horn or else a stuffed dummy (*mokukutoana*) is made of the calf's skin to "fool" the cow into giving milk. Occasionally the cow may be given a foster calf. Milking starts almost immediately after the cow has calved. The first milk is not taken home but is consumed at the *khotla*. Calves are not weaned until they have horns about half an inch long, because to do so earlier would make the cow dry up. This delay gives the calf a good start in life.

Formerly milk-pails were carved from wood. Nowadays they are small paraffin tins or galvanized iron pails bought at the stores. These utensils are usually scoured before and after use and the milkers generally wash their hands before milking. Standards of cleanliness in these respects are high. Women and girls are not allowed to milk cattle. Patrilineal descendants of Sekonyela are not supposed to drink the milk of a cow freshly calved, lest they become deaf—a fate which also befalls anyone who assaults old people or who takes gravy without eating meat.

In the old days, most of the stock was kept at the village except for surplus stock and cattle brought back from raids, which were kept at distant cattle-posts, hidden away in remote gorges and river valleys. Today, the growth of the population has so restricted grazing that most Lowlanders have to keep their stock at Highland cattle-posts, and even in the Highlands many people have to keep their animals at cattle-posts rather than at the village. Most of these cattle-posts lie in bleak and inaccessible areas above the 8,000 feet contour. They are scattered at varying intervals along the rugged mountain slopes and have no communication with one another except by rough winding paths. The

Roifel, Roinek, Donrag, Bigman, Bosman, Richmond, Basbanks and, of all names, Reduce. Cows and bulls on the other hand are given Sesuto names, such as *tlhakubele* (March), *serobele* (sparrow), *sekama* (antimony), *letsoala* (barbel), *tsoanatala* (ex-Natal), *thamaha* (red with white spots—bull's name). To some extent the animals respond to their names, as when calves are called out at milking time and oxen in ploughing teams are exhorted.

pasture boundaries are roughly defined by natural features, such as streams or mountain ridges, and sometimes by beacons, but these boundaries are rarely observed or enforced, except where grazing becomes congested, or agriculture encroaches. The post itself usually consists of a tiny hut, roughly built of undressed stone, often without mortar, badly thatched and provided with a raised stone platform inside, on which the herd-boys huddle to sleep. It is perched on a spur or knoll, exposed and windswept but commanding a magnificent view of the surrounding country. Cattle and other stock cluster at night on the patch of level ground outside the hut or take shelter from the bitter winds in the lee of the nearest rock or ridge. Occasionally rough stone kraals may be provided for them.

Owing to the intense winter cold and the absence of ordinary home comforts, life at the posts is far harder than in the villages. But it is free and invigorating and is, therefore, preferred by a few men who, having sown their wild oats, return with their wives to live there permanently. Mostly, however, herding is entrusted to boys and young men. Two or three usually live together, but occasionally one may be left temporarily alone. In such cases, the solitude is often too much for him and he sneaks away to a nearby post at night for shelter and company, leaving the stock to look after themselves. Herdmen live on meal sent up from the villages, milk from their cattle and goats, and meat of any animals which die or may be given to them for food or that they manage to kill. Sometimes they suffocate a sheep by pinching its nostrils. This apparently simulates death by disease and so confuses the owner who inspects the skins of all animals that have died to ascertain the cause of death. It is said that the colour of the inside of the skin differs according to whether the animal died of disease or was slaughtered.[1]

The herding is easy; indeed, as the saying goes, *Metebong ha ho lisoe* (one does not herd at the cattle-posts). The animals are driven out in the morning and, except when the rich valley grasses are reserved for cattle, all the stock is allowed to graze where it will. In the evening they return of their own accord. The herd-boys visit them occasionally to see that all is well, and for the rest just watch them from the door of the huts, or some other vantage point. Although they cannot, or do not, count their charges, they "feel" when some have strayed and go and look for the missing animals. Horses are seldom brought back to the post, but are left to graze where they will and seldom stray far. The only dangers to be feared are thieves and wild animals. The latter consist only of wildcats and jackals, and are so few that danger from them is nowadays almost negligible. Thieves are a curse. This is largely due to the fact that people take little trouble and care over their stock, seldom visit their posts and do not replace young herd-boys with men capable of defending their property against thieves.

[1] T. B. Kennan, personal communication.

An important incident in the cattle-post system is the winter migration of cattle from the Highlands to the Lowlands. This may be the only occasion in the year on which people see the bulk of their stock. Owing to the sparseness of the village pastures, the cattle can only come down from the Highlands at the end of the harvest, when the lands can be thrown open for grazing. Then, for a short time, the people can see their cattle around them as they love to see them, and can enjoy a relative abundance of milk. The animals cannot, however, remain long, for the grazing does not last more than a month or two and no winter fodder is grown. As soon as the pastures are exhausted or word comes that the mountain passes are open and the spring rains have fallen, the cattle return to the posts. They gather into huge herds under the control of three or four herd-boys and slowly wend their way back, taking anything from four days to a fortnight.

This exodus does not entirely deprive the village of cattle. Oxen required for ploughing are kept back and, where grazing is comparatively abundant, a few milch cows also remain. Thereafter, until the following January or February, there is a more or less continuous movement of cattle to and from the posts: as the grazing becomes poor, the cows are sent back, and if good rains fall, fresh ones are brought down; exhausted oxen are sent back and fresh ones fetched to replace them; and finally, at the end of the ploughing season, all the oxen are sent back, except for a few retained to thresh the ripened wheat. This movement used to take place on a large scale,[1] but nowadays, owing to the acute shortage of pasturage, it is limited mainly to oxen required for ploughing and a few milch cows. Highland villages usually have some grazing round them and so can keep a few cattle at home all the year round. There are also a few marginal villages, which are really cattle-post villages, where there is practically no movement of cattle at all. Sheep and goats usually spend the whole year at the posts, though from the most exposed areas they may move down to less inhospitable places for the winter. Sometimes, in spring and autumn, they may be taken down to the villages to be sheared in order to avoid the difficulty of transport or to guard against thieves, who often steal a flock solely for its wool. To combat thieving, the stock *bewijs* (permit) system has been extended to wool and mohair which can now only be sold on production of a permit.

Horses, particularly mares and colts, remain at the cattle-posts all the year round, except for a short break in the summer when they are taken down to the villages for mares to be served and colts branded and broken in.

The people are not particularly keen pastoralists and do not give their stock much more than the minimum attention required to keep them alive. They give their animals what grazing is available, water them as supplies permit, give them salt when they can afford it, and in

---

[1] For details, see Sayce, 1924.

a few cases feed horses or sickly animals on grain or beer strainings. They may also take some trouble to keep their stock away from poisonous weeds found in the local veld and from green mealie lands. But they make little attempt to improve their condition by supplementing the limited winter grazing with silage or other winter fodder, or by protecting the animals from the cold and wet with roofed stables and byres. Again, though they may notice that the pastures are being destroyed through over-grazing and soil erosion, they do nothing to remedy this condition and stubbornly resist Government proposals for reduction of stock or temporary closing of affected areas. They have responded slowly, suspiciously and apathetically to the various experiments which are being conducted by the Government and to efforts being made to introduce better methods. Recently (1946-7) a few chiefs, notably Matlere in Mokhotlong, have undertaken to enforce rotational grazing in their wards.

The traditional preference is for quantity of stock rather than quality. This is changing slowly owing to veterinary advice and force of economic circumstances. Many now try, by careful selection of breeding stock, to produce good sheep, goats and horses, even though the product, as in the case of merino sheep, is less prolific and requires more attention than low grade stock; and they are prepared to buy good and expensive rams imported by the Government or from neighbouring farmers. Some make a point of keeping the rams at a separate post away from the ewes until late summer, in order to delay the lambing season until spring, after the bitter cold of winter has passed. Similar care is shown in horse-breeding. Although few can afford to buy a good stallion, many are prepared to pay anything from a few shillings to a couple of pounds for the services of one, either privately or through the Government stud. They also try to prevent the casual and promiscuous service of their mares by insisting that stallions should be securely tethered and, in some areas, by making the owners liable for damages for failing to control their stallions.

On the other hand, cattle-breeding still largely follows the old traditional ways. Some might like their cows to be served by a particular bull, reputed to throw strong and healthy calves, but they rarely bother to keep the cows away from other bulls; and though they dislike their bulls running with other people's cattle for fear that this might weaken them, they have no objection to other people's bulls mixing with their herds. Sometimes they may single out a bull calf for future breeding purposes on account of its favourable build, strength and parentage, but in the final event their choice may well be determined by such genetically irrelevant factors as the colour of its skin. No effort is made to delay breeding from heifers until they are adequately mature and developed.

The reason for these different attitudes to cattle and other stock is mainly that the latter are directly economically valuable and often produce a cash return, whereas cattle are prized as much for their social as for their economic value. A considerable cash income is derived from the export of wool and mohair, whereas comparatively few cattle are exported, and there is thus no direct incentive to improve the quality of the meat; since there is little dairy-farming, there is no inducement to improve their milking qualities, and the oxen are considered strong enough for ordinary draught purposes. In other words, the people are satisfied with what they have, and they see no good reason why they should take trouble or spend money to improve what they consider to be adequately suited to their needs. Some, however, do make use of the Government cattle improvement centres and Government imported bulls which are lent to interested chiefs and headmen for the benefit of the people.

Though Basuto knowledge and practice of animal husbandry is indifferent, their veterinary lore, though simple, is extensive. They know how to castrate animals not required for breeding, and though they do not spey females, they occasionally reach much the same result by other means. For instance, should a barren cow not respond to the medicines given it, a heated stone is thrust into its vagina, cauterizing the *os cervix* and so preventing discharge of oestral fluid, thus turning the cow into a useful beast which can be used for ploughing and transport. Difficulties in calving and lambing are dealt with by giving the cow or ewe medicine to drink and, if this fails, an attempt is made to ease it by manipulation. Mares give birth very easily; so easily, it is said, that their afterbirth is used in medicine to assist women in protracted parturition. Minor fractures are mended by means of a rough splint of a stick or bundle of little sticks which is tied to the limb to hold the bones in place and the animal is rested as much as possible. The fracture must also be treated with medicine, called *thobeha*, which is injected through a hollow reed to reach the bone near the break. Some hold that the break can be mended merely by stabbing a hoofprint of the injured leg with a knife rubbed with the same medicine. In either case, the medicine is said to enter the fracture and heal it within a day or two and to be so powerful that it can be used without a splint.

Impotence is cured in various ways. The bull is taken into the kraal, tied by its horns and forced to jump the wall, while the senior herd-boy sings its praises. If this simple expedient fails, medicine is used. The stems of a stiff grass *thitapoho* ("strong as a bull") are broken into short pieces, smeared with medicine (*motsoso*—"the rouser") and used to stab the bull above its anus. The hair on the bull's tail is then parted and rubbed with more of the medicine. The bull should be kept away from other people's cows for the time being.

Medicines are used extensively to cure other diseases which are known and their symptoms described. For instance, gall sickness (*nyooko*) is diagnosed through "dry nose, lassitude and loss of appetite" and is treated by dosing with a potion made from the crushed roots of plants.[1] Diarrhoea in lambs is cured by a potion made from the root of another plant.[2] Horses are treated for bots (*papisi*) by dosing them with various potions. Proprietary veterinary preparations sold in the stores are also used extensively.

Sesuto veterinary practice does not stop at the treatment of ordinary disease, but goes further and tries to prevent the incidence of disease or other mishaps which might be caused by some "supernatural" agency. This involves the use of certain medicines and the prohibition of a number of actions. The most common means of protection is the doctoring of the kraal. This is done when the village is doctored at the beginning of the year to guard against bad luck, sickness or accident, especially such as might be caused by sorcery. The medicine, which is placed at the kraal entrance, is renewed at the beginning of each year and after any major calamity, such as a death in the village or the village being struck by lightning. Cattle-posts are doctored in the same way. Flocks and herds are sometimes protected from lightning, attacks by wild animals and sickness caused by sorcery, by vaccinating the leading animals with the same medicine as is used to "vaccinate" the villagers at the beginning of the year. Another protective medicine is *kubetso*; this is sprinkled on glowing coals placed in the kraal so that the fumes can fumigate (*kubetsa*) the cattle. It is used whenever necessary, for example, during an epidemic or when some misfortune is feared or is prophesied by the "bones". Protective medicines are also used against specific dangers; for instance, hunters sometimes vaccinate their dogs with medicine made from venom to protect them from snake bite.

The most common taboo is that women should not handle cattle: they may not go into the kraal to collect fresh cattle dung and *lisu* except when the cattle are out grazing, and not at all during their menstrual periods; nor should they at any time walk across the *lepatlelo*—the open space in front of the kraal where the cattle stand for milking. Breaking of these taboos releases the potency of whatever protective medicines have been used for the kraal and cattle, and causes the women to have painful menstruation; it may also make the cows slip their calves or stampede at night. A similar taboo is that a man should not approach the kraal immediately after having connection with an unpurified widow. These taboos are respected even where protective medicines are not used. The fact that other tribes, for example the Zulu, allow their daughters to milk the cows, is complacently attributed to the comparative impotence of their protective medicines.

[1] One recipe uses *hloenya*, *seboka* and *lebate*, and another *monnamotsu* and *khamane*.
[2] *Mosokelo*; Phillips, 1917, p. 364, says this plant is used to cure diarrhoea in humans.

The significance of cattle and other domestic stock was summed up by Casalis:[1] "The people of South Africa are above all pastoral. The herds which they possess have constituted until now their principal wealth. They provide for the expenditure incurred by weddings, marriage feasts, purchases, illnesses and funerals. To have no stock is to be worthless. The Basuto also call the bovine species 'the hairy pearl'... they set more store by their herds than their fields, but they count much more on their fields than on their herds for their maintenance."[2] This brief outline is still substantially correct. The people are at heart pastoralists rather than agriculturists; they find their stock more interesting than their lands and they look on their stock rather as a means of social exchange than as the basis of their "domestic economy"; they realize, however, that the possession of stock, particularly cattle, is as economically desirable as it is socially essential. As they put it, a beast is "the god with the wet nose" and "it is a disaster for a man to lack cattle".

This interest is reflected in linguistic usage. In Sesuto praise-songs frequent use is made of words and phrases associated with cattle to express esteem, value and outstandingly attractive qualities. Apart from about a dozen simple adjectives such as "large", "small", "long", "short", the only adjectives in Sesuto are those expressing colour which derive from descriptions of cattle, and all of these have a masculine and feminine form; thus, in addition to adjectives for simple colours, such as black, white, dark brown and fawn, they have many adjectives connoting colour combinations such as *phatsoa* (black and white), *thamaha* (red with small white spots), *chaba* (red or light brown shot with white), *khoaba* (white streak on the back), *tsumu* (white-faced), *tseka* (white spot on the forehead), *chitja* (hornless, round). Again the word *khomo* (cow, beast, etc.) is used figuratively for anything of worth or value, from *khomo ea fatse* (the ox of the earth, i.e. diamond)[3] to a term of praise *likhomo tseo* ("those cattle"—a form of address to a chief), or a "man" in the *marabaraba* game.

Early writers[4] give moving accounts of the people's absorption in and love for their cattle and describe how they used to sing the praise of their favourite animals, discuss their doings with such animation that they forgot about their games, and establish such intimate relations with them that they "could turn them out of the kraal just like calves... full-grown oxen with great horns indeed and cows," and lead them, playing the *lesiba*. They still have affection for their stock and spend hours at the kraal, looking over their cattle and watching them being milked, but they are no longer in such constant and intimate contact with them as they used to be, or so devoted to them. Nor do they now take as much trouble and care about them as they are said to have done, and not

[1] Casalis, p. 153.
[2] Ibid., p. 158.
[3] Mabille, 1937.
[4] Casalis, p. 196 and Mofolo, op. cit., 22.

uncommonly they are callous and neglectful—for instance, they will use their animals even when suffering from serious trek-chain abrasions and from saddle galls, and will leave their horses standing saddled for hours in the blazing sun without food or water.

CHAPTER X

LAND TENURE

AGRICULTURE and animal husbandry both depend on the use of land and so are closely related to the laws of land tenure. Indeed, they have been shaped by these laws almost as much as they have helped to shape them. This is therefore an appropriate place to describe these laws even at the cost of anticipating the description of the political system of which they are an integral part.

All the land of Basutoland belongs to the nation with the Paramount Chief as trustee. He controls its exploitation and distribution and is responsible for its protection, though he may delegate his authority to his subordinates—chiefs, sub-chiefs and headmen.

Every member of the nation is entitled to a share of the land for building, pasture and cultivation, and the last right has been embodied in the Laws of Lerotholi, No. 8: "All chiefs and headmen must by law provide people living under them with lands to cultivate."[1] These rights normally accrue on marriage, although unmarried adults of either sex may be given agricultural land, and bachelors are entitled to a house site independent of their parents. Payment of tax is sometimes claimed to be the basis of these rights, but here again exceptions occur; men do not forfeit such rights when they are exempted from payment of tax on account of poverty, old age or physical deformity, and widows or elderly spinsters, who are not required to pay tax, are nonetheless entitled to similar rights; on the other hand, many taxpayers have no land.

When a man wants to build a house for himself, after getting married or moving with his family to a new village, he approaches the local headman, through his father if resident there, and asks for a household or building site. The headman then inquires where he would like to build and accedes to his wishes if practicable; if not, he gives him another plot of land. If the applicant is prepared to live on his father's holding, he need not apply for the headman's formal permission to do so and should merely inform him of his intentions. When a stranger is given a site, the local headman should introduce him to his superior authority and inform him of what is proposed.

The site is roughly indicated to the applicant and his neighbours, and is not specially marked out or beaconed. It should be large enough for two or three huts—up to about one-eighth of an acre; an additional

---

[1] Laws, 1922, p. 5. The 1946 "Declaration" has switched the emphasis from the right to receive to the right to allocate. Law 7 (1): "Every chief and subchief and every headman has the power to allocate land in his area for cultivation."

plot may be granted for a small garden. The latter may be enclosed, walled or fenced, and used as a vegetable or tobacco garden, orchard or small plantation, and though most of them are not more than a few square yards in extent, some are an acre or more. Hitherto, little use has been made of these small patches but, with the encouragement given by the Government, they are now being widely used as kitchen gardens. If there is insufficient room for this garden patch around the huts, a householder may be given a small area on the edge of the village. The allocation of building materials is described later.

Application for arable land is made in the same way and usually at the same time. Formerly, when there was plenty of land available, everyone was allowed to have as much as he needed or could cultivate.[1] The original method of allotting such areas has never been described and is now forgotten in most parts of Basutoland but it was probably similar to that followed by the Tlokoa within living memory. The applicant would show the local headman an area he would like to have and was then either given what he asked for or else was told to run round the desired area; he was then granted as much as he could encompass without stumbling. When agreement was reached, the boundaries of the area were publicly and minutely described to the applicant by the headman or his caretaker in the presence of other villagers, and beaconed off.

These areas were much larger than were required or could be managed by one household and were regarded as family lands, vested in the family head for his own use, and that of his sons and brothers and other kinsmen living with him. Even though they did not cultivate all of it, no one else was allowed to use it without his permission and the uncultivated parts were usually kept for grazing. As the family grew, its new members would be given their own arable plots there by the family head, who would notify the headman. Nowadays, owing to the general shortage of land, few family holdings are left and practically all the land, especially the little remaining virgin land, comes under the headman's direct control.

Nowadays when applying for land, the applicant usually asks to be given certain unused fields or a particular piece of virgin veld. If possible, his request will be granted, but such is the demand for land that this is rarely feasible and he will usually have to be satisfied with whatever he can get. Where there is no virgin or vacant land available, he will have to wait, sometimes for years, for fields to fall vacant through forfeiture or the death or emigration of the holder. Alternatively he might get land taken from someone holding an excessive amount. Every chief or headman is enjoined to "frequently inspect all allocated lands in his area and is empowered to take away lands from people who, in his opinion, have more lands than are necessary for their

[1] Dieterlen, *Livre d'Or*, p. 80.

families' subsistence and grant such lands so taken away to people who have no lands or insufficient lands".[1] This method of ensuring the equitable distribution of land was adopted many years ago by the Basutoland Council, and enforced by the Paramount Chief who sent messengers to every district to investigate the position and adjust the most glaring anomalies. Opposition to this process may be heavily punished; for example, in 1933 Bereng's court imposed a fine of two head of cattle on a man who protested against his headman's taking away one of his four fields. This law is mainly applicable in the Lowlands where the land shortage is acute and I have no information as to how it works out in practice. It has rarely had to be applied in the Highlands as yet.

Theoretically arable land holdings should be limited to three good lands per household—one for wheat, one for maize and one for kaffircorn.[2] They are tacitly assumed to be equal in size, though the size is unspecified; in practice considerable variation occurs. As will be shown later, the arithmetical average holding is between five and six acres per household, which would give three equal fields of a little less than two acres each. Actually many people have four or more lands with an acreage of over six acres and some have very much larger holdings, while others have less than three fields or six acres and some have nothing at all.

It is widely recognized that widows are liable to lose one of the hypothetical three lands on their husband's death, but at a Basutoland Council meeting in 1938, Sekhonyana, the Paramount Chief's representative, denied that this was the law. "It would be persecuting the natives if widows were going to have their third land taken away from them and that they should remain with only two lands. Widows should continue to plough their lands until they die." Since then the Paramount Chief has formally declared that "no widow shall be deprived of her lands"[3] except under circumstances applicable to all land-holders.

Normally a person's lands are in the ward[4] in which he lives and fall under the jurisdiction of the headman to whom he owes allegiance, but exceptions may occur. If no land is available in that ward, but there is some in a neighbouring ward and the two headmen are friendly, his headman may ask the neighbouring headman to grant the applicant one or two fields. This puts the land-holder in a delicate position for he will have to show respect to the headman from whom he gets his land, and also remain faithful to his own headman. Provided relations between the three of them are friendly, the arrangement works

---

[1] Declaration of Basuto Law and Custom, No. 7 (2).
[2] Official Annual Reports, 1933-6.
[3] Declaration of Basuto Law and Custom, No. 7 (4).
[4] For a description of the ward see Chapter XIII. The term here refers to the smallest political unit, that under the control of a headman.

well, but should any conflict occur, he is likely to suffer and may either lose his dwelling site or his land depending on which headman is displeased. Again, neighbouring headmen sometimes cement their friendship by exchanging lands or by giving them to one another's followers. Occasionally, too, when a man changes his residence from one ward to another he may be allowed to keep his lands in the former. This occurs when the change is made for personal reasons, such as ill-health, or when the person is ordered to accompany a chief's son who is being "placed" elsewhere. In the latter case, the person concerned may be granted lands in the ward controlled by the chief's son as well as being permitted to retain his lands in his old ward. But where a man leaves one area because he does not like the headman and moves to another, to whose headman he promises allegiance, he will lose his lands in the former area and have to look to the latter for new lands. Land allocation is thus an important way of securing political loyalty and is a jealously guarded right. As the old law put it, "A person living under one chief, if he turns the door to the house against the chief and looks up to another chief, he must be aware that he will be deprived of his place, as such conduct has the effect of creating disturbances in this country."[1]

All allocations of land should be made in the presence of witnesses or be publicly announced. In a country where there are no written deeds, this is an obvious and necessary safeguard. Its neglect is the root of many of the land disputes which come before the courts.

Rights of tenure are less than full ownership, but they give satisfactory and secure title, and are admirably designed to meet the needs of the community. The holder has the right of occupation and use of his land for his lifetime and he may not "be deprived of his place or fields without good reason".[2] Two "good reasons" have already been dealt with, namely, possession of "surplus" lands and change of political allegiance. Another is failure "through continual absence or insufficient reason, for two successive years properly to cultivate or cause to be cultivated the land or lands allocated to him".[3] Should a man leave the district, his rights are unaffected provided his family remains behind; if he takes his family with him, his rights are forfeited unless he is going away for a specific period or for a special and acceptable reason, as in the case of an employee transferred from his home district, or if he notifies his headman and keeps in touch with him while he is away. In the latter case, his lands might be allocated to some one else during his absence, but on his return they should be given back to him or he should be given priority in the allocation of other lands. Allegations are often made that people are evicted by the local chief or headman for purely personal reasons or because the latter has taken a fancy to their lands, especially when their employment of good agricultural

---

[1] Laws, 1922, No. 9.   [2] Ibid.   [3] Declaration, No. 7 (3).

techniques has yielded outstanding returns. Although Law No. 9 expressly provides for appeal to the courts in case of unreasonable eviction, it is said that few victims take any action for fear of further reprisals. I was not able to get definite evidence of any such cases, but the belief that they occur is widespread.

It is sometimes said[1] that the land reverts to the nation at the end of the harvest and is then, theoretically, available for redistribution. This is based on a misinterpretation of the rule that at the end of each season, on the direction of the headman, the lands are thrown open so that the crop stalks and grass strips between the fields can be grazed by the local cattle. In so far as these communal grazing rights curtail the private and exclusive rights of individual land-holders, it can be said that "the land reverts to the nation"—but that does not mean that individual rights to these fields lapse: as soon as the grazing has been exhausted and the new season approaches, everyone is automatically entitled to plough his lands again. No authority would ever claim that he could redistribute lands annually, or say that the people's retention of the same lands year in and year out is due to his indulgence in not re-allocating them to others. As indicated above, once he has lands allocated to him a person is entitled to keep them for the rest of his life.

The land-holder has full rights of ownership in the grain, peas, beans, pumpkins and other vegetables sown thereon and in the fruit of all trees growing there, but rights to the stalks of his crops are somewhat curtailed. He is allowed to cut and dispose of wheat straw[2] as he likes, for thatching, stock feed or sale, but maize and kaffir-corn stalks must be left for communal grazing, with two exceptions: his headman may allow him to use some of them to feed sick stock or cows which have just calved; secondly, if he thinks the crop will fail to mature, he may cut and remove the stalks for fodder or for sale, provided he does so before the frosts. People may also use a few of their mealie stalks for fuel. Wild plants growing in the lands, such as spinach, are free to all, but self-sown grain springing up in a fallow land is generally regarded as belonging to the owner of the field, though some say it more properly belongs to the chief. Fruit growing in a field, whether self-sown or deliberately planted, belongs to the owner of the field.

Except for a few highly privileged persons, fencing is not allowed. This rule is maintained partly because fences might restrict the winter grazing of crop stalks, or lead to complicated claims if damaged by the cattle when grazing the stalks, and partly because it is feared that

---

[1] Hodgson and Ballinger, 1937, p. 12.

[2] This necessary curtailment of communal grazing rights caused Chief Jonathan for years to oppose wheat cultivation in his district. Not only did he not protect wheat growers, whose crops were damaged by trespassing stock, but he deliberately drove his stock into the growing wheat when the rest of the lands were thrown open after the harvest, and encouraged others to follow his example.

fences will set up demands for complete individual ownership. This might lead to the alienation of land, which is prevented under the present system, and to the political independence of the landowner. This is a crucial matter from the chiefs' point of view, for the right to give, withhold or take away land is an effective method of controlling their subjects, and they fear that any curtailment of this right might reduce their powers and position. Where there is no danger of this happening, fencing is allowed, and so small garden plots in and near the village may be enclosed with walls of sods or stone, hedges of aloe, prickly pear or quince, or wire fences.

The holder may dispose of his lands in certain limited ways with his headman's consent. If for some good reason, such as ill-health, he cannot cultivate all of them, he may lend or lease one or two to a friend for a few seasons, but not indefinitely. He may also exchange one or more lands with some one else for some good reason, such as proximity to the other's village, where they are liable to be damaged by his cattle. But he cannot sell them or otherwise alienate them, nor can he dispose of them by will or testament, although during his lifetime he may allocate one or more of them to his married sons. As the saying goes, *tsimo hase lefa la mosotho* (lands are not an inheritance). The law dealing with this last point is complicated. A widow is entitled to retain all her husband's lands although, as indicated above, some incorrectly claim that one should be taken away from her. After her death, her children if minors are entitled to cultivate them. "Also for orphans who have been left, the Paramount Chief has issued instructions because he sympathizes with orphans. He sends circulars to all the chiefs. Orphans should be allowed to plough their father's lands until they grow up to take their father's places."[1] In cases where the children are grown up at the time of their parents' death, the practice varies. If they have no lands, they may be allowed to take their father's lands and divide these between themselves, some preference being given to the elder sons. If they have already been allotted lands of their own, they may be permitted to exchange these for their father's. This is not invariable and it is quite legal for the headman to allocate these lands to other people. Where family areas are still recognized, as among the Tlokoa, the deceased's lands are re-allocated by the family head, usually to the deceased's children in order of seniority. Where the deceased was a polygynist, his sons are given priority only in respect of their own household's lands and not of the lands of other households, except that the senior son has preferential rights to the lands of households having no male issue. Women have no right to their parents' lands, although an old maid may be graciously allowed to cultivate a small field.

No rent is paid for land other than land hired temporarily from a private individual. But possession of land entails the punctilious obser-

[1] Sekhonyana, Basutoland Council, 1938.

vance of the political obligations due to one's headman: one should support and assist him in disputes involving his authority and jurisdiction, pay occasional courtesy visits at his court or village, take stray stock to him, obtain stock removal permits from him and pay one's taxes through him. This last is often taken as the touchstone of political affiliation. If a man persistently fails to do these things or does them to some other headman after being warned to mend his ways, he is said to turn his door on his headman. He then forfeits his rights to live and hold land in that ward, and will be turned out of his lands at the end of the harvest and driven out of the village.

Unlike arable land, pastures are used under communal not individual tenure. There are two main types of pasture, ward pastures and the mountain or cattle-post pastures. Every ward has some pasture land, although the amounts vary widely from practically nothing in parts of the Lowlands to considerable stretches in less densely settled mountain areas. Part of this is "open" grazing and part "reserved", the latter being called *letobo* or *leboella* (spare veld). All members of the ward are allowed to graze their stock, or stock of which they are in possession, in the open pastures all the year round. Theoretically, since all pasture land belongs to the nation, they should also be allowed to graze in the open pastures of adjoining wards, but in practice each headman tries to deny this right to his neighbours, and only lets them graze in his area as a special favour. Senior authorities claim the right to graze anywhere in their area, i.e. in their own personal holdings as well as in the wards of headmen and other junior authorities. They also claim this right for their immediate followers, but they deny reciprocal rights to the inhabitants of those other wards. These respective claims are often resisted and may lead to fighting and bloodshed, particularly when these headmen or junior authorities and their followers belong to clan groups who were the original inhabitants of the areas, and are on unfriendly terms with their senior authorities. Grazing rights to the crop stalks and to reserved pastures are defended even more jealously.

The *leboella* pasture is reserved for rotational and winter grazing and for useful grasses such as *loli* and thatching grass. Over-grazed veld may also be reserved to enable it to recover. The veld surrounding arable lands and the grass strips between lands are automatically treated as *leboella* from the beginning of the ploughing season until the fields are opened to grazing after the harvest. The same area is usually reserved every year although it may be changed, increased or diminished as necessary. The reservation is either publicly announced in *khotla* by the headman or by his representative who is charged with the supervision of the *leboella*, or casually told to the herd-boys in charge of the local cattle. The reserved areas are usually delimited by well-defined natural features or marked out by beacons. The *leboella* is sometimes entirely out of bounds to all stock, although, subject to the headman's special permission, milch cows, sick animals, horses and travellers' transport animals may be allowed to graze there. Trespassing animals may be impounded at a charge of sixpence per day per head, and those responsible for the trespass may be guilty of an offence and liable on conviction to a fine up to £3.[1]

Towards the end of the harvest, when the cattle are brought down from the cattle-posts, these pastures are thrown open, the herd-boys being told to "pierce" them, *punya maboella*. They often try to do this secretly in order to get the best grazing themselves before their neighbours hear of it, and when the latter come to join them, they may try to drive them back, sometimes being supported by their fathers and other men from their homes. To avoid this, neighbouring headmen sometimes make pacts with one another, according each other's followers full reciprocal rights to their grazing, and each promising to inform the other when he proposes to open his *maboella*. The same applies to grazing the crop stalks in the lands after the harvest.

The mountain or cattle-post pastures are treated somewhat differently. Parts of the mountain areas are deliberately reserved solely for pasture by prohibiting cultivation or settlement. Areas of this sort are the upper reaches of the Ketane and Maletsonyane rivers, and a large part of the western sections of Malingoaneng. There are doubtless many other areas, but my information here is scanty. A very few areas have fortuitously remained as pastures simply because, owing to their isolation, bleakness or altitude, they have not yet encouraged permanent settlement.

As they are separated from settlements, cattle-post pastures are not attached to each ward, or district, nor do they fall under the normal jurisdiction of ward authorities in the same way as arable lands and other pastures. Instead they fall under the direct jurisdiction of higher authorities, such as the Paramount Chief, chiefs and important sub-chiefs, and not all of these have such jurisdiction. The cattle-post country of the Tlokoa, for instance, comes directly under Mosuoe and three of his sub-chiefs, whereas a fourth sub-chief of otherwise equal status has no cattle-post country. Similarly, in other parts of Basutoland the cattle-post country falls under the Paramount and certain senior chiefs, to the exclusion of several other important chiefs.[2] Owing to this difference, grazing rights in cattle-post pastures are allocated and held in a somewhat different manner from that relating to ward pasturage, although the same general principles are followed. Stock owners are allowed to establish a cattle-post and to graze in the area controlled by their immediate chief, but this residential qualification is not as strictly enforced as in the case of wards, and a person wishing to establish a post in someone else's area, will usually be allowed to do so, provided they both come under the same chief. Where a chief has no cattle-

[1] Rules 11 (2).   [2] Staples, p. 20.

post country at all or cannot accommodate any more cattle, he should approach some other chief on his followers' behalf. The same sort of jealousy is found here as in the case of the ward lands, and many chiefs are very reluctant to let those who are not their own people have posts in their areas.[1] But some chiefs in the south-west districts, who have no cattle-post country, have been given preference by the Paramount Chief to specified parts of his mountain areas.

People are allowed to place their posts where they like, provided they are not too close to those of other people. They are not limited to a specific acreage of grazing and have no exclusive rights to any area. In practice, as the stock return to the post every evening, they do not wander far afield, and tend to keep in a rough circle round the posts. As the posts are not necessarily a day's grazing apart, these circles may overlap.

Other natural resources, such as uncultivated trees, reeds, grasses, minerals and earths are also communally owned. The first three are reserved and protected in the same way as winter grazing. Originally, on the advice of the missionaries, Moshesh placed people in charge of the exiguous forest areas to prevent their being wantonly destroyed.[2] To-day the natural bush or forest is regarded as the highest form of *leboella*. "Like all *maboella* it is placed under the protection of the local chief and is mainly a provision against the cold winter months. Once a year, at the beginning of the cold season, people are allowed to enter the wood for a single day and remove dead wood only. . . . Usually green trees may not be felled and the uprooting of live stumps is considered wanton destruction. Besides this, villagers may require wood or green poles at any time throughout the year. In such cases the individual must obtain special permission from his chief and he will be escorted by the so-called 'shepherd of the woods'. Bush and forest are thus communal property, but the wild olive (*mohloare*) and, to a lesser degree, *cheche* or *mosino*, are considered more or less the monopoly of important chiefs. The reason is that the olive wood gives a smokeless flame as compared with other native fuel."[3] The degree to which these indigenous woods are monopolized or cared for varies in different parts of the country; *cheche*, for instance, in the Malibamatsu valley is freely used by travellers.

In the mountain areas there are scarcely any indigenous woods except wild willow and a few patches of *cheche*. Among the Tlokoa, the few remaining specimens of the former are strictly preserved and may be cut only under permit from the local headman. Brushwood, such as *sehalahala* which is extensively used for fuel and is indeed the principal

---

[1] Ibid.

[2] Chief Jobo, Commission on Native Laws.

[3] Quoted from an excellent account of *maboella* by Dr. R. C. Germond, in Staples, *Ecological Survey*, pp. 24-6.

firewood, is not protected at all and may be gathered whenever required. In many areas, poplar plantations have sprung up. Those which were deliberately planted by an individual are the private property of the planter, but self-sown or abandoned plantations are communal and may be cut with the permission of the local headman. Large poplars are used for rafters, smaller trees for building or fence poles, and branches for fuel. Willows, both wild and weeping, which have established themselves along the river banks are communally owned and are controlled by the local headmen. Their wood is chiefly used for making sleighs and for the bars of kraal entrances.

Grasses of domestic utility, such as reeds and thatching grass (*mohlomo* and *qokoa*), are preserved at the same time as the ordinary *maboella* or spare veld. As they are not equally distributed throughout the country, they are not exclusively used by members of the ward in which they grow, but are shared by the inhabitants of a wider area, such as a sub-district or even a district. The areas in which they grow are opened towards the end of the harvest, and everyone entitled to a share may cut as much as he requires. As the quantity available is limited, there is a general rush on the opening day and the cutting usually lasts for only a day or two. Thereafter, the area may be grazed as ordinary opened *maboella* until closed again in the spring. Everyone has to give the local authority in charge of the *leboella* a portion of the reeds or thatching grass he obtains, the actual proportion varying and being defined by that authority, usually one bundle in ten. He is not supposed to sell any of the reeds or grass thus given him—although he occasionally does so—but is expected to give any surplus after his own thatching needs are satisfied to those of his people who were not able to cut enough grass for their own requirements. Private individuals may sell or barter away as much of their own share as they wish, although, if they do so, they are not entitled to ask for any additional supplies. Cultivated reeds or reeds growing in a cultivated land belong to the land-holder in the same way as an ordinary crop.

Grasses used for weaving, such as *moseme*, *loli* and *moli*, are not strictly preserved as they are not in general demand. The Tlokoa allow people to gather their requirements whenever they like, although Germond[1] states that in some cases this may only be done when the *leboella* in which they are growing is opened.

The main minerals used are coal, ilmenite (*sekama*) and red ochre (*letsoku*). Outcrops of coal occur in several places in the Lowlands,[2] mainly in Mohale's Hoek. People used to dig this for use as fuel, but I was not able to discover whether they had to obtain special permission to do so. Some years ago they were ordered by the chiefs to cease using it. Ilmenite comes chiefly from a deposit in the Leribe district at Sekameng,[3] and I gathered that anyone could go and dig it for his own

---

[1] Staples, op. cit., p. 25.   [2] Stockley, pp. 80-1.   [3] Ibid., pp. 81-7.

personal use and for sale. The same applies to red ochre, where found. There are no iron-ore workings or any known deposits of other minerals which could be used locally. Clays for making pots, and coloured earth for smearing and decorating the walls of the huts, may be dug from local sources without permission, although people coming from a ward other than the one in which the material is found should inform the local headman as a matter of courtesy. Residents may freely use stone, sods or earth found in or near the village for building their huts or kraals.

In view of the free provision of practically all housing material, property rights in buildings are slightly restricted. When a man builds his house from local materials, such as stone, plaster, rafters and thatch, acquired in the ways described above, he is entitled, when removing from one place to another, to pull his house down and take the thatch, poles, etc. with him to his new home. But "if all the building material of such house or houses was supplied by the chief's giving to the man who builds, poles, grass or reeds, such house or houses shall remain a property of the chief".[1] In such a case, the house must be left intact. It does not become the property of the chief in the sense that he can sell it or the materials in it, but he can allocate it to one of his followers or to a new-comer, or may allow them to dismantle it and use the poles and thatch as if they had cut them from local supplies. If the householder has bought the building materials or grown them himself—if the poles come from his own plantation or the roofing material is his own wheat-straw—he can dismantle his house and either sell these materials or take them away. He may do the same with fittings such as doors and windows. He does not have to demolish the house, but may leave the walls standing. Formerly, he could never sell his hut, but the recent *Declaration of Basuto Law and Custom* allows him to do so, provided he had purchased all the building material.[2]

Disputes over land and grazing are essentially civil matters. The person who considers that his rights have been infringed brings the case to his headman's court and the latter usually makes an order adjusting the disputants' claims. But where a person deliberately disregards another's rights or flouts a previous court order, he is liable to a substantial fine. The courts are also very ready to punish any retaliatory action, as the following cases[3] show:

1. *Qhalehang v. Lesaona, July 1936.*
   L deliberately ploughed a field belonging to Q. Fined 1 beast or 8 sheep. The

[1] Laws, 1922, No. 11.
[2] Declaration No. 9 (1).
[3] These, and other cases quoted in following chapters, are taken from the native courts. Unless otherwise stated, they come from the court of Mosuoe Lelingoana, Chief of the Batlokoa. The Bereng referred to is the late Bereng Griffith, Chief of Phamong.

crop awarded to Q. Q also fined 1 beast because, instead of reporting the matter immediately, he started ploughing the same field and might thus have provoked bloodshed.

2. *Tau v. Lesala, Bereng, 1933.*
L ploughed some of the 8 fields which had previously been the subject of dispute and which had been awarded to T. L fined 2 head of cattle, and T was given the crops sown by L on those fields.

Disputes originate in many different ways—deliberate defiance as in the above cases, encroachment, covetousness, ill-feeling, misuse, inheritance, inefficient granting of land, and political rivalry. The following cases illustrate some of these points.

1. *Mokete v. Kapara, November 1938.*
K was nibbling into M's field. M sued him in lower court, but K did not answer summons, so case taken to Mosuoe, where K was fined 30s. and told to keep to his own field.

2. *Lephoto v. Samuel, Bereng, 1933.*
S annually ploughed more and more beyond his original boundary, encroached on L's land, and seized the latter's oxen when they went to plough. S allowed to reap where he had sown and then ordered to withdraw.

3. *Ralithakong v. Rannekoe (his younger brother), July 1936.*
A quarrelsome pair. Some years before, Ran was given a very large area as a single field by his father. This was placed on the edge of the village as a barrier between Ran's stock and other people's fields. Ran divided it between his two wives. When the junior wife died Ral, who coveted it, tried to take it away saying he had authority over this family property and that Ran was interfering with his rights to his father's village by ploughing in the midst of it. Ran protests and points to the dead woman's children who have to be provided for. The matter is taken to the headman's court where field is adjudged to Ran but he is fined 30s. for not having any witnesses to the original transaction. Ral's appeal to sub-chief dismissed, so he appeals to Mosuoe's court. Messengers sent to examine the position, report that the field lies between their villages. Judgment—the field to be divided equally between them. No fine.

4. *Mokete v. Mazekane, January 1936.*
Mok is Maz's elder brother's son, whom he brought up as his own child after his brother's early death. Relations between them have become strained through property disputes. Maz now claims a field he had allotted to Mok. This field is close to Maz's village and kraal and thus liable to damage by his cattle. The court sends messengers to look into the matter on the spot. They propose that this field be exchanged with one of Maz's in the valley. This is confirmed by the court in spite of Mok's opposition. The exchange to be effected after the harvest.

5. *'Mamofelehetse v. her husband Montoeli, February 1936.*
M gave away 'M's three fields without consulting her; all given to the same man, one to pay for a white goat used to purify one of M's wives, another for a loan of 6 sheep to pay a debt of £3 and a bag of seed, and the third for helping

him with clerical work in court. These fields were to be lent to this man for three years. When 'M complained that this man was ploughing her fields M told her that the man was ploughing for her and it was only later that she discovered that these lands had actually been disposed of in this way. The court ordered these fields to be returned to her at the end of the season and fined M 1 beast.

M would have been within his rights to lend one field for three years provided he had consulted her, but he had no right to give them away or to dispose of them without consultation.

6. *Sebakeng v. 'Mamokhantsi, October 1935.*

S claimed 2 fields which had been given to 'M (a widow). These fields had originally belonged to his father. The latter had left the district and gone to the Lowlands for medical treatment, taking his wife with him. They both died two years later. S was away at the mines while this was happening. Shortly after his parents' death, he returned to their original home and got married. He thereupon tried to get his father's fields, two of which had been allotted to 'M and a third to someone else. His claim was dismissed on two grounds:

(i) S's father appeared to have migrated as he took his wife and cattle with him when he went to the Lowlands, and he did not tell his local authority where he was going or whether he was coming back. If he had said he was coming back the fields might have been kept for him and, on his death, his son might have been offered the first refusal. But as he and his family appeared to have migrated for good, the fields became free for redistribution.

(ii) *Mobu ha e etsoe lefa*—the soil is not inherited. Even if the lands had remained the father's property, his son would not have been able to claim them as his inheritance. S was given a letter to his headman, instructing the latter to give him some fields as soon as possible.

7. *Leqhekoana v. Khonyonyo, August 1936.*

L, on behalf of the local headman Monoana, sues K for ploughing a land he had not been allotted. K replies that when he immigrated he applied to one of the chief's counsellors for a place; the latter took him to Mosuoe who told another of his men to place him. Two of them then took K to Monoana's and told him they had come to place him. Monoana gave them a messenger as his representative and they gave him a village site and lands in the presence of this messenger. The latter then said he had been told Monoana would not accept this allotment as the men of his ward were absent. Mosuoe's men refused to accept this and said if he wished to dispute the matter he could. When K started ploughing, L on behalf of Monoana took it to their sub-chief. The latter decided that the placing was in order. L appealed to Mosuoe's court, which dismissed the appeal.

Note: Monoana used to be one of Lelingoana's caretakers and is now trying to assume greater authority as a full headman than he was originally given.

8. *Moshehlanyane v. Sello, August 1936.*

M claims a field which used to be his father's and which he ploughed himself after his father's death. S is the local headman, and shows that M had emigrated from the ward, having formally announced that he was leaving together with his children. S's father as headman later lent the field to the daughter of one of his followers. For a time M lived with this woman and ploughed this field for her, but he did not marry her. M then went off to the mines and returned home some time later and found that S had now taken the field for himself. M then sued S in S's own court, which found for S. M appealed. Appeal dismissed and M fined 5s. for having disputed a field he had not been allocated.

Note: This case illustrates the correct procedure in emigration and the subsequent reversion of the emigrant's fields to the common pool; also that fact that no permanent rights accrue in consequence of temporary loan.

9. *Daniel v. Sheta, October 1936.*

D, an immigrant, asked Mosuoe for lands in a particular district, where there was virgin ground, and also fallow lands of emigrants. So Mosuoe sent him with a letter to Molatoli, the sub-chief of that area, recommending his being allotted a site and lands. Molatoli called up the local headman who confirmed his statement. Molatoli then told him to place D in the presence of all the men of that area. This was done, everyone but S being present. When D later started to plough, S stopped him saying he was ploughing the fields of an adherent of his, which had been allotted by Molatoli years before. This adherent had been absent in Johannesburg for eight years and his wife had been with her people for four years, but he had not emigrated, as he, S, was in touch with the wife and their household property was still in the village.

Note: Case unfortunately not concluded—but quoted here as it illustrates correct procedure in granting land to new-comers and also difficulty in deciding whether a person has emigrated or not. The correct judgment in this case would be that D should continue to plough these fields until S's adherent returned, when the matter could be reviewed.

10. *Thaha v. Mahasane, June 1936.*

T and M are half-brothers. M's mother was given a small patch of land on the banks of the river to grow pumpkins. As this was flooded out, she gave it up. Later T's father obtained this patch, worked it by hand as it was too stony to plough and grew tobacco. As this got frosted he changed to poplars. They began to flourish so he built a wall as a boundary to his plot and to avoid encroaching on a neighbouring field. T helped him in this. The two brothers now dispute ownership. Case taken to the court of their sub-chief Molatoli who upheld T's claim, but said the property was to be administered by Molatoli whom their father had made responsible for all their property.

CHAPTER XI

MISCELLANEOUS OCCUPATIONS AND PURSUITS

Hunting used to be an important activity, both as a form of sport and as a source of food, and was one of the major pastimes for young men. Game such as eland, koodoo and zebra was plentiful and lions and hippo were there for the brave. Little is recorded of hunting organization and technique. So far as one can tell, people usually went out singly or in small groups, although occasionally the tribe led by the chief or his deputy turned out for a large battue. On these occasions, the animals were carefully rounded up by beaters and driven within easy reach of the "seigneur's spear".[1] The kill was shared between the hunters, with the best pieces going to the person who first wounded or killed the animal. The chest of each animal and the skin of lions, leopards and other "royal" game were given to the chief. The people hunted with spears, occasionally with bows and arrows,[2] and later with guns obtained from Europeans. They also trapped game in pits, dug near drinking places, and they used dogs, both for tracking and pulling down the game. The use of medicines to bring luck is not recorded, but prescriptions are still in use for protecting dogs from snake bite. Nowadays as the only game consists of a few vaal rhebok, hares and birds, hunting is no longer of any importance and is limited to a few enthusiasts who use shotguns and to herd-boys who use sticks, stones, snares, catapults and dogs.

Fishing has never been a popular pursuit. The rivers are poorly stocked and the few fish found, barbel and yellow fish, are rather unpalatable. Moreover, many Basuto have a strong distaste for fish, a personal fad unrelated to any totemic taboo. The only people who fish to any extent are herd-boys. They use hooks and lines (bought at the stores), fish traps and sometimes also spears, sharpened umbrella ribs being a favourite makeshift.

In the old days the Basuto made their own spearheads, hoes, adzes, scrapers, needles and knives. Most of this was done by specialists who had to undergo an apprenticeship, "mysterious purifications"[3] and special doctoring. They extracted the iron ore from limited local deposits and worked it up into the finished product. They could not temper the iron, which was consequently somewhat brittle and soft, but their work was of remarkably good quality. Their smelting and

---
[1] Casalis, 1930, p. 223.
[2] Ellenberger and MacGregor, op. cit., pp. 24, 53.
[3] Casalis, 1861, p. 173.

MISCELLANEOUS OCCUPATIONS AND PURSUITS

forging technique appears to have been similar to that of other tribes.[1] In spite of their skill, the art never really flourished and Casalis records that in his day the people had come to depend on the Zulu for their main supply of spears and hoes. As a result of the introduction of guns, ploughs, hoes and other European-made implements, metal-working has become practically extinct and is now carried on in an attenuated form by a few metal-workers who use hoop iron as their raw material and supply the diminishing demand for spears, battle-axes and similar out-moded articles. Formerly, people worked copper and brass, imported from the Thonga and other tribes, and made ornaments such as those described by the early travellers[2]—large anklets and bangles worn in great numbers "from ankle to the knees, from the wrist to the elbow" and ear-rings which resembled "spiral springs that had been drawn out beyond their strength"; also breastplates used in war "worked so smooth and bright that they would not disgrace a Birmingham manufactory".[3] Nowadays only a few small articles, of little artistic value, are made, such as small flat ear-rings of twisted pieces of wire, flattened and shaped at the ends; bangles of soft copper wire coiled round a core of iron or horse-hair; and spatulae made from teaspoons beaten out and shaped.

After serving an apprenticeship with a European smith or at a technical school, some Basuto set up their own blacksmith's shops, where they shoe horses and repair wagons, scotch carts and ploughs. There is still plenty of scope for this trade, in spite of modern motor transport, but few young men take it up nowadays as they prefer to become motor drivers and mechanics.

Formerly leather-work was almost entirely confined to the making of clothes, such as loincloths, skirts, aprons, cloaks, fur caps and sandals, and articles of general use such as skin grain-bags, karosses and pouches. Tanning and minor decorations were done by the owner of the skin, but more elaborate processes, such as matching skins, cutting them out, sewing and decorating them, were carried out by experts. These experts still survive although in insignificant numbers, as their work is no longer in demand except on special occasions such as girls' initiation when traditional clothing has to be worn. Details of the various processes of tanning and braying skins are given by Kohler[4] who pays generous tribute to their competence.

Cobblers and saddlers, who have learnt their trade from Europeans, mainly at technical schools, may be found working independently and in European employment.

---

[1] Casalis, op. cit., pp. 161, 173–4. Basutoland Records, pp. 27–8.
[2] See Basutoland Records, pp. 17–36, quoting extracts from James Backhouse's book, *A Narrative of a Visit to Mauritius and S. Africa*. He visited Basutoland in 1839.
[3] Basutoland Records, p. 28.
[4] Dieterlen 1912, pp. 64–9.

Pottery is limited to the making of household utensils, such as drinking-pots, water-pots, food dishes, beer-pots and, in the old days, cooking-pots. These vary greatly in size and shape. The drinking-pot, which is the smallest, is either round or oval and is often made with a stand or pedestal, sometimes designed in the form of human feet. The water-pots are plain and perfectly circular with a maximum capacity of as much as three gallons. Beer-pots are usually enormous and the largest have a capacity of as much as thirty gallons. The food dishes are wide and shallow and some approximate to a small water-pot. All of these pots may be glazed or highly polished and most of them are decorated with colour and simple geometrical patterns. A few vegetable stains and colouring clays are known and used, although nowadays some people prefer paints bought at the stores.

The making of pottery is confined entirely to women. The technique is similar to that used by other Bantu tribes and has been frequently and fully described.[1] Several processes are hedged about with secrecy and taboos. For instance, many women dislike men being near or watching their work, and some definitely refuse to let a stranger come near their kilns during the firing stage, for fear that they may use the evil medicine *seteipi* to destroy or damage the pots. Some women[2] do not fire their pots when the moon is on the wane for fear they will be "weakened". The traditional price of a pot is an amount of grain equivalent to the pot's capacity, but this is being superseded in favour of cash valuation, which is more elastic and allows a better price to be asked for the smaller pots.

Sesuto pottery is still in demand both at home and in the Union urban areas. But it is not as popular as it used to be, owing to the competition of European goods, such as iron cooking-pots, mugs, plates, paraffin tins and petrol drums. This is inevitable as these articles are more serviceable than the earthenware they are displacing. But the tendency to use the European article is easy to overrate and the position to-day does not appear much worse than it was over thirty years ago, when Dieterlen and Kohler pessimistically wrote "the native utensils tend to disappear".[3]

In spite of competition with European goods, Sesuto weaving and basketry still survive. Men, using the appropriate grasses, make large grain baskets (*lisiu*) with a capacity of up to 3,000 lb., smaller conical baskets, used for carrying grain, and various sorts of hats. Women make more intimate domestic articles such as sleeping mats, beer strainers, and the small mats used to cover food or catch flour falling from the grinding stones. They also weave, from *tsikitlane* fibre, skirts (*thethana*), necklaces and bracelets, worn by girls and formerly also by women. Men and women plait grass ropes for tying bundles or tethering horses, and each sex has its own special way of plaiting. There are

[1] Meyerowitz, 1936.   [2] Ibid., p. 10.   [3] Dieterlen and Kohler, 1912.

PLATE IX

(a) Funeral of Chief's son: the foremost beast is to be sacrificed to accompany the dead

(b) Herd-boys racing cattle

Photo: L. Lewis

PLATE X

(b) Girl carrying maize

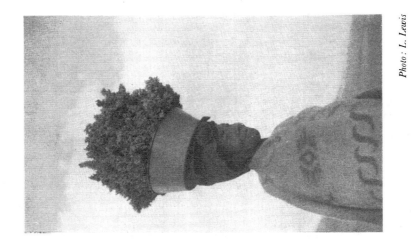

Photo: L. Lewis

(a) Woman carrying kaffir-corn heads

MISCELLANEOUS OCCUPATIONS AND PURSUITS 161

only a few indigenous grasses suitable for weaving, such as *loli* and *molikharatsa*; other materials, such as cane, osier or palm leaves, which play such a large part in basket-making elsewhere, are completely lacking, and this probably accounts for the paucity of Basuto basket-work. Some schools are trying to introduce new raw materials such as mealie leaves and aloe fibre, but not as yet with marked success, and the Government has recently tried to introduce osier willows.

Formerly, simple articles, such as milk pails, spoons and platters were carved out of wood. Many were decorated with geometrical patterns burnt into the wood or with sculptured designs, representing animals.[1] But by reason of the lack of material, which is even more scanty than in the case of basketry, this art never really flourished and has now practically died out.

Recently, under European instruction, a few people have taken up carpentry and simple joinery. Some of these have been able to fit themselves into the national economy, but others have had to take up work under Europeans in Basutoland and in the Union, since their work is of too high a standard and the cost of the materials they have been taught to work with is too great for them to practise it at home. A few of them, giving up all pretensions to skilled work, do odd jobs in the villages, such as making coffins, doors and rough *riempie* chairs.

Before Europeans came to Basutoland stone-working was limited to the building of kraals—an operation which was crude and unskilled and was done by the kraal owner and his friends, using undressed stone. With mission influence, however, western methods of house-building with mortar and dressed stone were adopted. As this work is comparatively difficult, it is more or less confined to specialists, who, in 1935, charged £1 to £3 to build an ordinary hut. Most of them learn their trade at the mines or in gaol, through labouring with a gang of stone workers, or at the technical schools. The latter reach a very' high standard.

Other forms of economic employment are those which have been created as a result of European contact. Some have grown out of modified indigenous institutions, and the rest are dependent on the various European organizations established in the country. Of the first, the only important ones are those connected with political affairs. Every important authority employs several more or less permanent officials. Though some of the posts, such as that of messenger, are traditional, their present status as permanent employees is due to modern conditions. Others, such as clerks and tax-collectors, owe their positions entirely to the modern requirements of government.

The second type of employment arises from the demands of the Administration, mission societies, trading concerns and other European

[1] Casalis, 1861, p. 181. See also illustrations in Christol, 1897, 1911, and Lagden, 1909.

institutions, for clerks, interpreters, messengers, mechanics, chauffeurs lorry drivers, policemen, agricultural demonstrators, education supervisors, doctors, nurses, orderlies, priests, teachers, nuns, evangelists, domestic servants and unskilled labourers.[1]

A third and more important type of employment is that provided by European industrial, commercial, mining and farming activities beyond the borders of Basutoland. This encourages tens of thousands of men and women to leave their homes every year and contributes as much to the material prosperity of the country as all the other economic pursuits of the Basuto together. It also creates social problems which are as serious as they are neglected.

Labour migration is not new to the Basuto, and is, in fact, nearly as old as their contact with Europeans. During the famines and the troublous times of the Free State wars (intermittently from 1851 to 1868), numbers of men sought employment with the Europeans in Natal and the Cape for money to buy food. After the political settlement of 1868, work abroad became more regular, and considerable scope for employment was offered only 180 miles away by the opening of the Kimberley diamond mines. Thither men flocked in their thousands to work for money for guns, clothes and agricultural implements and for the ten shilling tax imposed in 1869. By 1875, out of a total population of 127,325, of which the number of able-bodied men was estimated at 20,000, 15,000 men were getting passes to work outside the territory for long or short periods,[2] and by 1884 this number had doubled itself.[3] By 1908, 78,000 men out of a population of 350,000 "went abroad at intervals for work".[4] They were not all away at once and the periods during which they were absent doubtless varied considerably and probably averaged no more than six months in the year; this means that about 39,000 were away at any one time. In May 1936 the census revealed that 78,604 men and 22,669 women out of a population of 660,546 were "absentees at labour centres"; in 1946 the corresponding figures were 58,634 men and 12,144 women out of a

---

[1] According to the 1936 Census, there were:

	Men	Women	Total
Ordinary Labourers	878	88	966
Domestic Servants	186	686	872
Mechanics	977	306	1,283
Teachers and Evangelists	1,586	345	1,931
Total	3,627	1,425	5,052

These categories are vague. No explanation is given of what women "mechanics" may be and there is no mention of clerks, interpreters and others similarly employed.

[2] Smith, 1939, p. 206, quoting Rolland in *Cape Blue Book*, 1876.

[3] Pim, p. 21: "Over 20,000 Basuto were going out annually to work in the mines, chiefly Kimberley diamond mines, and on farms or railways".

[4] Lagden, p. 642.

population of 624,605. (The apparent decrease in absentees and in total population is discussed at the end of this chapter.)

Only the 1936 and 1946 figures have any pretension to accuracy. Nevertheless the earlier estimates are reliable enough to show that for over three generations a very high proportion of men have been going to work out of Basutoland. They also show that whereas formerly only a negligible number of women left the country, latterly thousands have done so. The great majority of these migrants go to the Union of South Africa, and the rest, an insignificant number, go to the Bechuanaland Protectorate or elsewhere. The type of work they do varies considerably.

Most of the women go to the Orange Free State to work on farms during the harvest; the rest go to the towns where they work as washerwomen or domestic servants, or earn a living as prostitutes or beerbrewers. Latterly many have left Basutoland to join their husbands.

Most of the men work in the gold mines; although it is not as well paid as other unskilled labour in industry, it offers food and accommodation which are valuable considerations. The main attraction of mining is that it is for definite periods, during which the worker can save most of his pay and at the end of which he can return home. Of recent years there has been an enormous increase in industry in the Union with a consequent demand for unskilled and semi-skilled labour. Many Basuto prefer this kind of work as the pay is higher and conditions easier.

Farm work is unpopular. Many who take it up are ex-miners, whose health prevents their return to the mines or who are tired of such work and want a change; a few are people who, from living on the border or on European farms (from which they migrated to settle in Basutoland), have had some experience of farm work and prefer to go back to it rather than face the towns. The pay is low, but the type of work may appeal to them, and though their work conditions are poor, they are permitted and even encouraged to bring their wives and families; they are housed and may grow their own grain and keep a few cattle. Some men also go to the sugar plantations and coal mines in Natal. This is not popular as the climate is considered uncomfortably hot and the pay unattractively low, and it is only when there is a scarcity of labour demand elsewhere that they take it. A few also go into domestic service or become casual labourers and some, suffering from wanderlust, drift round the Union, working their way from one town to another.

Some men go out of the country as itinerant doctors, others set up independent businesses in the Union urban locations as bakers, carpenters, shoemakers and traders, but the great majority become wage earners of one sort or another.

Formerly most of the labour for the mines and industries was recruited by traders and private recruiting agents who received a bonus of 30s. to £2 *per capita*. All recruiting for the gold mines is now done by the Native Recruiting Corporation through offices established in each district, although there are still a few private recruiters for other types of work.

The reasons why the Basuto seek work are mainly economic:[1] they go to work to supplement an inadequate income. Sons of wealthy families rarely go to the mines or other labour markets, whereas the sons of poorer families frequently do so, and those who have adequate lands and stock go far less frequently than those who have not. This is graphically shown by figures given in the 1936 census; whereas the proportion of the total male population of the country absent at labour centres is 25 per cent, that in the Mokhotlong district, where people are very much better off than elsewhere, is only 13 per cent—figures which are again reflected in village surveys made at Malingoaneng and Phamong (Mohale's Hoek).

Money is needed for various things. Tax is the most urgent and compelling because it cannot be postponed in the same way as other things. But it is not the only, nor indeed the most important, item for which money is needed,[2] and indeed long before any taxes were imposed (in 1869), the Basuto went out to work. People want money to buy food, clothing and miscellaneous articles such as ploughs and other equipment; to buy stock wherewith to get married or build up a herd, and, finally, to pay the expenses of marriage, relatives' funerals or children's initiation. Initially, agricultural production kept pace with these demands, thanks to the development of new techniques and the introduction of new crops whereby a sufficient surplus was produced for export; later it lagged behind and had to be supplemented by this export of man-power.

Though undoubtedly the most important, the economic motive is not the only reason for going abroad. Curiosity, a spirit of adventure, and admiration for returned miners with their airs, glamorous stories and enviable successes with the local girls, encourage youngsters to go out to work, and a spell of work in the mines has almost come to be regarded as an essential part of education, as a sort of initiation to manhood. Consequently, young sons of many well-to-do families go once or twice to the mines for the fun of it, and then return home to settle down to ordinary village life. Sometimes, however, sheer boredom or an acquired taste for urban life may urge them to return to the towns.

The length of the time they are absent from the country varies greatly according to the type of work and also with individuals. Mine workers who go on contract usually return on its expiration after about

---

[1] For a full discussion of the causes, consequences and channels of labour migration, see Prof. I. Schapera's *Labour Migration in the Bechuanaland Protectorate*, where the position is essentially the same as in Basutoland.

[2] Corroborated by Dieterlen and Kohler, 1912, p. 467.

ten months to a year, though some re-engage themselves on a further contract before returning home. Those joining under the Assisted Voluntary System may stay away from four months to a couple of years. Formerly they might stay away for many years at a time, but the Native Recruiting Corporation now undertakes to repatriate them at the end of two years. Similarly, their intervals of rest at home vary from a few weeks to a matter of months, sometimes years; in good seasons they usually stay longer, but in periods of drought they try to get back to work as soon as they can. If possible, they like to come home in the autumn for the harvest and leave again after they have seen to the ploughing; but owing to the mines' need for a continuous supply of labour, they can seldom indulge in such whims.

Farm labourers tend to stay away for longer periods. As rates of pay are poor, it takes them longer to amass enough to make their emigration worth while. Nor have they the same inducements to return soon because, unlike the miners who cannot bear the thought of their women being exposed to the vice and temptations of location life, farm workers often take their families with them, for their life on the farm is healthy and normal. Moreover, besides being pleasant, it is an economic asset to have them there, as they can earn money as well as help to cultivate the ground they are provided with as part of the conditions of their employment.

Until recently there was very little permanent emigration. The men went to work, not to stay, even though they might take their wives with them. Consequently, though some might spend long years away from their country, practically all made their way back home eventually. Inevitably, however, a few got "lost", formed local attachments and settled down for good. Industrialism in the Union has recently accentuated this tendency, for the reason that many industrial workers are no longer confined to compounds, but can live in the urban locations and slums where they can set up their own households. As a result many men now take their families with them with every intention of remaining there permanently. This tendency has been most noticeable in the past decade and is shown by the 1946 Census which reveals an actual decrease of 35,941 in the population. That so many people should have left or severed their connection with the country, in spite of the appalling slum conditions in the Union urban areas, is a reflection of the acute land shortage in Basutoland, the difficulty of making a living there and dislike of the restrictive discipline of the old tribal system, using this term in the widest sense of parental, family and political control.

CHAPTER XII

TRADE, EXCHANGE, WEALTH AND PROPERTY

IN the old days, the Basuto had few material wants and these scarcely went beyond the primary needs of food and shelter which could be satisfied by each family working for itself. Their food was the produce of their lands and herds, the spoils of the chase, and vegetables and fruit collected from the veld; their clothes were the hides and skins of animals, wild and domestic, and their homes were built of local earth and stone, roofed with reeds and grass. Their other requirements, such as implements, basket-work or pottery, they provided themselves or exchanged for surplus produce. Each family was practically a self-contained unit; consequently, there was little demand for specialization and industry, and none at all for such institutions as markets. The only early trade[1] which existed was with the Zulus with whom they bartered ostrich feathers, cranes' wings and panther skins in exchange for cattle, hoes, assegais, bronze collars and rings.

This closed family economy was gradually broken open as a result of European influence, by changing tastes and the recognition of new needs. The new articles that were first wanted were guns, wagons, spirits, horses, clothes, wooden doors and windows and corrugated iron for roofs. These could be had in exchange for cattle or surplus grain. After enough horses had been acquired, they could be bred locally, but the other articles continued to be in demand and slowly changed from luxuries to necessities, except for liquor which was first prohibited in 1869 and thereafter continued to be contraband. This change was due to habituation, to missionaries and other white men who insisted on clothes being worn, to the obviously superior efficiency of new articles such as ploughs, saddles and pots and other ironmongery, and finally to the rinderpest, which decimated the cattle and so completed the transition from skin clothing and blankets to cloth garments and wool or cotton blankets.

As indicated in the previous chapter, the Basuto economy was not developed enough to be able to meet this change from its own resources except for occasional heroic efforts as when the Basuto smiths cast cannon and made gunpowder during their desperate wars. The newly required goods and services remained essentially foreign and had to be imported, thus leading directly to the introduction of commerce and the expansion of trade.

[1] Casalis, 1861, p. 109.

At first, trade with Europeans was limited: a few pedlars came to Basutoland and the Basuto began to visit the small European towns that were springing up beyond the borders, such as Colesberg (the nearest in 1840 and some 200 miles away), Aliwal North and Winburg. Gradually resident traders established themselves in the country, and by 1871 there were six of these. With the rapid commercial and agricultural expansion that followed the proclamation of the British Protectorate, which ended the Free State wars, and the opening of the Kimberley mines, fifty-four new trading stations were opened during the next four years. Thereafter expansion continued and by 1937 their number had risen to two hundred. Most of these stores are owned by Europeans or European firms, except in the north where Molapo for a time gave equal facilities to Indians. Latterly the Basuto themselves have taken to trade and own or manage some of the district stores. One of the first to do so was the author, Thomas Mofolo.

The trading stores are all run on much the same lines, look very similar and contain the same kind of goods. They are usually plain rectangular buildings of stone and corrugated iron, and are flanked by large iron-roofed barns, used as granaries and wool sheds. Behind them is the trader's house, usually pleasantly surrounded with a garden and a belt of trees. The stores contain a wide assortment of goods. Half of the wall space is devoted to blankets, arranged in price groups, and the rest to clothing, cotton prints, and "kaffir" sheeting, tinned foodstuffs, tobacco, medicines and trinkets. The rafters are festooned with boots, bags, saddles, bridles, scarves, sunshades, shawls and a host of other oddments, while on the floor and veranda outside are ploughs and hand mills. Near the door, there usually hangs a mirror for the convenience and attraction of customers. Ordinary people are served at the counter, but chiefs and other élite are allowed to go behind and handle the goods themselves.

Most of the stores are licensed to sell any sort of merchandise except guns, ammunition and liquor, and to buy every sort of agricultural produce; but Basuto licensees are usually debarred from dealing in wool and mohair, in order to protect their inexperience from the risks of this particular form of fluctuating trade.

The business of the stores is subject to regular seasonal fluctuations. Winter is the busiest time, for it is then that people sell grain and buy most of their blankets and other clothing, and perhaps a few luxuries such as paraffin, sugar and tea. Trade slackens off about August and remains fairly dull for a month or two until the first spring wool clips are sold. With the proceeds, debts are paid and miscellaneous goods bought, such as blankets, ploughs and other agricultural equipment and minor articles such as beads, jars of vaseline and soap. Then, as the season progresses and food supplies at home get low, more and more people come in to buy maize and other grains. Later this trade dwindles as the new crops begin to ripen. Business revives again at the end of March when the second wool clip is sold and the winter trade begins. Throughout the year there is a regular trickle of business in dress materials, cheap blankets, sprouted grain for beer brewing, tea, pots of vaseline and beads. There are also occasional bursts of activity when people buy foodstuffs and clothes for some celebration or a mine worker comes home with money to burn. An actual illustration of these variations is given by the following figures, relating to the year 1928, when the crops and business were good. Since the war, the cash values have increased, but the proportions are probably much the same. No figures were available for maize bought from the people.

	Merchandise Sold £	Wheat Bought £	Maize in bags Sold £	Wool Bought £	Mohair Bought £	Credit[1] Allowed £	Repaid £
January	163	—	1,703	11	—	—	38
February	223	21	1,212	102	4	—	42
March	419	85	191	701	4	335	83
April	1,052	337	36	2,592	32	481	349
May	801	331	6	125	350	36	81
June	609	140	—	12	632	—	79
July	670	33	126	3	392	—	85
August	494	32	114	84	173	226	97
September	374	23	91	173	34	—	45
October	306	11	427	279	31	158	37
November	383	12	304	593	9	—	97
December	460	6	455	608	—	188	127

Merchandise sold by the stores consists mainly (about 80 per cent) of soft goods, of which about 70 per cent consists of blankets, the softest being aptly called "the otter skin" and "thigh of a young mother" (*serope sa motsoetse*).

In the large villages and Government camps, the stores do most of their business by means of cash, but elsewhere by barter of a peculiar variety. Barter pure and simple, the direct exchange of one commodity against another, scarcely obtains except for a few paltry transactions where wood, thatching grass or animal skins are exchanged for salt and tobacco. But in a modified form, under what is known as the "good for" system, it covers a large volume of business. When grain and sometimes wool is brought for sale, it is weighed and valued by the trader to the nearest threepence. The seller is then given a slip of paper endorsed as being "good for" the amount in question. Some traders do this simply as a temporary matter of convenience to avoid dealing with cash in the exposed and dusty veranda where they do their weighing, and they redeem the note for cash as soon as they can. Others only redeem the note for goods. This system encouraged traders to offer apparently high prices for the seller's produce, as they would at the same time

[1] Outstanding 1 January, £1,154.

mark up the price of their goods proportionately. It had a number of interesting features, some good, some bad, but as it may have changed considerably as a result of price controls during the war, no good purpose would be served by discussing it further.[1]

At one time credit was freely given, but owing to widespread defaulting during the pre-war depression and the decimation of stock from drought and disease, it is now only sparingly allowed. The only people normally allowed credit are those in regular employment, such as teachers, or chiefs and other influential authorities and important stock owners. Teachers are allowed credit up to one month's or one quarter's salary and as they have to liquidate their debts after each pay-day, they usually contrive to be overspent by one to three months' salary. Others are allowed to run accounts varying roughly with their wealth and reliability and are expected to settle their debts from time to time by the sale of cattle or wool. Some are required to deposit stock as security. Some chiefs are allowed to run up debts amounting to hundreds of pounds, partly because their security is considered good and partly to keep their goodwill.

Some Basuto are keen buyers and sellers and many of the more enterprising go from store to store in search of the best bargain. From the Highlands some take their produce down to the Lowlands, and even as far afield as the Free State or Natal. Some are also quick to appreciate differences of price, particularly of produce, and travellers are often asked for the latest prices, quoted by various stores or advertised on their handbills. Nevertheless, the majority do not take much trouble over their bargaining and tend to accept what is offered or asked, provided it is not obviously unreasonable. In some cases they are merely careless and indifferent; in others they take into consideration other things besides price, such as the nearness of the store, its generosity with *paselas* (free gifts of sweets and tobacco), its offer of services, such as free transport of wool and grain to the store or free ferrying across the river, and finally a most important factor, the personality of the trader. Furthermore, even though they haggle for hours over sixpence, their keenness is only superficial and, if they win their case, they flatter themselves more on the amount of the "special reduction" they have been allowed than on the lowness of the final figure obtained.

To most people the inner details of trading, especially the reasons for fluctuation of prices, are a closed book. If asked why prices vary, they shrug their shoulders and remark, "Those are White men's affairs"; they recognize that whatever the causes may be, they are beyond their control and they leave it at that. They usually attribute fresh changes in price to the policy of the store which first introduces them, but when they see other stores following suit, they may realize that it is part of a

[1] The barter system has now been prohibited by the Basutoland Chamber of Commerce. T. B. Kennan, personal communication, 1949.

wider movement, though they have little idea what it is. Their failure to grasp the problem is not surprising, considering the short experience they have had of the unstable European economic system, which contrasts so strongly with their own simple and relatively steady traditional system.

Traditional trading was confined to the exchange of comparatively few items, none of which were subject to violent fluctuations of supply and demand. The result was that their exchange values tended to become fixed and, when the European monetary system was introduced, these values acquired a constant monetary equivalent. For instance, under the traditional system a clay pot was worth as much grain as it would hold, one beast was worth four small stock, and one horse was worth two beasts. The subsequent cash values were similar; sheep were valued at 10s., cattle at £2 a head, and "tickey", "sixpence" and "shilling" billycans were considered to hold 3d., 6d. and 1s. worth of grain or beer. These values remained unchanged in drought and plenty; they were supported by *bohali* calculations, for example, that a horse equalled two cattle, and by the adoption by the courts of fixed equivalents for the payment of fines; thus one sheep was taken to be equal to 10s. and one beast as equal to £2 irrespective of the size, age or sex of the animals concerned. Gradually, however, experience with the stores and with the fluctuating prices has begun to modify this attitude and has produced an interesting ambivalence: fixed equivalents continue to be observed for formal transactions such as *bohali* or payment of court fines, whereas in private and purely commercial transactions considerable variations in prices occur. For instance, in 1935–6, while the courts maintained the constant value of 1 sheep = 1 bag of grain = 10s., the following business transactions took place: X sold a beast to Y for 3 bags of grain (market price probably about 12s. 6d. in that area), and another beast to Z for £2; A bought a horse for 8 sheep; C sold an ox for £6 10s. and bought 17 sheep for £4; in January D sold 2 sheep for 1 bag of grain; E refused an offer of £4 for a fat cow and went to a store two days away where he hoped for £6; F sold a large ox for £4 10s.; G sold a beast for £3 and bought two sheep for £1; a young beast was sold for £2 and a two-year-old for £3; H bought a beast for 28s. from K who was being pressed for his tax. Boom prices and postwar inflation have probably accentuated these differences and may even have begun to upset the fixed values, but I have no up-to-date information on this point.

One aspect of trading which Basuto find perplexing is the trader's need for early liquidation of debts. They do not understand that outstanding debt means the loss of capital or that this has to be covered by raising the credit price above the cash. Sheer ignorance is partly responsible for this, and also their familiarity with the *bohali* system, where the amount due may remain unpaid for many years and where delay is not penalized by claims to interest or to the progeny of the cattle withheld. Consequently, they do not see why they should pay immediately and so they may wait until they see that their creditor is in real difficulties, or else they gently postpone payment year after year until one day, maybe, they suddenly decide to settle it. Too much emphasis should not, however, be placed on these differences in economic concepts. The Basuto have fundamentally much the same attitude towards debt and commercial morality as Europeans and recognize that strictly speaking a loan should be repaid when due.

Trade is also carried on by pedlars and hawkers. They fall roughly into two categories: those who deal in a variety of goods and those who peddle a few small articles. The former operate under a hawker's licence which entitles them to sell goods, such as blankets, clothing and groceries, under certain conditions regarding their movements and areas of operation. Most of them used to be Indians or Indo-Basuto half-breeds, who were agents of Indian dealers, and few were Basuto, hawking on their own account. Latterly the Government has tended to restrict the issue of hawker's licences to Basuto only.[1] Pedlars are all Basuto; they deal with simple commodities such as matches, red ochre and salt, and are not licensed.

Hawking flourishes mainly in the Highlands where stores are few and far between. The hawker's usual technique is to spread the news that he will be found at such and such a village on a certain day. There he displays his wares in some friend's courtyard. The art of this trading lies in tempting people to buy a large number of small cheap things. The customers will shy off buying anything at all if faced by an expensive item such as a blanket, but they do not mind buying a large number of trifling, cheap articles, such as coloured handkerchiefs, lengths of print or jars of vaseline. One reason for this is that most of the hawkers' customers are women who cannot spend much money or part with much produce without their husband's consent and this may not be readily obtainable. Another reason is that people prefer to wait until they have a large order to execute, such as several blankets or many yards of print, and then make a grand expedition to the store, where they will have a wider selection to choose from and lower prices to pay.

Hawking is not an easy undertaking. Apart from the difficulties of trade, it involves continuous travel from one village to the next, and returns to the base, with such grain and stock as have been accumulated. Nevertheless, it appeals to some as offering an opportunity for travelling and making wide social contacts. Sometimes it is combined with doctoring, and many hawkers spend the slack period dispensing medicines and treating the sick.

[1] T. B. Kennan, communication.

Wealth and Property

The principal forms of wealth are stock, land, tools and agricultural equipment. In the old days stock was acquired mainly through tribal warfare, cattle raids and plundering expeditions.[1] This loot was handed to the chief, who deducted a substantial portion for himself[2] and distributed the rest to the leaders and others who had taken part in the raid. Stock could also be acquired in exchange for produce, by inheritance and by marriage. The advent of British control stopped the first and substituted employment and the earnings of labour.

Stock is the most popular store of wealth as it increases itself through natural means, is useful and can be liquidated when necessary. Its great disadvantage is that it is subject to rapid deterioration when most wanted, as in the times of drought and famine, and is also liable to depreciation or loss through theft and disease. Cattle are the favourite form of stock, chiefly for prestige and tradition's sake, and are often called "the people's bank". Some people, however, prefer small stock, particularly if they already possess a few head of cattle, as they can buy more animals for the same money and they feel that dealing in smaller units reduces the risk of heavy losses: at the same time their rate of increase is normally higher than that of cattle, and the prices paid for wool and mohair promise further profit. Other forms of stock, such as horses and pigs, are not usually kept in large numbers as they are not regarded either as stores of wealth or as investments, but are wanted for their immediate utility.

Many Basuto realize that stock as a store of wealth has disadvantages, but until recently they had no alternative. The introduction of the European money economy now offers them a means of converting their stock into cash, which can be saved in various ways. One of these is hoarding—the hiding away of money in cracks in the hut wall, or under the floor or the kraal wall. When notes are hoarded they are treated with ash to protect them from mice and mildew. The cache is usually known only to the head of the family and its whereabouts is only divulged on his death-bed. It is difficult to say to what extent hoarding was, and is, practised. Reports of hidden fortunes often end only in the discovery of empty brandy bottles.

Banking is another form of saving, especially the depositing of small sums of money with the Post Office Savings Bank. The depositors are mainly wage-earners such as domestic servants, teachers and clerks. Of these people, a high percentage are women, because they have not the same expenses as men, although they may contribute to the support of their families, and because they have not the same interest in stock. Other depositors are wealthy men, such as chiefs and important stock owners, and during the war every soldier opened a savings account.

---

[1] Casalis, 1861, p. 198.   [2] Ibid., p. 199.

A number of people bank with commercial banks such as the Standard or Barclay's Bank. A very few also take out life insurance policies.

Money may be acquired through inheritance and marriage, but mainly through the earnings of labour. Next to wool and mohair, wheat and cattle bring in the best returns. Maize and kaffir-corn also bring in some revenue but, as about the same quantities are re-bought in the course of the year, their cash value in this context is largely illusory. The acquisition of land, the third important form of property, is described in a previous chapter.

The people's wealth has never been equally divided and, so far as historical times are concerned, there have always been rich and poor. In the old days the richest people were the chiefs[1] and other important political authorities. Successful warriors and specialists came next, then the heads of small family groups, followed by the mass of the people. At the tail end came servants, who were mostly aliens. This uneven distribution of wealth continues to this day and has been intensified by the widening of the gap between rich and poor. Wealth is still a jealously guarded prerogative of political power. The end of inter-tribal fighting and of cattle raiding dried up the chiefs' special source of income through captured cattle, but they were compensated by the growing value of their prescriptive rights to all stray stock found in their districts, and by the steadily increasing revenue from court fines. They also continued to enjoy and, in some cases, unscrupulously exploited, their rights to land, grazing and free tribal labour; some also used their official position to further small private enterprises such as transport riding. Moreover, the more important chiefs received a cash allowance from the Government. The real value of these incomes was further increased by their growing disregard of the obligations that had traditionally been associated with wealth; instead of using the produce of their tribal lands and of their cattle to support the poor and to feed people attending the court, and those employed on the court work, many diverted it to their own personal use. In 1934, one chief, who kindly showed me his books, owned 200 cattle, 1,500 small stock, 90 equines, and 31 large lands, which in a fair year yielded 300 bags of grain; he had also a revenue from his court of about 200 cattle, 225 small stock and £20 cash, and an allowance of £100 (subsequently raised to £300) from the Administration. He was one of the wealthier chiefs, but not as wealthy as the late Chief Jonathan, who died leaving an estate worth over £20,000. The introduction of a Native Treasury in 1946 deprived chiefs of their rights to stray stock and court fines, but compensated them with increased allowances which vary from £130 to £3,600;[2] though limiting the scope of possible abuses, it did not fundamentally alter the position.

Wealth is not confined to the political authorities, although it is concentrated there, and a few wealthy commoners with considerable in-

[1] Casalis, op. cit., p. 199.   [2] Basutoland National Treasury Estimates, 1949-50.

comes and property may be found. Some have their own trading stores and others have large herds and flocks, reckoned in hundreds of head of cattle and thousands of sheep and goats.

At the other end of the scale, there are many Basuto who have no stock or land at all. Theoretically, the traditional land tenure system provides everyone with land; there are no means of telling whether it really did so in the old days, but it certainly does not now. The present landlessness is, however, nothing new—it was anticipated by observers like Mabille many years ago when the Basuto were threatened with the loss of their agricultural lands to the Boers and finally did lose them after the 1865-8 war; it was first remarked upon by Dieterlen[1] early in this century. Since he wrote the position has still further deteriorated. In the Highland district of Qacha's Nek, for instance, 80 per cent of a group of tax-payers of less than 5 years standing, 32 per cent of those between 5 and 10 years and 17 per cent of those over 10 years standing were recorded in 1934[2] as having no stock, and 84 per cent, 30 per cent and 9 per cent respectively, no land.

The bulk of the population lies between these two extremes. The average family holding in the years 1937-47 was about 3 head of cattle, 1 equine, 13-18 small stock and 5-9 acres of arable land, with rights to common grazing which averaged about 50 acres per family, if every square inch of other than arable land is included as grazing. These figures are averages arrived at by dividing the country's total wealth by the number of families.[3] They show that the "average Mosuto" is poor.[4] The actual division of wealth between different classes of rich, middling

---

[1] Dieterlen, *Livre d'Or*, p. 449.

[2] Pim Report, p. 41.

[3] The number of families is taken as a fifth of the total population, including both those present in the Territory and "absentees at labour centres". The actual figures are:

	Total Pop.	Cattle	Equines	Small Stock
1937	660,546	418,921	108,851	1,695,35
1947	624,605	429,158	162,150	2,349,990

The figures quoted in the text could be modified by a more accurate determination of the number of families, but such modifications would be very slight and would not alter the fact that the average holding is very small. The estimates of the areas cultivated are only rough. In 1938, they were said to be 750,000 acres and in 1946, 1,200,000. Whether either or both of these figures refer to the amounts actually cultivated only or to the amount of land broken to the plough is not clear. The total area of Basutoland is 7,498,240 acres. No estimate has been made of the acreage available for pasturage. The Basutoland Government is at present (1949) planning an agricultural survey of the whole Territory which will take some years to complete.

[4] Measurement of wealth by stock ownership is not completely reliable, as some people may earn large cash incomes and have no stock. This, however, is rare because the Basuto value stock for its social value as a symbol of wealth, quite apart from its economic value and so, if they have none, they try sooner or later to buy some. Moreover with wealth goes influence and with influence acquisition of additional lands. So those who have cattle are bound to have lands. On the other hand, the less stock they have the less land they are likely to have.

and poor is more difficult to arrive at; but a tiny sample in the Highlands in 1936 showed that only about 11 per cent had more than 20 head of cattle and 50 small stock (e.g. 30 large stock units), and 30 per cent had little or no stock.

The wealthier sections of the people are well off in terms of the satisfaction of their material and social needs. They have more than enough simple foods, such as grain, milk, meat, and they are able to buy all they want of other foodstuffs, such as refined meal, tea, sugar, jam and tinned foods. They are also able to clothe and house themselves comfortably and many still have something over. Formerly the chiefs, whose position was largely dependent on popular support, spent this surplus on feeding their people, helping needy but influential persons, and providing the poor with gifts, loaned stock (*mafisa*) and even, in a few cases, with wives. Now that political power is largely independent of popularity, there is no need for them to do this and they and other wealthy people can, if they wish, expend their wealth on advanced education for their children and luxuries for themselves, such as expensive tailor-made suits, large houses built on European lines, motor cars, travel, liquor and race-horses.

The "middling" groups are also able to satisfy most of their needs fairly comfortably. They feed, clothe and house themselves adequately, pay their tax without undue strain and have enough left over to buy iron pots, ploughs, trek-chains, etc., saddles, bridles and minor luxuries in the shape of European foods, salt, paraffin lamps and furniture; and they are able to educate their children.

The "poor" live at a low level. Most of them are adequately though simply housed, but a few live in hovels. They are poorly nourished and shabbily dressed, find difficulty in paying their tax, and can only afford one or two small cooking pots and implements such as hoes. Ploughs and other such things are beyond their means and only rarely can they buy minor articles such as salt and knives. Their incomes are often inadequate, even for their simple requirements, so that their womenfolk have to supplement it by selling beer, or labouring in rich men's fields or on European farms. In bad seasons many actually go hungry and literally dress in sackcloth.[1]

There are many reasons for the change from the old position. Formerly people's wants were few and simple and readily satisfied. Now they are many, complex and beyond the local resources. Dwellings were easily built with materials at hand; now some of these have become scarce, and substitutes have to be bought, such as corrugated iron in place of thatch, as well as new necessities, dictated by modern standards and ideas, such as wooden doors and glass windows. Clothing used to be simple, durable and cheap. Now the new types of clothing are less durable and more costly. This expense can be lessened by the

[1] For further details see Ashton, 1939; Dieterlen, op. cit., p. 76; *Doc. Inédits*, p. 5.

purchase of material to be made up at home instead of buying ready-made clothes, but the cost even then is a considerable item which cannot be avoided and few know how to make clothes. The people do not know how to spin and weave and so make no direct use of their resources of wool and mohair, though in the mountain areas a few uncouth garments of knitted mohair may be found, and "Home Industries" on a small scale are being introduced by the Government. In the past, although famine and periods of insufficiency were not unknown, they had on the whole enough land and stock to provide all the food needed to satisfy their hunger and to keep them in good health. "The harvests hardly ever failed and the quantity of grain which was reaped annually exceeded considerably that which the inhabitants could eat."[1] To-day there is insufficient land to satisfy these needs. Even though they may be able to feed themselves in good years, they cannot produce enough to tide them over bad periods, let alone to provide a sufficient surplus for disposal for the satisfaction of other needs. Even forty years ago they had to eat the ripening grain of the new crops "having nothing in the granary".[2] At the same time their other food resources have been impoverished by the extinction of game, and by the concentration of most of their stock in the Highlands, away from the Lowlands where the bulk of the population lives, so that little of it is available for the supply of milk. The maldistribution of stock, and the decay of customs mentioned above, which tended to counteract differences of wealth, mean too that the poorer people cannot enjoy the country's wealth to the same extent as before.

Finally, new needs have been created. Taxes have to be paid and new implements such as ploughs, iron pots and hoes have to be bought. School fees, dipping and inoculation costs have also to be paid (by some, though not by all), and there are in addition the many new interests and articles on which money may be spent.

To meet these demands the people have the produce of their stock and the earnings of their labour. The former applies to only a proportion of the people (about between a half and two-thirds) and covers only a fraction of their liabilities. The earnings of wages provide the rest and, as indicated in the previous chapter, well over half the adult male population is away at any one time, working out of the country.

The social consequences of this maladjustment are unfortunate. The men live a life divided between their rural homes and the urban areas of the Union and, floating between the two, they miss the full benefits of both. As mine or industrial workers, their intermittent employment makes them difficult to organize and so reduces the opportunity of bargaining for better wages; their instability keeps their productivity and therefore their wages low, and their life in the towns is squalid and unhealthy both physically and socially. On the other hand, the know-

[1] Casalis, op. cit., p. 148.   [2] Dieterlen, 1912, p. 84.

PLATE XI

Photo: L. Lewis

(a) Harvesting

(b) Threshing mealies in private courtyard

PLATE XII

Photo: Constance Stuart

(a) Gathering for a National *pitso* on the outskirts of Maseru

Photo: I. Lewis

(b) Women returning from the fields

ledge that they can always get temporary, if ill-paid, work, deprives them as peasants of any great incentive to farm properly or to make the most of their land and pastures, while their absence from home disrupts and impoverishes their social and economic life.

The Administration is trying to improve the position. Through extensive anti-erosion work, contouring, tree-planting and, latterly, controlled grazing, land is being reclaimed. The value of stock is being enhanced by the importation of selected stud animals, such as merino rams, bulls and stallions, the castration of undesirable breeding animals, the eradication of disease such as scab, the compulsory dosing of sheep, as well as by improved wool marketing schemes, including better shearing methods, classification of clips and direct export. Agricultural improvements are being introduced through better seed strains and more intensive cultivation. These efforts have undoubtedly improved the production of the country, but it is still far from achieving a balanced economy independent of labour migration. There is undoubtedly considerable room for further improvement—for instance, the increasing of crop yields by manuring and proper cultivation; but this postulates fencing and far more intensive farming than is practised and a virtual revolution in production methods. Alternative means of keeping the men at home, by the establishment of industries other than trifling Home Industries, are occasionally thought of, but no investigation of the matter has yet been undertaken. The recent geological survey indicates that the prospects of mining are remote.[1]

In conclusion, property rights of various kinds may be briefly sketched.

Private Property

Private property rights are of two kinds, personal and household. It is often difficult to draw a hard and fast line between them, but, subject to the modifications described later, the following broad distinctions may be made:

Personal Property.

(*a*) Personal effects such as clothes, ornaments, tools and equipment connected with a specialist trade (e.g. doctoring, leather-work, pottery).

(*b*) Gifts from friends, given for personal reasons and not in fulfilment of specific kinship or other social obligations; for instance, a pot given by one woman to another as a friendly gesture, but not a pot given to her at her wedding, as the latter is a gift to her household rather than to the bride herself.

(*c*) Gifts made in fulfilment of some personal kinship obligation, such as a blanket given by a man to his mother-in-law, or *bohali* cattle given to specific individuals, such as the *khomo ea letsoele* and the *khomo*

[1] Stockley, pp. 70–93.

ea seholoholo (the cow of the breast and the ox of the loins) which should be given to the bride's mother and father respectively, and the sheep called *setsiba* (the loincloth) which should be given to the father; similarly various gifts exchanged between a maternal uncle and his uterine nephew and niece.

(*d*) The proceeds of some part-time specialist activity or hobby, or the exploitation of some personal talent, such as singing, or powers of divination. It is difficult to determine where part-time earning ends and making a living begins. Generally speaking, the criterion is the nature and continuity of the work. Thus, running a business or wage-earning, even if discontinuous, as in the case of mine-working on contract, are undertaken to earn a living or contribute towards the family livelihood. A small part of the earnings therefrom may be retained by the worker himself, but the bulk of them should be treated as family income and used for the family. On the other hand, occupations such as doctoring are regarded as personal, so that the proceeds of them are also personal, even though the individual concerned practises them continuously. Women are allowed to treat their earnings as personal only where their work does not interfere with their household duties and occupations; as a full-time teacher, her wages should be used for her family's maintenance, but as a potter, herbalist or diviner, she may keep her earnings. Similarly, she may keep her profits when she only occasionally brews beer for sale, but not if she does so regularly and frequently, or if she uses the household grain for making the beer.

(*e*) Property inherited by personal bequest or in fulfilment of personal kinship obligations, such as a woman's clothes given to her daughter.

Rights to these forms of personal property are in most cases absolute. The owner can dispose of them as he likes without reference to anyone. The only exception occurs in the case of women's and children's clothing which was bought by the family head or with the proceeds of household property. Here its disposal is obviously a matter of household concern.

Formerly, bachelors and women, whether married or unmarried, were regarded as minors and therefore were not entitled to own or administer any property other than a few minor personal effects. Their earnings were regarded as belonging to the family. They were expected to hand these over to the family head, who could retain them all, but might return a small portion. Popular opinion in this matter is changing and unmarried men and women are now often allowed by their parents to keep private earnings and even their wages from continuous employment as domestic servants, school-teachers or mine-workers. They may also own stock and be allocated land. Some married women are also allowed by their husbands to keep the proceeds of their private work and even a small proportion of their other earnings. But this change has not yet achieved full legal recognition and if a father uses his unmarried child's property, or a husband his wife's, without his or her consent, the courts would support him in any action brought by the aggrieved person, provided the property was used for some legitimate family purpose, such as buying food, making up the requisite *bohali* cattle or paying a court fine. For this reason, some men working away from home do not remit their money to their parents, for safe keeping or for investment in stock, but prefer to send it to a friend.

Children are allowed to have a little property of their own such as poultry or minor personal effects which they can dispose of as they like. Girls are allowed to earn a little pin money by the sale of beer (*kongkotia*) made with gleanings or with *talane* they were allowed to reap for themselves. Boys are also allowed to sell or exchange gleanings.

Household Property

Household property is that which has to do with the maintenance of the family or household, such as stock, agricultural implements, produce of the lands allocated to it, furniture, tools such as cooking utensils, pots and hand-mills, and certain quasi-personal things belonging to the head by virtue of his being head, such as the family medicine horn, guns and saddles. These may be acquired by purchase, with the proceeds of the sale of household produce or with the earnings of its members, as a gift from the family head or by inheritance. Stock may also be acquired through a daughter's marriage, and household goods as a part of the trousseau given to a new household by the bride's parents, relations and friends.

This applies to both monogamous and polygynous households. In the latter case, each wife, except the one who may be attached to the senior household, has her own household, and each such household has its own property and its own fields. The polygynist concerned may also keep his personal property, mainly the proceeds of his specialist activities, quite separate from that of any of his households. Each household is entitled to the exclusive use of its property and its produce and to the proceeds of the sale thereof. It may use another household's stock only with the latter's express permission; it may, for example, borrow some of another household's cattle in order to make up the *bohali* cattle for a son's marriage or to pay a fine. Similarly, for ploughing and transport riding, all available draught animals and agricultural implements are pooled and used under the direction of the common head.

There is seldom any trouble over property such as grain or household equipment, as they are kept separately in each household. Agricultural implements are usually allocated to the senior household, except those that have been bought by the earnings of the members of another household and are retained there.

Quasi-personal property belongs to the senior household and should remain there—its removal from the senior wife's hut is tantamount to desertion and is an actionable wrong.

Stock belonging to different households is not kept in separate flocks and herds, but is herded and kraaled together both in the village and at the cattle-post, except where the wives live in different villages and have some of their household stock with them. Consequently, disputes over stock occur more frequently than over any other form of family property. Particular care has therefore to be taken to identify them. This is done by earmarking and/or branding the animals. Each household has an earmark of its own or a special combination of earmarks, and sometimes its own brand as well, although it is more usual for the brand to be shared. These earmarks (and brands, if separate) are taken as irrefutable proof of ownership (*vide* the case of Masenkane, quoted below). The most common marks used are a hole in the ear, a V excision (*lekeletsane*), a circular excision ("half moon"), a serrated or saw-like excision (*koena*), topping (*leripa* or *tlhomola*) and other marks such as *seneiki*, *letabo* and *bentlelaka*. Brands consist of the owners' initials arranged in various ways and are put on either the hindquarters or shoulders.

Household property is jointly administered by the man and his wife, her authority being subordinate to his. She may dispose of agricultural produce in small quantities as she thinks fit, but she should consult him and obtain his consent before disposing of substantial amounts, such as a bag of grain or wool. He should consult her when disposing of any of their property, but he is not bound by her views. He should also keep her informed of his proposals for moving stock from one cattle-post to another, or his arrangements for ploughing. In polygynous households there is no joint discussion between the husband and all his wives, but he deals with each one separately. He should treat his senior wife most punctiliously. If his son is grown up, he should also consult with him.

Maqetha v. Pipi (his father), November 1935.

M, senior son of P's senior household, complains that P refuses to let him and his mother use their household property, and is trying to squander it on his junior wife (*o hana ka lintho tsa ntlo ea 'me o rata ho li jela moqekoeng*). He also complains that P prefers to work with his uterine nephew (*mochana*) and other "strangers", rather than with him, e.g. P does not let him plough his mother's lands but gets this nephew to do so and he uses his senior household's cattle to plough the junior wife's lands. The court condemns P, saying, "You have turned away from your children, you have taken someone else and made him your son inside your own village, and you have put him in charge of all your property. You are sowing discord; this man is your *mochana*, not your son and heir—send him away for he is breaking up your family." After threatening to fine him heavily for such behaviour, the court orders him to consult and co-operate with M in everything.

Two days later M reported that P had totally disregarded this and had taken a span of oxen to plough his nephew's field without mentioning it to him. This was found to be quite untrue, so M was fined £1 for trying to get his father into trouble, and the witness who gave false evidence in support of this was fined 10s.

Two months later, M again sued his father for earmarking stock belonging to the senior house with the earmark of the junior household, and thus disregarding the previous judgment. P was ordered to return the stock he had marked in this way, and was fined 1 beast and £1.

Should the husband stay away for long periods, at the mines, for instance, his wife acquires greater independence and authority, though she should still consult with his senior male kinsmen. Sometimes, when family relations are strained and her husband is away, she may ask the court to give her permission to dispose of stock to buy food or clothing, and to "witness" the transaction, i.e. to take official note of it. The husband has exclusive control over his personal property, and his wife may not dispose of it in his absence, except in extreme cases when the household is in desperate need; she must then adopt the procedure just described.

Miscellaneous Property Rights

Wealthy people often lend part of their stock to their friends and retainers as *mafisa*. They do so to "spread" the risk of stock theft, to save hiring herd-boys, to take advantage of good grazing in areas to which they might otherwise be denied access, and above all to cement personal and political loyalties. *Mafisa* owners have very wide rights to such stock. They can use it for milking, riding transport or draught; they may sell the wool to their own profit; they may eat the meat of animals that die or have to be destroyed and, provided they look after it reasonably well and remain loyal to the owner, they should not be deprived of it in favour of someone else. The only conditions and restrictions are that they should occasionally report to the owner, though few people do so; they may not kill any of the stock except those that have to be destroyed by reason of old age, sickness or injury; they may not dispose of any except in exchange for breeding stock or when an exceptionally profitable opportunity occurs, and then the proceeds must be given to the owner; they may not earmark the stock as their own property; and they must return them when the owner wishes to look after them himself.

Other rights are those which people have to different parts of animals killed on various occasions, ceremonial and otherwise:

1. Formerly the chief was entitled to the breast (*sefuba*) of all game animals killed in his district, as well as the skins of lions and leopards.

2. The boys' *mophato* should be given the breasts of the cattle killed by each initiate's father and maternal uncle.

3. A maternal uncle is entitled to the right shoulder of the ox killed to "settle" his nephew's grave.

4. The *tlhabiso* ox killed at a wedding is supposed to be divided among various kinsmen according to detailed rules.

5. The head of any animal killed should be given to the *khotla* for consumption by those who helped to skin the animal and peg out its hide. These rights are customary rather than legal.

Inheritance

The property of an unmarried female is inherited by her parents. Her clothing goes to her mother to be distributed as the latter may wish, usually among her sisters and other female members of the household. Money and any stock go to her parents but, at the discretion of her father, they may be shared out among her brothers and sisters and other close kinspeople. The property of an unmarried man goes to his father and may be distributed among his brothers and other close kinsmen as the father may direct. The deceased's maternal uncle is entitled to certain intimate items, such as one or two pairs of trousers and other articles of clothing, one or two blankets, a watch or some other small personal possession, a gun and the deceased's best saddle and favourite horse. He should also be given an ox in exchange for the one he should slaughter to "settle" his nephew's grave.

The property of a married woman belongs to her household and is administered by her husband, except for her personal effects such as clothing, which should be given to her mother-in-law. The latter may give some of this to the deceased's mother or brother's wife. Her pots and other household utensils will continue to be used by her husband and children.

The property of a married man is inherited by his widow and children, except for the items enumerated above which go to his maternal uncle. In the case of a polygynist, each household inherits the property allocated to and owned by it during his lifetime. The balance of his personal property and all unallocated property is inherited by his senior household.

A monogamist's property is administered by his eldest son in consultation with the widow. If the son is not old enough to do so, she should take charge and administer it with the help of her husband's brothers. By virtue of his senior status, the elder brother should have most authority in this, but should one of his younger brothers cohabit with (*kenela*) her, the latter, by virtue of his intimacy with her, may possibly have the greater say. As her son grows up, he has an increasingly greater authority, until finally, when he marries, he becomes personally responsible for the property. He should consult with his mother and uncles, but may overrule them where there is a clash of opinions.

TRADE, EXCHANGE, WEALTH AND PROPERTY 183

Paul v. 'Ma Paul, August 1936.
'Ma P sold an ox to pay for her daughter's initiation. Her son P had agreed to the expense involved but had said he would pay cash as he did not want the ox sold. When she ignored his instruction and sold the ox, he sued her. She was fined 10s. for disregarding his wishes.

On the other hand, if the mother and son do not get on well together, and if he does not support her properly, the former has considerable independence of action, although she should always discuss proposed property transactions with her son before carrying them out. The following case illustrates this point and shows the weight that is attached to due observance of the formalities of consultation:

'Mamasiea v. Motsarapane, February 1936.
'M's food was running out so she bought some grain from M for a calf. (She is a widow. Her son lives about half a mile away from her village and does not support her.) As the calf was too young to leave its mother, it was agreed that she should keep it for the time being. Later, when M asked for the calf, 'M refused to give it up, so he sued her. She was ordered by the court to hand it over to him and was fined 10s. because her refusal smacked of theft, and a further 10s. for having sold the calf wrongfully by not discussing the matter with her son. M was also fined 10s. for dealing with her without any witnesses and without her son, and a further 10s. for earmarking the calf without getting a *bewijs* or stock permit authorizing him to do so.

'Mashoapile v. Shoapile (her son), June 1936.
'M went off to the Free State with a man, T, while her husband was away. When her husband heard about this he said he wanted to have nothing more to do with her, and so gave 30 sheep to his son S and told him to use them in maintaining her. She now sues S, alleging that he had used 9 of these sheep for himself and had disposed of 12 cattle from his sister's *bohali* and had failed to plough for her. His defence is that he put the 30 sheep in the charge of a certain herd-boy and, on their return from the Free State, T went to the cattle-post and took the sheep, saying he had been sent by 'M. He also treated S contemptuously so the latter in a rage and also fearing he would lose all the sheep, seized 3 of them and used them himself, in the thanksgiving ceremony for the birth of his child. There was no evidence that he had misused the cattle. The court found 'M responsible for any loss that may have occurred as she had permitted and encouraged her lover to take the sheep away from her son's herd-boy. It ordered S to forgive his mother and look after her, and it urged her to live peacefully with him. It also ordered T to return the remaining sheep and instructed him that under no circumstances was he to go into their kraal again.

The position is very similar where the deceased was a polygynist. Here each household has its own separate property, which is administered in the ways just described. The only difference is that where the senior son is of age, he may exercise authority over all his father's households (such authority being greatest where a household has no sons or only young sons), but as their sons grow up, marry and become responsible for their affairs, this authority progressively decreases to vanishing point.

Khauli's wife v. Samoele, February 1936.
K and S are half-brothers, each being the eldest in their respective houses. Their father is dead. During K's absence at the mines, S borrowed some of his cattle to make up the *bohali* for his own marriage, promising to return them when his sister got married. As he did not do so, K's wife sued him (K being still away). S refused to answer her complaint, saying it was a domestic matter, but the court ignored this, fined him 10s. for refusing to do so, then heard the case and ordered him to return the cattle immediately (i.e. to return an equivalent number of cattle to those he had borrowed).

This case shows the independence of a polygynist's households, once he is dead, and his senior son is not there to keep them together. It also shows the considerable authority and standing women can achieve in the conduct of their affairs and the administration of property.

"If a man dies leaving only female children, the widow shall be heiress to his estate and property, but she must work in conformity with the wishes of her deceased husband's people who shall in all matters be deemed her guardians."[1] This must not be taken too literally and means no more than that she has a good deal of say in the administration and disposal of this property—more so than where it is administered by her own son—but she still has to consult, and be consulted by, her husband's brother-in-law.

Two exceptions occur in the case of chiefs. Among the "Sons of Moshesh", only the first two or three households have any appreciable amount of property of their own and, except for this, the whole estate goes to the senior son. He is expected to maintain all his father's widows, except those of the principal households which have some property and whose senior sons will probably have been placed as chiefs on their own. The senior son is also entitled to *kenela* his father's junior widows and their daughters' *bohali* cattle will be his property and not that of their individual households. This principle that the senior heir is responsible for all his father's widows, rather than that the heir of each household is responsible for his own mother, placed a heavy burden on the Paramount Chief and other large-scale polygynists. It has now come to be regarded as a burden of office to be met from public funds, and special provision is made in the National Treasury Estimates for allowances to twenty-one widows of former Paramount Chiefs.

The second exception occurred in the case of the senior household of the Tlokoa chiefs. Here, if all went well and everyone lived long enough, the heir was not the son but the grandson. The chief's senior son would be placed on his own in the usual way. The latter's son, instead of growing up at home until old enough to be given a caretaking of his

---
[1] *Laws of Lerotholi*, No. 15.

own, grew up at his grandfather's place, remaining there when he became a man and helping the old man. On the latter's death, this grandson remained where he was, administered his grandfather's personal ward, and inherited his personal property and the property of his senior household. The property of the junior households was inherited by the senior son of each, in the normal way. It is doubtful whether this complicated arrangement was ever fully carried out. Lelingoana observed the necessary preliminaries by placing his son Mosuoe at Sememanyana and keeping his grandson Mokotjo with him at Malingoaneng, until the latter's illness forced him to move to a healthier area; but on Lelingoana's death, political considerations made it inadvisable for Mosuoe to remain in the remote area of Semenanyane and so he followed the usual Basuto custom and moved to Malingoaneng, sending Mokotjo to take his place at Semenanyana. As a result of this, Mosuoe also adopted the usual line of inheritance and inherited Lelingoana's property, although this was criticized by some of the Tlokoa traditionalists.

According to Chief Letsie,[1] Moshesh's son, Sesuto law and custom as long ago as 1870, recognized disposal of property by will, provided a man "disposes of his property justly, but not if he disinherits his legal heirs". But such a practice was very rare and the only instance he could quote was the case of Chief Moshesh. Jobo's reply to the question, "What is your opinion about a law providing that people can make wills?" suggests that Moshesh's action was an innovation rather than accepted practice. "I think it would be a very good thing; if there was such a law, I would make my will at once." Nowadays this is provided for in the Laws of Lerotholi:[2] "But if a man during his lifetime has disposed of his property by will or gift, his intentions must be carried out. Will or gift is a document made by a person during his lifetime, stating what he desires done with his property after his death, if the estate thus willed be his bona fide property and if that is in accordance with the laws and customs of the Basuto." The second proviso is much the same as that mentioned by Chief Letsie above, namely, that the heirs are not disinherited and no radical departure from the normal rules is made, such as bequeathing one household's property to another. In effect, personal property only can be disposed of by will. A significant change, which is admissible but may lead to acrimonious disputes in the courts, is the leaving of property to women.

[1] Laws Commission. This is fully discussed in Chapter XIII.   [2] No. 15.

CHAPTER XIII

POLITICAL ORGANIZATION

BASUTOLAND forms a single political unit. At its head is the Paramount Chief who "has full power and authority over natives resident in Basutoland".[1] Under him the country is divided into districts, sub-districts and wards. Each district is administered by a chief and is subdivided into sub-districts, which may also be further subdivided into lesser sub-districts. Each sub-district is administered by a sub-chief and is, in turn, divided into wards. These wards are the smallest political units in the country and consist of one or more villages plus ploughlands and pastures. In charge of each ward is a headman. In 1939, under the New Native Administration Proclamation (No. 61 of 1938) the country was divided into eighteen districts, varying in size from 30,000 to 130,000 inhabitants, 316 sub-districts, varying from 600 to 20,000 inhabitants and 1,006 wards, varying from less than 50 to over 500 inhabitants. This official division followed the traditional division fairly closely except where it eliminated many of the smaller sub-districts and wards.

This division of the country refers to the Basuto political organization and not to the organization of the British Administration. For governmental purposes the country is also a single unit, under the authority of the Resident Commissioner. It is also subdivided into nine districts, for each of which a District Commissioner is responsible to the Resident Commissioner. Two of these districts (Mokhotlong, and Quthing) coincide with a single district under one chief, Seeiso (now 'Mantsebo) being chief over the whole of Mokhotlong, and Sempe (now Qefate) over the whole of Quthing. The other Government districts include more than one chief's district. Usually the latter all fall within the governmental district, but in three cases there used to be some overlapping; that of Boshooane Peete lay partly in Leribe and partly in Teyateyaneng; Mohale 'Mahao's district lay partly in Mafeteng and partly in Mohale's Hoek, and Sekhonyana Bereng's district lay in the Maseru, Mafeteng and Qacha's Nek districts. So, too, Letsie Motsoene, Chief of Leribe, had jurisdiction over two chiefs in Butha Buthe, which at the time was a government sub-district under Leribe, namely, Kuini Mopeli and 'Matumane Matela. These anomalies have now been straightened out by revising the governmental district boundaries and, in the last case, by raising the status of Butha Buthe to that of a full district, and placing these two chiefs directly under the Paramount Chief, so that there is no overlapping between the two systems.

[1] Declaration No. 1.

The terms chief, sub-chief, headman, and district, sub-district, ward, are not always used strictly in accordance with the definitions given above, as the political organization is so complicated that strict adherence to them would encumber the narrative without really clarifying it. Besides denoting one of the major subdivisions of the country, the term "district" is often used for any large political unit or area; "sub-district" is often used to denote a comparatively small political area that is a subdivision of some larger area, whether such larger area is a "district" in the strict sense of the word or a subdivision of a district; "ward" is occasionally used to denote a very small political area such as a small sub-district of minor importance. The terms chief, sub-chief and headman are sometimes used in a similar way to denote "important" authority, authority of middling importance, and "minor" or "unimportant" authority.

The Basuto have terms for these divisions and authorities although they are not used with any precision. The Paramount Chief is *"morena o moholo"*, literally "great chief"; a chief is *morena*, and this term is also a courtesy mode of address given to anyone of importance; sub-chief is *morenana*, literally "little chief", and the English term "sub-chief" itself is often used. The term *khosana* is also used (diminutive of *khosi*—"chief") but is decried by the purists as being Sechuana and not proper Sesuto. A headman is *ramotse*, literally "father of the village". This term is applicable also to a village headman, but the two kinds of headman are sometimes distinguished by using the diminutive form *rametsana* (usually in the plural *"bo-rametsana"*) for the latter. The Sesuto terms for district, sub-district and ward are vague: words such as *naha, sebaka* or *setereke* are used, but they really mean little more than "area". A headman or sub-chief is sometimes referred to as *ra-sebaka*. The term *setereke* is often used to denote "district" or a large and well-knit "sub-district".

As the terms "chief" and "sub-chief" have definite connotations of status, many important authorities who are technically sub-chiefs, in that they are subordinate to chiefs, resent the title, feeling that it implies a degree of inferiority they are not prepared to accept. Thus it happened that when the authorities were gazetted in 1939,[1] several authorities who were under chiefs and should therefore have been called "sub-chief", such as Kuini Mopeli mentioned above, were by courtesy styled "chiefs". To meet this point in a bigger way, the National Council recommended in 1946 that the term "sub-chief" be abolished and that all sub-chiefs be called chiefs. This is a comforting salve to wounded feelings, but it does not solve the real difficulties of status. It also maintains the existing terminological ambiguities, for, to some extent, it still reflects "importance", in that the title "chief" is denied to some people who are in charge of sub-districts, but are not considered important enough to merit verbal promotion from "sub-chief" to "chief";

[1] High Commissioner's Notice, No. 171 of 1939.

instead, such authorities have been verbally demoted to "headman". In spite of the National Council's recommendation, the term "sub-chief", either in its English form or its Sesuto equivalent (*morenana*) is still used.

Attention must be drawn to one further difficulty. The Basutoland Government officially uses the term "ward" to denote not the *smallest* political division but the largest, i.e. the major divisions into which the country is split. My main reason for not following this is that in view of the basic similarity between the Basuto political organization and that of the Bechuana, as described by Schapera, I have deliberately tried to use terms similar to his wherever possible, in the hope of minimizing confusion between the two. Another reason is that the word "ward" is also used locally, both officially and colloquially, to describe parts of these major divisions, particularly in the phrase "personal ward", which refers to an area directly under a chief or sub-chief; this ambiguity is avoided by limiting the use of the word to the smallest undivided, or basic, political unit. For this reason, too, I have avoided the use of the term "ward-chief". This term is the official designation of the chief in charge of what I defined in the opening paragraph of this chapter as a "district", who is directly subordinate to the Paramount Chief. The term, *morena oa setereke* was also recommended by the National Council in 1948.

A further refinement introduced by the National Council at the same time is the classification of some of the "ward-chiefs" as "principal chiefs" (*morena oa sehloho*). Ten "ward-chiefs" were singled out for this honour. This differentiation seems to have been based on genealogical seniority modified by political importance, and to be a matter of prestige rather than of function; but I was unable to follow this up and so have not referred to it again.

The ten principal chiefs are:

'Mantsebo (acting Paramount Chief, widow of Seeiso, senior son of Griffith, second son of Lerotholi).
Bereng Griffith[1] (junior half-brother of Seeiso).
Theko Makhaola (senior son of Makhaola, who was third son of Lerotholi).
Jacottet Lerotholi (junior son of Lerotholi).
Mamohlalefi Bereng (widow of Lerotholi's brother's son).
Seeiso Maama (son of Lerotholi's half-brother Maama).
Qefate Sempe (grandson of Lerotholi's half-brother Nkoebe).
(All the above are descendants of Moshesh's senior son Letsie.)
Letsie Motsoene (senior lineal descendant of Moshesh's second son Molapo).
Gabashane Masupha[1] (senior lineal descendant of Moshesh's third son Masupha).
Ramabanta Api.

[1] Executed in 1949 after conviction for "ritual murder". I do not know the position regarding their successors.

POLITICAL ORGANIZATION

POLITICAL STRUCTURE: MOKHOTLONG DISTRICT
DIAGRAM NO. I: 1936

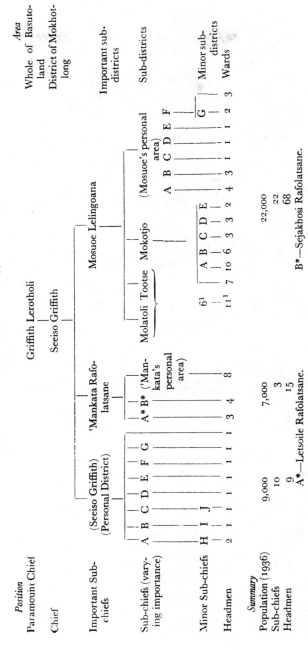

One final terminological point should be noted. The word "chief" is occasionally used in the sense of head of a tribe. For the most part, this refers to the early days before the break-up of the tribes and the amalgamation of their fragments under Moshesh, but it is still applicable to the heads of the few recognized and politically coherent tribes that still exist, such as the Khoakhoa and the Tlokoa. This meaning of the term has recently received statutory recognition from the Government; for instance, Mosuoe Lelingoana was gazetted in 1948 as "Chief of the Batlokoa". The full practical implications of this designation have not yet been worked out by the Government, so it is not possible to say whether it has any special meaning or is merely a courtesy title.

The basic form of the political structure is the same throughout the territory although it varies in some details from one area to another. This is illustrated from Mokhotlong in diagram I.

In 1936 Seeiso Griffith was head of the district and subordinate to his father, Griffith Lerotholi, the Paramount Chief. The district was divided into three major sub-districts. One of these was Seeiso's personal district, the second 'Mankata Rafolatsane's and the third, Mosuoe Lelingoana's. The first two originally formed one district under Rafolatsane Letsie, 'Mankata's predecessor and father-in-law; the circumstances of their division will be described later. The third sub-district was the Batlokoa area or district. Before 1925, both this and Rafolatsane's whole district came directly under the Paramount Chief.

Each of these sub-districts was divided into further sub-districts and into wards. Seeiso's was divided into seven of the former (A–G) and one of the latter, directly under him; three of these sub-districts (A, B and C) were divided into minor sub-districts (H, I and J), and all of these (D–J) were divided into wards, each under a headman. Besides this, each of these sub-chiefs, and Seeiso himself, had his own personal ward. This section of the Mokhotlong district thus had Seeiso at its head, ten sub-chiefs of varying importance and status and nine headmen. Another way of putting this is to say that this section of the district was divided into twenty wards, comprising the personal ward of Seeiso, the personal wards of ten sub-chiefs and the wards of nine headmen, and that these wards were amalgamated in the ways shown above, to form sub-districts of varying size and importance, and ultimately to form part of the district.

'Mankata's sub-district was simpler, but basically similar. There were eight headmen and two sub-chiefs directly under her, and seven headmen under the two sub-chiefs, making a total of eighteen wards in this area.

The position is similar in Mosuoe's sub-district (or the Batlokoa district, as I often call it, in view of its size and importance) although more complicated than in either of the other two. It was subdivided into four main sub-districts, one of which was Mosuoe's own personal one,

POLITICAL ORGANIZATION

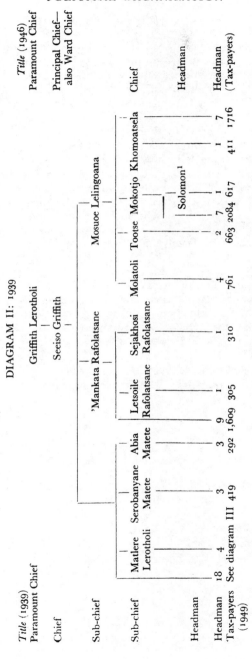

DIAGRAM II: 1939

[1] Solomon's importance is such that he is probably entitled to be called "chief" under the 1946 nomenclature.

the other three being under his uncle Molatoli, his brother Tootse, and his son Mokotjo. Each of these was again sub-divided in the usual way into further sub-districts and wards. The whole area under the control of Mosuoe thus has twenty-one other sub-chiefs and sixty-eight headmen, making a total of ninety authorities; in other words, it is divided into ninety wards, which gradually build up, in the way shown above, to form sub-districts of varying size and importance, and ultimately part of the district itself.

After the promulgation of the Native Authorities' Proclamation in 1938, some of the foregoing authorities and areas were not recognized, minor authorities (especially in the Tlokoa area) were eliminated and the whole structure was partially modified and simplified. This is shown in diagram II. The old terminology, used in 1939, when the recognized authorities were gazetted, is shown on the left of the diagram; on the right, the new terminology adopted by the National Council in 1946. The diagram incorporates various minor modifications and corrections of the original Government Notice, No. 171 of 1939.

To facilitate comparison with Diagram No. 1, the same names of the authorities have been retained, although in several cases the previous incumbent has died or been replaced.

One important change, made about 1945, should be mentioned. Matlere, the chief's right-hand man, was promoted to a more important sub-chieftainship, which had existed in Rafolatsane's time and was now resuscitated. Several headmen who had previously come directly under Seeiso were placed under him and his vacated position was given to his brother Makhahlela, the title being reduced in 1946 from that of sub-chief to that of headman. The new arrangement is shown below.

DIAGRAM III: 1946

Chief		Seeiso Griffith		Principal Chief
Sub-chief		Matlere	(as before)	Chief
Sub-chief		Makhahlela		Headman
Headman	9	5	8	Headman
Tax-payers (1949)	854	524	595	

The changes since 1936, apart from nomenclature, may be summarized as follows:

	1936	1939	1946
Chiefs	1	1	1
Sub-chiefs	35	12	13
Headmen	92	61	61

The numbers of tax-payers (1949) in each sub-chieftainship have been given to show the variation in size of these divisions. A complete list is given in Appendix V of the tax-payers under each headman, which shows how the wards also vary in size. Sub-chiefs, such as Mosuoe and 'Mankata, have thousands of people and many authorities under them; others have only one headman and few followers. In fact, measured in these terms, sub-chiefs such as Mosuoe are the equals of Lowland authorities such as Peete, whose status is that of full chief. The significance of this is that rank and title are dependent on position in the political hierarchy and are not correlated with clear-cut differences of function.

The chieftainship is one of the most important institutions of the Basuto and questions of succession are among the most burning and contentious matters in Sesuto public life. The law in regard to succession is given pride of place in the "Laws of Lerotholi" and appears at the head of that authoritative compilation.

"Succession to the chieftainship in Basutoland shall be by right of birth, that is, the first-born male of the first wife. If the first wife has no male issue then the first-born male of the next wife in succession shall be heir to the chieftainship. Provided that if a chief dies leaving no male issue the chieftainship shall devolve upon the male following according to the succession of wives."[1]

In other words, the chieftainship is hereditary in the male line and usually passes from father to son. This bare statement of the Law, though it accurately reflects the basic principles of succession, does not cover the many exceptions and variations which may occur.

Formerly, although succession remained within the chief's family, the law was sometimes modified by extraneous considerations, such as the popularity or ability of the claimants. Thus Moshesh himself succeeded his uncle as head of a small tribal group, before he created his unique position as Paramount Chief. Nor have his successors all been in the direct line of descent, for Griffith succeeded his elder brother Letsie II and ousted his nephew Makhaola, who was born posthumously to Letsie's second wife (his first wife having had no male issue) and was therefore the true heir according to this law. Many other such cases are cited by Ellenberger and MacGregor,[2] such as Moletsane's chieftainship over the Taung, acquired at the expense of the senior branch of his family, and the chieftainship of the Tsoeneng, which passed into the hands of Khiba whom "the people made chief in preference to his elder brother Lekhetho"[3] on account of his reputation for wisdom and courage. Similarly, the Tlokoa chieftainship passed some generations ago to the cadet line of the Ba-Lefe.

Nowadays, the first wife is always the senior wife, but formerly this was not always so. Sometimes a young chief was allowed to marry

[1] Declaration No. 2.   [2] *History of the Basuto*, pp. 57–9.   [3] Ibid., pp. 86–7.

women of his own choice, either with his father's help or at his own expense, and these women were not regarded as potential mothers of the heir. The "true" wife, the "mother of the tribe", was chosen by the chief in consultation with his relatives and counsellors; her name was publicly announced and the tribe contributed towards her *bohali* cattle and to the domestic herd to be attached to her household. She took precedence over her husband's previous wives and her son was the heir. For example, Ramokhele, founder of the Kubung or Baramokhele sub-tribe, a division of the Taung tribe, married his principal wife, mother of his heir, Leqhaqha, long after his first wife who was mother of Mosololi. Mosololi acted as chief during his father's old age, but[1] "there was no trouble about the succession for Mosololi himself was very old when his father died and did not live long after him so that Leqhaqha succeeded to the chieftainship quite quietly and as a matter of course".

Again, a wife who was genealogically senior to the others or came from a senior clan might take precedence, even though not the first to be married. Thus the second wife of Nkopane, a Koena chief, successfully claimed to be the senior "by reason of her being of the ruling house of the same tribe as her husband—she could not be preceded by a stranger at the first-fruit ceremonies".[2] Although great store is still set by the geneaological status of the senior wife and, as described earlier, marriage with one's father's brother's daughter is especially desirable for this reason, it is unlikely nowadays that a claim by a later wife to seniority based on such status would be entertained.[3] Precedence may nevertheless be given to later wives who are married by '*mala* or *seantlo* customs.[4]

Succession of the first son of the first or senior wife is not always automatic. According to traditional Sesuto law all children born to a man's wife, whether begotten by him or not, and even if begotten after his death, are regarded as his legitimate issue. This rule was probably never accepted without qualification, and nowadays is frequently challenged by those who regard paternity as the prime basis of legitimacy. This latter view is coming to be accepted by the courts, which sometimes allow a man to repudiate his wife's illegitimate children and place them in the custody of her people. Several cases have occurred

---

[1] Ibid., p. 65.
[2] Ibid., pp. 84–5.
[3] The question of Seeiso's successor is already the subject of discussion and intrigue, although the heir apparent is still a boy. The senior wife has no son, so according to the ordinary rules, the son of the second wife 'Mabereng should succeed. But in 1949 the story was being circulated in Mokhotlong that as 'Mabereng was a commoner's daughter, the succession should pass to the son of the third wife, 'Maleshoboro, who was a chief's daughter. Such gossip has little legal support, but it is significant that so much importance should still be attached to the woman's status.
[4] See Chapter V, p. 82.

where this view has coloured discussion regarding succession to an important position. For instance,[1] Peete, Moshesh's grandfather, who was born posthumously and should have succeeded his father, did not do so, partly no doubt because he was a posthumous child and partly because his genitor was a Tebele and therefore of low class. A similar case was freely canvassed among the Tlokoa in 1935; Mosuoe's senior son, Mokotjo, died without male issue, but at the time of his death his senior wife was pregnant. It was generally supposed that as Mokotjo had become impotent through illness, and as his wife had been consorting with a Tebele servant, the latter was the father; consequently there was a great deal of talk about refusing to recognize the child as heir, should it be a boy, as he would become chief of the Tlokoa and it was intolerable to have a chief of such lowly origin. The point was actually never put to the test as the child was a girl.

The case of Makhaola also illustrates the weakening of the traditional law regarding posthumous children. As the posthumous son of Letsie II and the child of a close kinsman of the house of Moshesh, he should have succeeded Letsie as Paramount Chief rather than Letsie's younger brother, Griffith. His claims have, however, never been tested legally. They would have little chance of success as they rest on too flimsy a legalistic basis which nowadays has scant public sentiment to support it. It is significant that when it was proposed that Griffith should take over the paramountcy unfettered by any restriction with regard to succession, i.e. that he should sit on his father's chair "with both buttocks" instead of as a regent, only one person objected on the grounds that this would prejudice the rights of any posthumous heir, and even this objection was eventually withdrawn.[2]

A peculiar case may also occur when the heir's mother was never actually married to the deceased. This may happen when a chief or a chief's senior son dies before he has married. In such an event, a woman is "married to the grave", and is taken as a wife in his name by his younger brother. By a legal fiction, her children are regarded as the deceased's children and the eldest son should succeed him. Isolated cases of this custom occur, but are seldom tested in court. At Phamong, a headman's senior son died unmarried, but later a wife was married to "his grave", and to her a son was born. While this boy was still a child, the headman died and was succeeded by his second son. The latter refused to give up the headmanship when the boy grew up. The rights of the matter were never clarified as the boy was not interested in the position and did not contest his uncle's usurpation. Another case concerned the eldest son of Mosuoe's second house. This son died and a woman was married in his name to his younger brother Qoqhoqo. The fiction was not, however, seriously observed and Qoqhoqo, who later married another woman, regarded the first as his senior

[1] Ellenberger and MacGregor, pp. 99-100.   [2] Judgment, p. 34.

wife and the second as his junior. This common-sense attitude was shared by everyone else.

Questions concerning succession are dealt with in the first instance by a council of the important members of the chief's family, together with the heads of the leading sections of the tribe. In the case of the Paramount Chief and the Moshesh lineage, this council is comprehensively known as the "Sons of Moshesh" and consists of the leading scions of the Moshesh lineage, and their leading councillors,[1] together with the few tribal chiefs who remain, such as the chiefs of the Makhoakhoa and Bataung. Lerotholi's succession (1891) was supported by sixteen chiefs, "all the principal chiefs of Basutoland, of whom one was actually a son of Moshesh, ten grandsons, four nephews and one more distantly related". His son, Letsie II (1905), was supported by thirty-one chiefs, including every chief of importance, and was announced to the Basutoland Council. The question of his successor was debated at length at a meeting of the Sons of Moshesh attended by all the principal chiefs, and their decision in favour of Griffith was finally conveyed to the Resident Commissioner by a letter signed by two sons of Letsie I (uncles of Letsie II and Griffith) "on behalf of the sons of Letsie and the Matsieng people".[2]

Formerly, if these family councils did not settle the matter, it was decided by fighting. Nowadays, a dispute concerning a minor chieftainship is referred to the native courts, and an important one to the Basutoland Council. If that body fails to reach a decision it is settled by the Government after due administrative inquiry. Dissatisfied parties may then contest this decision in the High Court, and finally, as in the Mojela case, take it to the Privy Council. Occasionally, the chief "points" out or nominates his successor before he dies, as Moshesh nominated Letsie I, but unless he happens to choose the heir according to the foregoing principles, this nomination has little practical effect. For instance, in 1927, Griffith nominated his favourite son Bereng as his successor. Seeiso, his other son, immediately objected. (Griffith's senior wife had no issue, his second wife was the mother of Seeiso, born in 1905, and his third wife the mother of Bereng, born in 1902.) Griffith thereupon convened a court of the Sons of Moshesh, consisting of seventy chiefs, to determine the matter. In the end only thirty-three voted, twenty-two supporting Bereng and eleven Seeiso. The High Commissioner was unwilling to accept their decision and announced that, while their views would receive due consideration, the eventual decision would lie with the nation; meantime he suggested a secret ballot, but this was not accepted by Griffith. On the latter's death, in 1939, the Government convened a meeting of the Sons of Moshesh to discuss the succession and the decision was in favour of Seeiso.

The question of Seeiso's successor was even more complicated. In

[1] Judgment, p. 41.   [2] Summarized from Judgment, pp. 33-5.

view of the rivalry between them, Seeiso did not nominate his brother Bereng to act for him during his illness in 1940 (which finally proved fatal), but appointed his principal counsellor Gabashane instead. On his death, Gabashane called a meeting of the Sons of Moshesh at Maseru where Seeiso died. Discord arose and the place of the meeting was challenged, so the proceedings were resumed at Matsieng, the Paramount Chief's headquarters, some days later. Feelings ran high and an attempt to single out a particular generation of counsellors, the Sons of Letsie, was thwarted by those present on the grounds that this was a national question. As the matter "was clearly incapable of peaceful decision" without Government direction, it was referred to the Government authorities, who summoned the Sons of Moshesh to the capital. Bereng, as "the successor and present head of the Sons of Letsie", protested, to no avail and without much justification, that this procedure was "very much against Laws, Customs and our precedents". The meeting, though virtually one of the Sons of Moshesh, was attended by all the leading chiefs, their councillors and people, whether they were descendants of Moshesh or not, and anyone who wished to do so was allowed to speak. It was overwhelmingly in favour of appointing Seeiso's widow 'Mantsebo to be regent rather than Bereng, Seeiso's son and heir being a minor, and the decision was accepted by the Government. This decision was subsequently challenged in the High Court on the grounds that the procedure followed, as summarized above, was irregular and illegal, but the learned judge found otherwise.[1]

The wording of Declaration No. 2, quoted above, clearly implies that the succession cannot be claimed through the female line, but cases have occurred where this has been attempted. For instance, Letsie I's senior wife had no male offspring, only a daughter Senate. Moshesh, "disliking the idea of going outside the great house for succession, adopted the strange device of marrying her to her cousin Joseph (Letsie's brother's son). Their second child was a boy, Motsoene, and Moshesh then called a National Pitso where "by his order it was authoritatively published that Letsie would succeed him and be followed in succession by the infant Motsoene who was held up to public gaze". The boy's pretensions were, however, never seriously canvassed although "encouraged by the enemies of Lerotholi (Letsie's son) whenever they might usefully serve as a screen to cover the intrigues directed against him".[2]

Occasionally a woman may become chief. Her succession is not by right of birth but by virtue of her marriage and the death, without male issue, of her husband. Two cases occurred in Mokhotlong. In the first case, Mokotjo, senior son of Mosuoe Lelingoana died in 1936 without sons (although he had four wives). As his next brother, who should have followed him, was not popular nor expected to make a

[1] Judgment, pp. 48-55.   [2] Lagden, pp. 583-4.

good ruler, Mosuoe allowed his senior widow Toeba to succeed him. She will probably hold the position until her death. It has been suggested that she might even succeed Mosuoe as chief of the Tlokoa, but it is doubtful whether this would be accepted by the tribe. The second case concerned Chief Rafolatsane who died in 1932. His senior wife was childless. His second wife produced two sons, the senior of whom, Pheko, married 'Mankata. Both these sons predeceased him, leaving no male issue. His third wife had a son, who was crippled and unambitious. On the death of the chief this son might have succeeded him but, for political reasons, 'Mankata was given the succession. Since 1936 she has been insane, and a regent has been acting in her name. The present regent is Lerato, widow of Rafolatsane's second son.

When a chief or the heir to a chieftainship is incapable of ruling properly for any reason, a regent is appointed to look after his affairs and rule in his stead. The regent has full rights of chieftainship except that of passing the chieftainship to his own son. He should hand over to his ward as soon as the latter can take over, although cases do occur where, for various reasons, such as outstanding ability or personality, the regent has retained his position until his death. Occasionally, the regent usurps the chieftainship and passes it on to his own heir, usually when the ward is a minor, whose claims to the succession are based on flimsy legalisms such as those described above.

The relationship between ward and regent differs according to circumstances. Where the ward's incapacity is due to senility or imbecility, sheer incompetence or prolonged absence, due, for instance, to active military service or imprisonment, the regency is usually given to his senior paternal uncle, younger brother or son, depending on their relative ages, or to his wife. If the ward is a minor, his regent is usually his paternal uncle or his mother.

There are no hard and fast rules determining whether the regent should be a man or a woman. Men are usually preferred as the conduct of public affairs is considered a man's function and privilege rather than a woman's. They are also preferred because it is feared that a female regent may jeopardize the chieftainship through her weaker grasp of affairs or through the rivalries that are likely to occur between her and her mother-in-law and her brothers-in-law. The personality of the people concerned and the political circumstances of the case usually settle the matter. Thus the famous Mantatisi, "Queen of the Tlokoa", as she used to be called, who ruled with skill and courage during her son Sekonyela's minority, simply swept her brother-in-law aside by sheer force of character. So, too, the ten women who occupied positions of authority and gave evidence in the Bereng regency case, owed their preferment to their character, ability and intelligence.[1]

Where there is a danger of an uncle being tempted to usurp his young

[1] Judgment, pp. 8-9.

nephew's position, the deceased's mother or widow may become regent to protect the boy's interests. The most outstanding example of this sort is that of the present Paramount Chief 'Mantsebo, whose appointment was largely due to the fear that Bereng would try to use the regency as a stepping-stone to the paramountcy. Yet another reason for the appointment of a female regent is the hope entertained by political schemers of deriving some advantage from the dissensions that are likely to follow her appointment. A case in point is that of 'Mankata, described above. Her appointment was supported by Seeiso who wished to use her weakness to strengthen his own position at Mokhotlong.

Where a polygynist is concerned, the regency must be held by the senior widow, even if, as in the case of 'Mantsebo, the heir is not her son. Since, and probably because of, the appointment of 'Mantsebo in 1941, there has been a tendency to appoint women as regents for minors rather than men. In all the five cases which occurred in Mokhotlong between 1939 and 1949, where the heir was a minor, his mother was appointed regent rather than his uncle.

Positions as chiefs, sub-chiefs and even headmen may also be acquired through appointment. People are given "caretakings" or "placed" in authority, as chief, sub-chief or headman over a particular area. This system is known to other Bantu, such as the Tswana, where the senior sons of a chief are given positions of responsibility as their father's representatives over a portion of his country; but it has been developed to such a degree by the Basuto and has become so characteristic of their political system, as well as being a serious administrative problem, that it deserves to be treated in detail.

The original custom was based on the sensible theory that the senior son, who would eventually succeed his father, should begin to learn the law and art of government as soon as he became a man, and that the best way of doing so was through the actual exercise of responsibility during his father's lifetime. Moreover, it was realized that the best way of reducing possible jealousy and friction between them and so of minimizing the danger that frustrated ambition would lead to intrigue and rebellion, was for the son to exercise this responsibility as far away from his father as possible. This latter point also encouraged the sending of some of the chief's other sons away, and so the practice grew of giving all but the most junior sons caretakings of their own. Moshesh developed the system still further as a means of governing his huge domain. At first he placed his reliable warriors over the more unruly sections of his people, and later, when things had quietened down, he divided the country into five parts, one of which he retained for himself and the other four he placed under his four principal sons, Letsie, Molapo, Masupha and Majara. He also placed some of his brothers and other sons over smaller areas and rewarded and strengthened the loyalty of his councillors and braves by giving them caretakings also. His successors carried this system to extremes, not only by placing their sons and favourites, but by allowing them to place their sons and friends as well. Owing to the extensive polygyny of many of the chiefs, the numbers of their sons and sons' sons multiplied exceedingly. As there was a limit to the carrying capacity of the country and the number of additional positions that could be created, many of these new authorities were imposed on or substituted for existing authorities. The position had become oppressive enough in 1906 for Dieterlen to write, "the 'royal family' has become cumbersome and sometimes dangerous to the public peace".[1] Nearly thirty years later, it had gone so far that Pim could quote, as fair comment, the remark of a speaker in the National Council, "that there are now as many chiefs in Basutoland as there are stars in the heavens."[2] A brake has been put on the proliferation of authorities by the Government's introduction of the Basutoland Native Administrative Proclamation,[3] but the system still continues.

The position of Mokhotlong, which has passed through all the above phases in sixty years, is typical and shows clearly how the system works. This district was first occupied by the Tlokoa shortly after 1880. Their chief, Lelingoana, who owed allegiance direct to the Paramount Chief, Moshesh's senior son and successor Letsie I, divided the occupied areas into four sub-districts of approximately equal size which he placed under his paternal uncle, his half-brother, his brother-in-law and himself. He also kept the unoccupied areas, which were used for cattle-post grazing, under his direct control. Within these sub-districts, his principal warriors and other relations were given jurisdiction over wards, in which they lived with their families, relations and friends. Clan heads were placed in charge of similar wards, predominantly occupied by members of their clans. Later, as the tribe grew, new areas were thrown open for occupation and placed under Lelingoana's senior son as a fifth district. Some of the wards also became large enough to be subdivided and were split into two or three sub-divisions, at the head of which sons or brothers of the original headman were placed as headmen. The original ward *ipso facto* became a sub-district and the head a sub-chief. Later, Lelingoana tried to re-group some of these sub-districts into a single larger sub-district over which he wanted to place another of his sons, but this appointment was vetoed by the Paramount Chief.

The Tlokoa were followed by a mixed collection of Basuto who settled in the vacant country between them and the eastern boundary of Basutoland. Rafolatsane, one of the then Paramount Chief's sons, was later placed as chief over them and the country they occupied. He divided the country into several large wards, over which he appointed, as headmen, men who had followed him up from the Lowlands or who were leaders of the people who had preceded him. Later some of these

---

[1] Dieterlen, 1912.   [2] Pim Report, p. 48.   [3] Proclamation No. 61 of 1938.

wards became sub-districts when they were subdivided to deal with the growing population. Later still, Rafolatsane placed his sons over some of these wards and sub-districts.

Until 1925, both Lelingoana and Rafolatsane were mutually independent chiefs, both subordinate to the Paramount Chief. In that year the then Paramount Chief Griffith sent his son Seeiso to be chief over them and their combined districts. He thereby reduced both to the technical status of sub-chiefs. Both protested strongly and the Paramount Chief was compelled to promise that for the rest of their lives they would both continue to be regarded as chiefs, although subordinate to Seeiso, to whose court appeals from their courts would now lie instead of proceeding direct to the Paramount Chief's court as hitherto. Lelingoana's area was left intact, but Rafolatsane was asked to point out a "small area" for Seeiso's village. Later, in 1935, after Rafolatsane's death, his successor was "asked" to give Seeiso an area for his personal holding. This, together with the previous excision, amounted to more than half of Rafolatsane's original district. There Seeiso placed several of his followers and kinsmen as headmen and sub-chiefs, degrading some of the previous authorities and wiping others out. After Lelingoana's death in 1934, the title of his son and successor Mosuoe was officially reduced from that of chief to sub-chief. Soon afterwards (1935) Seeiso began to try and enforce his rights as chief over Mosuoe and ordered his people to plough and gather firewood for him. Mosuoe refused and was sued in Seeiso's court, whence the matter was taken to the Paramount Chief's court at Matsieng. There an ambiguous judgment was given: the fine of two head of cattle inflicted by Seeiso's court was remitted, and Seeiso was ordered not to make Mosuoe plough as the Tlokoa would have to carry their ploughs across the river, but he might "invite him to scoffle". Seeiso was also authorized to order Mosuoe to deliver stray stock to him, but should accept what he gave "and not look under his blankets". Mosuoe tried to appeal to the Government court (the Resident Commissioner's court), but was not allowed to do so because the decision of the Paramount Chief's court was regarded as an administrative and not a judicial one. At a subsequent meeting with the Resident Commissioner, the position was further obscured by an official assurance that "no rights had been taken away from him and that he was looked upon by the Government as being of the same status as his father and that the only change was a verbal one, 'i.e. from chief to sub-chief'." He was further assured by the Government and the Paramount Chief that "it is not the intention to deprive you of any of your rights".[1] Quite what this meant was not made clear. Seeiso continued to insist that he had the right to make Mosuoe, as a subordinate sub-chief, work for him, and the latter insisted that the rights accruing from his father's status as chief included freedom from such subordina-

[1] Official correspondence.

tion. The matter finally came to a head in 1944. The Paramount Chief (now Seeiso's widow 'Mantsebo) asked Mosuoe to "give the chief a land and a knee-haltering area" (*bokhinapere*)—a euphemism for surrendering a portion of his district in the same way as Rafolatsane's successor had had to do. Mosuoe refused, saying "the bird's nest is full", so the Paramount Chief authorized an area to be taken, and this was done by representatives of the Paramount Chief and the Mokhotlong chief, who drew a boundary line round a part of Mosuoe's district. They excised approximately one-fifth of the district in area and one-third in population (1,619 out of 4,920 tax-payers). Mosuoe contested this in the courts, lost his case in the Paramount Chief's court, lost his appeal to the Judicial Commissioner's court and won his appeal to the High Court. The learned judge found for him on a technicality, but made the pertinent suggestion that the official assurance quoted above be clarified, "otherwise enforcement of the decision to make him a sub-chief may be regarded as a breach of faith and result in the creation of a lasting grievance and sense of injustice, for this assurance can hardly be reconciled with a step which, in effect, deprives appellant of all authority over a third of the Batlokoa people and about a quarter of the area under him."[1] Two years later, Mosuoe's title was amended and he was "recognized as Chief of the Batlokoa, Malingoaneng, in the Mokhotlong district subordinate to the Chief of Mokhotlong".[2] Quite how this affects the position is not clear and the action suggested by the judge has not yet been taken. And there the matter rests.

These events have been described at some length for they illustrate a process which has been happening all over Basutoland. Thanks to the longevity and the outstanding character of Lelingoana and possibly also to the peculiar circumstances under which the Tlokoa were accepted into Basutoland and given this area, Mosuoe has been luckier than most. As in Mokhotlong, each of the other seventeen districts of Basutoland is under a "Child of Moshesh", a brother, cousin or uncle of the Paramount Chief. Many of them have been placed over earlier and therefore junior scions of the Moshesh lineage who, though still important and ranking among the leading native authorities, have been reduced in grade. Practically all the old tribal chiefs have been degraded and although some are still tribal chiefs in the same way as Mosuoe is, namely the chief of the Taung and the chief of the Khoakhoa, others have been more or less completely eliminated. For instance, the descendants of Moroosi, chief of the Baphuthi, who were among the original inhabitants of the country, were systematically demoted and their positions whittled away, until to-day they are nothing more than rather junior headmen.

[1] High Court. No. 11-46. Mosuoe Lelingoana *v.* Paramount Chief.
[2] High Commissioner's Notice No. 161 of 1948. Some months earlier Chief Moeketsi Mokhele was recognized "Chief of the Bataung in the Mohale's Hoek District".

As intimated above, the chief advantage of this system is that it gives the chief's heir political training and experience, keeps him occupied and reduces the chance of his becoming restive and rebellious. It is also a convenient means of rewarding faithful service and of subduing and breaking up intractable tribes. This last point was important in the old days as a means of compelling and safeguarding the unification of the nation; but now that this has been achieved, the old dangers have passed and the paramountcy of the House of Moshesh is assured, its continued application is quite unwarranted. Properly used, it might prove a valuable sanction for efficient administration, but this is not likely to be achieved as the power is wielded by people who, too often, are inefficient and corrupt themselves.

The defects of the system and of its hypertrophy are obvious. One is that the placing of new authorities increases the gap between the people and the Paramount Chief, makes him more remote than ever and slows down political and judicial administration. Another is that the placing of an important chief in a settled area upsets the political loyalties and peace of the district and also leads to the undeserved suppression or supersession of junior authorities. This destroys the close clan, kin and personal relationships that often exist between smaller authorities and their people, and brings in outsiders who more often than not belong to a different clan or tribal group, have no personal feelings for or interest in their subjects' affairs and wellbeing, and are mainly concerned with what they themselves can get out of their position. The turmoil, heartburnings, intrigues and unhappiness created by a placing like that of Seeiso at Mokhotlong, with its unchecked plethora of subsidiary placings, may perhaps be dimly perceived from the bare details recounted above. Such important placings do not often happen, but the same kind of unrest occurs, though in proportionately diminished degree, every time a smaller authority is placed. Moreover, each authority naturally wants to be maintained in an appropriate style and so insists on his various rights, which are detailed below. The accumulated burden of these is intolerable.

The Government is opposed to the continuation of this system of placing on the scale hitherto practised, and has issued a directive to the effect that "before a Chief, Sub-chief or Headman is recognized in future the Administration must satisfy itself that the 'placing' is justified, that the allegiance of the people over whom it is proposed to 'place' the new Chief, Sub-chief or Headman will be freely given and that there is, in fact, room for the creation of a further Subordinate Authority".[1] The appointment of all authorities is now subject to the approval of the High Commissioner who is empowered to refuse or revoke any appointment and placing.[2] Hitherto, these powers have been

[1] Explanatory Memorandum, pp. 6-7.
[2] Proclamation No. 61 of 1938, Section 3.

sparingly used and placings, authorized and unauthorized, continue; nevertheless, the fact of their existence damps the chief's enthusiasm for making endless minor placings, and enables the grosser abuses to be checked. The basic principle involved—namely, that "the Authority is, in fact, recognized by the natives themselves"[1] has not yet been extended to the *bokhinapere* custom of taking away a large part of a subordinate authority's area and giving it to a superior authority as his personal area. The superior chief may well be recognized by the people as an authority in the area in that they recognize his general administrative authority over that district; but that is quite a different matter from their acknowledgement of his right to constitute himself their immediate chief in place of their own chief. The Tlokoa, for instance, freely acknowledged Seeiso's general authority over them as chief of Mokhotlong, but they do not acknowledge or accept his claim to detach some of them from their traditional chief Mosuoe and place them directly under himself.

The process of installing a new authority is simple, but differs slightly as between cases of succession and appointment. The death of an authority is immediately reported to his senior, who, in turn, if the deceased is important, reports to the Paramount Chief. The message in this latter case may be accompanied by a gift of cattle from the deceased's people to "console" the Paramount Chief for his loss. Public affairs are carried on by the deceased's son, brother, uncle or leading councillor until the family council decides who should be heir and when he should be installed. The decision has to be approved by the senior authority.

The installation takes place at a *pitso* (public gathering), when the senior authority's representative or the person who has been acting in the deceased's place presents the heir to the people. He calls upon him to rule wisely, firmly and fairly, and to heed the advice of his kinsmen and councillors. The people are also exhorted to support their new head. Other important relations and sectional leaders follow, speaking in much the same vein. Important chiefs are later summoned to Matsieng to greet the Paramount Chief.

Occasionally, a very old authority, who wishes to retire from his position, may bring his son and heir to the chief with the request that he be recognized in his place. If this request is granted, the heir is "received" by the chief who publicly announces his recognition of the succession and gives him a short lecture on his duties and obligations.

The heir of a minor authority usually does not have a previous caretaking of his own but lives in his father's village. On his accession, he continues to live there so that no change of residence is involved. The heir of more important authorities has usually had his own caretaking where he lived in his own separate village. On his accession, he should leave his previous home to come nearer the centre of things; but instead

[1] Ibid., p. 15.

of going to his father's village, he should build his own nearby and establish a new court there, and he should do so as soon as possible after the mourning is over. The site of the village is medically protected in the usual way and a small grass hut is roughly built more or less in the centre of it. The chief should spend the first night there, with his wife, in order to "establish" the medicines; thereafter, if he does not wish to live there himself until a more substantial house has been built, he should depute a favourite to "keep the place warm" in his stead. He must, however, use the new court forthwith.

He is now responsible for three villages—his father's, his own old one and his new one—and for three administrative and judicial areas, each with its own court: namely, the whole district, and his own and his father's personal caretakings. His senior son should now look after his old village and personal caretaking, or failing a son, some other kinsman or trusted friend, while his father's favourite son (*mosalalapeng*) "he who remains at home", should stay in their father's village to look after the widows and to "keep the old court warm". For a time this court continues to serve his father's old personal caretaking but is gradually eclipsed by his own. (Lelingoana's old court was, however, fortuitously given a new lease of life by the establishment of the National Treasury Courts, described in the next chapter; Mosuoe directed that this "newfangled Government court" be held there, lest its deliberations be disturbed by the old-fashioned Basuto ceremonies which he continued to hold in his own village.)

In the case of a "placing", the authority making the appointment has to obtain his superior's permission. If the Paramount Chief wishes to place one of his own sons, he is expected to discuss the matter with the "Sons of Moshesh"; should he disregard them or ignore their advice, there is nothing they can do about it except make trouble and resent his high-handedness. Chiefs making appointments must obtain the Paramount Chief's approval, except in minor cases, and he can veto any appointment made by them or with their consent, should the matter be brought to his notice. Similarly, sub-chiefs have to obtain their chief's consent, and so on down the line. Formerly, the Administration was notified of approved appointments by courtesy of the Paramount Chief and might be invited to send an official representative to witness the more important "placings", but since 1938 such appointments must receive the prior approval of the Administration.

The following description of the installation of a new authority is taken from an official report of the "placing" of a sub-chief "B" over a headman "A" in Mokhotlong. "I, X, who represent the Paramount Chief, and with the Assistant District Commissioner, who is the representative of His Honour the Resident Commissioner, at these placings of the sons of Chief Z, I confirm this placing on behalf of the Paramount Chief in the presence of His Honour the Resident Commissioner. I say, 'Here is the child of A. Look after him, look after his horse, make fire for him, carry out his orders, from to-day onwards you must respect him as your chief.' Now I say to you, B, I give you the following words, 'It has to-day pleased Molahlehi, the representative of 'Mankata and your late mother 'Makori, to place you, having consulted with the superior chief (Seeiso). Hence you see me and the Resident Commissioner at this your placing. I confirm it, I stretch forth my hand to place on your head this hat of Chieftainship, in the presence of His Honour the Resident Commissioner. I say give up *marabaraba*, sit in court, respect the rights of A so that he may respect you as his chief, leave the company of young men who will mislead you and set you against the law, respect the people. You must detest theft; you must respect the authorities above you; you must obey their orders and the orders of the Government issued through them; to-day I expect a push of the Tax Collection in this ward as you are a young man, which tax preserves the peace of Basutoland. I say to you, if you disobey any of these orders, I, the representative of the Paramount Chief and the representative of His Honour the Resident Commissioner, shall solemnly declare that we did not order you to be disobedient to the people or to envy their wealth. We therefore wash the hands of the Paramount Chief and the hands of His Honour the Resident Commissioner from your blood that they shall not be responsible for it but your own self. This crown of Chieftainship shall be taken from you, you shall be deposed, thrown away and you shall become a commoner.'

"A then made the following boundary between himself and B and showed B his personal holding."

Being a chief brings many privileges. A chief is "somebody", a fact which is popularly recognized both in speech and behaviour. People greet him and address him by the title "Chief", "Lion", "Fierce wild animal", "Those cattle". Formerly,[1] a chief used to be treated with little ceremony—"it never occurred to anyone to stand in their presence as a mark of respect or to give them a comfortable seat when they unexpectedly joined a circle already closed. People interrupt or contradict them without constraint and frankly call them by their personal names, reserving pompous titles and praises for great ceremonial occasions. This familiarity seldom leads to disrespect. People know that the lion has claws. If need be, a gesture, whose import is clearly understood, restores caution and respect. The chiefs usually carry, as a sign of their rank, a little club made of rhinoceros horn. When things are going too far, they throw this weapon down, saying, 'Enough—there's my rhinoceros. Let's see who'll pick it up.' Usually everyone scatters as fast as possible, scarcely daring even to look where the club was thrown. If, however, someone was bold enough to pick it up, he committed a crime, punishable by death." This free and easy relationship, which

[1] Casalis 1861, pp. 275-6.

may be tightened up with sudden abruptness, is now rarely found and the chief is usually consistently treated with deference and formality—the greater his importance, the more the formality. Nowadays, people salute the chief by raising their hats, sometimes by kneeling in the dust before him, and when he comes into the court they scramble to their feet murmuring greetings, adulation and applause. When he travels on official or ceremonial business, he is accompanied by a troop of horsemen; his approach to or departure from a village is marked by the trembling cry of the women and, on occasion, the men sing and dance his praises. On all social occasions he is met with more courtesy and fuss than anyone else. Minor authorities are treated with less consideration, but even they are better received than ordinary commoners, both under normal social conditions as well as at feasts and ceremonies.

Authorities also have the pleasure of being able to order other people about. They can send people on errands, and important authorities may call on free tribal labour to till, hoe and reap their lands.[1] These rights are explicitly and officially authorized only in respect of work parties on the chief's official lands, but wider rights are still claimed by the chiefs and it would be a bold person who flatly refused to obey his chief's "request" to bring him firewood, cut or transport building material or cultivate his wife's fields. The exercise of these rights is, however, being increasingly resented and passively resisted, and all official dues may now be commuted by paying one shilling per annum.[2]

Another advantage is that although theoretically everyone is equal before the law, in practice "the chief is the law", and he is allowed greater latitude in personal conduct than would be tolerated from ordinary individuals.

The most attractive aspect of a chief's position is the economic. Many have huge flocks and herds. The lesser authorities, of course, are not nearly so well off, though on the whole they are wealthier than the average Mosuto. Their stock mainly derives from the old days of cattle raiding when the chiefs were entitled to the largest share of the booty, but stray stock and court fines until recently provided a steady income. Traditionally, every authority had his court where he was allowed to inflict penal fines, and their takings provided a profitable income which might amount to as much as £500 a year in the case of an important chief.[3] Senior authorities were also entitled to the valuable privilege of keeping all stray stock found in their districts and not claimed within a year of being found. They own larger and more numerous lands than other people. The smaller authorities usually have only one or two lands more than the average, but others, taking advantage of their position,

[1] Rules No. 12.
[2] See p. 131.
[3] Mr. T. B. Kennan thinks this is an underestimate and that the incomes of the most important chiefs must have run into four figures.

cultivate a considerable acreage; one such chief, who had only one wife, had twenty large lands. Important authorities are also entitled to unpaid tribal labour for the cultivation of the *tsimo ea lira*, the tribal land, the produce of which should be used to feed messengers and other public officials, but which some now convert to their own private benefit. A few chiefs used to have rather an ingenious system, which is dying out, by which they allocated a field to various headmen to cultivate and share its produce. In this way they insured themselves against loss through locusts or hailstorms, and guaranteed a fair supply of grain without trouble to themselves. Chief Lelingoana had about ten such fields.

Other sources of income are various official allowances. Prior to 1946, 5 per cent of the tax collected from each district was set aside for payment of the chiefs and tax-collectors. The balance left after deduction of the latter's salaries was divided between the various chiefs, roughly in proportion to their seniority and the number of people under them, and this brought in a small steady income. In addition, about thirty chiefs, including three widows, received special allowances which varied from £5 to £300 a year and two received additional special allowances—Chief Motsoene, £400, and the Paramount Chief, £1,550. With the introduction of the National Treasury on 1 April 1946, this was modified, and thereafter 36 per cent[1] of the Native Tax, and all fines, court fees and stray stock were to be paid into the Treasury. Sub-chiefs and headmen are still paid on the old basis of a share-out of 5 per cent of the tax takings. Twenty important chiefs, heads of districts, are paid salaries varying from £130 to £1,238 to compensate them for the loss of court fines and stray stock, and as payment for their official services. The Paramount Chief is paid a salary of £3,600 and various allowances.

Occasionally a *sethabathaba* or *morokhoana* may be imposed on a district and, indeed, this used to be fairly common. This is a levy or "whip-round", and people are expected to pay according to their means and not at a fixed rate. It used to be imposed to collect funds for some local purpose, such as to finance a lawsuit involving the tribe, or to pay the chief's debts and to save him the disgrace of prosecution, but collections for this purpose have recently been prohibited by the Paramount Chief.[2] It is rarely used to raise money for constructive purposes, such as the building of a school, as frequently happens among the Tswana, although during the war a gift to the British Government and people was raised by this means.

In the old days the chiefs were entitled to tribute, such as the skins of leopards and the breast (*sefuba*) of all the game killed, but this right has now become obsolete. They have never attempted to exact personal tribute from their followers returning from work abroad.

[1] Increased from 31 per cent to 36 per cent in 1949–50.
[2] T. B. Kennan, personal communication.

The duties of the various authorities are essentially the same in all the different grades, the senior ones merely having wider jurisdiction and greater responsibilities than their juniors. In general terms the functions of a native authority are to ensure the smooth working of society, and "to maintain order and good government among the natives residing or being in the area over which his authority extends";[1] to protect, feed and shepherd (*lisa*) his people and, since 1938, to perform the obligations imposed by the Native Administration Proclamation. They have legislative, judicial and executive authority. In the exercise of this they are assisted by their relatives and counsellors, and they have at their command their wealth, the prestige of their office, the force of their courts and the support of the British Administration.

We do not know what legislative functions the chiefs exercised in the old days or how they exercised them, and speculation thereon would be idle. There are, however, numerous examples of legislation in modern times, that is, subsequent to European contact, for which records are available. These were times of stress and altering conditions, so changes in and additions to the laws were to be expected. An example of the first is Moshesh's abolition of the death penalty, and of the second his prohibition of the sale of European liquor to the Basuto. Legislative power has now been transferred to the British Administration, and the chiefs may do little more than issue orders, although, through the National Council and the Paramount Chief they have issued a code of customary law which is regarded by the native courts as binding. This whole question is discussed more fully later.

The chiefs' executive power is considerable and it is often difficult to say where their authority ends. They may order people to come to court, to carry their official messages and do such services as the law enjoins, such as bringing reeds or thatching grass for their senior wife's hut, or gathering firewood for the court. They may also issue such orders as are necessary for carrying out matters of public interest and benefit, such as the eradication of noxious weeds, and for maintaining order and good government. They have, for example, to allocate fields for agriculture, demarcate pastures, preserve special grazing areas, control the expansion of villages, and allot sites for houses, schools and other buildings; they control the holding of initiation ceremonies, and should send their messengers to feasts to prevent excesses, and to ceremonies such as weddings, to witness contracts that may be made. They supervise their junior authorities, control the placing of new authorities and demarcate their boundaries. Formerly, too, they used to decide questions of war and peace, organize their regiments and supervise the building of strongholds. Nowadays, they are expected to help the British Administration generally by executing its orders and in specific matters prescribed in the Native Administration Proclamation,

[1] Proclamation No. 61 of 1938.

such as eradication of noxious weeds, tree-planting, collection of tax and the investigation of crime.

Until recently their judicial functions were the most important. Every authority had his own court where he heard all cases, criminal and civil, falling within his jurisdiction. They had the power to compel the attendance of witnesses and parties and to enforce their decisions. These judicial functions were inherent in the chief's position as an authority and were to some extent complementary to his other functions. During the last decade the position has been revolutionized. Under the Native Courts Proclamation (No. 62 of 1938), the Resident Commissioner is empowered to recognize or establish such courts as he may think fit, and anyone exercising judicial functions without such recognition commits an offence punishable on conviction by a fine not exceeding £100 and/or, in default of payment, to imprisonment not exceeding twelve months. In 1939, just over 1,300 authorities were recognized as chiefs, sub-chiefs and headmen,[1] and were allowed to continue to exercise judicial functions and to have their courts. This was far too large a number to be properly supervised and controlled in terms of the Proclamation and close control was necessary, not only in the interests of justice and efficient administration but for the sake of the National Treasury established in 1946 into which all fines and court fees were now to be paid; the number of recognized courts was therefore reduced to 121. In 1949 this number was further reduced to 106. Those whose courts were not recognized, nevertheless continued as native authorities—but shorn of all judicial power. For the first time in Basuto history, the judicial and administrative functions of their authorities were separated.

At the same time two further changes were made. Hitherto judicial functions had been an integral part of an authority's duties, and the court was, in a sense, personal to that authority—it was his court. He could preside over it himself or appoint a representative to do so in his absence. This close relationship between things judicial and things political was further reflected in the fact that the system of appeals and jurisdiction followed the political line—the court of a headman was subordinate to that of the headman's sub-chief, and the sub-chief's court was subordinate to his chief's. In 1946 both these things were changed. Three classes of court were introduced—the Paramount Chief's court, Class A and Class B courts. District (ward) chiefs' courts were regarded as Class A courts and were still, to a large extent, regarded as personal to them. Class B courts were subordinate to Class A courts, and were placed in different areas, at the seat of the most important sub-chief. So far no great change in principle was introduced, but—and this is where the radical changes were introduced—that court was not automatically regarded as the sub-chief's; if he were appointed as its presi-

[1] High Commissioner's Notice No. 171 of 1939.

dent, it could be regarded as his, but if he were not appointed president, he could not, in terms of the Native Court Proclamation, have anything to do with it. It sat in his village, with jurisdiction over his area, but was independent of and ran parallel to him. If he happened to be directly under the district chief, the political and judicial hierarchy remained the same; but if he happened to have an authority intermediate between himself and the district chief, the two lines diverged—administratively he remained subordinate to this intermediate authority, but judicially his court now lay directly under his chief's court, and was no longer subordinate to his sub-chief. Moreover, as his appointment as a judicial authority depended on his chief's recommendation rather than on that of his sub-chief, his relationship to these two authorities was subtly altered and biased towards the former.

These points may be illustrated from Mokhotlong. In 1936 there were 128 authorities in the district, each of whom had his own court —1 chief, 35 sub-chiefs and 92 headmen; in 1939, their number was reduced to 74—1 chief, 12 sub-chiefs and 61 headmen, again, each with his own recognized court; in 1946, only 10 courts were recognized—1 "A" court and 9 "B" courts, and the latter were reduced to 8 in 1949. In other words, only 9 courts may now do the judicial work which, prior to 1939, had been done by 128. Even if allowance is made for the fact that very few of the 92 headmen and not all of the 35 sub-chiefs settled more than one or two cases a year, and that most of the work was done by a minority of the courts, this change was profound.

The divergence of the new judicial hierarchy from the political is shown in the following tables. To facilitate comparison with Diagrams Nos. I, II and III,[1] the same names have been used although some of the incumbents have changed.

TABLE A. POLITICAL HIERARCHY

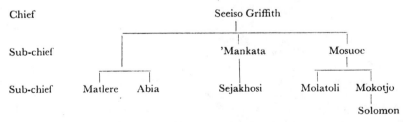

TABLE B. JUDICIAL HIERARCHY

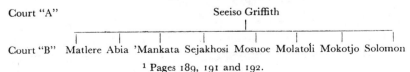

[1] Pages 189, 191 and 192.

As these changes have only recently been made, I am unable to say what actual effect they have had. Their potentialities are far-reaching, and not the least of these will be the enhancement of the position of district chief and the belittlement of those sub-chiefs who are administratively senior to other sub-chiefs or headmen, whose courts are now judicially equal to and independent of them. This will probably be accompanied by a shift of political and administrative influence. Considerable psychological readjustment will also be necessary both of rulers and ruled, and the psychological disturbance these changes must inevitably have caused is suggested elsewhere as a possible partial cause of the recent wave of ritual murders. Further details of the judicial organization and of the judicial function of the chiefs will be given in the next chapter.

Basuto chiefs have very scanty magico-religious functions. Their relation to first-fruit ceremonies, already described,[1] had no magical or religious significance. They are expected to protect the land from hail and frost, either with their own medicines or those of a hired doctor, and to secure rain in times of drought by organizing the tribal rain ceremonies, by hiring a doctor to make rain, or by setting aside a special Sunday for prayer for rain. These are purely personal and administrative acts and are not derived from any religious link with God or the tribal ancestors. The following is the only instance I have come across where the chief's position had some religious connexion: when the Tlokoa first occupied their present home, they made a medicine composed of ingredients culled from Sekonyela's grave and from their old home at Nkoe, where they had lived for several generations; with this they doctored their country, uttering at the same time an invocation to the chief's ancestors. Many chiefs were skilled doctors who performed their own magical rites; Lelingoana used to protect his people from lightning and hail, and Jonathan was the recognized rain-maker in North Basutoland.[2] A few chiefs still doctor their villages, and sometimes all their people, at the beginning of the new (Sesuto) year or after the village has been struck by lightning.

A chief is expected to use the material advantages of his position and his wealth for his people's benefit, and this was one of the main ties between a chief and his people. As Casalis puts it: "The chiefs instead of being fed by the community are its principal suppliers." Indeed, Casalis considered wealth so important a source of power that he suggests that they did not distribute the spoils of war on an equal basis because "wealth in changing hands compromised too much the stability of power. It is a fact that since the time that the natives have been able to acquire cattle, the repressive power of the chiefs has obviously diminished."[3] For public purposes the chief should draw on his own resources as well as on the produce of the *tsimo ea lira*. Formerly,

[1] See p. 128. [2] T. B. Kennan, personal communication. [3] Casalis, 1861, p. 198-9.

many conscientiously fulfilled these obligations; they kept a stewpot continually simmering in the court, or instructed their wives and other women of the village to supply the court with bread, milk or beer, so that, as in Lelingoana's case, the people in their court were as "flies round the milk pail". To-day there is less political need for such generosity and at the same time there are many more attractive ways of disposing of wealth; consequently the old open-handedness is now rarely met with; some chiefs do not even feed official messengers sent to them, let alone provide for the ordinary people who come to their courts.

In the old days, polygynists such as Mohlomi (an outstanding early chief and predecessor of Moshesh), Moshesh and Letsie, who had scores of wives, used to connive at the cohabitation of their followers with junior and less important wives, and even encouraged permanent attachments. They also[1] used to provide poor retainers with *bohali* cattle for a wife and some still do this. Some chiefs also, as a form of social welfare, support a larger number of dependants than strict economy requires, who help to herd their cattle and assist in household chores. Bereng, for instance, in 1934, apart from his own children and immediate family, had some sixteen people living with him, of whom half were orphans or widows who had come to him for support. Many lend stock to their people as *mafisa*—allowing the borrowers or holders to use them for their own purposes without other obligations than to look after them and accord the chief complete loyalty.

Few chiefs carry out their functions personally; most of them depute a principal executive officer to do their work for them and deal directly and on his own initiative with all important matters, save those connected with lands. This official interviews important messengers and visitors, supervises the administration, presides over the court—hence his title *molulosetulo* (president)—and directs its judicial work. As indicated above, this last delegation of power has been stopped—in theory at least—by the recent judicial reforms and the court president is now supposed to be independent of the local authority rather than his representative. In important chieftainships, this deputy has a number of assistants with whom he consults and to whom he leaves the petty details of everyday administration—the hearing of minor complaints, the examination of stock and the issue of stock removal permits. They may also act as secretaries, write out orders, summonses, court records and *bewijs*. Sometimes paid secretaries are specially appointed for this work.

These officials, to some extent, share with the chief the fruits of political office, but they also expect definite remuneration from him, which should bear some relation to his wealth and importance and to the weight of their own duties. A few of them used to be paid by Government and more are paid nowadays by the National Treasury. The Para-

[1] Ellenberger and MacGregor, p. 97.

mount Chief and other important chiefs have administrative clerks and a "*bewijs* and letter writer" at from £36 to £72 per annum. Courts also now have paid presidents at £48 to £96 per annum, assessors at £24 to £48 per annum and clerks and messengers at from £24 to £72 per annum.[1] Minor authorities, the volume of whose work is small, are helped by relatives and friends, including the local teacher who is often the only literate man in the village.

Some chiefs have officials with special duties. In the old days, the most important of these was the *molaoli*, commander of the fighting forces. He was chosen for his courage and skill and was usually a near relative of the chief.[2] Important chiefs, such as Moshesh, also had a town crier (*seboholi*). He called the people together for meetings, made public announcements from the top of a platform[3] built next to the chief's hut, and at night patrolled the village crying out, "*Kea le bona, kea le bona* (I see you)" to frighten off witches and evil doers. The failure of the Zulu attack on Thaba Bosiu is credited to Moshesh's watchman's stentorian cry: unaware of this custom, the Zulu believed that their approach on the mountain had been surprised and so they halted their attack, withdrew and hid themselves in a nearby valley, where their presence was discovered next day. Some authorities have a special land controller to distribute the agricultural land, deal with the pastures and spare veld and supervise the cutting of thatching-grass and reeds. Overseers of the cattle-post areas may be appointed to control the movements of stock and prevent animals straying down to the cultivated areas, and also to keep an eye on the people living up there.

Important chiefs have regular messengers who ply between themselves and neighbouring chiefs or whom they send on important missions. As Casalis says, "These are always skilful and shrewd men whose discretion is completely reliable. They try to have gentle and polished manners."[4] Some of these men are "political messengers" who go between the chief and the Government, act as observers for the Administration at the drawing of boundaries between authorities or at a placing, give effect to a court decision, or witness the enforcement of important judgments given by the chief's or the Paramount Chief's court. In the mountain areas they also act as postmen. Many of them are paid by the Government or National Treasury. Messengers are also employed by the principal courts to serve summonses, notify witnesses and give effect to court orders. Besides employing these regular, paid messengers, chiefs used to be entitled to the free service[5] of all adult men under them, whom they could send anywhere at any time on official business.

Lelingoana used to have a well organized relay system. Men living in his village were specially linked to the headmen of neighbouring

---

[1] N.T. Estimates, 1949–50.
[2] Ellenberger and MacGregor, p. 265.
[3] Casalis, *Mes Souvenirs*, p. 259.
[4] Casalis, 1861, p. 278–9.
[5] *Laws of Lerotholi*, No. 4. See p. 207.

villages; the latter were similarly linked to other villages and so on throughout his area, so that all these authorities were radially linked to him in this way, irrespective of their relative seniority. This network cut across the normal channels whereby the chief should communicate with headmen or junior authorities only through intermediate authorities such as sub-chiefs; it was therefore used only in cases of emergency.

A chief should be assisted by and pay heed to the advice and counsel of his people. Everyone is entitled to advise him but, in practice, very few take advantage of this privilege, except indirectly through their headman or a member of the chief's own entourage. A few, by virtue of their political standing or kinship relationship to the chief, have the right to expect to be consulted by him. They are the chief's near relations—his uncles, brothers and senior sons, and also the principal authorities of the district—the sub-chiefs, leading headmen and the heads of the principal tribal groups. In the old days consultation with them was essential, for the chief relied almost entirely on their support in carrying out his policy; to use Theal's phrase, "in agreement with them he was strong, in opposition powerless".[1] Other people who have the right to be consulted are the chief's executive officials, because they are responsible for enforcing his decisions. A young chief should also consult the advisers provided for him by his father, who are sent to live with him at his own village. All these advisers are often described as councillors but, as Schapera has pointed out in respect of the advisers of the Tswana chiefs, "they do not belong to any formally constituted body, their number is not fixed or limited in any other way, and they are not formally appointed as official advisers".[2] Meetings with these advisers are usually private and are held in some secluded place such as the chief's hut or office. Occasionally, at the chief's discretion, they may be held in public and then anyone interested may listen and, if he be bold enough, join in the discussion.

The chief may also consult individual tribesmen, who have some special knowledge of the subject under discussion, or intelligent strangers, for the sake of their unprejudiced opinion or their knowledge of affairs elsewhere. In addition, he has his favourites and confidential advisers. The latter may attend the meetings with his official advisers, but are usually consulted in private, for they are often unpopular and, in any case, generally prefer to deal with the chief alone. He may have private interviews with ordinary commoners to try to gauge public opinion, but as it is not in keeping with his position for him to do so, he usually leaves this sort of consultation to his principal advisers, and more especially to his favourites.

The chief may decide all minor matters on his own responsibility, with or against the advice of his councillors, but all matters of importance should first be discussed with the people at a public meeting

[1] Theal, *Basutoland Records*, Vol. II, p. 58.   [2] Schapera, *Handbook*, 1938, p. 75.

(*pitso*), to which all adult males are summoned. These meetings are held in his village and are presided over by him or his representative. The subjects for discussion, which will have already been discussed with his councillors, are introduced and elaborated by his relatives and other councillors, and then thrown open for general debate. The proceedings are finally wound up by the chief or his senior councillor (the part played by the chief being determined by his own activity and interest); his decision, if any, is announced and the meeting is closed with the words "*Le lumile*" (It has thundered).

Pitsos were frequently called by Moshesh and other chiefs, to discuss questions of policy and administration, and they played an active part in public life. Noteworthy examples are the *pitso* called by Mokhachane, Moshesh's father, to protest against the spread of Christianity (1841)[1] and one called by Letsie I to discuss the prohibition of *bohali* cattle (1888).[2] Discussion, according to contemporary observers,[3] was keen, great freedom of speech was allowed, and great weight attached to the opinion and attitude of the people. The people, as often as not, followed the line they judged the chief was taking, but if, for some reason, they opposed him, and he expected their opposition to be firm, he would not often risk forcing the issue. Moshesh himself constantly asserted that he could do nothing without consulting and gaining the consent of his sons and other chiefs, and in his announcements and proclamations he usually used such phrases as "Given with the advice and concurrence of our tribe", or, as in his proclamation against witchcraft, "This word is assented to by Letsie, by all my brothers and by all men of the tribe who spit on the lie of witchcraft and cover its face with their spittle." Tribesmen and chiefs were summoned to most of the meetings held with British or Boer officials, and they took an active part in them as, for example, the *pitsos* held to discuss the disarmament proposal of the Cape Government (1874), peace terms after the Gun War (1883), raising the tax to do away with the Cape Government's Grant-in-Aid (1898). Real consideration was given to the opinions expressed at these meetings. As Theal, writing of those days, says: "No native chief is despotic in the sense that he can carry out any measure in opposition to the will of his people, and of all the chiefs known to us at that time, Moshesh was one who could least afford to disregard the inclination of his subjects. He was merely the head of a number of clans, each with very large powers of self-government. Every one of his sub-chiefs expected to be consulted in matters of importance, and if his advice were neglected gave no support to his superior."[4] This also applied to every

[1] Casalis, *Les Bassoutos*, p. 293.
[2] Jacottet, *Livre d'Or*, pp. 200, 389.
[3] Dieterlen, *Livre d'Or*, p. 23.
[4] Theal, *Basutoland Records*, p. 48. By "clans" Theal refers here to what were described in Chapter II as tribes.

tribal chief, for they all depended on the support of the clan and lineage heads and the village headmen under them, and ultimately on the people—as the proverb puts it: *morena ke morena ka batho* (the chief is the chief by the people).

If the chief failed to conduct himself properly, to be just, generous and brave, amenable to the advice of his councillors and conscious of the welfare of his people, there was nothing to prevent dissatisfied tribesmen from joining a more promising chief elsewhere, or breaking away in a body and setting themselves up as a tribe under the leadership of the chief's more popular younger brother or son. In extreme cases they might even murder him. Basuto history contains numerous examples of such fissions and revolts.[1] The early missionaries also complained of the frequency with which people moved from one chief to another. With the tremendous growth of population in the last fifty years or so, and the fixing of the country's boundaries, the old freedom of movement has been restricted, so that people can no longer move away from an unpopular chief. The Government's protection of the chiefs has prevented their people from resorting to other and more drastic sanctions. So the chiefs have ceased to depend for their position on the support of their people and now have little incentive to consult them. They have, therefore, allowed the *pitso* to fall into disuse, except in a few tribally organized areas, as among the Tlokoa, where the practice of consultation has been kept alive by the need for tribal unity in the face of attacks by the Sons of Moshesh. This tendency was accentuated even in Casalis's day[2] by the Cape Government and by military commanders, who required quick decisions from the chiefs which rarely gave them time to consult their people, and which, as Casalis indicated, encouraged "despotic tendencies". Nowadays, *pitsos* are rarely held by chiefs except to announce orders that have been promulgated by the Administration or the Paramount Chief. In some areas, meetings are held in connection with the National Council to propose subjects for discussion at the Council, or to report on the Council's deliberations, but little scope is given for public debate. The Government has tried to revive the *pitsos* by encouraging the chiefs to hold them; some keen administrative officers call their own through the local chief to discuss matters of interest, such as the introduction of local Councils, or the establishment of agricultural improvement areas. Such *pitsos* are attended by the chief or his representative and by the Paramount Chief's representative. National *pitsos* are now only held on important ceremonial occasions such as the visits of the King (1947), Royal Princes or the High Commissioner, when huge spectacular gatherings are held at Maseru, the Administrative capital.

In 1883, and again in 1894, the Government suggested that a National Council of chiefs should be established to advise it and the

[1] Ellenberger and MacGregor, pp. 25, 59. etc.   [2] Casalis, op. cit., p. 296.

Paramount Chief. The proposal was rejected on both occasions by the chiefs who were jealous of their individual rights and opposed to any enhancement of the Paramount Chieftainship. But the Council was finally established in 1903, largely owing to the support of Lerotholi, then Paramount Chief, who knew he had not long to live and saw that it would be invaluable in buttressing the feebleness of his successor. The relationship of the National Council to the Paramount Chief was clearly shown in the official constitution proclaimed in 1910.[1] This provided for 100 members, consisting of the Paramount Chief, 94 members nominated by him and 5 nominated by the Resident Commissioner. Its functions were purely advisory, namely, "to discuss the domestic affairs of the Territory, including appropriation of money paid in taxes; to ventilate opinions and grievances, to deliberate on tribal disputes, and to confer with the Administration on tribal affairs." In addition, it could make recommendations to the Paramount Chief and advise his promulgation of orders to take effect as Sesuto laws.

The Council, as its constitution indicates, was representative primarily of the chiefs and their adherents and "so far as effective action is concerned, their outlook is limited to that of those elements of the Nation, though the sentiments expressed are often of the most lofty and altruistic character". The Council started off with a flourish and produced the interesting collection of Sesuto Laws known as *The Laws of Lerotholi*; from time to time it made valuable suggestions, which were taken up by the Administration. It also provided a convenient means of airing grievances covering the whole range of administration, and gave the Administration a valuable forum for clearing up misunderstandings and for discussing policy and such matters as agriculture, land reclamation, education and medical services. It inevitably suffered from the limitations imposed upon it by its constitution, and particularly from the fact that it was purely consultative, had no financial responsibility and no practical experience of many of the matters it handled.[2] Nor did it fulfil early hopes that it would restrict the chief's power "still too absolute".[3]

Recently the Administration has encouraged the Paramount Chief and Council to revise its constitution. An important step was taken in 1943 when the Council recommended the Paramount Chief to increase its representative character by including among his nominees elected representatives of the people and of various interests. This he did and the modification was statutorily recognized in the new constitution promulgated in 1948.[4] The Paramount Chief's ninety-four nominees now include two elected representatives of each District Council, and

[1] Proclamation No. 7 of 1910.
[2] Pim, pp. 28 et seq. where the Council is analysed in detail.
[3] Jacottet, *Livre d'Or*, p. 408.
[4] Proclamation No. 48 of 1948.

one representative from each of the following organizations: the Basutoland Agricultural Union, Progressive Association, Basutoland African Native Teachers' Association, Basutoland Traders' Association, Botsabelo Leper Settlement and the Basutoland Ex-Servicemen. The rest of the ninety-four are still "principal persons exercising authority as chiefs" selected from each district in proportion to the population thereof. Provision is also made for a Standing Committee of five members elected by the Council to act as an advisory body to represent the Council between sessions, to whom the Resident Commissioner or Paramount Chief can refer matters for consideration.

Another step towards encouraging the expression of the people's views was the establishment of District Councils in 1944. The members of these councils are drawn from three sources:

(a) *Members elected by the people.* At first the numbers varied from one to every 200 tax-payers to 1 to every 600 tax-payers. On this basis, the largest districts had 40 members and the smallest 10. The numbers are now decided upon by the Resident Commissioner in consultation with the Paramount Chief and have been considerably reduced.

(b) *National Council members.* These are members of the National Council, nominated by the Paramount Chief to be members of the District Councils. The numbers per district vary from 5 to 2, according to the size of the district.

(c) *Sectional Representatives.* The sections represented are the same as those now represented in the Basutoland Council.

These councils meet annually under the presidency of the District Officer. The matters placed on their agenda have been of the greatest importance, and in 1945 included "the adoption of better methods of land management and the declaration of Agricultural Improvement Areas", and an increase in the rate of Native Tax. The Councils were made statutory bodies in 1948.

The introduction of the electoral system, hitherto unknown in tribal law, and the representation of sectional interests which have sprung up under modern conditions, are radical innovations. The District Councils are outside the normal political organization and, as yet, have little control over the acts and policy of the chiefs, the Paramount Chief or the Government. But they do provide a forum, albeit infrequent, for public debate where the opinions of the people can be heard and their grievances ventilated. Moreover, as the District Commissioner is the Chairman of the Council, direct contact is established between Government and the people, and the tortuous channel of communication through the chiefs and Paramount Chief is short-circuited. No less important, they presuppose the holding of meetings or *pitsos* connected with elections, the hearing of prospective candidates and the reports of representatives on the Council's sessions, all of which may help to revive popular interest in public affairs. They may also give political experience to people other than the constituted Native Authorities. It is still too early to say what permanent effect the Councils will have upon the political structure of Basutoland, and much will depend upon the weight attached to their views and upon the responsibility given to their members by Government.[1]

The concept of the chieftainship is deeply rooted in the Basuto. Casalis wrote that they had "an almost superstitious respect for their chiefs"[2] and that they could scarcely conceive of any community being able to look after its own affairs without someone in authority at its head. They regarded chiefs as inevitable and indispensable and subscribed to a doctrine comparable to the old theory of the divine right of kings. This did not blind them to the human failings of their chiefs, nor prevent them from changing their allegiance from one chief to another, as has been described earlier; but it helped them to tolerate a degree of mishandling and injustice that they would not otherwise have borne. Casalis does not attempt to evaluate the institution or to assess the quality of the chiefs, but it is clear from his account of "government" that, on the whole, it served the people well and that the chiefs were like other humans, both good and bad. Some were just, public-spirited and accessible; others became preoccupied with the maintenance and increase of their wealth and were thus tempted to indulge in dishonest and unjust action; they obstinately opposed economic development that might enrich and emancipate their subjects, and were given, even then, to the practice known as "eating up a person": namely, punishing a prosperous man for some misdemeanour by seizing all or the greater part of his stock.[3] The controls described earlier were, however, strong enough to keep these defects within bounds and prevent the growth of that brutality, tyranny and overweening pride characteristic of the Zulu despots.[4]

The position is similar to-day, although it has in some respects deteriorated, especially in respect of the personal qualities of the chiefs. Owing to the breakdown of the old sanctions, the chiefs have little inducement to win the support and popularity of their people by the exercise of justice, generosity and graciousness; and, as indicated earlier, many are more interested in satisfying their own desires than in serving their subjects; they abuse their authority and the privileges of their position for their own selfish ends. Many are drunkards, corrupt and immoral, and, like their forebears, oppose developments and innovations proposed or introduced for the benefit of the country. Dieterlen wrote,[5] many years ago, of their "deplorable decadence", and his stricture still applies to-day.

[1] For a fuller account of popular participation in the old tribal government and in the modern administration, see my article "Democracy and Indirect Rule", 1947.
[2] Casalis, 1861, p. 269.   [3] Ibid., p. 272.   [4] Ibid. pp. 274-5.
[5] Dieterlen, *Documents Inédits*, p. 12, and *Livre d'Or*, p. 476. See also Pim, p. 48 and Hodgson and Ballinger, pp. 25-7.

During the last twenty years or so the Government has been trying to introduce reforms. At first it met with such opposition from people and chiefs alike that it had to drop its proposals. Later, thanks to the influence of the then Resident Commissioner, Mr. (now Sir Edmund) Richards, the Paramount Chief Griffith came to realize that reform was essential in the interests of the chieftainship itself, and of the country as a whole, and accepted the Native Administration and Courts Proclamations which were promulgated in 1938. This paved the way for the introduction of the National Treasury, through which additional changes were made which have been described above. The widening of the membership of the National Council and the introduction of District Councils were other reforms of the same nature which it was hoped would curb the worst abuses and faults of the old system. Unfortunately, I have had no personal experience of what real effect they have had.

The people often complain bitterly about the attitude of their chiefs, which they feel has deteriorated since the good old days, and many are very critical of their chief's failings, personal and administrative. There is, however, no real spirit of revolt against the chiefs and though they are strongly criticized in the vernacular press and in the National Council, there is no organized movement or real hostility. They are still too powerful on their own and with Government support, and too much revered for such an attitude to develop, and commoners who find the position intolerable can, and do, escape from it by migrating to the Union. Indeed, in spite of all its defects, the people are strongly attached and loyal to the institution which has served them so well in the past; they have a deep respect for what is both expressive of their traditions and representative of their national unity, and they are often apprehensive lest reform should weaken it and jeopardize the stability and safety of their country. It is probable that these attitudes are being strengthened by the growing racial tension and animosities of Southern Africa.

CHAPTER XIV

JUDICIAL ORGANIZATION

According to tradition, the exercise of judicial and of political authority are complementary functions. As briefly described in the previous chapter, every chief used to have his own court where he heard complaints and tried such cases as fell within his jurisdiction. Normally, he had only one court, but when pressure of business warranted it, he might establish a temporary additional court to help cope with the work. Thus Chief Seeiso, when in Mokhotlong, occasionally had a second court at Thabang, and Theko Makhaola once had a circuit court to hear cases in the outlying areas of his mountainous district of Qacha's Nek. The Paramount Chief, on the other hand, had so much judicial work that he had several permanent courts at Matsieng and other courts continuously on circuit. Their numbers fluctuated slightly, but until recently there were five permanent and three circuit courts. This number was reduced by the 1949-50 National Treasury Estimates to three of the former and two of the latter.

An attempt was made in 1946 to separate the administrative and judicial functions of native authorities, and only 121 out of over 1,300 were thereafter authorized by the Government to conduct courts. Even these were not supposed to be personal to these authorities but were called National Treasury courts. In 1949 this small number was further reduced to 106. The remainder were allowed to continue to function as courts of arbitration, that is, they could attempt to settle disputes, but their decisions were not final or binding, and could not be enforced by the infliction of fines or any other sanction.

Before the introduction of the foregoing reforms, when each authority had his own court, Sesuto law provided that: "Every chief is bound to preside over cases of any disputants, unless he is prevented by illness or some other reason, which should satisfy the disputants or members of his court."[1] This is still the law, although it must be remembered that except for the 106 recognized courts, all courts are now courts of arbitration only. In actual practice, only junior authorities presided personally over their courts. They were so jealous of this right that their courts did not function without them, unless they specifically appointed a deputy—a son, brother, uncle or favourite councillor—and rather than do this, they usually preferred to postpone a case until they could take it themselves. Chiefs and other important authorities did not share this enthusiasm and, either from sheer laziness or because they had other interests and activities, usually left their courts to a deputy or

[1] *Laws of Lerotholi*, 1922, No. 19.

chairman. This practice was confirmed by the establishment of the Basutoland Native Treasury, which provided for the payment of a permanent Court President.[1]

Every authority was assisted by relations and friends, who were senior members of the ward and had a right to help him. Important chiefs had an informal panel of assistants, known as the *banna ba lekhotla* (men of the court). Unless other arrangments were made, one of them acted for the President of the court when he was away. The organization of this panel was loose and variable. Chief Mosuoe for instance, used to have four or five assistants who attended court fairly regularly, and who, if unable to attend or if absent for a long period, excused themselves to the President. Chief Seeiso had a few assistants who worked continuously for short periods, from a month to three months, and then retired to go about their ordinary business, while others took their place. Some had two or three permanent deputies or close advisers, who called on others when needed. Bereng, for instance, had two such advisers who, in five months, invited over forty people to help hear cases, some as often as fifty times, others only once or twice.

There were no hard and fast rules as to who could become assistants. They were usually people who by birth or wealth were influential in the community; some of them were close blood relations of the chief and might or might not have had important holdings of their own; others were leaders of local tribal groups and usually related to the chief by marriage; others simply won their way to favour through personal qualities which appealed to the chief. Those given the most important positions, such as Court President, were almost always related to the chief either by blood or marriage, though occasionally they might be outsiders of exceptional ability. Normally, all these people lived under the chief, but a distinguished visitor might be asked to help in one or two cases as a mark of esteem.

The President and his principal assistants, who might from time to time act as President, should keep one another constantly informed of all that went on and of what they had done, both to preserve continuity and consistency of action, and also because they were supposed to be severally responsible for one another's acts. But they often failed to do so, and even if they did, they might try to avoid a ticklish matter previously raised by disclaiming all knowledge of it or by referring the complainant to their colleague who had dealt with it originally. This evasion

---

[1] The establishment of the National Treasury in 1946 led to the introduction of many reforms and modifications of the traditional organization. In order to avoid frequent repetition of the reason for such changes, they will simply be dated 1946, and this should be taken to mean that they were due to this important innovation.

. This account of the organization and procedure of the courts is based on my original field-work material, gathered in 1935-6. My information on the changes resulting from the 1946 reforms is superficial and incomplete, and many of their effects will take years to work themselves out.

of responsibility led to administrative delay and to grumbling dissatisfaction. Since 1946, provision has been made for the payment of two assessors to each court. This will stabilize the panel and, with a paid permanent President, will presumably encourage more uniformity and avoid the shirking of responsibility; on the other hand, it will also affect the flexibility of the old system and may discourage the voluntary attendance of local leaders who used to share the responsibility of conducting court business and hearing and deciding cases.

All important courts had one or more clerks. In addition to their duties, described in the previous chapter, they had to write out orders for the appearance of witnesses, keep a record of cases, check the payment of fines and see to the general clerical routine of court work. They rarely took part in the actual hearing of cases, except to record the evidence, but in the lesser courts they occasionally helped to try the cases. In these courts, where there was less formality and specialization, they were occasionally helped by one of the *banna ba lekhotla*, and even by the President.

Formerly, no officials of the court received any specific payment for their services. To some extent, they gave these voluntarily and freely, as this was recognized as one of the privileges and duties of a tribal authority and of those who occupied high positions in the tribe. It was an honour and a pleasure to take part in court affairs. But the position was not entirely without its material rewards. In the old days, the chiefs kept the court supplied with meat and other food, and though this obligation was increasingly neglected, most of the chiefs continued to allow some of the animals, paid as fines, to be killed and eaten by the men of the court. The chief also occasionally handed over a few beasts to the court President and others, who had greatly helped with its work. Being so close to the chief also gave one the chance of obtaining favours, such as the allocation of a good land or, after years of faithful service, placement over a ward or a caretaking of one's own. With the growing volume of work, the duties became more onerous and the officials began to claim more definite rewards. The panel system helped to spread the work and reduce the importunity of these demands. But where the volume of work made this impossible, the chiefs had to pay salaries and give honoraria, sometimes out of their own personal incomes, and sometimes from Government funds. The leading court officials might also be given stray stock, stock paid in fines or *mafisa* stock, and occasionally they were given or lent lands. Since 1946, the matter has been put on a more regular and definite basis, and the President, two assessors, clerks and messengers of each recognized court have been paid a monthly salary. These vary, with the importance of the court, from £300 to £48 per annum for the President, £60 to £24 for the two assessors and £84 to £36 for the clerks. Messengers all receive £36 per annum. The number of clerks varies from one to four, and of messengers from one to three, and the cost of each court from £492 to £168 per annum.[1] The higher-paid officials all belong to the Paramount Chief's Central Appeal Courts.

Other Judicial and Quasi-Judicial Institutions

Besides these courts there are other bodies which settle or help to settle disputes. One of these is the family council. All cases affecting family relations, such as disputes between husband and wife or non-fulfilment of kinship obligations, should be first discussed by the family, that is, by the near male relatives of the parties concerned, presided over by the most senior. "*Ke tsa lelapa*," as Laydevant says,[2] "they are matters of the household". Where women are directly concerned, female members of the family—the mothers, sisters and co-wives of the parties—may participate; even if they do not attend the meetings they should be consulted by their menfolk. The matter is, if possible, settled here. If it involves damages, the amount to be paid is agreed upon, in accordance with the usual scales, and a fine may even be imposed on the offender. No one can enforce obedience to the settlement, and the only sanction for payment of the damages and the fine is moral and social pressure and the offender's own good sense. If the offender refuses to have the matter discussed by the family council or to obey its decision, or if the parties cannot come to an agreement, the case is referred to the local court, either by the family head or by the complainant himself. Such cases do not necessarily have to be discussed *en famille* before they can be taken to this court, although the court may suggest that the matter be withdrawn for family discussion. For instance, in Mokhotlong there were two brothers, Ralithakong and Rannekoe, who were always quarrelling. It was useless having their disputes discussed *en famille* as the parties concerned were too cantankerous to accept so impotent a decision, and so these disputes were directly heard by the court. On the other hand, a young man, Lemeko, occasionally had a row with his father, Moithapalatsi, a half-brother of Mosuoe. It was unseemly for their bickering to be exposed in court and so, in one sordid case involving counter-accusations of the petty theft of 17s. 6d., the court ordered the dispute to be referred privately to Mosuoe in his capacity as family head—*ba ee ho morena Mosuoe ka lapeng*.

Another court is that of the *mophato* (initiation school). This is composed of the *mosoue* and *babineli* (head of the lodge and the boys' companions), assisted perhaps by other men, and is held at the lodge whenever necessary. It deals primarily with offences against the rules of the initiation school but may also deal with offences, such as theft and adultery, which are contrary to the ethical code taught to initiates, committed during the existence of the *mophato* by men connected with

[1] Basutoland National Treasury Estimates, 1949–50.
[2] Laydevant, 1931, p. 239.

the school. This court has the right to punish by thrashing or fining. It used to be an important disciplinary institution but nowadays, owing to the decay of initiation generally, its influence is negligible.

Yet another court is the women's court. This is presided over by the chief's senior wife, who is *ipso facto* the senior woman in the district and also the official head of all girls' initiation. It discusses matters affecting women and can also take disciplinary action where women misconduct themselves or break various sexual taboos. It can even take action against men who have offended against the women's initiation law, by spying on or blundering into some of their secret ceremonies, and it may punish such offenders by fining. In the latter cases, however, the women must be assisted by one or two men deputed for this purpose by the chief. The women's court still functions occasionally among the Tlokoa, but I have no information regarding its position elsewhere. The following is an instance of its use.

Sebolai v. Sefabatho, February 1936.

Sebolai wanted to initiate his daughter and killed five sheep as the *khomo ea lehlaka*.[1] His headman Sefabatho was not satisfied so Sebolai killed another two. Sefabatho still refused so he added another two. The series of initiation rites started and then Sefabatho refused to allow the women to proceed with the main ceremony—*ho ea malibeng*. As Sefabatho had partaken of the sheep, Sebolai wanted to sue him in Mosuoe's court. The court advised him to take the matter to 'Mamokotjo, the chief's senior wife—*ke litaba tsa mangope a basali*—"they are matters concerning girls' initiation".

Jurisdiction

The jurisdiction of the courts of the different authorities used to vary widely and corresponded with the position of the authority in the political hierarchy. The courts of headmen and other minor authorities could deal with every kind of case, provided it was not serious, such as land disputes (unless the authority concerned had no rights to allocate lands), trespass, theft, adultery, seduction and assault, and enforcement of marital and familial duties. There was no clear-cut definition of seriousness, but a case might be said to be serious when the issues involved were complicated or important (though this begs the question), when the persons affected were of equal or greater importance than the headman or when the damage done was extensive. The penalty inflicted afforded a criterion of importance, for a minor court should not inflict a fine of more than a few sheep or a beast, but even this was not infallible. The question was left to the good sense of the authority concerned and little confusion occurred in practice, as few headmen were anxious to take on more responsibility than they had to and, when in doubt, preferred to send the case on to a higher authority rather than

---

[1] The "beast of the reed", the opening feast signifying that the initiation is to take place, and attended by the parents of the prospective initiates.

risk a reprimand for having attempted to go too far. Furthermore, they knew that there was little likelihood of their decision being accepted by the parties if they went much beyond their jurisdiction, and so they preferred not to bother about it. Occasionally, a pushing person took whatever came before him, provided it was not glaringly beyond his jurisdiction, and heard cases that a less active authority of the same standing would have sent forward to a higher court. If he overstepped the mark, he might be reproved by a senior authority. Occasionally a chief specifically limited the jurisdiction of a junior authority when placing him. Any person attempting to adjudicate without authority could be dealt with by his local chief; for example:

Bereng v. Hlolo, Bereng, 1934.
H, a village headman, found a woman stealing, so punished her by making her weed his fields. As he had no judicial authority, B fined him one beast.

Some matters, such as the taking up of arms against another person, were reserved for the Paramount Chief's court.[1] This limitation was not strictly observed and important courts heard such cases, if there was no bloodshed, and especially if the taking up of guns was no more than a threatening gesture. Junior courts should, however, send on to their chief's court all matters involving the use of a dangerous weapon (*Fanyane v. Jeme*).[2]

The whole position has now been tightened up and more closely defined by the Native Courts Proclamation and the Native Court Rules.[3] Under the former, only such courts as are recognized or established by the Resident Commissioner may exercise judicial functions, and their jurisdiction is defined by warrant. They are divided into three classes—the Paramount Chief's Appeal Courts, Chiefs'[4] Appeal Courts (Class A) and courts of first instance (Class B). The Native Courts Proclamation excludes offences in consequence of which death is alleged to have resulted or which are punishable by death or life imprisonment, such as murder, rape and treason,[5] and civil cases dealing with marriage other than marriage "contracted in accordance with native law and custom, except where and in so far as the case concerns the payment or return or disposal of dowry". It also excludes all law other than native law and custom "not repugnant to justice or morality or inconsistent with the provisions of any law in force in the Territory",

[1] *Laws*, 1922, No. 18.
[2] Chapter XV.
[3] Proclamation No. 62 of 1938 and High Commissioner's Notice No. 32 of 1946. The Native Court Rules are based very largely on existing customs, to which they have given greater precision and definition and have added new formalities such as fees and writs.
[4] These chiefs are officially designated "Ward Chiefs". See Chapter XIII.
[5] Proclamation "B" of 1884, reiterated in the *Laws of Lerotholi*, 1922, No. 12, removed all homicide cases from the jurisdiction of native courts.

provided that the High Commissioner may confer jurisdiction "to enforce all or any of the provisions of any law". By 1949 native courts had been empowered to try cases of tax default arising out of the Native Tax Proclamation, and infringements of the Regulations for Compulsory Dosing of Sheep and Goats.[1] Some statutory laws have long been incorporated into the body of native law and are administered as customary law by the native courts, for example, the removal of stock only under permit issued by a competent authority.[2] The Native Court Rules also provide that "any dispute in which European law or trade usages are involved which, in the opinion of the court, it is unable to adjudicate upon properly because the facts are not covered by native law or custom" may be passed on to the District Commissioner's Court. Penalties (fines up to £100 and/or imprisonment not exceeding 12 months) are provided for adjudicating without authority.

The limitation of the native courts to only three classes, of which two are principally appeal courts, means that in effect the junior courts, B Class, are able to deal with all cases falling under Native Courts jurisdiction. The only official limitations are in respect of civil disputes, which may not exceed £200 in Class B and £500 in Class A courts, and of criminal penalties which will be dealt with later. It is quite possible, and more than probable, that important cases of both types are tacitly reserved to the Class A courts or even to the Paramount Chief's Appeal Courts, and are heard by them as matters of first instance, but I have no information on this point.

Serious criminal cases, such as theft or assault, after a preliminary hearing by the native courts are sometimes sent to the District Commissioner's court for trial, and sometimes remitted back to them. Cases which have been investigated by the police are not usually tried by the native courts, but may be remitted to them by the local police officer or by the District Commissioner. Civil claims for damages arising out of matters dealt with as crimes by the European courts, such as homicide or rape, may be referred to the native courts for settlement.

The geographical limits of a court's jurisdiction used to be co-extensive with the political competence of that authority. A chief's court had jurisdiction over the whole of that chief's district, a headman's court over that headman's ward. Such jurisdiction extended over all natives domiciled in that area, that is, over all men, with their wives and children, who were registered for tax purposes under that particular authority or who had lands and dwellings in that area, and the court could hear matters within its civil or criminal jurisdiction, in which such people were the defendants or accused, whether such matters arose within that area or not.

[1] High Commissioner's Notices Nos. 122 and 295 of 1948.
[2] Proclamation No. 80 of 1921. This was included in the *Laws of Lerotholi*, 1922, No. 24, and reiterated in Rules issued by the Paramount Chief, 1946, No. 17.

Shoapile v. Tsoloane, May 1936.
T left Basutoland with S's mother and sister and went with them to the Orange Free State where the latter became pregnant. On their return, S sues T for seducing her. Both parties are normally domiciled within Mosuoe's area.

Bata v. Kapoko, May 1936.
B lives in the lowlands, K under Mosuoe. They returned from the mines together. B left his goods with a friend near their dispersal point to keep while he went to fetch pack animals. After B had left, K returned to this person saying he was a relation of B's and had been sent to collect these goods, which were accordingly given to him. B traced them to K's home near Malingoaneng and sued K in Mosuoe's court.

The courts also had jurisdiction over persons not domiciled within their area when the matter in dispute, whether criminal or civil, arose within that area. As the saying goes, *"ntja e bolaeloa serobeng"* (the dog is killed in the fowl run). Thus a stranger who seduced a girl or who stole sheep or committed some other offence within the area could be dealt with by the court of that area. If he left the area before he was found out, he could either be tried in his home court, as in the above case of *Bata v. Kapoko*, or he could be sent back for trial on the request of the authority of the area where the offence was committed.

Mosalatsi v. Litsela and another, 1936.
M, a subject of 'Matumane, regent of the Makhoakhoa, traces sheep stolen from his cattle-post to L's post. As many of the witnesses in the case were at M's home, Mosuoe's court ordered L's headman to take him and his witnesses down to Butha Buthe to 'Matumane's court.

A case always had to be taken to the local headman's court. When it was beyond his court's jurisdiction by reason of its seriousness, it had to be forwarded to the sub-chief's court, and if beyond the latter's power, on again to the chief's court. This procedure might, however, be modified and the lower courts by-passed in the circumstances described below; this might also happen, improperly, when one of the parties concerned refused to recognize or deliberately wished to insult the junior court. Although these courts were debarred after 1946 from trying cases, they were still required to examine all cases falling within their jurisdiction. If unable to solve them to the satisfaction of the parties concerned, they had to forward them to the "B" court of the area, with a certificate to the effect that they had looked into the case and failed to settle it. If this certificate was not forthcoming, the court refused to accept the case and sent the parties back to get it. The purpose of this procedure was to keep the subordinate authorities interested in what was going on and to stop a lot of petty or simple cases from flooding the "B" courts; but owing to complaints that this delayed rather than expedited matters, the Paramount Chief, in 1949, authorized the "B" courts to accept cases which had not previously been examined by these minor courts.

The right of a dissatisfied party to appeal to a higher court has long been recognized. Formerly the decision of the chief, as head of the tribe, was final. When Moshesh established his paramountcy, he insisted on appeals being allowed to go from the chief's court to his, but met with little success until backed by the British Government. The position was clearly set out in the *Laws of Lerotholi* of 1922, from which the following extract is taken:

> "It is lawful for any person to have the right to appeal from the judgment of any court; but the Paramount Chief must be informed of such appeal. It is lawful that any person has the right to appeal from the judgment of any court to the court recognized as the one to which the appeals of the lower court lie, until the Paramount Chief's court is reached, so long as any of the disputants is not satisfied with judgments of the court below. It is the law that any person can appeal from the Paramount Chief's court to the court of the Resident Commissioner or an Assistant Commissioner as the case may be.
>
> "The Paramount Chief, Chief, Sub-Chief or Headman who has been given authority to try cases, and who will without reasonable excuse contravene this law by refusing any person the right to appeal, shall be guilty of an offence and liable to a penalty not exceeding £20."[1]

The Assistant Commissioner's court has been replaced by that of the District Commissioner (whose judicial work in hearing appeals from the Paramount Chief's court is now mostly done by the Judicial Commissioner) and the Resident Commissioner's court by the High Court. From the last two courts appeals have always lain to the Privy Council.

As indicated by the quotation from the *Laws*, appeals used to follow the political hierarchy. From a headman's court they lay to that of the sub-chief immediately over him and from this sub-chief to the chief or sub-chief over him, and so on upwards until they reached the Paramount Chief's court. The headman's court was thus a court of first instance only, whereas all other courts were, or could be, courts of appeal as well as courts of first instance. In 1946 this was changed by introducing Class B courts, which are courts of first instance only, and Class A courts which are courts of appeal only (although where the nearest "B" court is far away, the "A" court may be opened to litigants as an act of grace). Appeals from "B" courts go straight to their respective "A" courts and thence to the Paramount Chief's Appeal Courts, instead of through various intermediate courts.

Until recently the courts could deal with cases involving non-natives as complainants. The most usual cases of this sort were suits for debts owed to European and Indian trading stores or to Indian hawkers. It is probable that other types of cases also occurred, as a few Europeans

[1] *Laws*, 1922, No. 3.

and many Indians and Coloureds lived very close to the Basuto, although I have no direct evidence of this. The Native Courts Proclamation has now limited the native courts' jurisdiction to natives only.

Venue

The general rule about venue was that the case should be heard in the court of the defendant's headman. Thus, when giving notice of his intention to sue, a plaintiff asked the defendant where his hearth was—"*u besa kae?*"—and laid his complaint before the latter's headman. If the defendant failed to answer the summons, the court could force him to appear and fine him for his disobedience, usually one beast; if it was reluctant to do so, it gave the plaintiff leave to take the matter to the next court above. The latter court might either hear the case or return it to the lower court, ordering the defendant to appear before it; in either case, it might punish the defendant for his disobedience. There was no hard and fast rule as to which alternative should be followed. It would be strictly correct to refer the case back but, for practical reasons, the senior court might hear the case itself to avoid further delay, as the defendant's disobedience suggested that he would probably refuse to accept the lower court's decision and would appeal to the senior court.

Sehahabane v. Moleko, April 1936.
S sued M in Sehoete's court. M refused to answer the summons on the grounds that Sehoete had been placed in a supervisory capacity and had no authority to try cases. The case passed on to Thotofeane's court, but M again refused to attend. Thotofeane, who had just taken over his grandfather Lelingoana's personal ward court, was still weak, so the case was passed to Mosuoe's court, which heard it. As M was a tough customer it would have been a waste of time to send him back. For the same reason no fine was imposed.

If the defendant was sued in a higher court than his headman's, he was entitled to refuse to answer the suit, although he was still bound to answer that court's summons to appear. The plaintiff was then usually ordered to take the matter to the defendant's headman. An exception was made in the following circumstances: if a visitor were involved as plaintiff or witness, the case might be taken straight to the court of the chief of the area, sometimes after a cursory examination by the defendant's headman. This was done to obtain an authoritative decision immediately and so avoid the delay of possible appeals from the junior courts, which might prejudice the visitor who "has nowhere to sleep and nothing to eat". Where the defendant was himself a visitor, the case would normally be taken to the court of the headman under whom he was temporarily living or in whose jurisdiction the cause of the dispute arose. In criminal cases, the prosecuting authority (i.e. the chief) prosecuted the defendant (accused) in his (the chief's) own court or that of a higher authority, as it would be derogatory to him to have the case decided by a junior court and it would be invidious for the latter to have to decide it. Moreover, in the event of an appeal, the case would have to come to his own court for decision, so, as in the previous exception, it was expeditious to hear it there in the first place. The fourth exception occurred where the local topography was an important part of the evidence, as in stock theft cases. Such cases might be tried by the authority in whose jurisdiction the offence was committed, as he would be able to handle the case with greater competence than the defendant's headman who knew nothing of the country, as in the case of *Mosalatsi v. Litsela and another*, quoted above.

Court Procedure

Procedure varied slightly in different courts—the smaller the court the simpler the procedure; but the pattern was much the same throughout and the differences were largely those of detail. The headman's court was the simplest and most straightforward. When a person wished to sue another, he reported the matter to the latter's headman and asked permission to bring the case before his court. The headman then appointed a day suitable to both parties for the hearing. As his court only functioned intermittently, he also informed all the men of his ward so that they might attend and help him hear the case. On the appointed day the parties reported to the court. When everyone was ready, the plaintiff made out his case and called his witnesses. The defendant then replied and called his witnesses; after this, they were all examined by the headman and anyone else who might wish to do so. At the end of it all, the headman withdrew from the court accompanied by those whose opinion he valued. He first discussed whether the case was within his jurisdiction and, if he decided that it was, he discussed what the verdict should be. The judgment was then announced to the court by the headman or whoever was deputed to be his spokesman. If the case was beyond his jurisdiction, the parties were told to proceed to the next court. If it was obvious from the start that the case was beyond his competence, he would only briefly inquire into its details before sending it on. The procedure was much the same in the courts of minor sub-chiefs, except that the authority might be represented by a relative or councillor and only those of his subjects who lived in or near the village were expected to attend the court.

In the more important courts, procedure was more complicated and formal, and the same procedure is still followed in "National Treasury" courts. These courts sit every day except Sundays, public holidays and days of mourning. They open in the morning towards 8.30 or 9 o'clock and sit until late in the afternoon unless all their business is finished earlier. Every day part of their time is given up to hearing reports and complaints. Messengers report the results of their commissions, such as collection of fines, summoning of witnesses, assistance given to tax-collectors, and investigations into land disputes or cases of stock theft. Political messengers may also repeat official reports of public interest that have been delivered to the chief.[1] Complaints cover a vast range of topics. The most common are requests to the court to get on with some case that has dragged on for months, requests to subpoena a witness or opponent who has refused to answer previous summonses, allegations of injustice, complaints over land distribution, demands for maintenance or compensation for delays in cases to which they have been summoned, and pleas for the enforcement of judgments. To these remarks, some hotly, some suavely and others despairingly made, the judges make such reply as they can and arrange for such action as may be necessary. During this period of general business, would-be litigants announce their wish to bring a case to court. They briefly outline their cases and ask for the court to be "opened" to them. At Matsieng and other leading courts, a court clerk takes a written statement from them which is given to the Court President. If the court agrees to hear the case, it appoints a day for the hearing; if both parties are present, it orders them both to attend on the day appointed, together with their witnesses; if only the plaintiff is present, it orders him to inform his opponent of the arrangements made.

Under the comprehensive Native Court Rules, issued in 1946, the plaintiff must pay a fee of 5s. to "open the court", 1s. for the summons to each witness and 2s. 6d. for each day a court messenger is used. When these have been paid the clerk of the court sets down a day for the hearing of the case and issues summonses in duplicate on the defendant or accused and all requisite witnesses, which are delivered by the official court messenger.

On the day appointed, the parties announce their presence to the court and then wait for their case to be called. As they come into the court, they raise their hats and salute the President and the men about him: "Honoured Chief", "Chief and honoured court", "Chief and your circle of peace". They enter the court only by its defined entrance, and even though half the boundary consists of no more than a little line of stones, to walk over them rather than go in by the proper entrance would be grossly disrespectful. People of some political or social standing may go up to the President and other members of the court, shake hands and exchange greetings. The defendant and his friends and witnesses then go to one side of the court, where they sit down together, the plaintiff and his party go to the other side. Women are not allowed in the court, and those involved in a case sit outside, near enough to the palisade to be seen and heard by the President, and to hear and see him. At Matsieng, however, where the courts are purely places of official

[1] These reports would probably be omitted in the "Treasury" courts that are divorced from the political authority.

business and lack the social associations of the courts of smaller authorities, women sit in the middle of the court while being examined, but must leave when the examination is finished.

When the court is ready, the President calls on the plaintiff or appellant to state his case. Leaving his walking-stick, riding-crop or whisk in his place, and perhaps chewing a piece of a small plant called *molomo-monate*[1] (good mouth) to give his words sweetness, he walks to the centre of the court, uncovers his head, salutes the President and the court, and proceeds to make his statement (*setatemente*). When he has finished, he calls on his witnesses to speak, and is then followed by the defendant and his witnesses. Normally, they are allowed to make their statements uninterrupted, save for occasional interjections by the President or assessors, demands for explanation or a reminder to keep to the point. Then when both parties have spoken and all the witnesses have been called and the general trend of the case is clear, they are examined one by one, called and recalled as often as, and in whatever order, may be desired by the President and his assistants. The President usually examines first and, having finished, turns to one of his assistants with some such remark as, "I now leave him to you". When they have done, anyone present may ask further questions. Male witnesses giving evidence or replying to questions must do so standing in the centre of the court, women do so sitting, either in court or just outside. Those questioning witnesses do so standing in their seats.

Normally the parties do not cross-examine their opponents and witnesses, preferring to express disagreement by snorts of indignation and to refute their evidence later by criticizing or denying it in a further statement, although should they wish to examine their opponents or opponents' witnesses, they may do so. In a few of the more sophisticated courts, such as Matsieng, the wealthier people may have special pleaders (*akhente*) to help them conduct their case, but this is contrary to traditional practice and theory which place on the judge and the assistants the main task of sifting the evidence and arriving at the truth. Indeed, Sesuto conceptions of the role of the judge and the purpose of cross-examination differ profoundly from our own. To them, the judge is not an Olympian being, whose chief function is to referee the struggle between plaintiff and defendant and then decide whether, or to what extent, the case has been proven or refuted; they expect him to descend to the arena and to discover the truth himself with the help of his assistants. The employment of advocates or legal practitioners in the native courts has been forbidden by the Native Courts Proclamation.[2] At the end of the hearing and the examination of the parties and their witnesses, the party who first adduced evidence may address the court, summing up his version of the facts, and thereafter the other party may do the same.

[1] Cf. Phillips, p. 69.   [2] Proclamation No. 62 of 1938, Section 20.

When they have finished the President and his assistants go "into committee". The President clears the court and gathers his assistants round him or retires with them to the office, the chief's hut or some other convenient spot. They discuss the case, compare their findings and try to agree on their decision, on the damages to be awarded, or fines to be imposed. They are usually fairly quick over this, having gauged one another's attitude from the proceedings in court, but in important cases, they will discuss the matter thoroughly. I knew of one decision which was discussed for four days. There is no voting—the matter is decided by consensus of opinion, or, where there is a difference of opinion, by the President, who is not bound to accept the views of the others. The decision may be reported to the chief for information and approval if they think he would be interested; it should always be reported in land disputes and cases of assault accompanied by bloodshed, as *mobu le mali ke tsa morena* (matters of blood and soil are the chief's), and he should make the final decision.

When their deliberations are over, the court reassembles and the President, or one of his assistants, announces their decision with gusto and eloquence. Speaking in the name of the chief, he addresses first the plaintiff and then the defendant, praising those actions which met with the court's approval, condemning those of which it disapproved, and finally announces the terms of their decision. If damages have been awarded or fines imposed, he usually mentions a date by which they are to be paid. The following excerpts of two cases illustrate these points:

Moleleki v. Moloi, 1936.
Moleleki sues Moloi for committing adultery with his wife. This is the fourth time he has caught them. Moloi is fined two beasts and made to pay Moleleki four beasts as damages. In announcing the judgment, the President says to Moloi: "The chief says he finds you a child who will harm Sekonyela's village, because you have been warned by the late Chief Lelingoana to keep away from this house of Moleleki and yet you keep on going there. Leave this district and return to your parents. There is no law that says when a person joins a new chief he joins with his 'loincloth'." He then praises Moleleki for his self-restraint. "It is true you know that the heart is long-suffering, you have done well for you easily might have broken the law." Turning then to the woman, he says: "You are thoroughly wicked, you make our hearts sad, you are without shame, a person of whom it could be said, 'She is a witch'. The chief says to you, he finds it impossible to think of anything base enough to compare you with. You are like a dog or a pig, for in spite of having been reproved several times in front of Moloi for this very adultery of his, you have persisted in continuing to drag him into Moleleki's hut. He says to you 'Phooaha', you disgust him. You are the mother of trouble-makers, you are like Mankeeane who set the people against one another. Leave Moloi, this sorcerer of Mahao's."[1]

[1] Mahao was Moloi's headman.

'Makamoho v. Borife, August 1936.
'Makamoho sued her husband Borife for neglecting her and favouring his junior wife. Appeal case from Molatoli's court. After hearing the case, the judges went into committee. On their return the President said to the woman, "You have rightly sued your husband. I thank you in the name of the chief." Then, turning to the man, he said, "You, Borife, the chief says this woman was a virgin, her breasts were firm, it is you who have made them sag; you fetched a person's daughter saying you loved her, you defeated other young men who wanted to marry her, and now you are trying to free yourself. The chief says he orders you to sleep in this woman's hut. He has heard that your saddle is no longer in her hut, it is in your inferior wife's, now let it return to the chief hut. Plough for her, clothe her, buy food for her as you used to do when you first fetched her from her father's. The chief says that for throwing away your wife and for refusing to obey the judgment of Molatoli and his order that you should look after her, he now fines you £2 10s."

After the judgment has been delivered, the parties rise, and either thank the court for its decision and accept its judgment or bewail their misfortune and ask for an appeal. Dieterlen says[1] that in the old days "etiquette demanded that those who had been adjudged in the wrong, should thank the court even when they considered themselves the victims of rank injustice". This no longer obtains and aggrieved parties may give vent to their dissatisfaction in no uncertain terms; even if they do not wish to appeal, they may accept the judgment carpingly and grumblingly. If a person wishes to appeal, he is called to the office when the court rises and given a letter of introduction to the next court. This sometimes gives the salient features of the case and details of the judgment. The appellant is given a certain time within which to lodge his appeal—usually a week unless he asks for more—and if he fails to do so without adequate reason, he forfeits his right of appeal and automatically becomes bound by the original judgment. Formerly,[2] every appeal was supposed to be reported to the Paramount Chief, but this impracticable rule was rarely observed and has now been repealed. A formal and elaborate procedure for dealing with appeals has been laid down in the Native Court Rules, including a deposit of 5s. for appeal to Class A courts and £1 to the Paramount Chief's court.

The more important courts keep, and have kept for years past, records of their cases, though erratically and with varying fullness. The usual type of record contained the date of the hearing, a résumé of the judgment with reasons, the names of the parties and perhaps the names of their headmen and principal witnesses, the names of the President, his co-judges and helpers, the date on which the fines and damages were paid. Occasionally the judge's remarks and the statements of the parties and chief witnesses were also recorded. In some courts, notably the Paramount Chief's, copies of judgments were given to the parties and

---

[1] Dieterlen, *Livre d'Or*, p. 39.   [2] *Laws of Lerotholi*, 1922, No. 3.

sent to the court from which the appeal was taken. In appeal cases, a moderate check was kept on slippery witnesses by sending the appeal court a fairly full résumé of their statements in the lower court or by sending a messenger from the latter to attend the appeal court. Very occasionally a full record might be kept and sent to the appeal court. At Matsieng, a written statement was often taken before the case was called. The new Native Court Rules provide that full written records should be kept of the proceedings in every court and that all evidence, questions and answers should be recorded.

The period allowed for payment of fines and damages was usually a week, but has now been extended to thirty days.[1] Extension of time may be asked for and is usually given. Payments are received by one of the court officials who notes the amount paid in the record book. Before 1946, receipts were not usually given, as payment was supposed to be made publicly, thus safeguarding the payee, but they are now required by the new Native Court Rules. Where payment is made in the form of stock, the official also checks the *bewijs* and satisfies himself as to the ownership of the stock. The cash or stock paid as damages are then handed over to the successful party and those paid as fines to the chief. Formerly, one or more of the animals delivered in payment of a fine was given to the judges to be slaughtered immediately and consumed by the court, but this practice has languished for many years, and all the stock was kept by the chief, except for the few animals that might be given to the judges as payment for their services. Since 1946, all fines are supposed to be paid into the National Treasury, the revenue from this source being estimated at £22,000 for the year 1949–50. They also have to be paid in cash instead of in kind.

If payment is made in instalments, the damages awarded to the successful party should be paid before any fines are appropriated by the court, as its primary function is to see that justice is done and not to fill the chief's pocket. This sensible precaution was not always observed and officials sometimes deducted the amount of the fine from the first instalment and then, having got what they could out of it, lost interest in the case, and made little effort to enforce the rest of their judgment. The temptation to do this has now been reduced by the regulation that all fines must be paid into the National Treasury.

If the offender does not comply with the judgment, the court should send a messenger to remind him or should call him in and ask what the position is. If he does not obey the judgment after several reminders, the court may fine him for disobedience and order him to comply. Failing this, it may seize as much of his stock as may be necessary to pay the amount due; the messengers sent to do this may take an extra sheep or two for food and may also penalize him for contempt of court by taking additional stock. Should he try to resist them forcibly, or be-

[1] High Commissioner's Notice No. 32 of 1946, Section 22.

have rebelliously, he may be sued in the chief's court and fined one or more beasts. In extreme cases, he may be "eaten up", and most, if not all, of his stock would be seized and his huts burnt. The nature of the action taken greatly depends on the personality of the chief and his court officials. Some are prompt and exacting; others are lenient or lethargic and send out reminders at odd intervals, until either the matter is settled or they tire of it; others again order their subordinate authorities to collect what is due from those living in their areas, while others may wait several years until harvests are good and the people are comparatively prosperous, and then make out complete lists of defaulters and send messengers round the district to collect what is unpaid. The process of execution has now been elaborated in the 1946 Native Court Rules which formalize the old procedure. The Rules also provide various safeguards against abuse, such as that no execution of a judgment against property or stock may take place between sunset and sunrise, that the court messenger should make an inventory of all property and stock seized and hand a copy thereof to the owner, that various kinds of property shall be exempt from seizure under writ of execution, such as beds, bedding and wearing apparel, furniture and household utensils not exceeding £15 in value, food and drink sufficient to last till the next harvest, agricultural and other trade tools and equipment not exceeding £20 in value, immovable property, land or growing crops.[1] I have no information as to the extent to which these safeguards are effective. The occurrence of cases of spoliation or "eating up" clearly pointed to their desirability.

On the whole, promptness is not one of the characteristics of the courts; when roused or when they want to, they can act speedily and efficiently, but for the most part they are content to jog along and let things slide. This is due partly to temperament and partly to the scale of damages and fines imposed (described below) which is absurdly high in relation to the general standard of the people's wealth. A fine of a beast is quite common, but it represents about two-thirds of the average holding, so that the enforcement of even moderate judgments takes time and needs more compulsion than would appear at first sight.

Evidence

In hearing cases, the court is guided by certain principles of evidence. Though vague and variable, for they are not formulated in any recognized code and their application varies with the personality of the judges, they serve as a good general guide. Evidence should be more or less relevant to the issue, though great latitude is allowed for various reasons. One is that it is traditional for witnesses to give their evidence in a round-about rather than a direct way, the extent to which they are allowed to wander from the main point depending on the alertness

[1] High Commissioners' Notice No. 32 of 1946, Section 22.

of the judges and on the competence or astuteness of the parties. A second and more important reason is that the court is not obliged to deal only with the main dispute at issue, but may deal concurrently with any other wrongdoing, civil or criminal, that may be brought to its notice. It may, therefore, hear any evidence which, though irrelevant to the main dispute, reveals and bears on any such wrongdoing. The following example illustrates this elasticity:

Titisi v. Makhala, January 1936.

T sued M for some grain and money (£1) which he had left in M's village. The facts elicited were that T, a stranger, had been allowed to settle in X's village, X being away and M acting as his caretaker. T made a set at X's wife. He was warned several times by M to cease his attentions to her and was finally ordered to leave the village. After he had gone M found T's money and some grain there which he handed to the local headman for safe keeping. The latter consumed all of this save 2s. T meanwhile continued his attentions to X's wife. The court fined the headman 30s. for his dereliction of duty and fined T 30s. for his adultery with X's wife. M was commended for his restraint and correct behaviour.

The case of *Mamasiea v. 'Motsarapane*[1] also illustrates this point.

As regards what constitutes good evidence, court practice is fairly loose. The evidence of eye-witnesses is regarded as the best, indeed, as the only really reliable type of evidence, although slackly conducted courts, unless forcibly challenged by one of the parties or by some onlooker, are frequently satisfied with less reliable evidence. Hearsay evidence is often accepted, particularly if repeated by independent witnesses or if the alleged source of the information is unavoidably absent. Circumstantial evidence is also often accepted; the fact that a man was found alone with a married woman of whom he is known to be fond, or was seen coming out of her hut or courtyard, may be taken as evidence of adultery.[2] Sometimes, evidence of this sort is only accepted if supported by other facts, though if such facts are matters of common knowledge, they may be taken for granted, and not brought out specifically in court.

A special type of evidence is the confession. If a person admits liability on apprehension or at some time prior to the hearing of the case, his admission counts heavily against him, and should he subsequently retract, he will have to produce stronger evidence to prove his innocence than he would otherwise have done. The weight attached to a confession or admission varies according to the way in which it was made. It counts for little if it took the form of a boast, or was made under duress or fear. On the other hand, in theft cases, if it takes the form of carrying all or part of the stolen property to the local authority, it is taken as positive proof of guilt. In fact, so damning is this, that at-

[1] Chapter XII, p. 183.   [2] *Fanyane v. Jeme*, Chapter XV, p. 258.

tempts to make the person suspected of theft carry the *corpus delicti* frequently end in bloodshed. A written admission of liability is also strong evidence.[1]

In everyday life people believe the statements made by a witch-doctor from his interpretation of the "bones", or by seers who claim to have second sight. Some also accept deathbed statements made by a dying person, attributing his death to some enemy's sorcery. Casalis's mention of the occurrence of "smelling out" trials seems to indicate that formerly evidence of this sort was officially accepted by the chiefs, but this no longer is the case. No matter how firmly people may believe in sorcery, bone-throwing or the powers of seers as individuals, they would not, as judicial officers, accept such evidence in court. Furthermore, although they might privately credit circumstantial evidence of witchcraft or sorcery, in their official capacity as judges they reject such evidence.[2]

Normally, plain statements of fact are all that are expected and allowed from witnesses, and it is left to the court to decide what inferences and conclusions should be drawn from them, although in slackly conducted cases, witnesses may be allowed to run on and air their own speculations and opinions. Nevertheless, there are certain occasions when the opinion of witnesses is not only allowed but is actually sought. For instance, in a stock theft case, part of the plaintiff's case rested on the finding of charred bones in the defendant's ash-heap; the latter argued that these were the remains of a sheep he had killed a month or two before, whereas the plaintiff argued that they were fresh. To settle the matter, not only did the judge examine the bones to get some idea of their condition, but the court also asked for the opinion of a number of independent people. A common case when opinion is allowed or sought is that of disputed paternity; old women, supposed to be experts in such matters, are asked to compare the infant with the men supposed to have fathered it, and to judge from physiognomical likeness who might be the father. In one case, "A" sued "B" for adultery as his wife said she had conceived by "B". The latter denied this, so Mosuoe's court sought the opinion of local women as to whom the child resembled. Opinion was divided, but the majority said it looked like "B". He was ordered to pay three head of cattle as damages. He then appealed to Seeiso. The latter adopted the same procedure, but chose old women who knew nothing about the case and told them to pick the father out of a group of men including "A" and "B". They could not say the child looked like any of them, but they considered that it strongly resembled its mother!

Evidence about character may be allowed. The object of this is either to discredit one's opponent's evidence by besmirching his own or his

---

[1] *Bofofu v. Nkhala*, Chapter XV, p. 256.
[2] *Mokopu v. Motinyane*, Chapter XV, p. 265.

witness's character, or to enhance one's own evidence by establishing the good character of one's witnesses. In the lower courts where everyone knows everyone else, and the judges and court know from past judicial experience, as well as from their ordinary social intercourse, what reliance can be placed on the testimony of witnesses, these tactics are not often employed; in the higher courts, where individual reputations are not so well known, they are used to a greater extent.

Courts often make use of unexpressed evidence, when the facts are known to the court members or are common property. If, for example, it is common knowledge that members of a family are constantly quarrelling, the court usually treats actions they may bring against one another with considerable levity and gives a light-hearted decision which it has little intention of enforcing and scarcely expects to be observed.

All evidence produced in the court should be oral. Evidence so given must be given by the witness himself, except when representatives are allowed to appear and speak on behalf of their principals: for example, authorities are allowed to send their representatives to speak on their behalf to say what the judgment of their court was in a particular case, to describe how they had placed a junior authority or to answer an action brought against them. Old people are sometimes allowed to do the same when it would be a severe hardship for them to appear personally. Written evidence may be allowed in special circumstances, as in the following case:

Motseki v. Tau, June 1936.
Eight cattle were stolen and the thieves tried to dispose of them at the store of Mofolo (the well-known author). One of them confessed the theft to him and implicated T. T denied this to Mofolo, but other accomplices then confessed to Mofolo. As Mofolo was a man of considerable standing and was unable to attend the court owing to ill health, his written statement was accepted.

In stock theft cases or ownership disputes, *bewijs* or stock removal permits are accepted as evidence of ownership, and the person who issued the permit is not called on to substantiate the permit, unless there is some doubt about its authenticity. Again, reference is occasionally made to old court records to ascertain the terms of a previous judgment relevant to a present dispute. Certified copies of judgments of other courts, such as the Paramount Chief's courts at Matsieng, are also accepted.

Wherever possible, material exhibits connected with a case should be produced: for example, a garment of the offender (usually his hat) in adultery cases, or the implement with which an assault was committed. Similarly, the victim of an assault should show his wound to the court as soon as possible, so that the judges may have direct evidence of its seriousness. In some cases, such as stock theft, the production of the *corpus delicti* is essential, unless there is very strong circumstantial evidence linking the defendant or accused with the offence for which he is being sued.

Khabu v. Majone, March 1936.
K was sent to look for twelve lost horses. Two were discovered at M's cattle-post. The court found M guilty of the theft of these two but dismissed K's action in respect of the other ten as there was no evidence connecting M with them and they might easily have got separated from the other two before M found them.

Chaka v. Sebanyane and others, March 1936.
C lost seventeen sheep which were later seen being driven by S at night. On being challenged, S and the others ran away, but they were identified by S's hat found on the path and by their footprints. They denied the theft and one of them, a doctor, said that they were running over the veld in a trance (*phephetha*). Sixteen of the sheep were found. As it was reasonable to suppose that they had also taken the seventeenth, they were found guilty of the theft of all seventeen.

It is not necessary that the whole of the *corpus delicti* be produced in court. All that is needed is sufficient material to prove that an offence has been committed, or to identify an object suspected of being stolen, such as the skin of a sheep. In one case where the accused had no stock of his own, a small fragment of fresh bone found in his ash-heap supported an accusation that he had killed and eaten a stolen sheep.

Anyone may give evidence in court with the exception of the mentally deficient and the very young. The courts may call children as witnesses, but dislike doing so, and would rarely call them to give evidence against their parents. Wives and husbands are able to give evidence for or against one another, such evidence often being of great value in cases of theft or adultery. Accessories and co-defendants are entitled to give evidence for or against one another, but do not escape their liability. Turning "king's evidence" is repugnant to people's sense of what is fitting, and accomplices and accessories are expected to remain loyal to one another. Such loyalty is sometimes recognized as an extenuating circumstance, meriting a reduction of the penalty an offender would otherwise have deserved.[1]

Evidence is not taken under oath, but people are expected to tell the truth. They may swear to the truth of their statements by the usual oaths—"by my father", "by God", "it is God's truth"—but they rarely do so, partly because it is not etiquette and partly because they know that it will not greatly impress the court. To get at the truth the court relies on vigorous examination (as the Basuto say of an exposed liar "the questions have defeated him"). Witnesses should not be obstruc-

[1] *Tootse v. Maekane*, Chapter XV, p. 271.

tive nor lie deliberately, and serious or malicious false witness is penalized by fining.

Factors affecting Liability

Once it has been proved that an offence has been committed, and that the offender is in some way associated with it, the determination of his liability depends on the type of his connexion, and varies from one kind of offence to another. Liability usually depends on whether the offender intended to do what he did, or intended the presumptive consequence of his action. In some cases, such as stock theft, seduction and adultery, the mere fact that the offence was committed implies that it was intended. In other cases intent has to be specifically proved; for example, if a man sells a beast left in his trust, theft by conversion can be proved only by showing that he had no intention of replacing it at a later date. In some cases the offender may do more or less than he intended to do and here his intent, rather than his action, measures his liability. Thus, if a man deliberately insults another in order to goad him to violent retaliation, he may be punished for trying to provoke a breach of the peace, even though he did not succeed in doing so; lurking near a kraal or village at night is not in itself an offence, but if a man is found doing so in circumstances that suggest that he intends to steal, he may be found guilty of attempted theft. In one such case, the offender's ingenious plea that he had come *ka bohlola* (to commit adultery) was not accepted! On the other hand, a person sometimes does more than he intended; he may, for instance, insult or assault someone in a fit of temper or drunkenness. If he immediately apologizes and tries to heal the wound he has inflicted (*ho rotetsa leqeba*) by spitting on it, washing, anointing or bandaging it, or taking such other action as indicates remorse and a desire to make amends, his offence may be punished more lightly than it would otherwise have been and may even be entirely excused.

In a few cases, extenuating circumstances may diminish the offender's liability or exculpate him. An unprovoked attack on oneself or one's family, serious and unprovoked insult or the discovery of a person *in flagrante delicto*, sleeping with one's wife, are instances of provocation which may entirely exonerate a person charged with assault. According to the witnesses[1] before the Native Laws Commission, a thief caught at night breaking open a kraal or stealing stock, or a thief who resisted arrest, could be stabbed or shot without fault. In such a case the court may distinguish between civil and criminal liability and may fine the offender for having taken the law into his own hands; it will not make a civil award for damages to the person injured, as it was the victim's own fault that he was hurt.

That an offence was committed under the influence of liquor is

[1] Sofonia and George Moshesh.

seldom accepted as an extenuating circumstance, unless the offender apologizes and tries to make amends for his offence as soon as he is sober enough to realize what he has done. The courts take a serious view of drunkenness and often regard it as an aggravation of the offence.

Other forms of incapacity may reduce or annul liability. Thus incapacity to distinguish right or wrong or appreciate what the law is, due to insanity or extreme youth, may exculpate lunatics and children, though the court in its discretion may suggest that the child be beaten to teach it the law. The same may occasionally apply to people such as *mathuela* acting under the "influence of the spirit"; but as many people are sceptical about this alleged spirit control, the courts require exceedingly strong evidence to support it before accepting such a plea, and the more sophisticated courts would not entertain it for a moment. Occasionally, a plea "the devil entered into me" is seriously advanced to mitigate offences such as assault or petty theft committed on the spur of an impulse, but I have never heard of its being accepted.

We may now turn to another type of case where liability has nothing to do with intent, where indeed the offender may be quite unaware of the fact that he is committing an offence or that an offence, for which he is being held responsible, was committed. Only a few examples of this are to be found, but they are interesting as showing a high degree of juridical development. Thus, ignorance of the law is no excuse, and failure to obey an order of the chief is not exonerated by ignorance of the order. In the old days, the first situation rarely arose. All laws were traditional, and knowledge of them was acquired as part of the normal cultural heritage of the people. Nowadays, with the promulgation of new laws and the occasional resuscitation of old ones, it is possible for a person to be ignorant of a particular law and so to contravene it unwittingly. But since all new laws, and revivals of the old, are either publicly announced at a *pitso* or published in the press, everyone is presumed to know what the position is. Similarly, if a person fails to obey a command of the chief to turn out for work on the chief's field, or observe a day of mourning, he is guilty of an offence, even if he was unaware of the command.

A person may also be held responsible for acts done by his servants or dependants, and for damage done by his stock. In the former case his vicarious responsibility is of two kinds: he is responsible for all acts done by his wives, minor children, unmarried younger brothers and other dependants. He represents them in court and pays the fines and damages they may incur in respect of some offence, whether it was committed with his knowledge and consent or not. He is also responsible for their contracts, entered into with or without his consent, such as marriage or service. The application of this principle is breaking down in respect of adult unmarried sons and daughters, who are now trying to assert their independence; nevertheless, it was recently offici-

JUDICIAL ORGANIZATION

ally reaffirmed,[1] "The head of a family may be held liable for a wrongful act or debt of his minor children (i.e. unmarried children living in his house and under his control)".

The second type of vicarious liability covers liability for the offences of servants, agents and other subordinates, committed in the course and within the scope of their employment. Thus, a stock owner is responsible for the negligence of a hired herd-boy who lets his stock stray into another person's lands; but the employer is not liable for an offence, such as stock theft, which the herd-boy may commit outside the scope of his work. Similarly, a chief is liable for wrongful acts of his court officials, such as the issue of false *bewijs* or unjustified confiscation of stock, as well as damage caused by their negligence, such as death of detained stock which were not properly looked after. Many authorities try to evade this responsibility, but that does not alter the principle.

Collective responsibility, such as the famous spoor law of the Ngoni, was sometimes found among the Basuto[2] in the old days. In spite of the early attempts of the British Government to foster it, it has died out, largely, according to Jobo, because Moshesh disapproved of it owing to the ease with which it enabled people to "plant" incriminating evidence on innocent villages. Laydevant writes[3] that "here the family and his chief are responsible for the good conduct of individuals. It often happens that a whole village is sentenced to a fine for the fault of one or two people only." If this means any more than that a parent is responsible for the acts of his minor children, this statement greatly exaggerates the position. Under no circumstances nowadays would a village be held collectively responsible for the acts or faults of individual villagers. In 1948, the High Commissioner threatened in the Basutoland Council that this principle would be revived if ritual murders continued on the same scale as hitherto. Later, legislation was promulgated providing for the quartering of police on a village at the expense of the villagers if an unreported murder was detected there or an unreported body found.[4]

A person is liable for all damage due to stock supposed to be under his control. Thus, if a person's cattle stray into a field, he is responsible for the damage, whether they strayed as a result of his negligence or not. Similarly, the owner of an animal is liable for the damage it causes to other people's animals. Cases of this sort are discussed in detail in the next chapter.

The courts distinguish between the principal offender and accessories or accomplices. This distinction occurs mainly in theft cases. The former are made to pay the full fines and damages, whereas the latter,

[1] Declaration of Basuto Law, Section 6.
[2] Ellenberger and MacGregor, p. 268 and Commission.
[3] Laydevant, 1931, p. 277.
[4] Proclamation No. 57 of 1948.

whether they actually committed the theft or merely helped to conceal the stolen goods or traces of the theft, are not held to be liable in the same degree. Ordinarily the distinction is not drawn too fine, and all those implicated are held more or less equally responsible; but where a large amount of stock has been stolen by a number of thieves, the court discriminates between their liability according to the degree of their participation in, and responsibility for, the theft. Sometimes persons who have heard or seen something suspicious and failed to report their suspicions to the local authority, may be treated as aiding and abetting the offence they suspected; more often they will be indicted for attempting to defeat the ends of justice. People who eat meat knowing it to be stolen are also regarded as accessories to the theft.

Punishment

The courts' powers of punishment are limited almost entirely to fining and public ridicule. Fines are inflicted either in money or kind, and vary from 3d. to several beasts. Some offences were (and still are) punished by a more or less constant rate of fining and others with varying fines depending on the circumstances of the case. Theoretically there was no limit to the amount of the fine that a chief's court could impose, but in practice it did not exceed a few beasts for serious offences, since a heavier fine would encourage the offender to appeal to a higher court. The standard fine varies from one head of small stock (or 10s.) to one beast (or £2); heavier fines were rarely given except by the most important courts. Commenting on a fine of a beast plus 30s. inflicted on a man who had interfered with the chief's messengers and assaulted them to prevent them arresting a thief (a fine which to me seemed perfectly just in the circumstances), my assistant wrote, "These people fine harshly; that is why the tribe takes so many appeals. If a person sneezes, they fine him several cattle!" On the other hand, courts such as the Paramount Chief's sometimes fine very heavily, especially if the offence smacks of political insubordination. For instance, for failing to obey an earlier judgment, Moholobela Seeiso of Berea district was fined 50 head of cattle by the Paramount Chief's court in 1935; in 1942, Bereng Griffith was fined £150 by the same court for contempt of court.

Before 1946 fines and damages were usually given in terms of small stock or cattle, or their fixed equivalents; the payer could elect how he would pay it: whether in stock, large or small, or cash, or partly in the one and partly in the other. As regards stock, any size, kind or quality would do, provided it was not excessively young, old or thin. The fixed equivalents recognized by the courts, irrespective of current market values were: 1 head of small stock (sheep or goats) equalled 10s.; a large wether equalled £1; four small stock equalled 1 beast or £2; a horse equalled £4 or 2 beasts; and a bridle and saddle together equalled 1 horse.

JUDICIAL ORGANIZATION

The only fines which had to be paid in the denomination in which they were imposed were small money fines and fines in grain, though in the latter case, when it was a matter of bags of grain, the equivalent of 10s. to one bag was allowed.

All fines have now to be paid into the National Treasury; they may no longer be paid in kind, but must "be paid in cash to the clerk of the court who shall issue receipts on the prescribed form for the moneys so received by him".[1]

The weapon of ridicule is freely used by the courts and is applied to unsatisfactory witnesses as well as to litigants whose conduct is reprehensible. During the actual hearing of the case, the court may pass adverse remarks on the character and behaviour of the people concerned, but the really stinging remarks are reserved for the end, when the verdict is announced. At times, the judge, or an assessor acting on behalf of the President, rises to heights of irony, sarcasm and abuse, and I have seen his victims squirm in their seats as he flayed them with words.

In the old days the chiefs could inflict the death penalty for sorcery, conspiring against the chief and inveterate thieving. Execution was carried out by throwing the offender from the top of a high cliff. Casalis records that Moshesh put a stop to the death penalty for theft and sorcery, and later the British Government abolished it altogether, so far as native courts were concerned. Mutilation occurred occasionally, but was never practised regularly. Torture was occasionally resorted to. For example, in 1934 one of the leading Highland chiefs was said to have punished two thieves by branding them with heated needles and exposing them to the heat of a fire, in an effort to check the widespread growth of stock theft. Another chief was said to have punished a soldier, about 1944, for some misdemeanour by exposing him to the cold for nights on end in winter tied to a tree. But such forms of punishment are not tolerated by the Government and the perpetrators may be prosecuted under the ordinary criminal law of the country.

Flogging was not used by the courts in the old days, except in the case of juvenile offenders. Laydevant writes[2] "that corporal punishment may be administered to thieves and wrongdoers who own no property and cannot pay a fine". It may be that this punishment was used in the area with which he was conversant, namely, Mafeteng, but I did not meet any instances. Corporal punishment is forbidden by the new Native Court Rules except for "a moderate corrective chastisement for children too young to receive any other punishment".[3]

Drastic punishments occasionally suffered were banishment, being "eaten up" and having one's huts burned down. Banishment meant

[1] Native Court Rules, No. 3.
[2] Laydevant, 1931, p. 267.
[3] High Commissioner's Notice No. 29 of 1948, Section 29.

being ordered to remove from one area to another within Basutoland and was imposed for gross disloyalty to the local chief or other native authority. One case occurred in 1935 when three men were ordered by the Paramount Chief's court to remove from a certain area in the Berea district, and a more recent case occurred in the Quthing district. Nowadays such orders have to be confirmed by the Resident Commissioner. The burning of a person's hut is usually done to enforce a banishment order or an order to remove from one part of a district to another area within the same district: for example, to cease living in a cattle-post area and move to a proper village area. It also used to be done in order to speed the departure of a suspected sorcerer. "Eating up" means seizure of all or most of a person's stock and other property. This was sometimes done as a punishment for disloyalty to one's chief, but more often for failure to obey a court judgment or pay a fine, particularly if such failure was associated with a truculent or contemptuous attitude towards the chief. It was often abused by chiefs in order to ruin or cripple some wealthy or independent-minded subject, and was a scandal decried by the early missionaries as long ago as the 1860s. It is no longer permitted by the Government although a case occurred in Mokhotlong in 1946.

CHAPTER XV

LAW

THE Basuto have a number of terms for different kinds of rules of behaviour: *lesiko*, traditional custom, particularly one peculiar to a particular clan or group of people; *mokhoa*, a custom, habit or peculiarity; and *molao*, a custom or law. To some extent they interchange these terms and may, for instance, call a traditional usage *mokhoa* or *molao*; on the whole they tend to use the term *mokhoa* in a general sense for a way of acting or behaving, or a traditional form of behaviour; *molao* for rules of behaviour which are enforceable by some authority: *molao oa kereke* (the law of the church), *molao oa mophato* (the law of the lodge), *melao ea marena* (the laws of the chiefs). Schapera states that, if pressed, the Tswana distinguished *molao* from *mokhoa* as custom enforceable by the courts. I doubt, however, whether the Basuto actually do this quite so explicitly, but—and this comes to much the same thing—though they might talk of a custom not enforced by the courts as a *molao*, they would never talk of a *mokhoa* being enforced by the courts.

In some societies, laws may be distinguished from other rules of behaviour as those that are codified and embalmed in statutes, case records or the written opinions of recognized legal authorities. Sesuto law, for the most part, lacks such codification and must be sought where it is actually administered, namely, in the courts.

There are four sources of law—tradition, statutes, chief's orders and the courts. Although these sources are theoretically distinct, there is little practical difference between the laws which originate from them. Most law is traditional and is said to have originated with, or been established by, the "first Basuto" or to have been established by God. Some laws are known to have been originated directly or indirectly by Europeans, or promulgated by chiefs (such as Moshesh's abolition of the death penalty for theft or sorcery, and Letsie's order that the Tlokoa should observe Sunday as a day of rest), but they are accepted as part of the general body of laws and no longer depend for their authority on reference to the Government's or chief's enactment.

Statutory law is a comparatively recent phenomenon and could not have occurred before the people became literate. Moshesh was the first to have his enactments reduced to writing. Some were really customary laws which he caused to be recorded for reference and convenience; among them were laws "regarding the sale of brandy, circumcision, theft and also drinking native beer called *joala*".[1] Unfortunately, we know nothing more about them, as all existing copies were destroyed

[1] George Tlali Moshesh, in evidence to the Commission.

by fire during the 1865-8 wars. Others were statutes in the full sense of the word. They were published in the Government *Gazette* of the Orange Free State Republic. One entitled "Ordinance against the Introduction and Sale of Spirituous Liquors in the territory of the Basutos" was published in 1854; a second, "A Proclamation by Moshesh", dealing with sorcery, in 1855, and in 1859 a third, "The Law of Trade". This set out the conditions under which traders were to operate in the country and also reaffirmed the Liquor Ordinance.[1] The latter may be quoted in full, as besides being one of the first statutes of the Basuto, and therefore of historical interest, it also shows the extent of Moshesh's authority and illustrates his methods of consultation:

"Whereas the spirituous liquors of the whites were unknown to former generations of our Tribe, Matie and Motlomi until Bomonageng and our father Mokachane, now very advanced in age, has never used any other drink than water and milk; and whereas we deem that a good Chief and Judge cannot claim to be competent to execute his duties, if he makes use of anything of an intoxicating nature; and whereas spirituous liquors create quarrelling and strife and pave the way to the destruction of society (for surely the spirituous liquors of the whites are nothing else than fire);

"It is therefore hereby made known to all, that the introduction and sale of spirituous liquor within Basutoland is henceforth prohibited, and provided any person, whether white or coloured, contravenes this order, the spirits shall be taken from him and poured out on the ground, without excuse or indemnification.

"And this order shall be printed in the Basuto and Dutch languages, and posted up at all the places of public meetings, and in the villages of the Basutos.

"Given with the advice and concurrence of the great men of our Tribe, by us the Chief of the Basutos, at Thaba Bosigo, the 8th of November, 1854.

Signed,

MOSHESH, Chief."

In 1907 the Basutoland Council formally reduced some of the principal traditional laws to writing and published them as the *Laws of Lerotholi*. They were revised and added to from time to time; several were new laws which took account of prevalent social changes and others were Government statutory laws (proclamations) which were thus incorporated into Basuto law. For instance, part of Law 24 made it an offence, cognizable by the native courts, to drive stock without the stock removal permit (*bewijs*) required under Proclamation No. 80 of 1921. Other laws which reflected Government statutory law were Law 3 which provided that appeals could be taken from the Paramount Chief's court to the Government courts; Law 5 which provided that the Paramount Chief could send cases which he could not settle satisfactorily to the Resident Commissioner or District Commissioner; Law 22 which declared the 12 March (Moshesh's day) as a public holiday; and

[1] Basutoland Records, pp. 133, 152, 536.

Law 23 which authorized chiefs to order their people to eradicate burr-weed, because "High Commissioners have long been referring to the eradication of burr-weed and the Resident Commissioners have also spoken about it many times". From the strictly constitutional point of view, these "Laws" cannot be regarded as statutory law for the reason that neither the Paramount Chief nor the Basutoland Council had been granted legislative authority by the British Administration. But they had the effect of law, were legally binding in the native courts and were consulted and quoted by litigants and by the courts.

In 1946 a new version of the *Laws of Lerotholi* was published. This consisted of four parts: Part 1 is still, strictly speaking, customary or common law, but Parts 2, 3 and 4 are statutory in the full sense of the word.

1. *"Declaration of Basuto Law and Custom."* This re-stated some of the earlier *Laws of Lerotholi*, such as those dealing with succession to the chieftainship, allocation of lands, inheritance and Moshesh's Day, and introduced some new "laws" such as the definition of legal customary marriage, liability for acts or debts of others and criminal liability for being in possession of articles suspected to have been stolen.

2. *"Rules issued by the Paramount Chief with the approval of the High Commissioner under the provision of Section 15 (1) of the Native Administration Proclamation, No. 61 of 1938."* These include a revised version of several of the previous *Laws of Lerotholi*, such as No. 13 regarding seduction; No. 23, eradication of burr-weed; No. 12, compensation in theft cases; No. 24, issue of *bewijs* and stray stock. They also include several new laws, e.g. providing for pounds, ordering pigs to be kept in sties, reporting of lost property, reporting births and deaths, prohibiting the use of dagga, the drawing of sledges on roads and bridle paths, and the burning of grass and bush.

3. *"Orders issued by the Paramount Chief under the provision of Section 8 (1) of the Native Administration Proclamation, No. 61 of 1938."* These include a number of administrative orders dealing with matters such as the reporting of suspected cases of infectious diseases, destruction of wild oats, protection of anti-soil erosion works, brands and earmarks, control of habitual thieves and of smutty wheat.

4. *"The Native Court Rules."* This is a copy of High Commissioner's Notice, No. 32 of 1946. These rules are a formal and in some cases a modified version of traditional rules of procedure, and also include a few new features. They were dealt with in the previous chapter.

The division of the "Laws" into four parts is in some respects rather arbitrary. Different aspects of theft, for instance, are dealt with separately in Parts 1, 2 and 3, whereas they might quite as well have been included together in any one part. There is no practical or legal reason why the whole of Part 1 should not have been included in Part 2, and thus have become of equal legal status. The point is, however, of only theoretical importance as in practice the native courts will not differentiate between these *Laws of Lerotholi* and will regard the *Declaration of Basuto Law and Custom* as equally binding and authoritative as the "Rules" and "Orders".

The orders of the chiefs, particularly of the Paramount Chief, are the source of a good deal of law. They comprise not only executive orders of a purely temporary or ephemeral nature, such as requiring a person or community to cut grass for him or eradicate burr-weed, or orders reserving certain pastures (*maboella*), but also standing instructions of a permanent nature, some of which introduce new laws or modify old ones. They differ only in form from the statutory laws just mentioned, in that they are not gazetted and those issued by the chiefs prior to the introduction of the Native Administration Proclamation of 1938 were issued by virtue of their traditional right to govern and not by virtue of rights granted them by the Government in that Proclamation. Furthermore, most of them were not published and so their origin was soon forgotten and, unless they fell into disuse, they passed imperceptibly into the general body of customary and traditional law. The earliest of which we know anything are those of Moshesh—his public pronouncement of 1840 permitting a polygynist's wives to leave him on their conversion to Christianity; his abolition of the death penalty for theft; and his refusal to countenance the legal validity of sorcery. More recent laws of this sort are orders of the late Paramount Chiefs, Griffith and Seeiso, concerning the castration of "bastard" rams, the prohibition of beer-brewing for sale and of the growing of dagga (Indian hemp), and instructions regarding the maintenance of contour banks and furrows, modes of ploughing and other matters concerned with anti-soil erosion works (1936). In 1947 the regent issued orders forbidding men to take their families to urban areas in the Union unless they had a permanent job and suitable accommodation. As described above, some of these orders, notably those dealing with anti-erosion measures, were subsequently promulgated by the Paramount Chief by virtue of his powers under the Native Administration and Courts Proclamations and were published in Section 3 of the *Laws of Lerotholi* (1946).

The fourth source of law is the courts themselves, and derives from the judges' power to adapt the traditional law to changing conditions and new situations. Some of these changes are made imperceptibly and almost unconsciously in the day-to-day decisions of the courts, in response to new ideas that find current acceptance. Many examples have already been given, namely changes in the position of widows, the decay of the *kenela* custom and the gradual emancipation of unmarried adults from the control of their parents and older relations. Others, though introduced in response to the same trends, are effected by some authority who is in advance of the times, so that the innovation sometimes comes as a shock to public opinion; such are Seeiso's opposition to initiation schools among the Tlokoa and his order to the head of a *mophato* to release a child who had joined contrary to its parents' wishes.[1] The acceptance of these innovations or reforms and their incorporation into the body of Sesuto law depend less on their correct anticipation or reflection of public opinion than on the importance of the authority which makes them; for such changes need to have sufficient weight to impose themselves on, and be taken as a precedent by, other courts, and to stand the test of an appeal to some higher authority. Such abrupt changes, therefore, are made only by the most important courts.

Sesuto law may be divided into three categories: civil, criminal and a mixture of both. The Basuto used to make no verbal distinction between them and it is not easy to define them. Under the new Native Court Rules[2] a distinction has been based on the presence or absence of a penal sanction.

" 'Criminal cases' are cases in which the offending person . . . may be sentenced to a fine or imprisonment for the offence committed even though compensatory award may be ordered by the court to be paid by the offending person. . . ."

" 'Civil cases' are cases in which two persons are disputing or where a person is suing another for damages or compensation and where the court is not empowered to impose a fine or imprisonment."

This distinction is clear and unmistakable and is verbally recognized by the new courts, which now define a criminal matter as *tlolo ea molao*, literally a "breaking of the law", and a civil matter as *tsekisano*, literally "a disputing together". This division is useful for practical purposes and facilitates the keeping of record books under the new legislation, but it ignores the true sociological nature of Sesuto law, which took account of the character of the dispute, and the way in which it was brought to court as well as the sanction involved. Taking these into account, the following definitions may be made.

Civil laws are those which deal with private rights. They can only be invoked by a private person, acting on his own account or as guardian or representative of another private person, who has been or may have been wronged by another. The issue involved is essentially a private dispute between the two parties and one or other of them must take the initiative in bringing the matter to court. As the court is here in the position of arbitrator, no penalties will be imposed other than an award to the injured party of damages or compensation. Examples of these are the laws dealing with family obligations, ownership of property, inheritance and contracts.

Criminal law, on the other hand, consists mainly of matters which

[1] This innovation may reach the statute book as one of the amendments to the *Laws of Lerotholi* proposed in 1949.
[2] High Commissioner's Notice No. 32 of 1946.

are of public or official concern. The person wronged is not so much a private individual as the community as a whole or an official institution of the community. The matter is, therefore, brought to court not by a private individual but by someone in his official capacity who represents the community or the institution concerned, or else by a private individual, not because he personally has been wronged, but because he is concerned that the public interest should be protected (*vide Mosebi v. Mohanoe*, quoted below). A penalty is imposed, not as a compensating award to a private individual or to the prosecutor personally, but as a punishment for breaking the law. It is, therefore, appropriated by the chief, as the representative of the public, and should be used for public benefit. Examples of these are the laws concerning the official prerogatives of the chiefs, the administration of the courts, the maintenance of law and order, and general laws protecting the community, such as the prohibition of the sale of liquor or use of drugs, and the protection of communal property.

The third group is a mixture of the other two, and has both civil and criminal aspects. The issues involved are primarily of a private nature and the initiative in bringing the matter to court rests on the person concerned; he may be awarded damages or compensation for the personal wrong he has suffered or the damage which has been done to him or his property. But as the action of the offender endangers the community or some official institution, as well as encroaching on a private right, the court may take advantage of the private suit to punish it. Some civil wrongs fall automatically into this category, as they are punishable *per se* by the courts and such punishment is almost invariably inflicted; such are offences against the person or property, such as homicide, assault, seduction, insult and theft. Others, which normally fall into the first group, may also become crimes if they occur in such a way as to threaten a disturbance of the peace or are otherwise harmful; for instance, where a debtor wilfully and unreasonably delays payment, he may be fined, as his behaviour "discourages people from lending to one another".

Unlike ordinary criminal cases, cases such as these are normally dealt with by the courts only when brought to them by a civil action. Thus, even though an authority knows a punishable offence has been committed, he is not supposed to deal with the matter in his court unless and until the injured person brings it before him. Even then, if the latter chooses to drop the case after reporting it to him or while the court is dealing with it, he can do nothing about it. But some courts are becoming sufficiently aware of their functions as "guardians of the peace" to be dissatisfied with this position, and are now trying to make some of these offences independent of private litigation. Examples of cases of theft and assault dealt with (in 1935–6) purely as crimes, are given below.

Civil Wrongs

The most important of these are various offences against the person, such as homicide (*polao*), assault with intent to do serious bodily harm (*phutuho*), ordinary assault, and rape or indecent assault (*peto* or *petello*), seduction (*chobeliso*), adultery (*bofebe*) and defamation (*ketseletso*).

Homicide is the killing of a person, directly or indirectly. It becomes culpable only when done unlawfully. Killing is regarded as lawful in a few cases such as the execution of sorcerers or other malefactors by order of the chief; killing members of the opposition in cattle raids or inter-tribal disputes; and a father's killing his child for disgracing the family by running away from the initiation school. A thief, surprised in a cattle kraal at night or resisting arrest, could also be killed without blame.[1] Abortion and infanticide were not regarded as lawful but, as they were cases primarily affecting the family, they were dealt with by the family rather than the courts. Death arising from a pure accident is not culpable. Apart from these cases, homicide is unlawful. There are degrees of unlawfulness and culpable homicide becomes more serious as it passes from accidental killing due to negligence, through unintentional homicide, as in a drunken brawl, to cold-blooded deliberate murder.

Culpability does not depend on death following immediately from the unlawful action, but may be alleged when death occurs some time after, provided it is directly attributable to that action; for instance, if a woman, who has been seduced, becomes pregnant and dies in labour, her seducer is held responsible for her death[2] and is liable to pay her parents damages up to twenty head of cattle. In the absence of post-mortem examination, the cause of death will be presumed to be due to injury inflicted by an assault only when the injury failed to heal or where the deceased complained of pain, caused by the assault. For this reason, courts insist that the victim of an assault should show them his injuries as soon as possible after the assault so that they may ascertain their seriousness.

The offender is liable to pay ten head of cattle as compensation to the deceased's family in all cases of culpable homicide, except in the case of the death of children, where the damages are four or five head or whatever may be determined by the courts. The compensation is the same whether the deceased is a man or a woman,[3] although Segoete writes that the damages were five beasts for a man and ten for a woman because the latter's loss is greater as she is the producer of children. Where someone is killed by a member of his own family, as when a man kills his wife, or a woman her child, no civil action can be taken as the offender and the victim are one and the same legal person.

[1] Native Laws Commission.
[2] *Laws of Lerotholi*, Rules Nos. 4, 5 and 8.
[3] George Tlali Moshesh; Evidence to the Commission, and *Laws of Lerotholi*, No. 13.

If the case is taken to court, the offender may be punished as well as ordered to pay damages. Such punishment varies, according to the degree of culpability, from a reprimand for carelessness in the case of an accident to a heavy fine for murder.

Formerly, even if the case was not taken to court, one or two head of cattle had to be sent to the chief "to report the death of his subject and that he, the chief, might drink the blood of his dead subject",[1] except in the case of a woman, "because a woman has no chief but her husband or her father".[2]

Nowadays, "it is compulsory for every chief to forward cases of accidental or wilful homicide, which may occur in his ward, to the courts of the Assistant Commissioners, and further the chief is bound to notify the Paramount Chief of such cases."[3]

The District Officer then conducts a thorough inquest or preparatory examination, at which representatives of the local authorities, and sometimes also of the Paramount Chief, are present. If a criminal prosecution for murder or culpable homicide is decided upon, the case is heard under the Territory's criminal law by the High Court or Subordinate Court; if no prosecution takes place, the matter is referred back to the chief. In either case, civil action for damages may be brought to the local native court. This court may also punish the offender if he has not already been punished by the Administration's courts, although some people say that if the offender is punished, no civil action should be taken at all. I was unable to ascertain to what extent, if at all, civil actions for damages are actually brought in the native courts against those who have been convicted in the European courts of murder or homicide. Such offences do not give rise to any sort of blood feud or other system of retaliation.

Homicide cases are rarely dealt with by the native courts, but the the following interesting one occurred in Mosuoe's court, October 1936:

Bofofu v. Nkhala.
N committed adultery with B's wife as a result of which she became pregnant. N wrote to B, who was at the mines, admitting his responsibility. When she died in childbirth, N again wrote to him. On his return from the mines, B did not discuss the matter with his family, as he was angry with them for not having told him anything about the matter, but went straight to N and discussed it privately with him. He pointed out that the full compensation was 10 beasts, but said he would accept 4 head as N was his cousin and had been as frank and helpful as he could about the whole matter. N delayed paying the cattle so the matter was then formally discussed *en famille* (*lapeng*) by B's family. The letters were read and full compensation claimed. N agreed to pay this but said he had

---

[1] Commission. Evidence of George Tlali Moshesh and Sofonia Moshesh.
[2] Jobo Moshesh, ibid.
[3] *Laws of Lerotholi*, 1922, No. 17, now covered by the Native Courts Proclamation No. 62 of 1938.

to consult his elder brother. The latter persuaded him to deny the whole business. The matter was then taken to the local court; N refused to appear and managed to bribe B's elder brother's wife to give him his letters which he destroyed. The case was then taken to Mosuoe's court which ordered N to pay 10 beasts compensation and fined him 2 beasts for his bribery, plus 10s. for refusing to answer the summons of the lower court. B's brother was fined 2 beasts for not taking proper care of the letters and his wife was fined 1 beast for giving them to N. N appealed but the others accepted the judgment.

Assault is an unlawful act of violence committed against another person. As with homicide, there are acts of violence which may be committed lawfully, such as a parent beating his child, a man flogging his wife, *babineli* whipping initiates at the *mophato* and herd-boys fighting with one another. There are also various degrees of assault. These degrees are assessed according to whether or not blood has been shed, the gravity of the injury, the nature of the assault, the degree of provocation given by the injured person, the relative social status of the parties and the wilfulness of the offender. The nature of the weapon used is also a material factor. The use of firearms is the most serious as it indicates reckless intention to do serious injury and—so far as assessing the penal fine is concerned—savours of insubordination. Using knives is more serious than using other weapons such as spears, knobkerries or sticks, for the Basuto have a horror of knifing and regard it as a cowardly form of assault introduced by the despised Pondomise.

The case should be heard as soon as possible after the assault, but if the injuries are serious judgment should be deferred until they have healed.

The offender is liable to pay the victim damages to "heal the wound" and also to be punished by fining. The amounts of the damages and of the fine vary with the seriousness of the assault. Where the assault was not serious, no compensation or fine will be awarded.

'*Mamorkeo v. Mofelase, Thothofeane, May 1936.*

'M, a widow, sues her stepson M because his son assaulted her grand-daughter by throwing her to the ground and beating her with a strap. This was the culmination of a quarrel between them in which they swore at one another. As the assault was a squabble between two youngsters who were kinsmen and no serious injuries were suffered, no damages or penalties were awarded and the court ordered them to go home and keep the peace.

Similarly, no damages or fine will be awarded where the assault was accidental and/or took place on a privileged occasion:

Maqebo v. Mokoto, November 1936.

The two men quarrelled over some meat. Next day the exciting opening feast of the initiation ceremonies occurred, during which Mokoto got very excited and fired off a revolver which by mischance hit Maqebo's son in the leg. Maqebo, suspecting that this was deliberately done because of their previous quarrel, sues for damages. The court finds no intention of deliberate assault and so merely orders Mokoto to buy medicines to heal the wounds, but warns him that he might have to pay damages if any permanent injury is discovered.

Note: Had this taken place anywhere else than at this ceremony, Mokoto would almost certainly have been fined for carrying a revolver as well as for carelessly discharging it.

Where the offender is seriously provoked by the plaintiff, he may be released from paying damages, as the latter has only himself to blame for his injury; but he may be fined for taking the law into his own hands. The plaintiff may also be fined for having provoked a breach of the peace.

Fanyane v. Jeme, February 1936.

J suspected that F was having an affair with his wife, as he heard that F and F's father, had given her medicine for bronchitis when he was away, and his child medicine for diarrhoea, thus indicating a high degree of intimacy between them. One day he saw F coming out of her hut and attacked him with a spear. F overpowered him and tied him up. As he had suffered considerable provocation, J was fined only £1 for the assault and was not made to pay any damages. F's father was fined 10s. for giving medicines and a third person was fined 5s. for helping to administer them. The case originated in a lower court, which sent it to Mosuoe's court as soon as the serious nature of the attempted assault, i.e. the use of a spear, was disclosed.

In sixteen cases, for which I have records, the amount of damages awarded varied greatly. In seven cases no damages were awarded; 10s. in one case, £1 in two cases, £2 or 1 beast in two cases, 5 small stock in two cases, £3 in one case and 2 beasts (=£4) in one case. Fines also varied: in two cases no fines were imposed. There were three cases of 10s. fines, two of £1, five of 1 beast, three of £3 and one of 3 beasts. There was also the purely criminal case quoted below (*Mosuoe v. Molapo* and *Setaka*) where a fine of 5 beasts was imposed. In two of these cases, the plaintiff was also fined 10s. These examples are concerned with assault pure and simple; they do not include more complex cases—such as land disputes, or suits for damage to property, or resistance to court messengers—where one of the parties is fined for using violence or for doing something which might provoke a breach of the peace. In such cases, fines of 1 or 2 beasts are usually imposed.

The use of threats is a form of assault, even if no violence was actually offered, provided that there was reason to believe that the threats would have been carried out but for the intervention of a third party or the retaliation or capitulation of the person threatened. Similarly, if a person deliberately and seriously frightens another.

July v. Ramabanta, October 1936.
One night when J was away, his wife heard someone stamping round her hut and then someone moving softly. She lighted a lamp and saw R on a horse. Without greeting her first, he told her in a low growling voice three times: "Come out of your hut, you 'Mantela'. She became thoroughly frightened at this unwonted behaviour and asked if he had come to kill her. He then came towards her and she shouted to her child to bring a spear. He made off then, dropping a stick and his saddlebags. R was ordered to pay 2 beasts as damages for "attacking" J's wife and children in this way, and was fined 1 beast and £1.

The essence of rape is forcible ravishment. The relevant facts considered by the courts are the nature of the previous relationship between the two, the degree of force used and any matrimonial intentions of the man. As pre- and extra-marital sexual intercourse are common, the courts are very sceptical about allegations of rape and require very clear evidence that the alleged offender had received no encouragement. Where this is proved, he may be heavily fined, in addition to being ordered to pay the usual damages for seduction or adultery to the woman's parents or husband. But if it can be shown that the offender wished to marry the girl, and that the alleged offence took place while he was abducting her, his act will be treated as mere abduction rather than as rape, even though he may have used a considerable amount of force. Nowadays all cases of rape should be reported to the police and tried in the Administration's courts.

The following is the only case of rape recorded at Mosuoe's court (1935–6):

Mongama v. Lemeko, October 1936.
L enticed M's daughter into a hut and there raped her. At first he denied it, then said she had consented to intercourse and finally admitted he had raped her. He was ordered to pay 6 beasts damages and fined 1 beast (i.e. the same as ordinary seduction).

Note on procedure: M tried to have the matter settled *en famille*, but L refused to admit his guilt so the matter was then taken to court. When he paid the first instalment of the damages, L asked for the girl in marriage, but M refused saying he did not want to be connected with him. M later informed the court that he had heard rumours that L had further designs on her, so the court formally warned L to behave himself.

Other sexual offences are abduction or seduction. These commonly pass under the blanket term *chobeliso*; formerly the courts made no distinction between them, and the 1922 version of the *Laws of Lerotholi*[1] treated them in the same way. The 1946 version[2] attempts to distinguish between abduction (*chobeliso*) and seduction (*kemariso*; literally "making pregnant") and provides slightly different scales of compensation and penalties, but I do not know to what extent the courts follow this new

[1] *Laws of Lerotholi*, No. 13.   [2] "Rules", 2–7.

distinction. The following account may, therefore, be somewhat out of date.

As indicated in Chapter V, the term *chobeliso* covers a multitude of sins which vary considerably in seriousness. The lightest of them is the elopement of a girl with her husband after the marriage ceremony and before she has been formally taken to his home. The worst is the forcible abduction of the girl and sexual intercourse with her, which is practically indistinguishable from rape.

Fundamentally, *chobeliso* is the commission of some act which publicly spoils or brings in question a girl's reputation for chastity. Thus, discreet seduction of a girl, in the sense of inducing her to grant sexual favours, is not an offence, even if it leads to some scandal-mongering, provided nothing is done publicly to spoil her reputation. But whenever seduction results in the girl's pregnancy, an offence is committed—a fact that is made clear in the Sesuto version[1] of the relevant rule in the 1946 *Laws of Lerotholi*; here the term used is *kemariso*, which means "making pregnant". Similarly, elopement is a public acknowledgment of intimacy, and even though no sexual intercourse takes place, as is often the case where a man takes the girl straight to his mother, such intercourse is presumed and is sufficient to spoil her reputation. The fact that publicity is the main factor is illustrated by the following case:

Motsamai v. Lekholo, October 1936.
M found L's younger brother in a hut at night with his daughter. They admitted that they were in love with one another and that they wanted to be married. The boy had given her his hat and they had exchanged scarves. They denied having had intercourse. M nevertheless sues L for his brother's act of seduction and claims the usual compensation. As L contests this, the court orders the girl to be examined by some impartial women. They report that she is intact and has no blemish. As the girl's reputation is thus publicly upheld, the case is dismissed, but the boy is ordered to return the girl's scarf and is fined 10s. for having jeopardized her honour and given her presents "as if she were his wife".

Formerly "seduction was settled by a fine. The man had the option of marrying the girl, in which case the fine was small, but if he refused to marry the girl, the fine was double".[2] Later (1912), the law changed and provided that a man "who seduced or tried to seduce an unmarried girl, had to pay two head of cattle; if she became pregnant, the penalty was six head, but if he afterwards married her, this was reduced to two head over and above the regular dowry."[3] The present position is dealt with in detail by Rules 2–9 of the 1946 *Laws of Lerotholi*, which are

[1] The English version is, indeed, somewhat misleading.
[2] George Tlali Moshesh, Commission. He probably meant damages rather than penal fine.
[3] Ellenberger and MacGregor, p. 269. Here again civil damages are undoubtedly meant rather than penal fines.

essentially the same as No. 13 of the 1922 version. The parents of the girl who is seduced (i.e. made pregnant) or abducted for the first time, may claim damages up to a maximum of six head of cattle, unless the abduction has taken place at the instance of the girl's parents, when no compensation should be granted. This has long been the accepted figure, and usually[1] the full amount is claimed and awarded. If the girl is seduced (made pregnant) a second time, the maximum compensation is ten head of cattle, unless the first seduction was by another man; in the latter event the maximum compensation is reduced to three head of cattle which is equivalent to that for adultery. Where she is abducted a second time by the same man against her parents' will, the amount of compensation is left to the discretion of the court, which may also order the dissenting parents to arrange the marriage.

Two cases of repeated abduction were dealt with in Bereng's court in 1933-4. In the first, the offender who had paid six head of cattle for his first abduction or elopement (the Basuto use the same term, *chobeliso*), was ordered to pay a second lot of six head, and was fined the usual fine of one head. In the second case, after the first elopement, the offender's elder brother succeeded in getting the girl's parents to agree to their marriage and gave them five head of cattle. A sixth head was given a little later. There was then some delay in completing and arranging the wedding, so the boy eloped with the girl a second time. Her parents sued for six head compensation, but were told by the court that as they had agreed to the marriage they were not entitled to further damages and should expedite the wedding.

If a girl is injured as a result of her abduction or seduction her parents may be awarded compensation not exceeding six head where she is abducted and eight head where she is seduced (i.e. made pregnant).

Formerly, all the foregoing offences were punishable by a fine of one head of cattle and in every case for which I have court records (eight) this fine was imposed. The Rules now provide new and heavier penalties. For abduction, they provide for a fine not exceeding £50 and/or imprisonment not exceeding twelve months; there are similar penalties for the abduction or seduction of mentally defective women or of girls under sixteen. For the seduction of girls boarding at a school or proceeding to or returning from school or a church service, the maximum penalty is halved. Strangely enough the new Rules do not provide for the punishment of other kinds of seduction, but I have no doubt that the courts will continue to inflict the traditional fine of one beast. The provisions dealing with mentally defective women, girls under sixteen and girls at church or school are innovations. Those dealing with girls under sixteen are based on local statute law. Unfortunately, I have no information as to whether the new provisions differentiating between

[1] In five out of six cases in Bereng's courts, and in one solitary case in Mosuoe's court.

abduction and seduction reflect the actual judicial practice of some courts (in my limited experience the courts do not distinguish between different kinds of *chobeliso*) or whether they represent new concepts which, it is hoped, will guide the courts in future.

Many classes of *chobeliso* are settled out of court by the parties concerned, the boy's parents agreeing to pay the girl's people the traditionally prescribed six head of cattle as damages. An attempt is usually made by the former to get the latter's consent to the marriage of the boy and girl and such overtures are seldom rejected, except in unsavoury cases, such as that of *Mongama v. Lemeko* (above), or where the two families are not friendly. If the marriage is agreed to, the six head of cattle payable as damages, and which should be paid immediately, are then counted as part of the *bohali* marriage-cattle, and a seventh head is usually sent as an earnest of good faith. The rest of the *bohali* may then be paid at leisure later. While these negotiations are proceeding the girl's parents usually ask for the return of the girl, if she eloped, and the boy's people must comply with their request.

Mposi v. Masekesela, February 1936.
T's son eloped with M's daughter. When M sent for her, T's people hid her, whereupon he got very angry and insisted on her return and on payment of the maximum damages; as T was away, they approached T's elder brother Mp to give him the 6 cattle from T's kraal. Mp then appealed to the court, saying it would be wrong of him "to go into another kraal and marry off another's child". The court agreed with him, but told him to return the girl, and advised M to calm down and the matter would be dealt with on T's return.

If the marriage has been agreed on, no damages are payable for any further abduction of the girl by her fiancé, as indicated in the example given above from Bereng's court. A similar case occurred in Mosuoe's court:

Tieho v. Doka, June 1936
T's son eloped with D's daughter, and as D then agreed to their marriage, T gave him 7 cattle, and D took his daughter back, saying T should "follow" him, i.e. complete the arrangements. Before he could do so, he was arrested and imprisoned for a year, and his son, tiring of the delay, abducted the girl again. D then seized 6 of T's cattle as further damages. On his release T sued for their return. The court ordered D to return them so that T could pay a further instalment of the *bohali* cattle and arrange the marriage in the proper manner, and fined D £3 for seizing them unlawfully and £2 for taking them without a permit.

If the girl is married by her seducer the child becomes his child; if they do not marry, the child remains with her until she marries and then remains with her parents. If the full damages have been paid, and she eventually marries someone other than her seducer, her husband should not be required to pay more than fourteen head of cattle as *bohali* (i.e. the full number of twenty less six) as she "has been spoiled" and her parents have been compensated for this spoiling. But if her husband wishes to take her illegitimate child and adopt it, as sometimes happens when the man concerned is old and childless, he may do so, provided he pays the full *bohali*. Although her parents thus get the full *bohali*, plus the six head paid as damages by her seducer, there is no question of returning these six head to her seducer.

Adultery is the infringement of a husband's marital rights and an affront to his dignity. It is thus an offence only when committed by a man, married or single, with a married woman and not when committed by a married man with a single woman. The offending man is liable to pay the injured husband damages. These usually amount to three head of cattle, but they may be more for repeated adultery.

Moleleki v. Moloi, December 1935.
Moloi was caught four times committing adultery with Moleleki's wife and warned each time by Moleleki. The fifth time, Moleleki brought the matter to court, which ordered Moloi to pay four head of cattle as damages, and fined him two head.

Damages are also higher in cases of adultery with a chief's senior wives. Laydevant[1] says they should be ten head of cattle. Mosuoe claimed and obtained, without going to court, damages of six head of cattle from a man caught sleeping with his second wife. In the old days adultery with the chief's principal wives was punishable by death or banishment.[2]

Some people do not bring cases of adultery to the courts as they do not wish to be exposed to the publicity involved and because their pride revolts against the idea of accepting the compensation "branded with dishonour". They prefer either to give the offender a thorough beating themselves or to let him go altogether; sometimes they take the matter to court and ask that the offender may be ordered to cease his illicit attentions. If the matter is taken to court, the offender may be punished by a fine. The usual fine is one head of cattle, but, as in the above case, this may be increased for repeated offences or other aggravating circumstances, such as being likely to provoke bloodshed. According to Segoete,[3] adultery with a nursing mother might be fined with an additional goat, *poli ea boluma*, which would be used to obtain medicines to cure the child of colic caused by his mother's intercourse.

Insult (*hlapa*), or the use of abusive, insulting or derogatory language towards a person ("to speak badly to a person") is an offence. Typical

[1] Laydevant, 1931, p. 240.
[2] Ellenberger and MacGregor, p. 269.
[3] Segoete, p. 17.

insults are to call a person a sorcerer, "one who habitually prays to Satan", or a bastard (*ngoana ea lingoetsi lefohlatsebe*), to accuse him of a misdemeanour such as adultery, or to swear at him by his or his mother's "private parts" or excrement.

Maliengoana v. Thulo, August 1936.
M is T's father's sister. Her son is known to be T's wife's lover. T went with a friend to ask M to reprove her son and stop him causing dissensions between him and his wife. M affects righteous indignation, so T loses his temper and calls her, "Dog, wild dog, I'll stab you so that the blade goes right through you, you are an adultress, and sin just as your son sins." Fined two head of cattle—appeals. Note: The fine here was harsh and should not have been more than 30s.

Another virulent curse is to call a person Satan (*Satana*), which, besides being offensive in itself, is also synonymous with an obscene expression for sexual intercourse.

Sehahabane v. Moleko, April 1936.
M interrupted a conversation between S and another telling the latter not to talk to S—"He is Satan". When S threatened to sue him, M got angry, shouted at him and tried to assault him. Fined 30s.

Insults can be offered through quite harmless expressions, if uttered in an abusive or disrespectful manner, or used by inferiors to their social superiors; deliberately breaking a taboo or convention, or behaving outrageously may also constitute an insult.

Rabuti v. Mokalinyane, September 1936.
After a quarrel, R rode his horse into M's *lelapa*. Subsequently he apologized and his apology was accepted, but M sued him in court. The headman's court fined R £1—on appeal to the sub-chief's court, the fine was increased to 55s. On further appeal to Mosuoe's court, the fine was reduced to 10s. No damages were awarded to M as an apology had been tendered and accepted, but he was fined 10s. for having brought R to court after forgiving him.

Insults are wiped out by apology. This is usually verbal, but may also include an offer of compensation; in one case where a man's herd-boy accused another of theft, the former offered him 10s. "to clean his name". Failing this, recourse can be had to the courts. Except in serious cases, the injured person is not awarded damages, but the offender is ordered to make a public apology and is soundly berated by the court. In serious and provocative cases he may also be fined, as shown in the above cases. (Bereng's court, in 1933, fined a man a beast for cursing his elder brother during a dispute over some trees.) The following case is of interest for the complicated form of insult and the award of damages, which were subsequently returned.

Paul v. Masekesela, June 1936.

M accuses P of stealing his sjambok, and then goes on insultingly, "I'll ruin you myself, I'll burn your hut down at night when you are with your wife, and when you both come out naked to put the fire out, I'll go and reap your fields." P sued in the headman's court but M refused the summons, so the matter was taken to Mosuoe. P was awarded 1 beast damages and M fined 1 beast and £1. P, honour now satisfied, asks the court to remit the damages, which it does.

A similar type of offence is defamation (*tlontlollo ea lebitso* or *ketseletso*). This is the spoiling of a person's reputation by maliciously attributing something evil to him, misrepresenting his words or actions or spreading false rumours. Such cases are dealt with on the same lines as the foregoing; the action is brought primarily to vindicate the plaintiff's reputation rather than to obtain damages, and the offender may be fined. The following cases illustrate the kind of defamatory remarks made and the action of the court. As the first one shows, it is not easy to draw a clear dividing line between this class of offence and the previous one.

'Mamafu v. 'Maneheng (two women), August 1936.

'Mamafu sues 'Maneheng for calling her a witch, a Christian (using the word *Lejakane* with contemptuous tone) who bewitches and prays to Satan. The court ordered 'Maneheng to pay 10s. damages and fined her 5s. "to cut off her tongue". 'Mamafu did not think this fine heavy enough and wanted to appeal, but was persuaded by her son to accept the judgment.

Mokopu v. Motinyane, February 1936.

The wives of these two men were working in the fields together and got into a heated argument, during which Mokopu's wife said, "*Thokolosi* will tread on someone". Later, the fire they had made to cook their meal spread to Motinyane's threshing floor and burned some corn. He attributed this to Mokopu's wife, insinuating that she had a *thokolosi* or witch. Mokopu then sues him for this. The court sympathized with Motinyane, but refused to convict, saying, "It is known that people are witches but unless one is caught red-handed, there is no theft," and ordered the parties to go home and live together in peace.

Tsekana v. 'Mantlameng, February 1936.

T sues his headman 'M for saying quite unjustifiably that he had refused to carry out his orders and thus giving him a reputation for disobedience. Some members of the court wished to fine 'M, but eventually the court decided merely to warn him.

Abimael v. Tootse, January 1936.

A, a priest, sues T for saying that he had taken part in recent initiation ceremonies, whereas he had actually opposed T's proposal to establish a lodge in front of his school and managed to get it established away from his mission.

Malicious reports and/or prosecution constitute an offence similar to the foregoing. But this rarely comes before the courts as a separate suit, and usually arises out of another dispute, or when the court finds that the prosecution is entirely unfounded. The offender is usually punished by fining. A good example occurred in the property dispute, *Maqetha v. Pipi*.[1] Similarly in the case:

Monoana v. Paul, January 1936.
M sued P, complaining that P had prevented him from ploughing a field and had brandished a gun and threatened to shoot him. It was proved that P had not carried a gun and had not threatened to shoot. M, a headman, was fined 30s. for malicious prosecution and his three witnesses were fined £1 each for giving false evidence.

Offences Against Property
Offences against property fall into three main groups: theft, wrongful use of property and wrongful damage to property.

Theft is the wrongful taking or retention of property with intention to deprive the owner of his ownership. There is no offence where this intention is absent, i.e. where a person merely takes and keeps someone else's property for temporary use and in such a way that it can be reasonably assumed that he intends to and can restore it to the owner.

Every kind of movable property can be stolen and, in fact, most kinds are stolen. Of twelve cases recorded from Bereng's court in 1934, seven were stock (four small, three cattle, horses, etc.) and one money, food, hide, wool and *bewijs* book. Of thirty-four at Mosuoe's court in 1935–6, twenty-five were stock (eleven small stock, fourteen cattle, etc.), two food, wool and ploughs, and one money, *bewijs* book and saddlery. The preponderance of stock cases is not surprising as stock is readily movable and is the principal form of property. Sheep are stolen, often in large quantities, for their wool, and having been sheared are let loose and driven into the veld, except for one or two which are killed for food. Cattle and horses are stolen for use and are seldom killed. Theft of food is regarded as a shameful matter—except as between herd-boys in the mountains—and is rarely brought to the courts.

The evolution and modification of the law relating to theft may be briefly traced. Evidence to the Commission in 1873 baldly stated that theft was punished by a fine. Later, it was more explicitly stated[2] that "theft was punished according to the merits of the case; usually the thief had to pay fourfold—two to the court and two to the owner (one in restoration and one in compensation for the trouble caused). There was a saying, '*Pinyane ha e senye motse*' (Petty theft destroys no village) by which the Basuto used to justify their leniency towards this kind of crime; but if one of the culprits confessed and denounced his comrades, much ill-will would ensue, even to the extent of 'destroying the village'."
A fuller statement of the law was made in the 1922 edition of the *Laws of Lerotholi*:

[1] Page 180. [2] Ellenberger and MacGregor, p. 270.

"It is the law that thefts of any kind or description whatever shall be punishable by the law of Moshoeshoe, which is the only one that satisfies the nation, to wit: a beast to be repaid by a beast, a second beast for compensation, and a third as a fine to be paid to the court. If the person so fined continues to steal, the court has the right to increase the amount of the fine."[1]

and,

"Any person who will steal for a second time shall be liable to a fine not exceeding 10 head of cattle. If the thief has no property to pay the fine he shall be sent to the Paramount Chief. Judgment in such cases shall be at the discretion of the Paramount Chief and the Resident Commissioner."[2]

The principles involved are those noted by Ellenberger and MacGregor—restoration, compensation and punishment—and qualified by the *Laws of Lerotholi*, in that they should all be of the same kind and number, or of equal value. If the article is intact, it must be returned, but if damaged or destroyed it must be replaced. Besides this, an equal amount must be paid as compensation. The concept of compensation, idiomatically expressed, is that when the thief returns the animals he has stolen, he should drive (*qhoba*) them with an equivalent number to keep them company. These principles are rigidly enforced: in every case for which full details are available (twelve in Bereng's court and twenty-four in Mosuoe's), the object stolen was returned when it was still intact, or replaced where it had been destroyed, and compensation was paid, equal in amount or value to the thing stolen: a beast was compensated with a beast, wool with its cash value, a mare with two horses.

There is a tendency to view theft from the thief's angle rather than the owner's and to insist that where there is more than one thief, each of them should make compensation, as is shown in these two cases:

Mochati and 2 others v. Mosala and 2 others, February 1936.
For the theft of 4 horses. As these were recovered intact they were returned, and each of the three thieves had to pay compensation with 4, so that each owner, besides getting his horses back, received threefold compensation.

Mosalatsi v. Ketleng and 3 others, July 1936.
Two sheep belonging to M were killed and eaten by K and three others. Each of the four thieves was ordered to replace the 2 sheep and then pay compensation with 2 more, so that the owner received 16 sheep.

In another case where sixteen sheep were stolen and were returned by order of the court, each of the three thieves involved had to *qhoba* them with an equal number, thus giving the owner forty-eight sheep as compensation. (See also cases 6, 7 and 9 of Mosuoe's court, p. 270.)

[1] *Laws of Lerotholi*, No. 12.   [2] Ibid., No. 24.

In one case, however, the court recognized that the basic principle was being misapplied and that the owner was being ridiculously overcompensated. It re-enunciated the law that the owner should receive compensation equal to the value of the thing stolen, but instead of making each of the thieves pay an equal proportion of this, it ordered that each should pay the full amount of compensation and itself appropriated the difference: where three men combined to steal four sheep, each of them had to pay four as compensation, making a total of twelve; the owner was given four and the court kept the remaining eight. In other words, it gave expression to the tacit implication that the so-called compensation is not really compensation at all, in the sense that it has any real relationship to the actual damage suffered by the owner; it is more in the nature of a fine, that is, it is penal rather than restitutive: therefore, since the owner is properly compensated by receiving an amount equal to the theft, the balance of the so-called compensation should go to the court rather than to the plaintiff. Where the co-defendant is only an accessory, the full duplication is not enforced (see No. 2 of Bereng's court, p. 269). This sort of judgment was imposed in all the cases occurring in Mosuoe's court in which more than one thief was involved.

In inflicting ordinary fines, the courts do not observe the same rigid uniformity in equating the amount of the fine to the amount of the theft, as they do when enforcing payment of compensation. In only one out of ten cases involving first offenders did Bereng's court inflict a fine equal to the value of the object stolen and so preserve the ratio set out in the *Laws of Lerotholi* of 1 : 1 : 1. In Mosuoe's court, only one case out of twenty observed this ratio. In both cases this was probably fortuitous as the thing stolen was a beast and this happens to be the usual fine.

Nor do the courts observe the same leniency that Ellenberger and MacGregor formerly noted. Heavy fines are the rule rather than the exception. The normal fine is one head of cattle; this was imposed in six out of eleven cases in Bereng's court and in eight out of twenty-three in Mosuoe's. It is seldom that no fines, or small fines, are imposed: one case in Bereng's court where a herd-boy was reprimanded for selling wool in his keeping, and three in Mosuoe's. In the latter cases, the fines were £1 (half the normal), but in two of them this was twice the value of the thing stolen. Heavier fines were imposed in all other cases. Apart from the tendency to fine heavily, such fines may be imposed for repeated offences or as a general deterrent; Mosuoe's court, in six cases, imposed fines of one beast plus £1 or more in an attempt to reduce the incidence of stock theft. Fines are also imposed where elements other than theft enter in, such as when the theft is accompanied by violence either in its commission or in the thief's refusal to confess his guilt by carrying the *corpus delicti*, or where there is some degree of insubordination. Thus Bereng's court imposed a fine of three beasts for the theft and consumption of two sheep, where this was a second offence; and in another case, where a headman seized, killed and ate an ox from a herd of another headman, who deliberately tried to open his spare veld, the court fined him five beasts and those who helped him, two beasts. Mosuoe's court fined the thief of a horse and a mare three beasts for resisting the court messengers and ignoring its summons. The following table shows the variety of cases dealt with and the frequency of the standard fine.

TABLE

Bereng's Court

	Case	Fine	Remarks
1.	2 sheep stolen and eaten. Principal to restore 2 and *qhoba* 2 sheep. Accessory—brother (first offence)—*qhoba* 2 sheep	3 beasts	Repeated offence
2.	Headman for killing and eating 1 ox to restore 1 and *qhoba* 1 ox. Those who helped	5 beasts 2 beasts	Case aggravated by defiance.
3.	Theft of food valued at 6d. Return 6d., *qhoba* 6d.	1 beast	
4.	Theft 3 horses which died through ill-treatment. First offence. Restore 3 horses, *qhoba* 3 horses	2 beasts	Case aggravated by ill-treatment of animals
5.	Theft and consumption of 1 sheep. Restore 1 and *qhoba* 1	1 beast	
6.	Theft of money. Money to be returned	1 beast	
7.	Theft of untanned hide. Return the hide and *qhoba* 2 sheep	1 beast	
8.	Herd-boy selling wool and misappropriating the money. Refund twice the amount of money	Nil	Reprimanded

Mosuoe's Court

	Case	Fine	Remarks
1.	2 sheep stolen and eaten. Return 2 and *qhoba* 2	Nil	Ordered to leave mountain area—a heavy punishment in itself.
2.	1 goat stolen and eaten. Return 1 and *qhoba* 1	1 beast	
	For helping to kill goat, accessory	£1	
3.	1 sheep stolen and eaten. Return 1 and *qhoba* 1 (herd-boy). Master of herd-boy did nothing about the theft and refused to help bring him into court	£1 30/-	
4.	Theft 10 sheep. Return them and *qhoba* 10	1 beast	
5.	Theft 1 donkey. Return it and *qhoba* 1 donkey	£1	

Mosuoe's Court—*contd.*

	Case	Fine	Remarks
6.	3 thieves stole 4 horses. The 4 to be returned and each thief to *qhoba* 4 horses	1 beast + £1 each	
	Herd-boy for helping	1 beast	
7.	2 thieves stole and sheared 30 sheep, killed and ate one, 8 died. To return 30 and each to *qhoba* 30, each to restore 9 and *qhoba* 9	1 beast + £1 each	
8.	Theft 4 sheep. Return them and *qhoba* 4	1 beast + £1	
9.	4 thieves stole and ate 2 sheep. Each to restore 2 and *qhoba* 2	1 beast each	
10.	Theft 1 horse and 1 mare. Return horse and *qhoba* 1. Return mare and *qhoba* 2 horses	3 beasts	Case aggravated by fighting and ignoring summons
11.	1 sheep stolen and eaten. Restore 1 and *qhoba* 1	1 beast	
	For refusing to catch thief	1 beast	
12.	Theft saddle and bridle. Replace them with 1 beast, *qhoba* 1 beast	1 beast	Inveterate thief

The revised version of the *Laws of Lerotholi*, 1946, is more realistic and more closely related to the practice of the courts than the original version. This version reads as follows:

"In cases in which a person is convicted of theft the court giving judgment may, in addition to any punishment imposed, order the convicted person to replace the article or stock stolen, or to pay to the owner of the stolen article or stock an amount equivalent to the value of such article or stock."[1]

An inveterate thief may be ordered to remove from the remote mountain areas to a more closely populated area. This traditional power has been embodied in the new *Laws of Lerotholi* in the following terms:

"Every chief is empowered to order any habitual thief whose hut or huts are situated in an isolated area of his ward to remove such huts and reside in the chief's village or in any other village ordered by the chief."[2]

As indicated above, inveterate thieves are liable to a heavier punishment than first offenders and may, according to the *Laws of Lerotholi*, be fined up to ten head of cattle. The heaviest fine of which I have record is three head of cattle for the theft of two sheep, imposed by Bereng's court; but, according to George Tlali Moshesh,[3] formerly, notorious thieves who were likely to involve the country in war by stealing from neighbouring nations were sometimes put to death. He

[1] Rule No. 16. [2] Order No. 8. [3] Commission 1873.

knew of four who had been executed by Moshesh. Sofonia[1] testified that incorrigible thieves might be put to death. Such drastic action no longer occurs, although, as mentioned in the previous chapter, inveterate thieves are occasionally tortured.

Sofonia also testified that thieves caught in a kraal at night could be killed with impunity and he quoted a saying, "A thief is a dog that must pay with its head". This offence is not regarded so seriously now and Mosuoe's court, in one such case, confirmed a fine of only two sheep imposed by a lower court. But if a thief was injured while being arrested in such circumstances, he could make no claim for redress.

Sofonia also stated that "the receiver of stolen property, knowing it to have been stolen, can be fined as a thief; this applies to all who partake of the meat of stolen animals, knowing them to have been stolen." This is still the law, but the fines imposed on the receiver are less than those imposed on the thief. Accessories are treated in the same way as thieves, but again with less severity. An interesting case occurred in Mosuoe's court, on appeal from Tootse.

Tootse v. Maekane, October 1935.
T sued M as an accessory to the theft of a plough. The thief, who was a friend of M's, left the plough with him saying he had just bought it. Later when the theft was reported, T by chance picked on M to investigate the matter and to make inquiries at the chief's village. M did so and reported that he had found nothing. The plough was later discovered in his possession and the thief convicted. T then brought a separate action against M for trying to shield the thief and not reporting that he knew where the plough was. T's court found him guilty, but taking into account his loyalty to his friend, it fined him only 3 goats. M appealed to Mosuoe's court, but the appeal was dismissed.

Where a person assists in a theft under duress, he is punished more lightly than the principal thief, as in No. 6, Mosuoe's court (p. 270) where the herd-boy was fined 1 beast only and did not have to pay compensation.

Where an accessory interferes with the administration of justice by hindering the search for stolen goods or the apprehension of suspected thieves, he may be punished heavily:

Mosalatsi v. Keleng and Piete, July 1936.
M traced the spoor of sheep lost from his cattle-post to another cattle-post where he found the skinned head of one of his sheep. P confessed to having stolen two sheep with three others whom he named. M rounded them up and tied them up. Two others then arrived and made him untie them and encouraged them to deny the theft. Finally the situation was saved by the headman's messenger arriving and getting P to carry the skin and so reaffirm his admission. The four thieves were ordered to "restore" 2 sheep and compensate M for the theft by paying 4 sheep each and were fined 1 beast each. The other two were fined 2 beasts for their interference.

[1] Ibid.

Robbery, or theft with violence, occasionally occurs, as when thieves terrorize herd-boys in remote cattle-posts or keep them in the hut at night by throwing stones on the roof or door and threatening to burn the hut or to kill them if they try to come out, while they rustle the sheep away. In such cases, the offence is dealt with in the same way as ordinary theft in so far as civil action and remedies are concerned; the victim does not get any extra compensation by reason of his having been subjected to violence or threats, although cognisance may be taken of these threats or violence in punishing the offender.

Mokete v. Lekhokhotsane, July 1936.
L robbed M of 2 horses. He was ordered to return them and *qhoba* them with 2 head of cattle, and was fined 2 head of cattle "for provoking bloodshed in a man's village" plus £1 "to make you respect the law".

Liau v. Monnamoholo and Khoto, June 1936.
M and K robbed L's herd-boy of 2 bags of wool. The court ordered them to return it with 2 bags and fined each 1 beast plus 10s. for theft. For the assault K was fined 2 beasts as he is a headman and M was fined £3 10s.

Theft by conversion is occasionally found. This mainly occurs in connexion with *mafisa* stock where some of the stock is sold or given away or killed for food beyond the quantity tacitly or explicitly agreed upon by the owner. Cases may occur where a guardian misappropriates his ward's property or where an authority misappropriates property given to him to hold in trust during a dispute. Ellenberger and MacGregor record[1] that because such theft involved breach of trust "any person in charge of cattle belonging to another, who tried to appropriate them for himself by theft or by means of false marks was almost as severely dealt with" as a warrior hiding booty captured in war, the penalty for which was death. But in the cases of which I have records no great differentiation is made between this and other forms of theft. For instance, Mosuoe's court fined a headman 30s. for eating some grain and spending all but 2s. of a pound which had been entrusted to his care. Similarly, Bereng's court ordered a person who had sold another's cow without his consent to restore it and fined him one beast.

Another type of theft is the misappropriation of lost property, i.e. appropriating it without taking the proper steps to return it to its owner. Ordinary articles, such as clothing or blankets, found on the road should be reported to the headman and returned to the owner as soon as it is known who he is; and no claim for reward should be made. If the owner is not found within six months the property may be retained by the finder. Stray stock should be handed to the chief or reported within two months of arrival. No obstacle should be put in the

---

[1] Ellenberger and MacGregor, p. 270.

way of people looking for their lost stock.[1] Breach of these rules is punished by fining and/or imprisonment and the offender may be ordered to pay compensation for any damage or loss suffered by the owner of the lost property.

Damage to Property

A person unlawfully damaging another's property or interfering with his enjoyment of such property is liable to pay the owner damages. As in other cases, the courts can impose a fine where the damage was done maliciously or provocatively, or was accompanied by some other reprehensible circumstance. For instance, in Bereng's court in 1933, a plaintiff sued a man whose dog had killed his sheep. The court ordered the defendant to replace the sheep, and then fined him two sheep for slackness in not reporting the killing to his headman or the complainant. So, too:

Lethapa v. Moji, June 1936.

L sued M for driving 12 cattle into his crops. The court ordered M to pay £1 plus 1 bag of grain for the damage, and fined him 1 beast for deliberately causing this damage.

Two cases occurred in Bereng's court of subordinate authorities being fined for damage to stock kept in their pounds: in one, the authority was fined for keeping a horse two days without letting it graze; in the other, he was fined one beast for gross negligence leading to the death of two sheep, and was also ordered to compensate the owner by replacing the two sheep.

An action for damages will be sustained by the courts only when the damage is done unlawfully.

Rankhonoane v. Nrebe, July 1936.

N was found sitting in R's hut with R's wife by another man who was enamoured of R's wife. A fight started between them in the course of which they smashed the door of the hut. R sued N as it was his presence in the hut which provoked the fight. N was ordered to pay R £2 for the damage to the door and was fined 30s.

Where it is done lawfully, there is no liability to pay compensation.

Mposi v. Mosebi, October 1936.

Mp unsuccessfully sued M and three others for breaking down the door of his hut. Their defence was that they were sent by the chief to his village to fetch him in connexion with suspected theft. On finding he had run away from home on their approach, they broke into his hut to search for the stolen goods and found the skin of one of the stolen sheep.

The amount of damages to be paid is usually assessed by the courts

[1] "Rules", No. 21.

and should be equivalent to the actual damage done; there is no additional "compensation" for any theoretical loss by deprivation or inconvenience as in the case of theft. Where there is no damage, there is no award:

Isaak v. Moiloa, etc., July 1936.
I unsuccessfully sued the parents of several boys for damaging his field. They had not done any damage as they were hunting a bird there and as they were only young boys, who meant no harm, his rights had not been seriously flouted.

In the case of damage to crops, the arbitrary figures of 1s. per head of large stock and 3d. per head of small stock were laid down in the 1922 *Laws of Lerotholi*:

"For trespass by any beast, horse, mule or donkey in any garden or tree plantation, the owner or caretaker of such animals will pay to the owner or caretaker of such garden or tree plantation the sum of 1s. for each beast or horse. Should, however, the damage be found by the assessors to be small the chief or headman shall only award a sum of 3d. per head."

"No charge for trespass shall be made in respect of any sheep or goat, but if any damage is done to crops or trees the chief or headman shall cause the owner or caretaker of such sheep or goat to pay the owner or caretaker of such crops or trees a sum of 3d. per head."[1]

Nevertheless, the courts adopted a more realistic attitude and where considerable damage had been done, they attempted to assess it more equitably:

Mokete v. Mazenkane, February 1936.
Mok claimed 32s. damages to his crop done by 12 cattle. The court awarded £1 instead of the prescribed 12s. to "console" him for the extensive damage done.

The old fixed rate has now been abolished and the courts are allowed to use their own discretion.[2]

The official rates were known to most people, but the two parties sometimes agreed on a higher rate of damages. If they quarelled about this later, the court would enforce the agreement:

Lebula v. Makokotla, February 1936.
Thirty of M's sheep grazed L's crops during the day. M sent a messenger to view the damage and agreed to pay 2 bags of grain as compensation. As he failed to honour his agreement, L sued him. The court first suggested that L should accept 7s. 6d., i.e. 3d. per head, but when he refused, it ordered M to fulfil his agreement and pay the 2 bags of grain or the equivalent (£2), although it considered this excessive.

The following is the usual procedure for obtaining compensation when crops are damaged: the owner of the crops reports the incident

---

[1] *Laws of Lerotholi*, 1922, No. 25 (2) and (3).   [2] "Rules" No. 13.

to the owner or person in charge of the stock, and the two inspect the damage together—in person or by proxy—and try to agree upon the extent of the damage and the amount of compensation to be paid. If the owner of the stock refuses to view the damage or if they fail to reach an agreement, the owner of the crops should appeal to his headman. The latter should then send reliable messengers to assess the damage before giving judgment. Under the new Rules, the person claiming damages should inform his headman of the amount claimed, and if the owner of the stock disputes this, the headman should "depute two independent persons to assess the damages; provided that if either party is dissatisfied with the amount assessed, such dissatisfied party may take the matter to court."

In the foregoing cases the damage had been caused either by the deliberate act of the offender or through his negligence. Liability may, however, extend further to cover cases where the damage is done through no fault of the person concerned. Thus, if cattle break out of a kraal at night and damage crops, their owner has to pay the same damages as described above, even though the cattle were properly secured for the night. If they break out repeatedly, the owner is presumed to have been negligent in securing them and may be fined as well; formerly, the cattle could have been taken to a kraal and one beast slaughtered there. Similarly, if a stallion breaks loose and covers someone's mare, the owner of the stallion is liable for damages, which may be assessed at 30s. Other cases of this sort are a bull goring another bull or a dog barking and frightening a cow and causing it to injure itself. Where, however, the owner of the injured animal was negligent and his negligence contributed to the accident, he is not entitled to damages.

Sekate v. Leshota, March 1936.
Appeal from lower court. L seized a beast belonging to S to pay off the tax arrears owed by S. When it was being driven off, it fell over a cliff and was killed. S sued L for damages, saying it had "died in the chief's kraal". The court rejected the claim since its fall was due to an attempt by S to turn it back.

Criminal Offences
One group of criminal offences consists of offences against the tribal authorities, such as refusal to obey lawful instructions given by the authority in his official capacity. Disobeying orders given by the authority in his personal capacity is not strictly punishable in law, but so wide are the powers of the bigger chiefs and so extensive the privileges they claim and try to enforce, that such disobedience would probably be punished in their courts, although the punishment might be set aside by a higher court if the offender were bold enough to appeal. The following are the sort of offences that occur: ignoring a summons to attend a general tribal gathering or *pitso*; refusal to carry messages;

refusal to accompany a person investigating suspected theft or following the spoor of lost stock; refusal to cut reeds or perform other forms of labour which the authority is entitled to exact.

Offences against the courts and the administration of justice form another important group, and include the following cases: refusal to obey the court's summons or to carry out its orders as to payment of fines or the surrender of disputed property; contempt of court, misbehaviour in court, impudence to the judges or refusal to give evidence; defeating or attempting to defeat the ends of justice by giving false evidence, suborning witnesses, hindering court messengers, sidetracking the investigation of offences such as theft, giving shelter to thieves or otherwise helping them to escape.

These categories of offences are part of the traditional law, but some have also been incorporated in the *Laws of Lerotholi* (1922), as in Law 2:

". . . Whatsoever chief or person shall disobey the summons or command of the Paramount Chief or other chief lawfully over him, shall be liable to be punished by the chief's court according to the gravity of his offence."

and Law 4:

"It is lawful for the Paramount Chief or any chief to call the chiefs or sub-chiefs under them or their people to take messages for them or to cultivate their lands. Any chief or sub-chief or man refusing such lawful summons shall be liable to a fine not exceeding ten shillings (10s.) or in default, two days' work."

Many cases of this sort are brought to the court by the aggrieved authority, and are dealt with as a separate, distinct issue. But others arise and are dealt with incidentally in the course of other issues or disputes. Where the matter is dealt with as a separate issue, it is usually prosecuted personally by the lesser authorities and by proxy by the more important authorities.

Theoretically the fines imposed for these offences vary with the gravity of the case, as provided in Law 2, quoted above, but in practice the standard fine is one beast. In Bereng's court, in ten out of fifteen cases where the offender was prosecuted for refusing to obey a summons, fines of one beast were imposed; other fines were: one for two sheep, one for three sheep, one for four beasts for ignoring four summonses, one where six men were each fined five sheep, and one where the elder brother was fined five sheep and the younger two. Disobedience in three other cases was treated more variously—for bringing only ten bundles of reeds instead of a larger, unspecified number that the chief expected, the offender was warned and ordered to bring more; for failing to plough for the chief, one offender was fined 5s. and another one beast. The punishment for false witness depends on the mood and general standard of the court and on the seriousness of the falsity. In the only case recorded in Bereng's court, the fine was one beast; in several cases in Mosuoe's court it varied from 10s. to 30s.

Opposition to court messengers, disregard of court orders or contempt of court may be punished more heavily as these are serious offences, though even here a substantial number of cases are punished with the standard fine of one beast. Fines of this amount were imposed, in six out of twelve cases, for the following offences: opposing messengers sent to enforce payment of a previous judgment; disregarding a previous judgment to cease ploughing a disputed field; disregarding an order to remove stock from an enclosed area; not paying damages (in one case the damages amounted to only 5s.). Fines of two beasts were imposed in three cases, for obstructing messengers and ignoring summonses, and for disobeying an order not to plough land and doing so defiantly with a gun in the hand. (The local headman who assisted the offender was fined one beast plus five small stock.) In yet another case, a subordinate authority was heavily punished for eating certain fines instead of handing them over; he was ordered to replace the three beasts he had eaten by eight, and the two goats by four, and he was fined five head of cattle. In only two cases were moderate fines imposed, "six half-crowns" and two sheep respectively for disregarding a previous judgment—in one case refusing to pay a fine and in the other for ploughing a disputed field. All these cases occurred in Bereng's court.

Mosuoe's court showed more variation and also more leniency. Out of twenty-two cases where fines were imposed for similar offences, eight were for 10s., one for 15s. two for £1, two for 30s., seven for one beast, one for one beast plus 30s., one for three beasts. In five cases no fines were imposed.

Cases of this sort may be prosecuted in four different ways. Take the case of refusal to answer a summons, for instance. The court concerned may repeat its summons to attend; if this is successful and the person does attend, the court will hear in the normal way the case for which that person was required, but will include in its judgment an order fining him for his disobedience. Seventeen of the twenty-seven cases referred to above were dealt with in this way as incidental to a civil case. Alternatively, the court may specially summon the offender for having refused the previous summons and thereupon deal with his refusal as a straightforward offence. This is done mainly by important and powerful authorities—it happened in only three of the foregoing cases in Mosuoe's court. If the court does not feel strong enough to deal with it in either of these ways, it may either prosecute the offender in a superior court (two such cases were brought to Mosuoe's court) or it may allow the plaintiff an "appeal" to that court. In either event, it shifts on to the superior court the onus of summoning the offender. In the former case, the superior court will deal with the matter as a straightforward offence and if it finds the offender guilty, it will punish him with a fine, which it will retain. In the latter case, it will deal with the defendant's disobedience to the lower court as a matter incidental to the civil complaint by the "appellant" in exactly the same way as if the respondent had disobeyed its own summons.

Continual disobedience and deliberate neglect of one's duties constitute a form of disloyalty known as "turning one's door" on the chief. This is punished by depriving the offender of his lands and expelling him from that authority's area, and sometimes by fining him as well. In the old days serious disloyalty, amounting to rebellion or conspiracy against the chief, was punished by death or by banishment and confiscation of property.

Another group of offences are those against other rules of the political and judicial organization. Cases of this sort are, the failure of native authorities to carry out their obligations or the exercise of powers to which they are not entitled. For instance, Bereng's court meted out the following punishments: a fine of two beasts to a headman for bad administration and insubordination, to a sub-chief for refusing to grant an appeal, and to another headman for gross negligence contributing to the death of two sheep in his pound and for failing to preserve the skins; and a fine of one beast to yet another headman for inflicting a punishment on one of his followers when he had no right to try cases at all. Seeiso fined an important sub-chief two beasts for the careless way in which his officials were issuing *bewjis*.

A third group of offences are statutory offences. Many of the offences described in the first and second groups now also fall into this group, as they have been incorporated in the Native Administration and Courts Proclamations, the promulgated Rules of Court and the *Laws of Lerotholi* issued under the Native Administration Proclamation. Such offences are: disregard of the Paramount Chief's, chief's, sub-chief's or headman's lawful order[1] or disregard of a court summons;[2] refusal to grant an appeal,[3] or cultivate the chief's lands,[4] and misappropriation of stray stock.[5] These new laws also list as offences various civil wrongs and criminal matters that were formerly punishable only under the common law, such as unlawful confiscation of property,[6] abduction and seduction,[7] grazing of *leboella*,[8] unlawful collection of levies,[9] destruction of trees.[10] They also include regulations made by the Para-

---

[1] Section 12, Proclamation No. 61 of 1938 and No. 2, *Laws of Lerotholi*, 1922.
[2] Section 16, Proclamation No. 62 of 1938 and Nos. 10 and 19, *Laws of Lerotholi*, 1922.
[3] Ibid., No. 3.
[4] No. 4, 1922 version and No. 12, 1946 version of the *Laws of Lerotholi*.
[5] Ibid., No. 24, 1922 version and No. 20, 1946 version.
[6] "Rules", No. 1.
[7] Ibid., Nos. 2-8.
[8] Ibid., No. 11.
[9] Ibid, No. 24.   [10] Ibid., No. 31.

mount Chief concerning matters such as eradication of noxious weeds,[1] prohibition of the sale of kaffir beer and other intoxicating drinks[2] and provision of stock removal permits (*bewjis*).[3] As with other criminal cases, offences against these provisions can be prosecuted directly by a native authority or can be dealt with as a side issue to some other case. The method adopted depends on the way in which the evidence regarding the offence is obtained. If the commission of the offence is revealed during the hearing of some case, it is punished then and there. This often happens with *bewijs* cases, which come to light during the hearing of theft cases or disputes over property.[4] On the other hand, if it is reported in some other way, it will be separately prosecuted.

Since the promulgation of the Native Courts Proclamation, the number of statutory criminal offences that the courts may try has increased. Elaborate court rules have now been promulgated, any breach of which is a punishable offence. The courts may also try offences arising under certain of the Territory's proclaimed laws, e.g. under the Basutoland Native Tax Proclamation and Compulsory Dipping of Small Stock.[5]

The last group consists of offences against the community. The main distinction between these and the third group is that these are offences against common law whereas the others are against proclaimed law. There is no practical significance in this distinction, which is useful merely for purposes of classification. In most cases, the prosecution is brought by a tribal authority in his official capacity, though there is nothing to prevent a private individual reporting the commission of an offence to the courts and the latter then taking action thereon.

A serious crime in the old days was hiding stock captured in war with a view to keeping it for oneself. This was punishable by death, for "as the saying is, it is booty which kills the village".[6] Witchcraft was also punished by death or by banishment.

On rare occasions, the chiefs or their courts may take cognizance of a civil wrong that has been committed and, in default of a suit brought by the injured person, they may prosecute it as a crime. The prosecution is undertaken either in the name of the chief or by the person who reported the matter. The former is the more usual. I believe that this transition of actionable wrongs to crimes is a new development, which is still in its infancy. No such cases were recorded in Bereng's court in 1933-4, and only three in Mosuoe's court. These are summarized below.

[1] No. 23, 1922 version, No. 26, 1946 version.
[2] No. 21, 1922 version, No. 25, 1946 version.
[3] No. 24, 1922 version, No. 17, 1946 version.
[4] See '*Mamasiea v. Motsarapane*, p. 183.
[5] Jurisdiction conferred by High Commissioner's Notices No. 122 of 1948 and No. 295 of 1946.
[6] Ellenberger and MacGregor, p. 270.

1. Assault

Mosuoe v. Molapo and Sekata, October 1936.

Mol. and S are normally close friends but at a *letsema* beer-drink they got quarrelsome, threw a pot of beer down and started a drunken brawl. They were separated but later S followed Mol. to his home, where he attacked him, hit him on the face and bit his cheek. Mol. ran to his hut, got his gun and shot at S, who joined with him again and struggled with him till they were separated. Mosuoe prosecuted them in his court and fined Mol. 5 beasts for starting the fight, for behaving badly at the beer-drink, and for taking a gun. The gun was confiscated. S was fined 3 beasts for fighting and for continuing the fight in Mol.'s village after they had been separated.

2. Theft

Mosuoe v. Masheitsi and others, September 1936.

M, a boy of 13, was carrying some wool in a blanket to sell at the local store. Some men met him on the road and asked him, in the usual sociable manner, where he was going and what he was doing. He answered their questions peculiarly, so they became suspicious and reported to Mosuoe. When interrogated by the court, he admitted that this was the wool of 2 sheep he had found straying in the mountains, brought into their cattle-post and sheared. He had killed them both, eaten one with his father and another man, and left the other to the birds. As the owner of the sheep was not known, the three of them were prosecuted in the name of the chief by one of the principal men of the court, saying, "what are not known are mine" (*tse sa tsejoeng lia ntokela*). M was fined £1, his father and the owner of the cattle-post were fined £2 or 1 beast each.

3. Theft: accessory

Tootse v. Maekane, October 1935.

T sued M in his own (T's) court for hiding a stolen plough. The court fined M 30s. M appealed to Mosuoe's court—previous judgment upheld and fine retained by Mosuoe's court.[1]

The following are the only two cases of "offences against the community" that were recorded in Mosuoe's court. There were none in Bereng's.

1. Drugs[2]

Mosebi v. Mohanoe and others, February 1936.

Mosebi, one of Mosuoe's principal men, saw Mahanoe and others smoking dagga (Indian hemp) and reported the matter. The court fined each of them £1.

2. Tribal Taboo

Mohlakola v. Monyane and others, July 1936.

Monyane gave a *letsema* during a period of mourning, i.e. he organized it

---

[1] For fuller details, see p. 271.

[2] As this is an offence under the "Habit-forming Drugs Proclamation", some officials regard it as improper for a Basuto court to have tried the case. Dagga-smoking is, however, regarded as an offence against Basuto law and so is cognizable by their courts.

after the mourning started. Mohlakola, a headman, brought the matter to Mosuoe's court. Monyane was fined 50s. and those who took part in the *letsema* were each fined 30s.

Since 1946, all recognized courts have to keep written records of their cases. For this purpose they have been given a "Civil Record" book and a "Criminal Record" book. At first, Mosuoe's court was undecided about which book to use for civil wrongs such as theft and slander, sometimes recording a case in one book and sometimes in another. Eventually, presumably after official guidance, it recorded[1] all theft, insult and assault cases as "criminal", but remained inconsistent about slander, sometimes recording such cases as "civil" and sometimes as "criminal". Procedure remained essentially civil in all these cases, in that the cases were brought to court and prosecuted by the person who had been wronged. I was unable to go into them deeply enough to find out whether the chief or the court itself had prosecuted any offences, as had been done in the assault and two theft cases quoted above. The separate recording of criminal and civil cases in this way did not, however, prevent the court from continuing to inflict penal fines in "civil" cases or from punishing offences that were discovered in the course of a "civil" hearing. It would therefore seem that, although the courts are adopting the formal European division of law into criminal and civil law, justice is still administered on the wider and more flexible basis of traditional Basuto law.[2]

[1] In Appendix IV the kinds of cases tried in Bereng's and Mosuoe's courts are summarized. This summary clearly shows the considerable volume of judicial work undertaken by the Basuto courts and the wide variety of cases tried.

[2] Some courts have gone so far as to list their ciminal cases as "Rex versus . . .". When one such case went on appeal to the High Court, the judge ruled that this was improper and advised that such cases should be listed as "Basutoland Native Administration versus . . ." or as "X" charged with the crime of . . . on the complaint of "Y". Marwick records that "this decision has been severely criticized by some Basuto who regard it as wrong since an offence committed in the Territory is an offence against the crown" and the native courts are so much an integral part of the Territory's administration of justice that they should be regarded as agents of the Crown. (Thioanya *v.* Rex: Basutoland High Court, 1950, quoted by Marwick, 1950.)

CHAPTER XVI

MEDICINE, MAGIC AND SORCERY

MEDICINE, magic and sorcery play an important part in Basuto life and form one of the most pervasive aspects of their culture. Though the first two are sociologically distinguishable, the Basuto do not differentiate between them; for simplicity's sake, therefore, I have adopted their terminology, using the term "medicine" in place of the more usual "magic". They do, however, distinguish between medicine (*moriane*) and sorcery (*boloi*), the former being the use of substances for socially approved ends, and the latter their use for ends not approved by society, and this differentiation has been followed.

Medical Practitioners

The *ngaka* (witch doctor, herbalist) is one of the most important individuals in society, judged by what he does rather than by his social status. He diagnoses and prescribes remedies for the ordinary ailments and diseases, alleviates and prevents misfortunes, gives protection against sorcery and accident, and brings luck and prosperity. He is expected to help in practically every situation which people cannot control by their own unaided efforts or where they feel insecure. To do this he relies on medicines, occasionally helped out with other means. He is an expert who has greater knowledge and experience than ordinary people and is called on professionally by them when the small store of medical knowledge which they or their friends possess is exhausted. He is not a sorcerer, as Christol and others[1] have asserted, and though his position as a doctor gives him more opportunity for dabbling in sorcery, it would be as wrong for him to indulge in such activities as for any one else.

Many doctors learn their profession by being apprenticed to a reputable herbalist. At first, as an apprentice (*lehlahana*), he collects his master's fees and carries his bags; later, in return for his assistance, he is shown where and how to dig for roots and how to prepare medicines, and is gradually taught to diagnose and cure diseases and to handle other aspects of his art. When he has learnt enough, he may set up on his own, but if his master likes him and is old and about to retire, he may, on payment of ten head of cattle, teach him his most secret and important medicines and give him his horns[2] containing the different sorts of *mohlabelo* (burnt medicines).

[1] Dieterlen, 1930, p. 20; Christol, 1900, p. 64.
[2] Those doctors who are purely herbalists and do not also use *mohlabelo* and other medicines that are kept in horns, are called *ngaka chitja*, the "hornless" doctor.

Doctors also increase their knowledge by observing other doctors, by cadging a prescription here and by buying one there. The price of a prescription varies from one sheep to ten head of cattle, depending on the nature and value of the medicine and on the relationship of the two doctors. A doctor may also inherit prescriptions from his parents or uncles, usually protective medicines used to promote the family's welfare. He may also invent or discover new medicines by mixing known medical substances in novel ways or by introducing new plants and substances. Whether they are the fruit of experiment, the result of chance or of the adoption of European medicaments, these medicines are usually attributed to dream revelation by God or by the ancestor spirits (*balimo*). Some doctors also attribute their adoption of this profession to dreams and miracles.

Another type of doctor is the diviner or bone-thrower (*selaoli*), who uses the bones to help his diagnosis and treatment. This knowledge has to be formally taught by another *selaoli* who is paid for his instruction. He is taught the names, praises and meanings of the various positions or "falls" of the bones, and he is also taught the symptoms and cures of the commoner ailments and the use of protective medicines against sorcery. This course is sometimes preceded as well as completed by a brief ritual—a chicken or sheep is slaughtered, and the initiate is given a potion made from the wild "forget-me-not" to strengthen his memory. The *selaoli's* medicines, though made of the same substances and administered in similar ways, are distinguished from those of ordinary doctors and are called *lithato* instead of *meriane*. They are also considerably cheaper. The diviner's approach to disease and trouble is also somewhat different and he tends to attribute them to sorcery and to the agency of supernatural factors, such as the wrath of *balimo* or breach of taboos, rather than to natural causes.

Then there is the seer (*senohe*). He is a person who "tells things that are not known, that are hidden: he diagnoses illnesses affecting people and he foretells things that are going to happen." This power of second sight may be improved and perfected through practice, but it is not a skill which can be acquired. It is a gift from God or the ancestors and is exercised intuitively or "through the mind". A special type of seer is one who can see in deep water; he is mainly of value in locating people who have been drowned or seized by the water serpent (*khanyapa*).

Another kind of diviner is the *lethuela*, *leqekha* or *mokoma*. These are comparatively new to the Basuto and have not been described by Casalis or any other writer on the Basuto, except Motlamelle in 1938. They are similar to the Pondo *amagqira*[1] and represent a foreign culture trait introduced by Thembus and others, who have come in from the Cape Colony. They are mainly to be found in the southern and eastern parts of Basutoland, from Mohale's Hoek round to Mokhotlong, where

[1] Hunter, M., *Reaction to Conquest*, pp. 320 et seq.; Maclean's *Compendium*, p. 82.

Thembu immigrants are most numerous and where contact with the "Colony" is greatest.

A *mokoma* is a person who has undergone the ritual and treatment required to cure an illness called *motheketheke*. This is an unaccountable sickness, which often continues for months; it is accompanied by fits, fainting, loss of memory, shooting pains in the head, and may finally cause the patient to wander about the country as if in a trance or dream (*phaphatheha*). The patient may also have repeated visions or dreams of deceased friends and relatives, and is said to be visited by a spirit or to be "spiritually upset". This illness can only be cured through special ritual treatment. Sometimes the symptoms are so pronounced that the nature of the affliction is obvious, but in other cases a diviner has to be consulted.

As soon as it is decided that the patient should undergo the full treatment and should "enter the churning" (*kena lefehlong*), friends and other *bakoma* are invited to a small feast. Two goats are selected (sheep should not be used as they are said to "darken" the patient's sight), and before they are killed in the morning they are made to drink a medicine that has been beaten into a froth. This will enable the patient to see the *balimo*. The doctor, dressed in his finery, then again churns the medicine into a froth, bedaubs the patient and other *bakoma* present, and gives him the rest of it to drink and wash his body while his kinsmen sing praises of the living and the dead. The goats are stabbed with a spear. The longer they take to die the better the omen. In the evening dancing begins. It is accompanied by drumming on a dry, rolled ox skin (*sekupu*) and by endless *bokoma* songs. The dance is a special one with a quick jerky step whose tempo gradually gets faster and faster until one of the dancers suddenly stops with a cry and chants a *bokoma* song, or rushes hysterically into the night. Then, after a slight pause, the dance starts again and so through the night until sunrise, when the last of the beer is drunk and the guests depart. The patient is then doctored with "black" medicine mixed with chyme to protect him from sorcery. Thereafter, the patient should have a séance every evening at which he dances for two or three hours, attended by neighbours and by the village children (except those who have been forbidden by their teachers to attend), who help to beat the *sekupu* and watch the proceedings intrigued by the songs and weird contortions of the dancers.

This goes on for several months until sooner or later the patient dreams that his doctor or senior kinsman or the *balimo* say that the séances should cease and that a particular animal, which they describe minutely, should be killed for the final ceremonies. Many people, particularly the owner of the chosen beast, are sceptical about these instructions, but if the patient continues to have these dreams, the owner of the beast, fearing reprisals from the *balimo*, will reluctantly give it to him as a present. Another feast is then held. Early in the morning the patient is washed with medicines at the riverside. When he returns to the village, the animal is killed, its gall is poured over his head and hands, and the inflated gall-bladder tied on to his head or round his neck. The tail is severed and put aside and is later made into a whisk which will form part of his ceremonial accoutrement. He is now given more medicine to drink to complete his cure. In the evening dancing starts again and continues throughout the night, punctuated by tests of the patient's psychic powers and his ability to find small objects hidden in the hut.

Besides being cured through this protracted treatment, the patient acquires powers of divination, and is placed *en rapport* with the *balimo* who reveal medicines to him and teach him how to doctor, and especially how to cure others suffering from *motheketheke*. Only a few take advantage of this cure to become professional doctors, but to those who do or who are already practising as ordinary doctors, it gives excellent publicity, especially if their séance performances were impressive.

An interesting feature of *bokoma* is the extent to which women are affected. Although many women are experts in simple home remedies, they are handicapped by tradition, ordinary female duties and occupations, popular prejudice against women and the taboos against their handling *mohlabelo* medicines, so that very few become doctors, and still fewer bone-throwers. But the majority of *bakoma* are women and among the Tlokoa the proportion of women to men was well over five to one. *Bokoma* is more a social affair and less concerned with practical and professional doctoring and so is more attractive to and less difficult for women. Indeed, it is now so much regarded as a woman's affair that the only men who become *bakoma* are either important doctors who go through the ritual as an additional professional qualification, or men of low social standing who do it to boost their egos.

The preponderance of women may possibly be due to some connexion between female physiology and the emotional disorders which characterize *botheketheke*. The Basuto also offer a psychological reason and explain that *botheketheke* and the desire to become a *mokoma* is a conscious or unconscious reaction to neglect or boredom; that by becoming the centre of these ritual dances and by forcing their relations to give them an occasional feast, people hope to attract attention and to enliven their existence, and that the predominance of women is due to their comparatively dull lives and to their being the passive element in social and sexual relations, and so liable to neglect. This is a plausible theory and in its support, I may mention that of the five *bakoma* I knew well, two were widows, two neglected wives of polygynists, and the fifth (one of the few men), the chief's hired herdsman who occupied a very lowly position.

A further point on which people have remarked is that *botheketheke* is "infectious". It seems to come in waves; for a time no cases occur and then suddenly several people are affected within a short period. Thus, during the early part of my stay at Malingoaneng no cases occurred; then one woman began to have séances, and within eight months at least seven other women in the immediate neighbourhood complained of the affliction and wanted to be treated. This phenomenon was cited in support of the psychological reason given above: "They see other women having feasts, so they say: Why shouldn't we have one for ourselves?" One Mosuto put it even more bluntly—"They want meat."

Recently, these people have been singled out for special attack in the name of the Paramount Chief. Theko Makhaola, chief of Qacha's Nek area, when acting Paramount Chief in 1948, accused them of being responsible for ritual murder and outlawed them. Referring to previous circulars of the Paramount Chief dealing with these murders, he said, "I have noticed with regret that I have forgotten to mention in these circulars the cause of witchcraft which is the *smelling-out* doctors (*mathuela*). Smelling-out (*bothuela*) is the source of witchcraft (*boloi*) because it believes in the existence of witchcraft. Therefore, I give an order that smelling-out should not be allowed in Basutoland by a male or a female person. Stringent measures will be taken against any person who is found practising smelling-out methods."[1] Later, he indicated that he was opposed to them because they believed in "*melimo* and other things which pushed the people backward". There is no evidence connecting *bokoma* with ritual murders or linking *bakoma* more closely with sorcery and accusations of sorcery than other kinds of doctors or diviners. Unfortunately I did not have an opportunity of finding out the real reason for this attack nor what effect this circular has had.

Although doctoring, divining and *bokoma* are separate activities, they are not necessarily practised by different people. Some specialize in one and some in another, but many practise all three.

Doctors and diviners have no particular status as a class or profession. Some individuals have considerable prestige, but this is due to their inherited social position, their personality or their success. Formerly, there used to be official doctors, who were attached to the chief as rain-makers, diviners and keepers of war medicine and ranked next after him in importance. Their office has now disappeared and, though doctors may be employed by a chief, they have no official standing though naturally they acquire some prestige on account of such employment. Doctors do not form a definite group and they have no corporate or co-operative activities; they are strong individualists who work by themselves and in competition with others. Recently, however, various associations have been formed in South Africa to protect and further their common interests, and to these some Basuto doctors belong. One such association is the Orange Free State African Herbalists'

[1] Circular No. 8 of 1948, dated 9 April 1948. Words in brackets appear in the Sesuto original.

Association. It is pressing for official recognition and for the registration of doctors on the grounds that it is otherwise "difficult to distinguish between a herbalist and an impostor". The Association itself unofficially registers doctors on production of a letter of credentials from a chief, testifying that the candidate has been practising as a herbalist or "medicine man" for more than ten years.

In the course of time, successful doctors work up a regular practice and have their regular patients. Some of them are paid a retaining fee by the heads of families. In return for this, they keep them supplied with medicine, such as *'meseletso* or *moupello*, which is needed periodically to protect the crops or villages, and attend to members of the family who are ill or in trouble; but if required to provide some unusual medicines or treatment they would be given an additional payment. Apart from this, no doctor has a monopoly over any particular area or section of the community and every doctor is entitled to work where and when he can. Many are great travellers and wander from village to village, impelled by various motives, such as the need to earn a living, wanderlust and desire to acquire new medicines, to enrich their experience and enhance their prestige. Some travel as far afield as Bechuanaland and the northern Transvaal and many visit Zululand. Some dream of a special plant to be found in a distant place and undertake a special journey to fetch it. One woman walked all the way from Malingoaneng to the coast on such a mission, a round journey of about 600 miles. Wherever they go, they can be sure of being called in by the local people, as the fact that they have come from afar is a good advertisement and guarantees that they will have potent medicines, culled from strange lands.

Doctors, on the whole, are ordinary people, although probably above the average in intelligence and alertness. Most of them go quietly about their business and it is exceptional to find one who flaunts himself before the public or dresses, according to the common European conception, in a wild and picturesque costume such as described by Dieterlen: "To strike the popular imagination he wears a head-dress of monkey skin adorned with feathers, gall-bladders and eagles' claws; a necklet of charms, horns, pebbles, chips of wood, animal claws, sea-shells and other trifles; a shoulder belt of black glistening horns of different beasts filled with powders and ointments of every kind; these horns with roots and other debris borrowed from the animal and vegetable kingdoms constitute the stock-in-trade of those who say, 'I know' (for this is one of the names that people's malice applies to such doctors). Last, but not least, a packet of divining bones much in evidence shows that thanks to this possession the doctor has the means of discovering with absolute certainty both the trouble his client is suffering from and the means of securing his deliverance."[1]

[1] Dieterlen, 1912, p. 104.

Bakoma are more partial to display and have a special dress which they wear on ceremonial occasions connected with *bokoma* treatment. This consists of a skirt made of baboon, rock-rabbit, or meercat skins and tails, a fur cap, perhaps a cloak as well, of the same skins, and numerous strings of white beads. They carry a whisk, usually made from the tail of the animal killed at their initiation, and sometimes a short spear, both decorated with white beads. Round their legs they wear anklets and little leather bags containing stones or seeds that jingle as they dance. They observe a few minor customs. They should always wear a necklace of white beads; they may not eat "black" foods, such as roasted maize, liver or other dark meats, or spinach (which has black seeds), or black beans; they may not use sheep-skins for clothing or sleeping mats, and when they die their bodies should be washed with a lotion of the *lefehlo* medicine. While undergoing treatment, they may not use "black" medicines, such as *mohlabelo*.

Doctors should be paid a consultation fee of a goat or sheep "to open" their bag of medicines. They may later be paid a further fee of up to one beast, provided they effect a cure. This principle of "no cure, no pay" has now received statutory recognition, as far as "medicine men and herbalists" are concerned.[1] In other cases, fees vary with the type of treatment. For agricultural medicine, a basket of grain should be given for each field treated; for protecting the village, one or two beasts, and for successful rain-making two or more beasts by the local chief or, according to Dieterlen,[2] a basket of grain from each family who benefited from the rain. In Bereng's court, in 1933, a doctor was awarded two basketfuls of grain for protecting fields from hail, as the defendant himself admitted that his "crops were not damaged by hail". Ten head of cattle were demanded by another doctor who was asked for medicine to locate hidden treasure. During his dispute with Seeiso, Mosuoe engaged an Indian for £50 to doctor the petition he sent to the Resident Commissioner, and a further £200 if it succeeded.

Diviners should be paid a chicken (or 1s.) for each divination, 1s. for supplying medicine, and a head of small stock for special treatment, but they often charge considerably more. Formerly, doctors who were asked to protect or cleanse a village used to insist on a black sheep (called *tsotso*) being killed for them to provide fat to mix with their medicines, but this is now regarded as a blatant form of extortion and few doctors have the temerity to insist on it. Another fee, *liphehiso*, is sometimes demanded when medicines have to be cooked.

These charges are extremely high in relation to the people's wealth and though, as the proverb puts it, doctors can do anything except secure their fees, it is surprising how often they are paid. Usually, however, the full fee is only claimed from chiefs and other wealthy

---

[1] Proclamation No. 44 of 1948, Section 4. [2] Dieterlen, 1930, p. 39.

PLATE XIII

Photo: L. Lewis

(a) Sheep

Photo: L. Lewis

(b) Scene at Paramount Chief's village, Matsieng

PLATE XIV

Photo: L. Lewis
(a) The late Paramount Chief Seeiso Griffith

Photo: L. Lewis
(b) Basuto type

Photo: Constance Stuart
(c) A Basuto blanket and grass hat

people or for the more important medicines, and the poorer people are charged a sheep for ordinary treatment.

The services of a doctor should always be engaged in the presence of witnesses. Disputes frequently occur over payment of fees, either as to the amount agreed on by the parties or as to the nature of the services rendered; in one case a man denied he had consulted a doctor professionally and said he had merely asked for medicine as from a friend. Witnesses are also necessary to remove any suspicion of sorcery. This is especially important where the doctor is engaged to provide protective medicine for an individual or for a village. (Bereng's court, 1933, fined a person two small stock for omitting to do this.) The consent of the patient's parent, if a minor, or husband, if a woman, is also required. If a villager wants to doctor his house, he should obtain the headman's permission so that the latter should know what is being done and that no sorcery is contemplated.

Sorcerers

Sorcerers (*baloi*) are people who use, or are alleged to use, medicines for anti-social purposes and to cause harm. They either use special medicines or reverse the effects of ordinary medicines normally used for beneficial purposes. They operate in much the same way as doctors, but as Dieterlen[1] has said, "it is in the realm of intention that the difference lies between these two activities (doctoring and sorcery), in many respects so similar". For instance, *seteipi* is normally used to protect infants, but in the hands of a sorcerer and applied with malevolent intent, i.e. smeared on a stone and left near the child, it will do it serious harm. So, too, the malicious and malevolent use of the medicine called *tseheletsa* will cause sterility instead of curing it.

Sorcerers can also gain their ends by sheer, unaided malevolence. Thus, if a man deliberately ignored the warning signs outside her hut and approached a *motsoetse* and her new-born babe, he would be regarded as a sorcerer, trying to kill the babe by his action. So, too, to threaten (*boletsa*) a person in certain ways is tantamount to sorcery; and to say, with appropriate gestures of ill-will, "You will see", or "I'll fix you", can be as effective as using medicines. Basuto cite cases where threats of this sort were followed almost immediately by illness or death, or by serious accident or misfortune. For example, a man tethered his horse near the field of another who, in a rage, cursed him, saying, "If the horse does not die, a person will". The horse did not die, but the man himself fell ill that night and died a fortnight later. I did not come across belief in the "evil eye".

It was formerly believed that sorcerers could harm the community at large by causing disasters, epidemics and drought; nowadays, such widespread calamities are attributed to other causes, such as the *balimo*,

[1] Dieterlen, 1930, pp. 22, 26-7.

being sad and angry at the abandonment of so many old customs; the incalculable design and purpose of God, fate, European influences or simply "unknown". Similarly, trouble occurring in a village, such as a series of deaths or accidents, is regarded less as a general attack on the people than as a personal attack on the headman. In short, sorcery is almost always aimed at a particular individual, whom it may harm directly by causing his misfortune, illness or death, or indirectly, by harming his family and friends.

As sorcery is pre-eminently an affair of darkness, it is scarcely to be expected that authentic instances of its occurrence can be obtained or that people will claim to be successful sorcerers; rumours of such claims are occasionally to be heard, and some doctors claim to possess medicines to conjure up lightning, or to do other harm. For instance, a doctor, whom I knew, claimed that the following procedure would cripple a man. "Three substances, one of which is potassium permanganate (*makhonatsohle*—'can manage anything'), are mixed with fat from a pig's back and rubbed on two pins which are fixed to straws and planted on either side of a path traversed by the victim. As this is being done, his name is called out, so that only he and not other passers-by will be affected by it. When he passes, the pins will break away from the straws and the medicine will enter his legs. At the same time as the pins are treated, some of the medicine is rubbed on the blade of a clasp knife. This is kept, half open, in a warm place. When the pins break off, the knife will shut and fall from its place and thereafter, as long as it remains shut, the victim will be crippled, unless he is treated by some doctor with more powerful medicine or by the sorcerer himself." This is a comparatively mild form of sorcery (*boloi*) which is used to cause minor hurt in revenge for some injury done by the victim, and not to kill.

In spite of the fact that sorcery can practically never be proved, people strongly believe in its existence and have little hesitation in attributing to it misfortune, accident, unusual illness, chronic sickness and sudden death—in a word, any mishap or abnormal occurrence savouring of mystery. For instance, when an enterprising agricultural demonstrator scratched his hand on a plough and nearly died of blood poisoning, this was ascribed to the sorcery of his jealous neighbours; the sudden firing of my assistant's cattle-post,[1] when no one was about and no clouds were in the sky (i.e. no lightning), was attributed to sorcery; Mosuoe's fourth and favourite wife became chronically ill soon after marriage, supposedly owing to the sorcery of his jealous third wife, whom she had replaced in his affections.

For the most part, people are content merely to assume that sorcery was the cause of the mishap or illness, if they are satisfied from the circumstances of the case that this is the most reasonable and likely ex-

[1] The apparently inexplicable burning of huts is a fairly common occurrence. It is probably due to spontaneous combustion of old, decaying thatch.

planation. Occasionally, however, corroboration is sought. Sometimes this is derived from the nature of the case. For instance, diarrhoea or stomach-ache is shown to be caused by sorcery, if worms or little snakes are found in the stools. So, too, the fact that a woman, who had had six miscarriages and no successful pregnancies, reacted to treatment which had been successful in other cases, by menstruating twice a month, clearly indicated that she had been bewitched—probably at her wedding. Bruises and scratches on the throat of a patient suffering from convulsions, or his complaints of a feeling of being strangled, are unmistakable evidence that the convulsions are caused by sorcery, probably operating through a *thokolosi* (a familiar). In a case of death from lightning, the cause can be determined from the nature of the injuries. If the body is not marked, it is natural lightning, God's lightning, for it is believed that a person struck by this is stunned by the flash and then choked by his tongue being driven into the back of the throat; if the tongue can be pulled forward immediately, he will recover. If, however, the body is severely lacerated, the lightning is believed to have been caused by sorcery and the injuries inflicted by the sorcerer himself who descended from the clouds (also conjured up by sorcery) and attacked his victim with an axe. Evidence of sorcery may also be adduced from deathbed confessions of sorcerers or if illness follows close on a quarrel. Thus, on hearing that his brother vomited blood after a beer-drink, a man who said, "Well, it serves him right, he is a stingy brute, he never shares his beer", was immediately accused of having bewitched him.

If evidence of this sort is lacking, confirmation can only be given by the "bones" or divination. Formerly, public "smelling-out" trials occurred, but these were stopped by Moshesh's "Proclamation against Witchcraft", quoted below, and his intransigeant attitude towards allegations of sorcery. Nowadays, diviners or bone-throwers are privately consulted by those who are worried by some illness, misfortune or untoward event. Occasionally specific allegations are made, that "So-and-so has bewitched you", naming a particular person, but usually the diviner contents himself with vague insinuations, hinting at sorcery and at its probable author, such as, "There is trouble in the village"; which means that co-wives are quarrelling and one has bewitched the other or her child; or "A stranger hates you", which means that the patient, usually a woman, is being bewitched by her lover's wife. As the diviner usually has a good idea of what jealousies and dissensions there are in the domestic circle, it is not difficult for him to make innuendoes which can readily be interpreted to confirm the patient's own suspicions.

The treatment to counteract sorcery and the steps to be taken to prevent its recurrence are left to the people's own discretion, although if a diviner has been consulted he will either say what should be done or will hint that he should be asked to prescribe the cure. For this a further fee is payable. The following is an authentic example.

R's married daughter came on a visit to her parents and her maternal uncle. One morning while she was at the latter's place, she felt drops of water fall on her. It was a cloudless sky and no one near her could have done this. Everyone was astonished and she became afraid. R then consulted B who threw the bones and said it came from a *thokolosi*, which belonged not to her home or her maternal uncle, but to her husband's people. R then asked him to treat her. B told him to bring a sheep which he killed and caught the blood, and with this he washed her blankets in the river. As she suffered no ill effects from her experience and nothing further untoward happened, B claimed to have cured her and was paid 1 head of cattle for doing so, in addition to £1 consultation fee.

Usually one of the first things to be done when sorcery is suspected is to renew all protective medicines, by scarifying the patient and his immediate family circle, and possibly renewing the village *moupello*. If that fails to improve the position, stronger medicines will be used or additional measures taken. A common ruse is to try to get beyond the sorcerer's reach. The patient is secretly taken away and hidden in a cave or in a friendly village, where the sorcerer will not find him or where he will be protected by that village's own *moupello*. When there is trouble between co-wives or kinsmen, one of them should be moved to another village, to reduce the friction between them and to minimize the sorcerer's power. In certain illnesses, special treatment is required. For chronic colic (*sejeso*) caused by eating bewitched food,[1] the patient must first be cleansed and then given medicine to remove beetles or snakes which are causing his colic and which were introduced through the bewitched food; as a precaution against re-infection, he should have his tongue and throat scarified to reveal tainted food before it is swallowed. If a village is repeatedly struck by lightning, it should be removed and rebuilt elsewhere as its present site is clearly unlucky.

Formerly, the sorcerer himself might be removed and Casalis recounts[2] the brutal torture and execution of an accused sorcerer. Moshesh seems to have been resolutely opposed to this sort of thing and, though he could not stamp out belief in sorcery, he forbade the exaction of this extreme penalty and heavily punished diviners who accused a person of sorcery and those who, on the word of a diviner, killed an alleged sorcerer. In the words of his Proclamation: "When anyone is killed in a case of witchcraft, the murderer will be most severely judged and sentenced to death."[3] Nevertheless, belief in sorcery is so strong that

[1] The term *sejeso* is primarily applied to the bewitched food, and secondarily, by extension, to the malady itself. Strictly speaking it is quite distinct from poison (*chefo*), although when talking loosely, some Basuto may equate the two.
[2] Casalis, p. 351. See also Basutoland Records, pp. 152-3.
[3] Dated 27 August 1855, Basutoland Records, p. 153.

occasionally a person who believes himself to be a victim of sorcery is driven to desperation and murders the suspected sorcerer.

The following case, reported by my assistant, illustrates the type of family discord that produces a state of mind ready to interpret sudden illness in terms of sorcery, and the steps taken to deal with it. It involves "L" and "T". L is the senior wife of D, who recently married a second wife, and so she is somewhat jealous and touchy. She is also a *mokoma* and doctor of standing. T is the widow of D's younger brother, a middle-aged and somewhat "disappointed" female.

One day L quarrelled with her sister-in-law T and asked why she told her husband that she (L) was having an affair with another man. T denied she had done so. They then scolded one another and L accused T of wanting to make trouble between her husband and herself. T denied this; D's mother then told them to stop talking like this, and asked what people would think if they heard of it. So they stopped. T went to her work.

When she returned in the evening, she went to her hut and went to bed. Then something—as it might be a needle—pricked her thigh and went down her leg; at the same time she began to feel cold. She called D's mother, who found her ill. She asked what the matter was and T told her there was something the matter with her leg, it felt paralysed. The latter then raised the alarm. All the villagers gathered there, for her leg was swollen. She then said to her mother-in-law, D's mother—"You see, I was clearing the matter up when you stopped me. Because you stopped me, I have been afflicted with this illness by D's wife." Her mother-in-law was much distressed and asked how she could have known it would turn out like that.

D's mother then called a diviner who lived close by. The latter divined and said, "The person who is ill quarrelled with her sister; her sister then got medicine called *litoromo* from a certain Zulu, and then went and poured it on the threshold of T's hut where she would have to pass when she returned from work." He then told them to get her some *litoromo* medicine for herself, and he gave them some medicine, telling them to vaccinate her. They vaccinated her, but it did not help her at all. She then thought she was going to die and said to D's mother, "Look after those children. I am going to join my husband." D's mother then went to divine with another doctor. The latter said the illness was caused by *litoromo* which she crossed when returning from the store. This diviner gave them more medicine with which to fumigate her and vaccinate her. And then she began to feel better.

D's younger brother, who is a doctor, then arrived. He scarified her with medicine, pricking it in with pieces of dry grass. Another medicine he poured into water and sprinkled it in her room and round her hut. He then fetched his own doctor. When the latter arrived, he asked for two chickens, a cock and a hen. These he scarified. He also made them bleed, letting the blood fall on his medicines. Then he scarified the woman again, using these medicines and the blood with which it was mixed. The woman T recovered completely.

Witches

The Basuto apply the term *baloi* to sorcerers as well as to others whom we may distinguish as witches. Witches are not downright dangerous and anti-social as are sorcerers, but are rather mischievous and immoral and, though they may sometimes harm their fellow-men, on the whole, they use their powers solely for their perverted amusement. It is, however, impossible to draw a hard and fast dividing line, and when witchcraft becomes malignant it really turns into sorcery.

Witches are believed to be ordinary men and women (mainly women) who have acquired powers of flight and/or possess familiars. They usually behave as witches only at night, when they fly about, visit their friends in different parts of the country and foregather in a secluded donga, where they disport themselves naked, and dance and sing. They are able to fly through their knowledge of appropriate medicines or because they have acquired wands, on which they can ride, in much the same way as European witches rode on their broomsticks. They can also fly on the backs of fleas. They have two wands, one black and the other red. With the former they cast the living into a deep sleep or raise the dead from their graves and turn them into ghosts; with the latter, they undo these spells and restore the *status quo*. Occasionally, they may visit a village, whose inhabitants they cast into sleep, and there they hold a feast, slaughtering an ox for their entertainment. As dawn approaches, they resurrect the animal with medicine, remove the spell on the villagers and return home. They usually leave no trace of their visit, but if they should hurt the beast by gnawing a bone too savagely or by resurrecting it carelessly, they may cause it to limp and thereby betray their visit. The beast will be none the worse for its experience, but the villagers, alarmed by this evidence of a nocturnal visitation, may renew the village *moupello* lest worse befall.

These midnight revels are supposed to be invisible and inaudible to ordinary mortals. But travellers are said occasionally to come upon a group of witches dancing in a donga or hear them singing faintly and eerily in the distance. They then flee as fast as they can go, lest they be captured and used for purposes known only to the witches, but believed to be "too horrible to describe". Instances of attempted capture are freely quoted in conversation, but though the witches always appear to be foiled, many people believe in their powers and are afraid of travelling at night, except in company or when protected with appropriate medicine.

Witches are said to have a taste for human flesh, preferably of the dead, and this they satisfy by violating newly made graves, which have been inadequately protected. They also have power to raise the dead and to capture a departed spirit before it reaches the spirit home, particularly if it is delayed or handicapped by any irregularity in the funeral rites; they turn it into a ghost with which they annoy and frighten other people, particularly the kinsmen of the deceased.

They have the power of turning themselves into animals, such as a monkey, snake, owl or crow, and in this form they visit and frighten people whom they want to annoy. No immediate harm is done by this, but people get scared and worried when they see these creatures in unusual circumstances, for instance, if a crow settles on their hut, as it is a sign that they are being molested by some form of *boloi*, which though frivolous at the moment, may become sinister.

Witches possess familiars and this is, perhaps, their most important characteristic. These familiars, loosely called "animals" (*phoofolo*), include creatures such as those just mentioned and, particularly, *thokolosi*. This is a tiny little man, eighteen inches to three feet in height, ugly, covered with long hair, looking very like a monkey and possessing an enormous penis which he can wrap round his waist or sling over his shoulder. *Thokolosi* may sometimes be seen, usually in the evenings, and his image may also be seen reflected in an afflicted person's eyes.

These familiars are acquired through medicines, as gifts from other witches or by inheritance from a parent (usually the mother). Sent by their owner or master, they can annoy people by breaking pots and upsetting milk-pails and cooking vessels, or frighten them by throwing stones and producing other poltergeist phenomena; they may make horses shy by suddenly materializing in front of them or by turning into fireballs, cause children to have convulsions by throttling them in their sleep, and give adults dreadful dreams of a murkily sexual character. They may also be made to do real harm—causing sickness, accidents and death, doing damage to crops, driving cattle out of the kraal at night and setting huts on fire. Moreover, *thokolosi* is such a lecherous little beast that he can act independently of his master and rape women in their dreams and cause various kinds of sexual perversion. In fact, he is largely associated with and blamed for women's sexual troubles and disappointments. Thus frigidity (female aversion to normal sexual intercourse) is attributed to his destroying a woman's natural desires by giving her secret sexual satisfaction, and spinsterhood (inability to procure a husband) is due to his jealousy which drives men away from her. He also causes other kinds of perversion. In one case, where a young mother let her baby die of neglect, she was said to have been prevented from suckling it by her own *thokolosi*'s unbridled jealousy. Another case was that of a chronic invalid, who had no sex appeal, was unmarried and likely to become an old maid. Some said her illness was due to *thokolosi*, and when her petticoat was found mysteriously buried under the hearth, their suspicions were confirmed. It was even said that her shadow was not a proper one, but was *thokolosi* itself. Others, however, attributed her trouble to her blood being spoilt because her maternal uncle had not fully carried out his obligations at her initiation.

Once one has acquired a familiar, it is difficult to get rid of him and for this reason, as well as because of the pleasure and comfort his owner derives from him, there are very few instances of attempts to destroy or dispose of a familiar. He cannot be killed, but certain medicines can dissolve him to nothing. Those who are plagued by other people's *thokolosi* are protected by being fumigated and vaccinated with appropriate medicines or treated in some other suitable manner. Christians believe he can be removed by prayer. A priest holds a special service in the plagued person's home and, after hymns have been sung and prayers said, he anoints the person with holy water, pronouncing the words, "In the Name of the Father, the Son and the Holy Ghost. Christ died for our sins. Amen".

Belief in familiars is widespread and to them or to sorcery are attributed every form of unnatural or abnormal behaviour, uncanny events, accidents and misfortunes; and many claim to have seen them and experienced their activities.

Divination

Divination by bones (*litaola*) has been frequently described, so that there is no need to enter into technical details of the bones themselves or of their various positions; it will be sufficient merely to describe the general characteristics of the art.

Divining sets contain varying numbers of different pairs of bones, ranging from four to twenty. Each pair has its own name and each bone is differentiated by size and markings. Among them[1] are carved pieces of the hoof and horn of an ox and a cow, astragali of the ant-eater, springbok, sheep, goat, rhebok, monkey and steenbok, sea shells, conchshells and tortoise-shells. They are threaded on a string and kept in a special bag. Diviners add to their collection from time to time as opportunity offers.

The typical procedure adopted may be briefly quoted from Laydevant's account.[2] "When they are divining, the person who comes to ask for this service sweeps the ground where he has to throw them. Then the diviner loosens them from the string and gives them to the one who comes to consult. This one tosses them and lets them fall on to the ground. The diviner examines them carefully in order to see the positions they have taken. When he sees that they have fallen in a certain position, he praises that fall for a good while. Among those praises he mixes the affairs of people, of things and of animals and sickness. When he has finished the praises, he says to the person who comes to consult him, 'Make me divine, my friend'. This one says, 'With these words, when you were making the praises, you pointed exactly to my case and my sickness.' And the diviner says, 'So it is, and this special position of the bones says the same.' Then the diviner gives a charm to

---

[1] For fuller details, see Laydevant, 1933, p. 342 and Dieterlen, 1930, pp. 41-2.
[2] Laydevant, op. cit., pp. 343-4.

the consulting person and receives a small fee from him in exchange." If the bones foretell bloodshed or death, they must be purified before being used again and if the client dies, they must be washed with *seharane*.[1]

The denouement is not always as naïve and simple as this, and the diviner usually has to battle hard before he satisfies his client. Occasionally the diviner may be clairvoyant, or may know what the trouble is and so arrive at his diagnosis without beating about the bush, but mostly he feels his way through his knowledge of the local situation, guided by his audience's reactions to his systematic probing. The "praises of the falls" (*lithoko tsa maoa*)[2] contain conventional prophesies and statements which are vague and ambiguous. For instance, the phrase "They die, they kill each other in the chief's village. White ox I die, I die for the land," is capable of many explanations centring round the chief, strife and land. As many people are familiar with these "praises", and readily note and exclaim when passages are recited which appear to meet their case, the diviner uses the *lithoko* discriminatingly, and selects them, not so much in accordance with the actual fall, as with reference to the situation he suspects he is being called upon to divine. A good diviner thus elicits what he wants to know by watching his audience and noting their reactions to these songs and to the remarks which he interjects, seemingly, at random. The majority, however, are not so subtle and depend on the more obvious co-operation of their audience, who must "make them divine" (*laolisa*) by responding to their remarks, softly or indifferently if they are off the track, loudly and feelingly when they are on it. They recite the praise song, either to get a clue or simply to create the right atmosphere, and then under cover of a close scrutiny of the bones, work through "the affairs of people, of things, of animals and sickness", gradually discovering what is troubling their client through the warmth of his responses.

The following satirical account given by my assistant illustrates this point:

The diviner (molaoli) says:	*His client replies:*
"You have come to consult the bones."	"I have come."
"You have come about a person."	"No, I haven't."
"You have come about an animal."	"It is so."
"You have come, you have come about something."	"Molaoli."[3]
"It is something which walks."	"Molaoli" (softly).

[1] Phillips (1917), pp. 112–13.
[2] Mapetla (1928) and Laydevant, op. cit.
[3] A common alternative to the word "*Molaoli*" (a polite word for Diviner) is the phrase "*sea foma*", which comes from an Nguni phrase, meaning "We agree". This phrase is used when replying to a *mokoma* initiate's attempts at divination and is also a part of the chorus to *bokoma* songs. In the latter case, the *mokoma* suddenly stops chanting and says "*Chaea*", to which the audience replies with a spirited "*Sea foma*". This may be repeated several times, with rapidly increasing tempo.

"This thing doesn't walk, it is something of yours and it has something the matter with it which perplexes you."
"It is an object of wealth."
"Why do you refuse me? You must make me divine, you will handicap me if you don't contradict when you don't agree with me. Come now, you say you are perplexed about something of yours."
"It is a thing which walks."
"It is a thing with four legs."
"It hasn't got four legs. It has two."
"It is a thing which walks on two legs, it lives with people at home."
"It is a thing which walks on two legs. It is a chicken."

"It is a chicken which has perplexed its owner."
"This chicken is lost. What has it done?"
"This chicken is lost . . . if it is not lost, deny it, don't agree with me."
"Come now, don't sit silent, man, when I am wrong you must contradict me. Now I say this chicken is lost."
"It is a chicken and you agree that it has perplexed you."
"This chicken is dead."
"This chicken has died, and now you are wondering what killed it that it should die at night."
"It didn't die at night. It died at mid-day."

"It died in the evening. It died early in the morning. When did it die?"
"You agree it died in the morning."
"It died of a louse in your blanket. I can't tell you how. Give me my shilling. It is finished."

"Molaoli."
(Silence)

"Molaoli."
"It walks, Molaoli."
"Molaoli" (softly).
"Molaoli."

"Molaoli."
"Molaoli ! ! ! "(excited).
"Molaoli" (softly).
(Silence)
"I am asking you, Molaoli."

"It is not lost, Molaoli."
"It has perplexed me, Molaoli."
"It is dead, Molaoli."
"It didn't die at night."
"It didn't die at mid-day."
"It died in the morning, Molaoli."
"Molaoli."

"Molaoli."

"Then the client gave him a chicken in place of the shilling and then asked him, 'Should I throw it away or may I eat it?' The diviner replied, 'You may eat it provided I give you some medicine, with which to sprinkle it. You must watch out otherwise your village will become weak. You should get someone to go round it with medicines.' The diviner said this, knowing that his client would call on him."

In addition to, or instead of the "bones", some diviners use more modern and up-to-date instruments and methods to reveal their clients' troubles. For instance, they use mirrors in which they "see", sea-shells held over the ear or stethoscopes by which they "hear", and watches by which they are "told" these mysteries. Some also hold the client's hand or wrist to "feel" the trouble, just as a doctor feels his patient's pulse.

Diviners are expected to divine anything and everything but, in practice, they are called upon to solve only two types of mystery, namely, illness and misfortune, such as accidents, the inexplicable burning of a cattle-post and loss of stock or clothing. Moreover, they are only required to explain what has happened; I have never heard of them being asked, or expected, to forecast the future.

People usually take straightforward cases of illness to an ordinary doctor for diagnosis and treatment. If the doctor cannot cure it, or if the case develops unusual features, they will consult the diviner. When he has diagnosed the trouble, he should be asked to treat it or prescribe the remedy. If it is an ordinary medical case, he will treat it in much the same way as an ordinary doctor, but in other cases he will advise what should be done. The main difference between him and an ordinary doctor—or rather between their respective methods of approach—apart from his jargon, is that the diviner tends to lay greater emphasis on sorcery or action by the *balimo*, as in the following case: "Soon after a man began to build a hut, a splinter from a stone he was shaping embedded itself in his eye. When it was well again, he resumed his work, only to have another splinter enter the same eye. When it was well, he went to a diviner who advised him to 'purify' his father's grave which he had failed to do after the funeral. This he did and suffered no further mishap."

Belief in diviners is by no means universal, but this is mainly due to their incompetence. Most people are prepared to believe that divination is possible, either through personal powers or through intelligent interpretation of the bones, but many are sceptical about the claims of the diviners they know. They recognize that the results are usually disappointing and they complain that for the most part they are incompetent, if not downright dishonest. As one informant put it: "You have to help them divine, and if you do not, they are lost." Another informant once deliberately tested a diviner by refusing to answer his questions and by giving misleading replies; when the unfortunate diviner finally gave up in perplexed disgust, he mocked him for being an impostor. Nevertheless, such failures do not shake the people's faith in the possibility of divination, and even the sceptics counter any suggestions that it is impossible by citing cases of accurate divination which they or their friends have experienced. They also explain that the art of divining is a delicate one and that modern diviners, by prostituting it for the sake of gain, are fast coming to lose it. "God", as one man said, "gave our ancestors a gift of wisdom which was good, strong and true; it was a rare gift, which is lacking in these times of 'Light'." ... "Furthermore," he went on, "earlier diviners did not ask anything, they just consulted the bones, their client remaining silent; they divined what their client came for and did not question him. This practice of questioning, followed by modern diviners, has been acquired from the Zulu"—and he used an expression of profound contempt.

Criticism from another side comes from educated or Christian Basuto. They mock the diviner and his bones, his *lithoko* and the other paraphernalia of his trade, and his jargon about *balimo*, sorcery and neglected customs, as being out of date and belonging to an old order which they like to think they have left behind them. Sometimes they may actually deny the possibility of divination, but often their scepticism is merely skin deep, and the diviner has only to change his technique and make it more up to date in order to regain their support.

Divination for gain has recently been made a punishable offence.[1]

Doctoring

Owing to their familiarity with the dissection of animals, the Basuto have a fair knowledge of anatomy, and distinguish with some exactitude the different organs and bones of the body. Their knowledge of physiology or the functions of the different parts of the body is less accurate and sometimes quite fantastic. The more important organs are held to control and influence the emotions and feelings. People are, therefore, described as hard-hearted, hard-headed, soft-hearted, bilious or splenetic, and these terms have the same meaning for the Basuto as for us. This correlation between physiology and temperament is often carried further. Thus a white heart indicates or causes kindness; a black heart, anger and sadness; a long heart, tolerance; the liver is the seat of patience, the lungs of irascibility (derangement of the lungs also causes hysteria) and the kidneys and spleen of irritability. Except in the last two cases, these beliefs are not related to current aetiological knowledge or to treatment of disease. Here, as in other aspects of their culture, the Basuto are empiricists and show little interest in theory or speculation.

A man's normal state should be that of good health (*bophelo bo botle*), but he is liable at any time to be ill, feel unwell or have his bodily functions disorganized or upset. Dieterlen says[2] that every illness and death is attributed to the malevolence or sorcery of enemies, but he exaggerates the position, for many illnesses are recognized as being due to natural causes, and death from these causes is attributed to God—*lefu la Molimo*.

Natural illness can be caused in a number of simple ways: a surfeit of certain plants, such as *mabelebele* and *manakalali*, may cause constipation; green fruit and badly cooked food may produce acute stomachache, colic or diarrhoea; some roots and herbs are poisonous to sheep, horses and cattle, and even to human beings; snake venom can be fatal. Some diseases are recognized as infectious or transmissible, such as venereal disease and typhus, the former being caught through sexual contact and the latter through association with affected people,

[1] Section 10 (1), Proclamation No. 44 of 1948.
[2] Dieterlen, 1912, pp. 104, 148 and 1930, p. 23.

although the way in which infection spreads is unknown. Other illnesses are regarded as due to some organic disorder, and may be described by reference to that organ. Biliousness is attributed to the spleen; colds, asthma, tuberculosis and bronchitis to the lungs; insanity to the head; heartburn to the heart; colic to the intestines; and hysteria to the lungs. A few of them may also be described more specifically. Thus rash, pimples or sores may be attributed to overheated blood or to internal sores, which have been driven by treatment from the stomach and are now breaking out of the body; biliousness to an excess of bile or to sluggishness of the spleen and kidneys; sterility to sexual promiscuity; children's colic to the curdling of milk in the stomach, especially of mother's milk tainted through sexual intercourse. Other diseases, such as leprosy, syphilis, gonorrhea and influenza are merely identified by name.

Most people can diagnose and treat various common ailments such as colds, coughs and mild constipation. They may also know what is the matter with themselves in more serious cases and buy the appropriate medicines from a doctor or the local store. If they are on friendly terms with their doctor, they may be given the prescription as well as the medicine, so that in future they can collect the proper ingredients themselves. When these ordinary remedies fail, or when the patient is not sure what is the matter with him, he goes to the doctor for a serious consultation. The latter will then base his diagnosis on such data as the seat of the pain, giddiness, vomiting, constipation or internal bleeding. Pain is the most definite and dependable symptom and clearly indicates which organ is affected. Giddiness and vomiting usually indicate sorcery, emotional disorder or spiritual visitation, except in the case of pregnancy of which they are the natural accompaniment. Internal bleeding usually denotes sorcery.

Methods of treatment and kinds of medicinal substances known to and used by doctors are varied and numerous. Some diseases can be cured in different ways or by different medicines, and many medicines have various uses. In numerous cases, the actual medicine or method employed depends on the doctor's own predilection although, on the whole, there seems to be a fair degree of uniformity.

Most medical treatment involves the use of medicines (*sehlare*, *meriane*). These are applied in many different ways. Some are taken orally as a fusion, potion or powder, and either cure the complaint directly or deal with it indirectly by removing the cause of the trouble and cleansing the body by purging or vomiting; others are introduced into the body by inhalation, fumigation (penetrating through the skin), scarification or by means of an enema; others again are applied externally by aspersion, or as an ointment or lotion rubbed on the skin over the affected part or on an open sore. Other medical techniques are the use of splints to support a fracture, lancing to open an ulcer, cupping to extract snake poison from a bite or to let blood to relieve headache or swellings, and manual manipulation in difficult childbirth. These techniques are often accompanied by the use of some sort of medicine. Scarification or vaccination (*ho phatsa*) is perhaps the most common, and is usually resorted to as a sort of shield to counteract sorcery, while the other medicines deal with the actual physical basis of the complaint itself. Scarification involves making two light incisions on various parts of the body, usually the cheeks, forehead, chin, tongue, throat, breast and pit of the stomach (called the "home of the blood") and on all joints other than fingers and toes. When the incisions have been made, medicine is rubbed into them. The whole range of incisions, just described, is made only when important protective medicines are used, otherwise they are limited to the head and the affected parts.

Theoretically every substance that exists may have medicinal properties, but up to the present only a limited number have been discovered. The commonest ingredients are herbs or some other vegetable substance, such as the root, leaves, fruit or bark of a plant or tree, and almost every medicine contains one or more of these vegetable substances. Other ingredients that are actually used, either alone or, more commonly, in association with these, are human and animal flesh and blood, and inorganic substances, such as sea water, salt, ochre, potassium permanganate and mercury.

The following examples, which are by no means exhaustive, illustrate the range of illnesses and troubles treated by doctors and the variety of their techniques. For simplicity's sake, many details of the parts used, such as leaves, bark or berries, or of the state of the plant, whether fresh or dry, are omitted. These details are nevertheless important and, as shown in some of these examples, some parts of the same plant may be used for one medicine and other parts in another. Unless otherwise stated, they are applied as infusions or potions.

Colds are treated by snuffing a powdered root which produces violent sneezing, by stuffing the nostrils with the fresh leaves of *koena* or *lengana*, by drinking a potion of *lengana* or by eating the roots of *koena* and *lesooko*; stomach-ache by chewing the root of a grass or by drinking various potions; diarrhoea by drinking a potion of *hloenya* or *lenoku*, or in serious cases, of *lenoku* mixed with *qoojoana*, *pohotsehla* and *seletjana*; constipation by various potions or, in the case of infants, by an enema blown into the bowel through a reed or syringe; stomach troubles by various emetics or by purgatives made of *pohotsehla* and *tsebe-ea-pela*; painful menstruation by a potion of *hloenya* and *selomi* (the "biter"); male impotence by *motsoso* (the "rouser"); sterility by a potion of *tsikitlane* mixed with three plants, which is also used for painful menstruation, but is weaker than *hloenya* and *selomi*; pregnancy pains by a potion of *selomi* or *papetloane* and others; difficult childbirth by a potion made from a mixture of a mare's afterbirth, dried and powdered, crocodile skin and a plant, or by the powder of *khapumpu* mixed with red ochre from Bopeli and rubbed on the various parts of the body, or by fumigation with smoke of crocodile skin; erratic menstruation with two or three tablespoons of *mahleu* and the juice of *hlabaroana*; headache by inhaling the smoke of peach tree roots, by snuffing powder made from a root, by cupping or by tying a string round the head; boils by lancing, hot fomentation, or a lotion of *serelile*; syphilis by *phoa* and by dusting the sores with the powdered plant; scabies by a mixture of *phoa* and *selomi*; rash, ulcers and sores with various lotions and, if these fail, by the patient's uncle "laying hands on him", spitting on the sores or washing him with water or the bile of a goat specially killed; earache and the ejection of earwigs by pouring into the ear whey or the milk of a nursing mother; snake bite with an emetic of *bohloko* ("venom") mixed with flesh of snakes and porridge, or with potassium permanganate followed by cupping and by rubbing the wound with the powdered plant *bohloko*. The vomiting is regarded as the essential part of this treatment, as the venom is supposed to come out through the lungs. If these medicines are not available, paraffin should be drunk and rubbed into the bite.

Fractures are mended by means of a powder of *mosala-supine* and *tobeha*,[1] mixed with the fat of a goat. One way of applying this is to insert it into the flesh next to the break through a hollow reed. Another way is to smear it on an axe and then strike the imprint made in the dust by the injured limb. In either case the fracture will mend although sometimes, to give the medicine added strength, the fracture may also be set in a splint.

The treatments for various animal diseases have been mentioned in a previous chapter.

The use of medicines does not stop at the curing of sickness but extends far beyond, to almost every situation where a man requires help to control natural and social phenomena, or is faced with difficulty, danger and uncertainty. Some examples have already been given, but to give a complete sketch of their range, a few more may be added.

Love philtres (for men and women) (*bolao*) are in fair demand. In order to win the beloved's affection, the amorous one must first wash himself with a lotion of the plant *moelela*, then be scarified and anointed with an ointment containing *moelela* and his loved one's "dirt" (*litsila*, i.e. sweat, blood, hair or nails). Then when he is near her, he should sprinkle his handkerchief with the *moelela* lotion or hold it in the fumes of the burning plant, and then wave it near her or let her hold it so that the essence of the philtre will waft over her. Alternatively, he should let his shadow fall on her and so transmit the essence of the *moelela*. Wives who wish to

[1] *Tobeha* is said to be such a strong medicine that it has to be kept away from the village lest it cause many fractures. (Dieterlen, 1930, pp. 37-8.)

recapture their husbands' affections should smear *moelela* juice on to a pin and stick it into the wall of their hut, saying, "This man must never go out of here again; let him remain here." Several alternative medicines may be used, one of which, *folabahleke*, can overcome people's hatred and make them friendly. A lotion made with a plant *bolao* may be used by a bride to wash herself when she first goes to her husband's home, in order to ensure his love. Other medicines have the opposite effect, and may be used to prevent men making love to one's wife or mistress. One is made of the plant, appropriately called "the fire extinguisher" (*setimamollo*), mixed with other plants. The man washes himself with it and while it is still fresh sleeps with his loved one so that it permeates her body. Thereafter, other men wishing to sleep with her will be made to feel inordinately tired and so reduced to impotence. It is so strong that one should be careful not to use it when committing adultery, lest one "shut the woman off" from her husband and so arouse his suspicions.

Medicines are also used for luck and to bring help in difficult enterprises, for example, to locate hidden treasure (p. 288 above). An informant and his schoolfellows used medicines to help them through their examinations. They were instructed to wash and put medicated ointment on their faces and then borrow a threepenny-bit from their teacher, smear it with the same ointment and rub it over their examination books. This would prevent the teacher examining their answers too closely and make him grant them generous marks. But, "Alas, the threepenny-bit failed a whole lot of us, including those who had used it."

Stock thieves use medicine to make themselves invisible; they also burn some near the herd-boys who are guarding the stock they wish to steal, in order to throw them into a deep sleep. Medicines are used by litigants to strengthen their case. *Molomo monate* has already been mentioned. Another medicine is *seteatea* or *moferefere* (disorder). The client is scarified in the morning; he then bathes and washes his eyes well with *seteatea*—"so that he may see his opponent's argument clearly"; then, on his way to court, he buries some of it in a hole and urinates on it, chews another bit of it and spits it out to the east, north, south and west, saying, "*Seteatea*, let the person I am suing seek without finding,[1] and let those I am going with also be unsuccessful".

Sometimes more powerful medicines are used; for instance, in 1934 one of the parties to a land dispute murdered a woman to get the fluid from her eye for medicine. Some of this was then smeared on seven stones which were placed on the seven hills surrounding the disputed area; the rest was used to give the litigants strength in arguing their

---

[1] Seek without finding = *teatseha*. Here, as in many other instances, the name of the principal ingredient is synonymous or associated with the purpose to be achieved or the affliction to be cured.

PLATE XV

(a) General scene of Court

(b) Court in session: member of court questioning witnesses

PLATE XVI

(a) Girl initiate in traditional dress

(b) Female witch doctor

case. This type of case is dealt with in greater detail in the discussion on ritual murder.

A chief will sometimes protect and strengthen his position with medicines. For instance, a certain chief, during a crisis in his dispute with a neighbouring chief, placed medicated stones and sand on either side of his village and on all paths leading from the other's village to his own in order to prevent the inroads of the other's "power"; and he had his guns doctored for use in case fighting broke out. He also put medicine on a written petition to the Resident Commissioner to strengthen his case and secure the Commissioner's favourable attention. Chiefs may also bathe themselves with appropriate medicines to protect themselves from the jealousy of rivals and to secure the loyalty of their people. They also protect their courts by burying medicated stones or pegs at the entrance and back. Special *mohlabelo* (burnt medicines) are used for these purposes, and the most powerful of these medicines are believed to contain human flesh.

People also use medicine to bring them luck in employment. For instance, a doctor scarified his client for a fee of £1 and successfully "beat the forms", i.e. got his client passed as medically fit for a mine contract for which he had previously been rejected. A clerk, sacked from his position on a Johannesburg mine in 1944, returned home and participated in a ritual murder to get ingredients for medicine to reinstate himself. A teacher, while working as a labourer, was envied for his supposed "popularity" medicine, as he was the only one of the gang who was not roughly treated by the farmer. This last example is typical of the way in which success is attributed, by unsuccessful and jealous rivals, to the effects of medicine rather than to intelligence, ability or probity.

Other important medicines are those used to protect villages, huts and people against sorcery. Details of method vary slightly with different doctors, but in general follow these lines. Pegs, smeared with *mohlabelo*, are driven into the ground at the back of the hut and behind the door, and a besmeared river stone is buried at the entrance to the courtyard. This is done to each hut or household. The village is then circled by besmeared *mofifi*, *cheche* and wild willow pegs, and river sand is mixed with the *mohlabelo* and broadcast on the roofs and ground. Finally, all the villagers are scarified with the *mohlabelo*. The site of a new village is protected in the same way, beginning with the three varieties of pegs placed together at the centre of the site. Some doctors insist that while they are working everyone must keep perfectly quiet and they should be assisted by two naked children, a boy and a girl below the age of puberty, i.e. sexually pure. Many doctors also smear a cross or line on the hut doors and lintels and on large stones which encircle the village. Christians, who are forbidden to use such medicines, sometimes surreptitiously apply *mohlabelo* by smearing it on coloured chalks with which little crosses and dots are then drawn on the hut walls in patterns which look like decorations rather than applications of medicine. Formerly, these protective medicines were renewed every New Year, but now they are only renewed when necessary, for instance, when the village has been struck by lightning, or after several deaths have occurred in quick succession. Some varieties of *mohlabelo* have to be renewed if water or fire (such as flames from lighted straw, but not glowing coals) are taken from a hut at night, as their potency is thereby destroyed.

Individuals may also be protected by wearing a root, seed or other "charm", by being scarified or by undergoing a slightly more complicated treatment, such as the following, which was given to an efficient and therefore unpopular tax-collector. After he had washed himself with medicines, the man knelt on the floor holding a spear between his knees (a posture sometimes adopted when being treated with war medicines) and after a *motsoetse* had squeezed her milk on to his chest and back, he was thoroughly scarified with *mohlabelo*. He was also given special medicine against lightning, as well as a piece of white chalk smeared with *mohlabelo* to put on his horse's hoofs when travelling at night and with which to draw a line round his sleeping mat, when he slept away from home and was therefore unprotected by his own *moupello*.

The medicines used for the protective purposes just described are known as *mohlabelo* and *lenaka* rather than as *meriane* and *sehlare*. The name *lenaka* comes from the fact that they are usually kept in an ox- or goat-horn (*lenaka*). Other terms for them are "burnt" or "black" medicines, so called from the manner of their preparation. They consist of different herbs, compounded with animal and mineral substances. The mixture is charred or burnt in a potsherd until it is black and is then ground to a powder, mixed with certain fats and kept in a horn. When required, it is smeared on to the object to be treated: sticks used to ward off hail; pegs, sand and stones to protect a hut, village or district; guns and spears used for war or boys' initiation; the lintel or door of a dwelling, court, cattle kraal or stable. When people or animals are scarified, it is smeared into the incisions. It may also be smeared on to parts of the body without incisions.

Details were obtained of the ingredients of three different *mohlabelo*. Although I cannot vouch for their authenticity, they are given here to show the kind of stuff they are made of, or are believed to be made of, and to illustrate the powers they are believed to derive from their ingredients.

(*a*) Three plants from Bopeli (believed to be one of the early homes of the Tlokoa): *lethektheke* ("difficulty", unidentified), *boleba* (a species of *helichrysum* or "everlasting"), and *setlemo* (unidentified); 4 plants obtained in Basutoland: *lira-ha-li-bone* (enemies don't see), *tsitaboloi* ("hinder the sorcerers"), *mohato* ("keep down by witchcraft"), and *mohatollo* ("remove an oppression"); mercury ("which runs about freely"), shiny, black powder (*sebilo*) and clay (*khato*—derived from the same verbal root as *mohato* and *mohatollo*).

(*b*) In addition to plants, animal substances are included, such as the fat of *thokolosi* (probably baboon) and of a lion, and flesh of a vulture, cut-throat lark and *norokapore*,[1] together with *moretele*.

(*c*) In addition to plants this *mohlabelo* contained the flesh of a bat, wild cat, owl and leopard.

Others again, particularly those used for war or initiation, contain the fat of lion, buffalo and other brave and ferocious animals. Those used for the chieftainship, war and serious litigation must include human flesh.

In several of the above, the power of the ingredient is suggested by its name, especially in the case of the herbs used, such as *lira-ha-li-bone*.[2] The power of others is suggested by association with the beast, e.g. the strength of the lion, the ferocity of the wild cat, the nocturnal habits of the owl and bat. The use of human flesh is an extension of these ideas. The animal world is superior to the vegetable or mineral world, and man is superior to the animals; therefore man is the greatest thing in the world. Consequently, medicines containing human flesh and blood will be superior to those which do not, and so it is essential that the strongest medicines should contain such ingredients. For *mohlabelo* or a *lenaka* required for general purposes, no special part of the body is required, though, if they are procurable, the best parts are the heart, bowels, generative organs and blood, as they are all sources of man's power and activity. Other organs may be particularly valuable for medicines required for special purposes, such as to influence the courts, e.g. eyes and ears to help one see and hear the weak points of one's opponent's case, tongue and lips to help one speak well. Furthermore, just as the living are better than the dead, so the living flesh is better than the dead, and the power of these parts is enhanced if they are obtained from a living victim. For these reasons, those who are bold and powerful enough to risk the dangers involved, resort to murder to obtain the requisite human ingredients for their *lenaka*.

Ritual murders, as these murders have recently been termed, have latterly received such publicity and present such grave administrative and moral problems that they deserve to be discussed in detail.

It is sometimes said by Basuto and by Europeans who have long been in the country, that the use of human parts is not a genuine Basuto custom, but was recently introduced by Zulu doctors, and that murder for the purpose of getting such parts is a very recent development.

---

[1] Unidentified.

[2] I should have liked to work this whole question out in much more detail and I am afraid some of my deductions are pure speculation which I have not had the opportunity to test in the field.

Neither of these propositions is, I think, true. Casalis,[1] writing nearly a century ago, states that the bodies of men killed in battle were mutilated to provide ingredients for medicines "to compose a powder which would transmit the courage, skill and good fortune of their enemies". An early recorded case is that of a British officer who was captured at Lancer's Gap in 1852, and later killed and mutilated,[2] presumably for medicine. Some Basuto assert that human ingredients have been used from time immemorial for the chiefs', war, and boys' initiation horns, although many of them say that such ingredients were taken from men killed in war and not from victims specially murdered for the purpose. This may well have been so in the case of war and initiation horns, both of which required some association with battle, but not necessarily in the case of the chief's horn; and many Basuto believe that so-called ritual or medicine murders have been going on for a long time. It is said that strangers were usually selected as victims for two very good reasons: firstly, they presumably belonged to a clan different from the local one and were therefore usable, and secondly, they would have no nearby friends or kinsmen to ask awkward questions; and that, to avoid this fate, travellers used to adopt the clan name (*seboko*) of those among whom they journeyed, and pass themselves off as relations of neighbouring villagers. It is possible that this happened—it is quite consistent with Basuto belief and way of life—but whether it did or not, there is now no way of telling. It is at any rate quite certain that such murders have been going on for the past fifty years at least. One was discovered and punished by a collective fine in the Butha Buthe district at Kukune in 1897, involving (at least) mutilation of the fingers, and another occurred the following year in the Berea district. Since then they have been discovered with increasing frequency—a few are known to have occurred between then and 1910; between 1910 and 1939 at least ten were brought to court and many more suspected; since 1940 at least sixty have been reported and of these more than half have been brought to court.

A number of factors may account for this apparent increase: the increased efficiency of the police; the modifications made in 1947 in the earlier system of reporting deaths to the police and of undertaking criminal investigations; the growing independence of the people and their impatience with the restrictive power and control of the chiefs, which have stimulated them to overcome their previous fears and to report crimes about which they would formerly have kept silent; and

---

[1] Casalis, 1861, pp. 321-2.

[2] Basutoland Records, Vol. II, p. lxvi. My reason for assuming that this mutilation was to obtain ingredients for war medicine is that the Basuto were clean fighters, in that they did not indulge in torture or other atrocities. Lagden refers to their "reputation for chivalry" and the "conspicuous absence as a rule of barbarous acts such as characterized other Kaffir races in their frenzy". (Lagden, op. cit., p. 629.)

finally, the unrest among native authorities created by the recent reforms and the dissensions over the paramountcy, following the death of Seeiso in 1940. This whole question is now the subject of a special commission, so it would be inappropriate to discuss it any further.

The following description of these murders is based on an analysis of thirty-four cases. They follow very much the same pattern. Most murders are doubtless prompted by a doctor, though this is rarely proven. In all except three cases the leaders were proved, or were suspected, to be native authorities of one kind or another (i.e. chiefs or headmen); in these three cases, the leaders were doctors who wanted human parts for their stock-in-trade. The leader is usually present in person and either directs operations himself or watches while they are carried out at the orders of some deputy.

The more important the leader, the more numerous his accomplices, and where he is a man of standing they usually exceed ten in number—presumably their number is a measure of his importance and of his confidence that he will avoid detection. They usually include the president of the leader's court and the headman of his village, a number of trusted followers, his doctor (although many doctors prefer to remain in the background) and one or two close relations of the victim. There may be some esoteric reason for the inclusion of the latter, connected with the efficacy of the medicine to be made, but an obvious practical reason is that their participation will deter his other kinsmen from making too searching inquiries, for fear of making matters worse.

As a rule, the victim must belong to a different clan from that of the person requiring the medicine, on the grounds that to use one's own fellow-clansman or kinsman for medicine savours of cannibalism. The "Sons of Moshesh", who are Bakoena, are said to favour Basia or Bafokeng. The scanty information available confirms this: of six victims of whom details were obtained, one was a Mofokeng, two Thembu (many of whom were originally Bafokeng), one a Mosia and one a Mohlakoana. The sixth was a Mokoena, deliberately chosen because of this clan affiliation (it is said, on a Mokoena chief's instructions), possibly with the idea that this would intensify the medicine. (This is so contrary to the general pattern that I would have liked further corroboration.[1]) It is often said that only strangers are selected, for the reason given earlier. Actually, however, recent records show that this is rarely the case nowadays, and that though the victim might be a stranger to the area or village where he was killed, in the sense that he did not permanently live there, in no case was he a new arrival from some distant part.

In most cases, the actual victim is chosen quite arbitrarily or for some reason known only to the doctor. Age and sex seem to be irrelevant;

[1] See note, p. 16.

nineteen out of twenty-nine were males, and ages ranged from four (a girl) to seventy-five (a man). Occasionally some peculiarity appears to be significant, such as that the victim was a twin, or a woman with a new-born babe and therefore sexually pure, or, in one revolting case, the leader's "best friend". Sometimes he is chosen because his habits or state of health, for example, drunkenness or epilepsy, could corroborate the ostensible cause of death—that he had strayed from his path and fallen over a cliff. Sometimes, too, he is chosen for personal motives of hatred or revenge. In one case the victim had been causing trouble in the chief's court, and in another he was the lover of the principal accomplice's wife.

Occasionally the murder is preceded by a "war of nerves". Bands of young men roam about at night, howling like wolves, naked and with their faces bedaubed with white clay. They beat on people's doors and molest and terrify travellers.

The murder is usually planned to follow a feast or beer-drink. This has two advantages. The victim is likely to be drunk—indeed, some one is usually detailed to see that he does get drunk—and so will be more easily assaulted, and secondly, his death can be attributed to his stumbling off the path and falling over a cliff or into the river. When darkness sets in, he is decoyed out of the village, ambushed in some secluded spot, overpowered, mutilated and killed. There are, of course, many variations of this procedure. Some are killed in broad daylight. One man was caught when he was fishing; a child was kidnapped in the afternoon, drugged and kept two days before being killed. The victim is usually battered or throttled into insensibility, but in three cases he was drugged, and in at least one even this consideration was denied him. Sometimes, when the victim is a woman, the male accomplices have to have sexual intercourse with her first. Operations are then directed by a doctor, if present, otherwise by the leader. If only blood is required, it is collected from one of the wounds inflicted during the original assault or from a puncture made on the head, arm, breast or back with a sharpened umbrella rib. If flesh is needed, the eyes, ears, lips, tongue, throat and skin are taken from the head (which is sometimes completely severed); biceps or calf muscles, sexual organs and bowels may also be used. Occasionally, an arm or finger or ribs are severed and the heart and lungs also taken. These mutilations should be done to the living body, but may be continued after death has taken place; in only one case were any parts removed some time after death. When the operation has been done the wounds may be staunched by laving them with boiling water or by cauterizing them with hot stones or burning sticks.

The body is usually kept hidden for some time in a hut or cave or in the woods. A possible reason for this is that it may be necessary for the medicine to be prepared before the murder is discovered, lest its strength be impaired, and this delay gives the doctor time to do so.

The delay also ensures that the body has started to decompose before it is found, and thus makes it more difficult for post mortem examination to reveal the cause of death or the nature and extent of the injuries and mutilations. Sometimes it is kept for an embarrassingly long time—embarrassing, that is, to the accomplices who have to keep it hidden in spite of its growing offensiveness and who have finally to carry it away. Whether it is kept like this or not, it must finally be left in some exposed position in the veld, such as on an open hillside where death might be attributed to exposure, under a cliff or high bank over which the victim might be supposed to have fallen or in a river bed where the deceased might have drowned. Although this ruse is transparent enough in many cases, it has succeeded sufficiently often to be worth while, and it also gives the local chief or headman a reasonable excuse for attributing death to natural causes and having the body buried without delay. Apart from this, such public exposure of the body is said to be necessary to test the strength of the medicine and prove, through the non-detection of the crime, that it will be satisfactory and also to infuse it with additional power.

These murders are characterized by an almost complete absence of personal motive. They are committed in order to get human flesh and blood for medicine. The purposes for which the medicine is required may be briefly summarized from thirty recent cases.

1. *General lenaka.* 6 cases. A typical case is that of Rex *v.* Tabola Nkutu (No. 196/44). Tabola and his uncle Lejaka were headmen and firmly believed in medicine. Their horns were empty and so needed refilling. There was no evidence to suggest that this was anything other than a routine requirement. In Rex *v.* Tsotang Griffith, etc. (No. 301/46), the principal, Tsotang, was a petty sub-chief. He had been promised a ward which he had not been given; in expectation of this he had acquired a date stamp which he was not allowed to use; he was not recorded as a ruling chief in the explanatory memorandum to the National Treasury; his people were insolent and disobedient. To remedy these troubles, he wanted medicine, and for this his doctor said he needed a human being.

2. *Placing.* 10 cases. In four of these, medicine was wanted because the person feared his position would not be recognized by the Claims Commission, or because he had previously been demoted for drunkenness and misconduct and now wanted to be reinstated. In Rex *v.* Manapo, etc. (No. 272/46) medicine was required for the placing of a headman and for ousting another headman in favour of his younger brother who had been acting for him.

3. *To influence the law courts.* 4 cases. In Rex *v.* Selemo Posholi and ten others (No. 217/45) Selemo was a sub-chief. Bereng wanted to move from Phamong to his village as it was better situated and was nearer the government offices at Mohale's Hoek. If he did so, it would mean either that Selemo's status would be reduced or that he would have to move. Selemo also wanted to place his son and he was in some trouble over stock theft. To help him in these disputes he resorted to medicine.

4. *Undetermined.* 7 cases. Insufficient evidence was adduced to indicate what

medicine was required for, although in several of them chiefs were indirectly implicated.

5. *Doctors.* 3 cases. In these cases the prime movers were doctors who wanted human parts for their ordinary stock-in-trade.

In five of the above cases, accomplices took part who wanted human parts for their own purposes. Three of them were doctors (other than those in 5 above) who wanted human parts for their ordinary stock-in-trade, one was the ex-mine clerk referred to above and the fifth was a Government policeman who wanted medicine to protect him from the hazards of his profession.

For the past two or three years, the Basuto have become acutely conscious of these murders. They are so much afraid of becoming involved in a medicine murder, whether as witness, victim or accessory, that they are extremely reluctant to go about at night and lock themselves in after sunset. Owing to their fear of witches and of sorcery, they have always been scared of travelling at night, and this fear has now been accentuated. Children's evening singing and dancing are now rarely heard, people hurry home from feasts and beer-drinks to be indoors by dark, and never before have the villages been so quiet. This atmosphere has even affected church attendance at early morning and evening services.

The authorities and all who have the good name of Basutoland at heart are deeply concerned about this evil and many remedies have been proposed. There has been a succession of articles and letters in the Basuto press since 1946; private people and public bodies, including the Progressive Association and the Orange Free State African Herbalists' Association, have expressed concern and suggested reforms; district Councils and the National Council have debated the matter at length and have made recommendations; the High Commissioner felt constrained to address the National Council in person in September 1948 and gave a stern warning that unless the position improved, drastic action would have to be taken.

The principal perpetrators of these murders, if convicted, are usually hung. It is generally recognized that this is no real answer and many possible deterrents and remedies have been suggested. As one of the terms of reference of the Commission is to make recommendations for dealing with this problem, no attempt will be made to discuss them here, beyond giving a brief summary of the various proposals that have been made. These include further reforms of the Native Administration, ranging from closer control of placings, disallowance of female regents and the creation of "Vigilance Committees" to the disinheritance of the heirs of convicted chiefs, deposition of chiefs who are involved in such murders and unable to prevent their occurrence, and government appointment of all native authorities; public hangings of those convicted of these murders; control of witch-doctors (this has recently been attempted through Proclamation No. 44 of 1948); collective punishment, in terms of Proclamation No. 57 of 1948, of chiefs and people who do not promptly inform the police of the presence of a dead body believed to be that of a victim; abolition of boys' initiation schools; establishment of industries to combat poverty, and finally, educational development to enlighten the darkness of ignorance in which belief in medicine murders flourishes.

An interesting "defence" reaction that has recently developed is the allegation that "ritual" murder does not occur at all, that it is a figment of official imagination and that the cases brought against various chiefs are trumped up charges, based on false evidence extorted by third degree methods. These allegations have been made by members of the *Lekhotla la bafo*,[1] who are bitterly opposed to the Government, and by chiefs, such as Bereng and Gabashane, who were convicted and executed in 1949, and by others who have been closely involved. There may also be some popular support of this view from those who, suspicious of the Government, may fear this is a gigantic "frame-up" intended to destroy the chieftainship and the nation. But for the most part the people hate and are worried by these events.

The prevalence of these murders raises the question—how deeply do the Basuto believe in medicine and use the kinds of medicines that have been described in this chapter. This is difficult to answer. Basuto doctors say everyone does—but possibly they exaggerate to enhance the importance of their own position. Other people, both Basuto and knowledgeable Europeans, say that 90 per cent do so. Direct observation is obviously inadequate as one cannot possibly see all that goes on, especially as so much doctoring is done in private and even in secret. This applies particularly to the use of protective medicines, as their efficacy depends partly on secrecy of application, and to Christians who are forbidden to use *mohlabelo* or to deal with diviners. Gossip, hearsay and the frequency of court cases dealing with doctors, the use of medicine and fears of sorcery, provide an inadequate basis for judgment. In Bereng's court 4 out of 125 cases dealt with these matters and in Mosuoe's 6 out of 138; the incidence of ritual murder has already been discussed. Judging from these rather inadequate criteria, I would say that almost everyone believes in and uses ordinary medicine; that fully half the people use *mohlabelo* and other protective medicines, of whom only a tiny minority are concerned with the most potent of such medicines containing human flesh; and that the vast majority believe in and fear sorcery and witchcraft. Education, the impact of new ideas

---

[1] The *Lekhotla la bafo*, literally, the "People's court", is a political association which is very critical of the British Administration and usually of the chiefs. But since about 1948 it has allied itself with the chiefs in publicizing the view that the Government is trying to destroy the chiefs. The association is also anti-European and preaches a "back-to-the-ways-of-our-forefathers" policy.

and the mockery of Europeans have made some people critical and selective. Such people may doubt the more extravagant claims of doctors and question the efficacy of certain medicines but, except for a few, even they share the general belief that medicine can do all that has been claimed for it. They accept the theory that medicine is all-powerful, but they doubt whether the doctors are skilled enough to discover or to use the right medicines to deal with the more difficult situations; their quarrel is not with the theory of medicine but with its practice. They do not distinguish between what we might call the medical and the magical—to them it is all one.

This lack of differentiation is understandable. All forms of what the Basuto call medicine have the same basic structure. All depend on the use of substances and every substance has its own particular property which produces certain effects when used in the correct manner on the appropriate occasions, either singly or in combination with others. A very few are used with spells or formulae, or associated with prayers to the *balimo* or to God, and this does not set them apart as a different variety of medicine, but is merely a special condition to be observed, similar in kind to other conditions such as silence or sexual abstinence.

The power or property of different substances to produce different results is regarded as inherent in the substances themselves or as deriving from God. These views are not contradictory or mutually exclusive, but are simply different aspects of the same thing, and depend on the context of the particular case or on personal predilection. Beer intoxicates; mother's milk, tainted by sexual intercourse, gives a babe colic; *lengana* cures a cold; a *mofifi* stick wards off hail—they are all the same sort of phenomena, operating through the same laws of cause and effect; each of these substances has the power to cause a particular effect, a power which is inherent and (which is the same thing) derives from or was placed there by God.

It is also recognized that a particular agent sometimes does not produce its usual effect. This is explained as due either to some counteracting agent or to God. God, being all-powerful, may, in His discretion, withdraw or increase the normal power with which he has invested everything.

The only distinction the Basuto make is between medicine that works and that which fails. This is not an easy distinction to make in practice; it depends on a far wider knowledge than the Basuto have and on far more rigid and accurate standards of judgment than they use. The effectiveness of some medicines is obvious to anyone and can, moreover, be demonstrated by bio-chemical or pharmacological analysis, e.g. that *hlaba* is a purgative, *poho-tsehla* an emetic or tonic, *lengana* a cure for colds.[1] Many others that have been found effective in practice

---

[1] Watt, J. M. and Breyer-Brandwjik, 1932, pp. 15, 82-3, 147-8, 161-2, 181, 197 and 210.

have not yet been analysed and may well have genuine therapeutic properties, such as *koena, selomi* and *bohloko*. On the other hand, there are many medicines which have no therapeutic properties but which are effective, for psychological reasons, in curing illness, giving confidence or causing trouble. The fact is that they work or, rather, they appear to work. These and many other medicines, which appear to have been successful owing to fortunate coincidence, could be shown to be valueless and quite incapable of producing the results claimed for them, because they do not possess the necessary properties or because the expected results are unobtainable by means of medicine. This applies to some of the medicines used to cure disease or impart various qualities as well as to medicines used to make rain, ward off hail, strengthen the chieftainship, bring luck, influence the courts, prevent misfortune or produce a heavy crop. But the methods that would have to be applied in order to distinguish the effective from the ineffective, the true from the false, are beyond the experience of the Basuto and depend on a far stricter assessment of probabilities than they are able to appreciate at this stage of their development. Moreover, the whole problem is complicated by the difficulty and sometimes the impossibility of correctly assessing whether some medicines are true or false, effective or ineffective; for there are innumerable border-line cases where the medicine may possibly produce the desired and expected result although this cannot be proved. There is no clear cut practical or logical division between them. Therefore, granted the premise that God's power, expressed through various kinds of materials or substances, is unlimited, nothing is impossible; thus, there is no reasonable basis for distinguishing between the effects that can be produced by medicines and those that cannot, between the medical and the magical. To us it may seem, as Dieterlen has put it, that they are explaining "the natural by the supernatural, the reasonable by the absurd",[1] but their system of thought in this is logical, coherent and reasonable; it simply starts from different premises from our own. Their beliefs are, therefore, difficult to destroy by reasoning, and though the little education they have had might be expected to have produced more results than have been achieved, it must be remembered that there are considerable psychological factors buttressing their beliefs and discouraging doubt. These factors are: the sense of insecurity, fostered by exposure to the dangers and chances of this mortal life and rendered more acute by the poverty of their material and mechanical resources; the limitations of their knowledge and experience; the barrenness of their religion; the uncertainty of their political and social position under European influences, and the drastic and profound changes caused by these same influences. The recent development of racialism in South Africa may also have had an effect in encouraging the Basuto

[1] Dieterlen, 1912, p. 144.

to turn away from European thoughts and attitudes, back to their traditional beliefs.

Christianity has made little headway against belief in medicine in spite of a century of activity. Dieterlen considers they are mutually exclusive. "Favoured by ignorance and fear, they occupy the place that ought to belong to religion."[1] This, I feel, is a false antithesis. Both Christian belief and belief in medicine share the fundamental characteristic of ignoring the conventional limits of "natural" causation and of going beyond and behind materialistic explanations. Both postulate an omnipotent God who created and, at the same time, can over-ride the normal relationship between cause and effect; whose help can be solicited by man in situations beyond his own normal control. The use of medicine is not inconsistent with the use of prayer and many Basuto regard it as entirely a matter of personal preference whether one uses one or the other, or both. Some Christians, in particular members of the Apostolic Church, go to one extreme and rely entirely on prayer to the total exclusion of medicine; but others say that so far as possible man should use the medical means of controlling his environment that God has placed at his disposal, and should resort to prayer only in extreme cases and not keep bothering Him with the petty problems of day-to-day existence. They see nothing inconsistent in using medicines for rain-making, to overcome sterility, produce good crops and maintain good health, and in praying for rain, for children, health or good crops; in asking a priest to bless their seeds, and in using sanctified olive sticks to ward off lightning or to protect them against sorcery, or placing a medallion of the Blessed Virgin to protect their crops. It is, therefore, scarcely surprising that another missionary could write seventeen years later, "paganism is still very much alive and has deep roots".[2]

The only attack that can shake it is the moral one, by subjecting the use of medicine to moral evaluation or making the use of some good and of others wrong. Some Christians and others have abandoned various protective medicines and no longer doctor their huts or themselves, or use medicine against lightning and sorcery. Instead they rely on prayer and on God's protection, and some, particularly Roman Catholics, use blessed medallions or holy water. But as the belief in medicine, which is what the missions mean by paganism, is strongly entrenched and is rationally and emotionally satisfying, the battle is being long and difficult. Dieterlen's *cri de cœur* still echoes down the years: "O liens du vice et ténèbres de l'erreur, quelle puissance céleste il faudra pour vous déchirer!"

---

[1] Dieterlen, 1912, p. 144.   [2] *Le dessouts*, 1929, p. 10.

APPENDIX I

(a) *Glossary of Sesuto Words*

Babineli (sing. *mobineli*): lit. "those who sing for one"; companions of boy initiates, while undergoing their initiation.

Bakoma (sing. *mokoma*): persons who have successfully undergone the ritual cure for the "spiritual" and nervous disorder *motheketheke*, and are thereby qualified to treat others suffering from this, and who acquire special powers of divination.

Balimo (collective plural): departed spirits, ancestor spirits, spirits of the dead.

Banna-ba-lekhotla (collective plural): lit. "men of the court"; the chief's principal advisers and helpers in judicial matters; those who help to adjudicate cases.

Bentlelaka: a kind of earmark.

Bohali: marriage.

Bokhinapere: lit. an area where a horse can be knee-haltered; an idiomatic and euphemistic term for a stretch of country given, in response to a formal "request", by a subordinate authority to a chief or other superior authority, who is placed over him.

Bokoma: (n.) the state of being a *mokoma*; (adj.) associated with the state of being a *mokoma* (q.v.).

Bothekethehe: the state of being ill with *motheketheke* (q.v.).

Bothuela=bokoma (q.v.).

Kenela: lit. "to go in for", to practise the *kenelo* (q.v.) or levirate custom.

Kenelo: the levirate custom, by which a man lives with his brother's widow, usually his elder brother's widow.

Khomo ea khurumetso: lit. "the beast of the covering"; the ox or cow killed by some Basuto at mortuary ceremonies, from which the second stomach is taken to provide a head covering or "hat" for the deceased.

Khotla: abbrv. for *lekhotla* (q.v.).

Lefehlo: churning reed or stick; the ritual treatment given to *bakoma* (q.v.).

Lekhotla: court where men sit in the village, where public business is transacted and public ceremonies held; court of justice.

Lenaka: horn; horn in which a doctor keeps his drugs and medicines, usually burnt medicines or *mohlabelo* (q.v.); medicine so kept or belonging to the category of medicine that is usually kept in a horn, i.e. protective medicines.

Leqhekha=mokoma (q.v.).

Lesheleshele: thin porridge.

Lesiba: feather; hence a musical instrument made from a quill stretched by a cord from the ends of a stick.

Letabo: a kind of earmark.

Lethuela=mokoma (q.v.).

Letsema: an organized work party.

Lisu: dry cattle dung dug out of the kraal and used for fuel.

Lithoko: praise-songs, praises.

Mabele: kaffir-corn, sorghum.
Mafisa: stock put in the care of a person who, in return for looking after it, has the usufruct thereof.
Mahleu: a soft drink, made from maize.
'Mampoli: the head herd-boy.
Marabaraba: a board game, a cross between draughts and noughts-and-crosses.
Mathuela=bakoma (q.v.).
Melimo=balimo (q.v.).
Mohlabelo: medicine which is reduced to ashes and mixed with fat; burnt or black medicine, usually rubbed into incisions when applied to humans and animals, or on to sticks, pebbles, door lintels or chalk, when applied to inanimate objects, and mostly used for protection against sorcery and misfortune, and for good luck and prosperity.
Mohoha: an ox killed during mortuary rites, to purify the grave and speed the departed on his journey to the next world.
Mokoma: sing. of *bakoma* (q.v.).
Mokorotlo: a solemn, ceremonial men's dance.
Molutsoane: ritual hunt undertaken to make rain.
Mophato: boys' initiation lodge.
Mosuoe: circumciser; the leader in charge of the initiation and of the *mophato.*
Motheketheke: illness caused by the *balimo* (q.v.) or by sorcery, the symptoms of which are hysteria, headaches, etc., which makes the victim wander blindly about the country, and which can only be cured by the *bokoma* (q.v.) treatment.
Motsoetse: a woman who has recently given birth and who is suckling her baby, a woman who has recently been confined: such women are supposed to eschew sexual intercourse and so are ritually pure.
Moupello: medicines used to protect a dwelling or village from sorcery and misfortune.
Pitso: a calling together, a public gathering called by the authorities.
Qhoba: lit. to drive; to compensate for theft by paying the owner of the stolen goods an equivalent in kind or value.
Sekama: antimony, ilmenite, black powder.
Seneiki: a kind of earmark.
Seteipi: a medicine used to protect children, which can also be used with malevolent intent to harm them.
Setoto: porridge used for making beer, before it has started to ferment.
Thethana: a short petticoat made of fibres, worn by women and girls.
Thokolosi: a familiar.
Tsipo: frog-hop, a game played by small boys.

(b) *Botanical Names*

This list of plants referred to in the text is taken from the Sesuto-English Dictionary, 6th edition, which, in turn, derives its identifications from work on which Phillips's *Flora* was based. My doctor friends gave me the Sesuto names for the plants they said they used, and I

APPENDIX I

looked these up in the dictionary and checked against Phillips:[1] I did not have any of these plants identified from specimens collected from the doctors. It may be reasonably objected, therefore, that the plants which these doctors denoted by particular Sesuto names are not necessarily the same species of plants as those referred to by the same Sesuto names by other Basuto, or by the collectors on which Phillips's *Flora* was based, and that therefore the identifications given here are quite valueless. The only counter plea to this that I can offer is that the Basuto have a deep and accurate knowledge of plants, to which a generous tribute is paid by Phillips himself,[2] but which is by no means infallible.

The comments on uses, etc., given after each title are culled from Phillips and show the essential uniformity of Basuto practice and the variety of ways in which plants are used (cf. uses mentioned in text and obtained independently).

Betheu: unidentified.
Bolao: Lightfootia denticulata, Sond. Used as a love philtre (*bolao* is a general term for love philtre).
Boleba: Helichrysum latifolium, Less. Phillips's Sesuto name is *papetloane*; used to doctor people to conceal a deed.
Bolila-khomo: Rumex Woodii, N.E.Br. "Sorrel of the cattle." Used to prepare a medicine to cure calves of diarrhoea. Plants eaten raw by herd-boys.
Cheche: Leucosidea sericea, E. and Z. Phillips says *cheche* is a Zulu name. The only use he records is as a vermifuge, with other plants. Used also largely for firewood.
Folabahleke: unidentified.
Hlaba: Aloe ferox, Mill. One of the ingredients of a doctor's *lenaka*.
Hloenya: Dicoma anomala, Sond. Used for colic and toothache.
Hloko: Elyonurus argenteus, Nees. Used for colic.
Khamane: Rumex ecklonianus, Meisn. A hot decoction used for washing wounds.
Khapumpu: Eucomis undulata, Ait. Powerful charms used in the same way as Urginea capitata—*moretele* (q.v.).
Khashe: unidentified.
Koena: wild mint: Mentha longifolia, Hudson. Used with other mints for colds and chest complaints.
Lebate: Cymbopogon validus, Stapf. Used for chest complaints.
Lengana: S.A. wormwood: Artemesia afra, Jacq. Given as an enema to children suffering from constipation.
Lenoku: unidentified.
Leshoma: Boöphone disticha (L.f.) Herb. Formerly hollowed out for use as a pot to warm milk.
Lesooko: Alepidea amatymbica, E. and Z. Roots chewed or decocted for chest complaints.

[1] The synonymy has been checked through the kindness of Mr. H. Wild, of the Dept. of Agriculture and Lands, Salisbury.
[2] Phillips, *Flora*, p. 11.

Lirahalibone: unidentified. "Enemies do not see."
Lokola: unidentified.
Mabele: kaffir-corn, sorghum.
Mabelebele: Rhus dentata, Thunb. Berries eaten.
Mathethebane=*khapumpu* (q.v.).
Moelela: wild garlic: Tulbaghia alliacea, Linn.
Moferefere: trouble, tumult: Lycium Kraussii, Dunal. Smoked to cure headache; branches burnt and crushed and rubbed into incisions to cure rheumatism.
Mofifi: Rhamnus prinoides, L'Her. Branches placed on top of huts, in cattle kraals or in the *Lekhotla*, to prevent harm befalling the inmates. The dictionary also records its use as a peg "planted as a charm at the entrance of a hut".
Mohato: Crassula natans, Thunb. Used to make a medicine called *mohatollo* (meaning deliverance from oppression) and is used as a charm when a person is suspected of being bewitched. Also used as a charm in cases of illness. If a child is ill, incisions are made on its body as well as on the body of the mother, in which the "medicine" is placed, and some of the child's blood is put into the mother and vice versa. In the case of a grown-up person the same process takes place between him and his nurses.

    Also Berkheya onorpodifolia, (D.C.), Burtt Davy. Used as a charm to detect an evildoer and prevent him from doing harm. Also in many feverish illnesses and, together with Euphorbia basutica, to cure leprosy.
Mohatollo: Pittosporum viridiflorum, Sims. Much used by native doctors. Also when working the divining bones to prevent a sick person being harmed by other people.

    Also Berkheya montana, Wood and Evans: lotion for bruises; and B. (Stobaea multijuga, D.C.).
Mollapiso: unidentified.
Mohhomo: Hyparrhenia hirta, Stapf. Used for thatching grass and to make large grain baskets (*lisiu*).
Moli: generic name for plants of the genus Hypoxis: H. Rooperii, Moore. Used for making ropes and large grain baskets (*lisiu*).
Moli-kharatsa: Hypoxis costata, Bkr. *Also* H. Rooperii, Moore.
Molila: Eragrostis plana, Nees. An ingredient in many "strengthening medicines". Used to make very strong baskets and hats.
Molomo-monate: Lotononis eriantha, var. obovata, Scott-Elliott. A Mosuto before visiting a chief bathes in water in which a bruised or crushed plant has been dipped, or a bit of the plant is chewed, the belief being that it will bring luck and act as a charm in obtaining the favours of the chief or other important person visited. It is said to give a "good mouth" (*molomo o monate*) in speaking in such a way as to fascinate the chief.
Monakalali: Cyperus usitatus, Burch. Bulbs eaten.
Monkhoane: Heteromorpha arborescens, Ch. and Sch. As in text: also intestinal worms.
Monnamotso: Myrica aethiopica, Linn. Used for painful menstruation. Used as a fuel.
Moretele: Urginea capitata, Bkr. "He who causes to glide." Of all the Basutoland plants, this is perhaps the most esteemed by native doctors, who pre-

pare from it a powerful charm able to bring good fortune to friends or inflict harm on enemies. By the use of this charm the natives believe that they can "glide" among their enemies unnoticed and unharmed. By its use, sorcerers are kept away from huts, illness and death can be sent to enemies, and the country can be made to flourish or otherwise. Basuto chiefs are vaccinated with it.

Mosalasuping: Lithospermum cinereum, D.C.

Also Malva parviflora, Linn. Lotion for bruised limbs. Used to mend broken pots.

Moseme: unidentified.

Mosino=cheche (q.v.).

Mosokelo: Pellaea involuta, Baker. To cure diarrhoea and bites of spiders, the rhizome being crushed and mixed with milk and drunk.

Mothaleho: unidentified. This name means the mark made on the head of a child to protect it from evil spirits.

Motsoso: unidentified. Generic term for an aphrodisiac.

Papetloane: Haplocarpha scaposa, Harv. Used when consulting the divining bones. Also by women "as an article of their toilet", as a slip or loincloth.

Pheta: Oligomeris dregeana, Presl. Used when consulting the divining bones. A witch-doctor is supposed by this means to be able to avenge a man who has been bewitched by a distant enemy who has sent lightning to him or his cattle.

Phoa: Aster hispidus, Bkr. non. Thunb. Mixed with Helichrysum callicomum, Harv. (*motoantoanyane*) and H. Rugulosum, Less. (*motoantoanyane o monyenyane*), as an enema for colic. Used with H. callicomum, for a *lenaka*.

Pohotsehla: Xysmalobium undulatum, R.Br. Eaten as a spinach.

Also Pachycarpus rigidus, E. Mey. For colic. Eaten as spinach.

Also Phytolacca heptandra, Retz.

Qokoa: Andropogon auctus, Stapf. Said to be the best and most lasting of thatching grass.

Qoojoana: unidentified.

Seboka: Scilla rigidifolia, var. Gerrardi, Bkr. Used for child's constipation.

Also Gerbera viridifolia, Sch. Bip. Smoke inhaled as a cure for colds in the head.

Sefeamaeba: Gymnosporia buxifolia, Szysz. Mixed with parts of a snake as a cure for snake bite.

Sehalahala: eight different species are called by this Sesuto name, of which the most important are Aster filifolius, Vent., and Chrysocoma tenuifolia, Berg.

Seharane: Galium wittbergensis, var. glabrum, Phillips. *Also* G. dregeanum, Sond. and Rubia orientalis, Bullock. Used for colic, sore throat and chest complaints: also to wash the teeth. If a witch-doctor loses a patient by death, he washes his 'divining bones' in the decoction to purify them. A man wishing to become a witch-doctor drinks the decoction; this will give him intelligence and judgment, and the various ways of using the divining bones will become clear to him.

Selepe: unidentified.

Seletjana: Hermannia depressa, N.E.Br. Used when working the divining bones. A much renowned medicine for colic. Also a charm against witchcraft.

Selomi: Scabiosa columbaria, Linn. Mixed with Rhus divaricata, E. and Z. and Cussonia paniculata, E. and Z. (*kholitsane* and *motsetse*), used for colic pains and painful menstruation, also difficult confinement.

Senyarela: Ajuga ophrydis, Burch. Painful menstruation.

Sephephetho: unidentified.

Serelile: unidentified.

Seteatea: Polygala rarifolia, D.C. "The deceiver." Used for love philtres and as a charm to rid one of tormentors.

Setimamollo: Pentanisia variabilis, Harv. The fire-extinguisher, so called because it relieves the burning pain of boils; also used to rub the breasts of a woman after confinement and, in feverish illnesses, the body of the patient is bathed with the lotion. As a charm against witchcraft it is mixed with other plants and rubbed on pegs placed around the *lelapa*; this prevents the sorcerer from finding the door of the hut.

Teele: Moraea edulis, Ker. Cattle, if not accustomed to the plant, die in a few hours after eating it, but if dosed in time with the ashes from the incinerated plants, mixed with the dregs of Kaffir beer, they can be cured.

Thitapoho: Eragrostis gummiflua, Nees. Used for brooms. An ingredient in medicines for keeping or bringing luck. *Also* Pennisetum sphacetalum, Durand and Schinz, and Fingerhuthia africana, Lehm.[1]

Thobeha: unidentified. Name of medicines used for mending fractures.

Tsebe-ea-pela: Gerbera piloselloides, Cass. "Rock-rabbit's ear." Used to fumigate hut of person with a cold in the head.

Tsikitlane: Gazania serrulata, D.C. Fibres used for making *thethana*. Crushed and wetted, is put in ears to cure earache.

Tsitabaloi: Wahlenbergia depressa, W. and E. "Too much for the witches". A love philtre.

(c) *Colloquialisms*

Bewijs: stock removal permit; also includes permit for removal of animal produce such as wool. This permit is tantamount to a certificate of ownership and is issued by the stock-owner's chief or headman. It has to be obtained when a person wishes to remove his stock from one district to another and when he wishes to sell or otherwise dispose of it, as when he pays a fine or exchanges *bohali* cattle. The sex, coloration, horns and earmarks of the stock are described on the permit, together with the name of the owner, the purpose of the removal or transfer, and the name, if known, of the transferee.

Doeks: kerchief head-dress; a head-dress made of a strip of material wound round the head. Worn by married or elderly women only.

Donga: eroded gulley, nullah.

Kraal: byre or enclosure for cattle, calves and other livestock. *Not* village or homestead—a meaning frequently given in South Africa to native villages or homesteads.

Riempie: thong, made in Basutoland from ox-hide.

[1] Staples and Hudson, 1938, p. 58.

APPENDIX 1

Span: a team of draught animals, such as oxen or donkeys. Hence the verbal use "inspan" and "outspan"—to yoke or unyoke oxen, etc., to a wagon, plough, etc.

Spoor: track of a person, animal, vehicle, etc. Under the "spoor law" inhabitants of a village to which the tracks of stolen animals were traced and beyond which no further trace could be found, were assumed to be guilty of the theft unless they proved the contrary.

Tickey: a threepenny-bit.

APPENDIX II

KINSHIP TERMS

THIS list is incomplete. So far as it goes, it is based on actual terminological usage as noted in the field. Except for those in brackets the terms are those of address. The following abbreviations are used:

B.=brother	c.=child	co-w.=co-wife	d.=daughter
F.=father	H.=husband	m.=mother	o.=older
p.=parent	S.=son	si.=sister	w.=wife
y.=younger	m.s.=man speaking	w.s.=woman speaking	

(a) *Relationship through Father*

F.: *ntate*.
F.F.: *ntate moholo*.
F.F.B. (o. or y.): *ntate moholo*.
F.m.: *nkhono* (*nkhono ea tsoetseng ntate*, my grandmother who bore my father).
F.m.B.: *ntate moholo*.
F.m.B.d.: *'me, motsoala oa ntate*.
F.m.B.c.S.: *ngoaneso* (m.s.).
F.m.B.c.S.c.: *ngoanaka* (m.s.), *ngoana ngoaneso*.
F.m.B.c.d.c.: *mochana* (m.s.), *ngoana khaitseli*.
F.m.B.c.d.: *khaitseli* (m.s.).
F.m.B.w.: *nkhono*.
F.m.si.: *nkhono*.
F.o.B.: *ntate moholo*.
F.o.B.w.: *nkhono*.
F.y.B.: *rangoane*.
F.y.B.w.: *mangoane*.
F.B.S.: *ngoaneso, moroeso* (m.s.); *khaitseli* (w.s.); (*ngoana'ntate moholo*); *ngoana' rangoane*.

F.B.d.: *khaitseli* (m.s.); *ngoaneso* (w.s.); *ngoana' ntate moholo, ngoana' rangoane*.
F.B.S.w.: *ausi, mosali* (m.s.); *ausi* (w.s.).
F.B.S.S.: *ngoanaka, ngoana' ngoaneso* (m.s.).
F.B.S.S.w.: *ngoetsi* (m.s.).
F.B.S.d.: *morali, ngoana' ngoaneso* (m.s.)
F.B.d.c.: *mochana, ngoanaka*.
F.B.d.S.c.: *ngoana' ngoanake*.
F.B.w.si.: *mangoane* or *nkhono*, depending on whether B. is y. or o.
F.B.w.si.c.: *khaitseli, ngoaneso, ngoana' mangoane* or *ngoana' nkhono* (as above).
F.B.w.B.: *malome*.
F.B.w.B.w.: *malome*.
F.B.w.B.c.: *motsoala, ngoana' malome*.
F.B.w.B.S.w.: *malome*.
F.F.y.B.S.: *rangoane*.
F.F.y.B.S.w.: *mangoane, mohatsa rangoane*.
F.F.B.d.: *rakhali*.
F.F.B.d.d.: *motsoala*.

Note: There is no difference in the terms for father's older and father's younger brother's descendants.

F.si.: *rakhali*. There is no difference between older and younger sister.
F.si.H.: *rakhali*.

F.si.c.: *motsoala, ngoana*.
F.si.c.c.: *ngoana motsoala*.
F.si.H.B.: *motsoala, mokazi*.

324

APPENDIX II

(b) *Relationship through Mother*

m.: *'me*.
m. senior co-w.: *nkhono*.
m. junior co-w.: *mangoane*.
m.F.: *ntate moholo*.
m.F.B. (o. or y.): *ntate moholo*.
m.F.si.S.: *ntate, motsoala' 'me*.
m.F.si.S.c.: *ngoaneso, khaitseli, ngoana' motsoala' 'me*.
m.F.si.d.: *'me, motsoela' 'me*.
m.m.: *nkhono (nkhono ea tsoetseng 'me,* my grandmother who bore my mother).
m.m.si.: *nkhono*.
m.B.: *malome*.
m.B.w.: *malome, mohatsa malome*.
m.B.c.: *motsoala (ngoana' malome)*.

m.B.c.c.: *ngoana' motsoala*.
m.B.w.B.: *malome*.
m.B.w.B.c.: *motsoala*.
m.o.si.: *nkhono*.
m.o.si.H.: *ntate*.
m.o.si.c.: *aubuti, ngoaneso, khaitseli, (ngoana' 'me), (ngoana' nkhono)* (these terms are used by and to males and females as with B. and si.).
m.y.si.: *mangoane, 'me*.
m.y.si.H.: *rangoane, ntate*.
m.y.si.c.: *ngoaneso, khaitseli (ngoaneso ka 'mae, ngoana' mangoane)*.
m.o. or y.si.S.w.: *khaitseli, ngoaneso*.
m.si.H.si.: *rakhali*.
m.si.H.si.c.: *motsoala, ngoana' rakhali*.

(c) *Relationship through Brother*

O.B.: *aubuti* (m.s. and w.s.); *(moholoane* (m.s.), *khaitseli* (w.s.)).
o.B.w.: *molamo, khaitseli, ngoaneso*.
y.B.: *ngoaneso* (m.s.); *aubuti, 'nake* (dear) (w.s.); *(moena, monyane* (m.s.); *khaitseli* (w.s.)).
y.B.w.: *ausi, ngoaneso* (m.s. and w.s.); *molamo* (w.s.).
B.w.si.: *khaitseli, 'nake* (m.s.).

B.w.F.B.d.: *ausi, ngoaneso, 'nake* (m.s.).
B.w.B.: *soare*.
B.w.B.d.: *ngoanaka, (ngoana' soare sa ka)*.
B.S.: *ngoanaka* (m.s.).
B.S.w.: *ngoanaka* (m.s. and w.s.); *(ngoetsi oa ngoaneso* (m.s.)).
B.d.: *morali, ngoanaka* (m.s.).
B.d.H.: *mokhoenyana, ngoanaka* (m.s.).
B.d.H.si.: *ngoanaka*.

(d) *Relationship through Sister*

o.si.: *khaitseli, ausi* (m.s.); *ausi, ngoaneso* (w.s.).
y.si.: *sisi, ausi, 'nake, ngoaneso* (m.s.); *ausi, 'nake* (w.s.).
o.si.H.: *soare* (m.s.); *molamo, mohatsa* (w.s.).

y.si.H.: *soare* (m.s.).
si.H.si.: *soare, ngoaneso, 'nake*.
si.c.: *mochana* (m.s.); *ngoanaka* (w.s.).
si.S.w.: *ngoetsi* (w.s.).
si.c.c.: *ngoanake* (m.s.).

(e) *Relationship through Husband*

H.: *mohatsa, monna oa ka*.
co-w.: *khalitso, mohalitsong*.
H.o.B.: *ntate*.
H.o.B.w.: *'me*.
H.y.B.: *aubuti*.
H.y.B.w.: *ausi*.

H.B.c.: *ngoanaka*.
H.si.: *molamo*.
H.si.H.: *soare*.
H.si.c.: *mochana*.
H.p.: *matsale*.
H.F.B.S.: *khaitseli, ngoaneso*.

(f) *Relationship through Wife*

w.: *mohatsa, mosali oa ka.*
w.o.si.: *ngoaneso, khaitseli.*
w.y.si.: *mohatsa, ngoaneso, 'nake.*
w.si.H.: *mofobe.*
w.si.c.: *ngoanaka.*
w.B.: *soare.*

w.B.w.: *soare.*
w.B.c.: *ngoanaka; (ngoana 'nake, ngoana soare).*
w.F.: *mohoe, ntate.*
w.m.: *mohoehali, 'me.*

(g) *Relationship through Children*

S.: *ngoanaka; (mora).*
S.w.: *ngoetsi, ngoanaka.*
S.c.: *ngoana' ngoanake; (motloholo, setloholo).*
S.w.p.: *mokhotsi.*

d.: *ngoanaka; (morali).*
d.H.: *mokhoenyana, ngoanaka.*
d.c.: *ngoana' ngoanaka; (motloholo, setloholo).*
d.H.p.: *mokhotsi.*

(h) *General*

1. Siblings of same sex: *ngoaneso.*
2. Ortho-cousins of same sex: *ngoaneso.*
3. In polygynous marriages, children of one wife call relatives of other wives by the same name as relatives of their mother.
4. A wife uses the terms *nkhono* and *mangoane* for the same people as her husband does. His uncles and aunts are also classed as her own, his parallel cousins as his siblings and his cross-cousins as cross-cousins (*motsoala*), wives of the former being classed as his brother's wife, and of the latter as *motsoala*.

(i) *Use of Kinship Terms Between Unrelated People*

The following kinship terms are used in addressing people to whom the speaker is not related:

1. *Ntate* is used for an older or senior man, by both sexes.
2. *'me* is used for an older or senior woman, by both sexes.
3. *Nkhono* is used for a woman much older than oneself, by both sexes.
4. *Ngoanake* is used for a junior or child of either sex by both sexes.
5. *Mokhotsi* is used between older people of more or less equal status with a friendly connotation.
6. *Soare* is used between young men on friendly terms and sometimes by young women and by girls in their later teens to young men.
7. *Aubuti* is used by young men or women, boys and girls, for an older man as an alternative to *ntate*, especially when they are friendly or he is not so much older as to merit the more formal address.
8. *Ausi* is used by young men and women to women or girls of more or less the same age and status.

APPENDIX III

KINSHIP MARRIAGE

FIVE hundred and sixty-nine marriages recorded from the Tlokoa are analysed in the following tables: 184 of these marriages are between kinsmen and 153 are between people who are not related to one another. The remaining 232 marriages are between people whose kinship status was doubtful; enough was recorded about them to show that they were not patrilineally related, but not enough to show definitely whether they were related in any other way or not.

Each table has been divided into three main groups: "chiefs", "Tlokoa" and "Tebele". The first includes Chief Mosuoe, his immediate family and all other Ba-Lefe; the second includes all Tlokoa, other than Ba-Lefe and Tebele, and comprises the Ba-Tsotetsi and Basuto clans such as Koena, Fokeng, Taung, Tloung and Phuthing; the third is confined to those of Nguni origin (Zulu or Tembu), such as Koenehatsi, Khala and Sakong. This division is roughly one of status: the Ba-Lefe on the whole are of higher social status than other Tlokoa, and the latter, in turn, are higher than the Tebele. There is some overlapping, as junior Ba-Lefe are less important than senior Tlokoa of other clans and than a few senior Tebele, but not so much as to vitiate the divisions as a whole. It is impossible to draw a more accurate dividing line between different degrees of status.

Each group is divided into two parts, "A" and "B". Part "A" is "past generation" and includes all those marriages where the man was more than about sixty years old in 1936, or would have been if he had still been alive. Part "B" is "present generation" and covers the marriages of men of less than sixty years of age or who would have been less, if they were still alive. This division is also a fairly rough one, as the ages of very few people were accurately known. All Chief Lelingoana's children are placed in group "B". The relationships given in the tables include classificatory as well as actual relationships.

This table shows that an appreciable proportion (nearly one-third) of marriages are kinship marriages, even if all those classified as "doubtful", are disregarded. It also shows the greater incidence of kinship marriage in the higher social group. This would have been even more clearly shown had it been possible to classify degrees of status more accurately. The marriages of Lelingoana and his male descendants are analysed below and it will there be seen that the less important the marriage the more frequently it is not a kinship one.

The table also suggests that there is a higher proportion of kinship

TABLE A

KINSHIP MARRIAGES

Social Group	F.B.d.	F.si.d.	m.B.d.	m.si.d.	Dist.	Own Generation	Miscellaneous Daughter's Generation	Mother's Generation	Total	??	Nil	Total
Chiefs "A"	15	7	6	2	5	—	3	1	39	37	9	85
Chiefs "B"	18	8	5	2	3	16	6	1	59	35	21	115
Tlokoa "A"	5	2	2	1	—	1	—	—	11	36	5	52
Tlokoa "B"	19	7	12	4	—	11	6	2	61	66	63	190
Tebele "A"	...	—	—	—	—	1	—	—	1	4	3	8
Tebele "B"	—	1	5	—	—	7	—	—	13	54	52	119
Total	57	25	30	9	8	36	15	4	184	232	153	569

Abbreviations: F.=father, B.=brother, d.=daughter, si.=sister, m.=mother, Dist.=distant; relationship undetermined, ??=doubtful, insufficient evidence; *Nil.*=no known relationship.

TABLE B

KINSHIP MARRIAGE: "FATHER'S BROTHER'S DAUGHTER" TYPE

Social Group	1 generation removed F.B.d.	F.½B.d.	2 generations removed F.F.B.S.d.	F.F.F.½B.S.d.	3 generations removed F.F.F.B.S.S.d.	4 generations removed F.F.F.F.B.S.S.S.d.	More remote	Total
Chiefs "A"	3	8	3	1	—	—	—	15
Chiefs "B"	4	1	3	4	1	2	3	18
Tlokoa "A"	4	—	1	—	—	—	—	5
Tlokoa "B"	3	2	6	—	6	2	—	19
Tebele "A"	—	—	—	—	—	—	—	—
Tebele "B"	—	—	—	—	—	—	—	—
Total	14	11	13	5	7	4	3	57

marriages among the "present generation" than among the "past generation". This, I feel, is misleading, and the figures here suffer from the fact that a higher proportion of "past" marraiges than of "present" are "doubtful". The reason for this is that as people are not interested in their maternal relations it was difficult to obtain full genealogies on the mother's side. I believe that complete genealogies would have revealed quite a number of kinship marriages such as F.si.d. and m.B.d. which are now lost in the "doubtfuls". This applies even more to the "miscellaneous" kinds of kinship marriage, of which very few are recorded for the "past" generation.

For much the same reason, I think that the proportion of F.B.d. marriages to other kinds of kinship marriage appears unduly large. The Basuto are more interested in paternal ancestry than in their maternal lines, so it is comparatively easy to trace the former back for several generations and thus obtain more connexions on the father's side than on the mother's. Furthermore, the F.B.d. type of marriage can be extended back indefinitely, as indicated in Table B—although after two or three generations the connexion ceases to have any great meaning; other relationships, such as F.si.d., can only be traced further back by stretching the classificatory system to its utmost; they also lose almost all their significance beyond the first generation; for example, F.F.B.d.d. can be classified as F.si.d., but it means very little to the person concerned even if he is aware that this relationship exists. A truer picture of the socially significant kinship marriages is given in tables B, C and D. Marriages of the F.B.d. type occurring more than two generations back may be disregarded, as may other types occurring more than one generation back. Nevertheless it is clear that F.B.d. marriages predominate, and F.si.d. marriages are more frequent, in the upper classes. This is one of the many byways of kinship study which I should have liked to follow, but did not have time to pursue. The extent to which these types of kinship have been traced back is shown in tables B, C and D:

TABLE C

KINSHIP MARRIAGE: "MOTHER'S BROTHER'S DAUGHTER" TYPE

Social Group	1 generation removed m.B.d.	1 generation removed m.½B.d.	2 generations removed m.F.B.S.d.	3 generations removed m.F.F.B.S.S.d.	Total
Chiefs "A"	4	—	—	1	5
Chiefs "B"	2	1	—	—	3
Tlokoa "A"	—	2	—	—	2
Tlokoa "B"	7	—	2	—	9
Tebele "A"	—	—	—	—	—
Tebele "B"	5	—	—	—	5
Total	18	3	2	1	24

APPENDIX III

TABLE D

KINSHIP MARRIAGE: "FATHER'S SISTER'S DAUGHTER" TYPE

Social Group	F.si.d.	F.½si.d.	F.si.H.B.d.	F.si.co-w.d.	Total
Chiefs "A"	5	—	—	2	7
Chiefs "B"	7	1	—	—	8
Tlokoa "A"	2	—	—	—	2
Tlokoa "B"	4	2	1	—	7
Tebele "A"	—	—	—	—	—
Tebele "B"	1	—	—	—	1
Total	19	3	1	2	25

Apart from the qualifications made above, other factors must also be taken into account in assessing the significance of the figures given in Table A. One of these is that not all kinship marriages are preferential marriages or were contracted because of the type of relationship existing between the couple. A few cases have been included in the table where the kinship aspect was fortuitous, as when a man married his F.B.d., not because of this relationship, but because he loved her. This is a preferential marriage in the sense that it is warmly approved by the parents of the couple because of their relationship, but not in the sense that it was prompted by that relationship. It is possible that the couple were influenced by the conventional behaviour associated with their relationship and wanted to marry one another because they knew such a marriage was socially desirable and would be approved; but I cannot say to what extent, if at all, this was so.

A special difficulty arises where more than one interrelationship occurs. For instance, Lelingoana was closely related to his sixth wife in five different ways, and more remotely connected in still other ways; she was his F.si.S.d., 4th w.B.d., 1st w.½B.d., senior d.H.si., si.H.B.d. Which of these relationships should be recorded in Table A? I adopted the rule that where the marriage had been prompted by a particular relationship, this was recorded; where the nature of the connexion was irrelevant, the closest one was taken. As Lelingoana had married this particular wife as a helpmate for his senior wife, who was getting old, and chose her because she was the closest of the latter's kin available at that time, I selected the first relationship because it was the most direct; but it would have been just as reasonable to choose the third as being the closest tie between her and his senior wife. In some cases, the relationship to be selected was obvious; in others, as in the above case and where a man had married a woman who was both his m.B.d. and his F.si.d., the issue was not clear and I had to use my discretion.

The close correlation between status and kinship marriage is shown in the following list of marriages contracted by Lelingoana and his male descendants. It will be seen that the senior wives of the senior males are kinswomen, whereas their junior wives and the wives of the junior males are usually not related. The former tend to be married to fulfil family and, occasionally, political obligations, the latter from personal choice, and it is usually just a coincidence if they happen to be related.

The genealogical relationship of Lelingoana's male descendants who are married is given in the following table:

Lelingoana: 1st house, Mosuoe.
              Mosuoe: first house, Mokotjo, no male issue.
                    second house, Thothofeane, sons young.
                    third house, Nyooko, just married.
                          Qhoqhoqho, just married.
                          Hemi, just married.
                          Tlontlollo, just married.
                    fourth house, Lehloba, just married.
     2nd house, Tootse. Tootse's descendants and brothers not enumerated.
     3rd house, Joalaboholo. Children young.
     4th house, no male issue.
     5th house, Semai, son Mosamelo.
              Qaqailane, sons young.
              Mokopuntja, sons young.
              Thuke, sons young
     6th house, Ntjabokone, sons young.
              Mohlabakobo, just married.
7–10th houses—sons not married or else no male issue.

Details of these marriages are given below:

Name	Wife's position	Wife's Relationship	Wife's clan	Comment
Lelingoana	1st	F.si.co-w.d. Also si.h.½si.	Taung	Daughter of important sub-chief and clan head
	2nd	Distant patrilineal ortho-cousin. Lelingoana and his brother married sisters or cousins—records incomplete	Lefe	
	3rd	Possibly related through father's mother—records incomplete	Taung	
	4th	F.si.d. (same F.si. as in 1 above)	Taung	
	5th	F.si.co-w.d. (same F.si. as in 1 above)	Taung	
	6th	F.si.S.d. (same F.si. as in 1 above). Other relationships referred to in text	Taung	Married as companion and help to 1st wife

APPENDIX III

Name	Wife's position	Wife's Relationship	Wife's clan	Comment
	7th	m.F.F.B.S.d. (possibly closer, but records incomplete)	Tloung	
	8th	Records incomplete, probably not related	Tloung	
	9th	m.B.d. Distantly related to 7th and possibly to 8th wife	Tloung	Daughter of important sub-chief and clan head
	10th	No relation. Granddaughter of great friend	Khala	Married as domestic help to 1st wife, now very old
Mosuoe	1st	m.B.d. Other relationships traceable through L.'s 4th, 5th and 6th wives, and through the intermarriage of their children	Taung	Arranged match
	2nd	F.si.d. Also m.½B.d. Other involved relations traceable	Taung	Arranged match
	3rd	si.H.si.	Tsotetsi	Love match
	4th	Records incomplete—probably no relation	Tsotetsi	Love match
Mokotjo	1st a	F.si.d. (when she died her y.si. replaced her)	Tsotetsi	Arranged match
	1st b	F.si.d. Sister of above. Although married after 2nd wife, she takes precedence	Tsotetsi	Seantlo
	2nd	F.si.d. (A different F.si. from former)	Tsotetsi	Arranged match
	3rd	F.si.d. (A different F.si. from both 1 and 2 above)	Taung	Arranged match
Thothofeane	only	Records incomplete, but probably no relation	Tsitsi	Arranged match
Nyooko[1]	only	Records incomplete	Sia	Arranged match
Qhoqhoqho	1st	m.B.d. She was engaged to Q.'s e. br. who died before the marriage took place. Q. was supposed to marry her in his e.B.'s name, but he and everyone else now regard her as his full wife	Tsotetsi	Arranged match
	2nd	No direct relation—F.m.co-w. si.d.	Sakong	Love match
Hemi[1]	1st	No direct relation—F.si.co-w. B.d.	Tau	Love match
	2nd	Records incomplete, but probably no relation	Phuthing	Love match
Tlontlollo[1]	only	Records incomplete, but probably no close relation—common great-great-grandfather and some connexion through f.si.	Lefe	Love match

Name	Wife's position	Wife's Relationship	Wife's clan	Comment
Lehloba[1]	only	Records incomplete—common great-grandfather	Lefe	Arranged match
Tootse	1st	F.si.d.	Phuthing	Arranged match
	2nd	Records incomplete, probably no relation	Konatsi	Love match
	3rd	Records incomplete, probably no relation	Tloung	Love match
Joalaboholo	only	m.si.d.	??	??
Semai	only	Records incomplete. Her sister and Lelingoana's 9th wife's sister married the same man	Khala	Arranged match
Mosamelo[1]	only	F.F.½B.S.d.	Lefe	Arranged match
Qaqailane	only	F.si.d. Also m.½B.d. and more distant involved relations	Taung	Arranged match
Mokopuntja	only	F.F.½.B.S.d.	Lefe	Love match
Thuke[1]	only	Records incomplete—distant relation through cousin's marriage	Thutsi	Love match
Ntjabokone	only	m.si.d. When she died in childbirth her younger sister replaced her	Tau	Arranged
	only	m.si.d. See above	Tau	Seantlo
Mohlabakobo[1]	only	No relation		Love match

The prevalence of preferential kinship and arranged matches is, I believe, closely associated with and dependent upon polygyny. I am unable to pursue this point very far and can only suggest these two possibilities. As the foregoing analysis shows, almost all arranged matches are with kinsmen and almost all "love matches" are with people who are not related or only distantly related; furthermore, most of those whose marriages were arranged, subsequently married women of their own choice and, as they occupied fairly high positions in the family hierarchy, expected to be able to do so. This suggests that polygyny acts as a sort of safety-valve to a restrictive custom and enables a man to accept as his first wife a woman chosen for him for family reasons, as he knows he will have a chance later of being able to marry the wife or wives of his own choice. This hypothesis can only be checked by a comparative analysis of Christian Basuto marriages of more or less equal status elsewhere, as Christians assume they will marry only one wife; unfortunately, I do not have the necessary information.

The second possible reason is that polygyny encourages large families and creates wide family ties, and so extends the field of available kins-

---

[1] These marriages occurred between 1936 and 1949 and are not included in the 569 marriages analysed in Tables A–D. The information I obtained in 1949 was so highly selective, being almost entirely confined to the marriages of Mosuoe's children, that its inclusion in those tables would be wrong.

men. In this way it increases the chances of a man's parents finding him a congenial wife from among his cousins and reduces the danger of his rebelling against their wishes and choosing his wife for himself.

The relationship of intermarriage and interbreeding is another question that merits attention, but is one on which I have little information. The prime object of intermarriage is the union of two families of more or less equal status and this equality is best guaranteed by keeping to kinsmen. The genetic implications of this are not seriously considered and few bother about the fact that it leads to in-breeding. Mosuoe, however, had decided views on the matter. He regarded in-breeding as undesirable and he cited instances of families and of cattle which had deteriorated because of in-breeding and of others which had improved through the introduction of new blood. But to him, in-breeding only occurred when the relationship was traceable patrilineally through the males, as he considered that the family blood was transmitted only by the men. He therefore disapproved strongly of marriage with one's father's brother's daughter, but commended marriage with one's mother's brother's daughter and father's sister's daughter, also but to a lesser extent with one's mother's sister's daughter, as such relationship is regarded as more distant than the other two. He and his father adhered strictly to this viewpoint, as the foregoing details show, and only two cases of marriage between close patrilineal kinsmen occur in his family: one is that of Mosamelo, son of Semai, which took place after Lelingoana's death and was beyond Mosuoe's personal control; the other a marriage (not recorded in the above list) between Mosuoe's daughter and his F.$\frac{1}{2}$B.S.S., which he strenuously opposed for a long time and finally agreed to only because he was convinced that the young couple really were in love with one another. This attitude is in marked contrast to that of the Koena chiefs whose preferential marriage is with one's father's brother's daughter, or others classificatorily equivalent. For instance, Griffith's first four wives were sisters, all daughters of his father's half-brother, and Seeiso's senior wife was his father's father's half-brother's son's daughter (and also his mother's brother's daughter). In the latter case, the former relationship was considered the more important.

In conclusion, the composition of the kinship marriages shown in the "Miscellaneous" column in Table "A" is analysed below. They are divided into three main groups: "own generation", "mother's generation" and "daughter's generation"; this division refers not so much to the relative age of the couple as to their relationship. Each group is further divided according to the different types of relationship[1] involved. This clearly brings out the widely differing types of connexion

[1] In all cases, the relationship described is the closest kinship connexion between the couple; occasionally more distant connexions occurred as well, but these have been ignored.

that are covered by the same kinship term. Half-brothers and half-sisters are not here distinguished from full brothers and sisters.

(a) Own Generation

1. Classificatory sister (*khaitseli, 'nake, ngoaneso*)
    (*a*) Brother's wife's sister   1
        Class. brother's wife's sister (B.w.F.B.d.)   3
        Class. brother's wife's sister (F.B.S.w.si.)   3
        Class. brother's wife's sister (m.si.S.w.si.)   1
    (*b*) Wife's sister (also called *molamo*)   2
    (*c*) Mother's cross-cousin's daughter (m.F.si.S.d.)   1   11
2. Classificatory ortho-cousin (*ngoaneso, khaitseli*)
    (*a*) Maternal aunt's daughter (*ngoana' mangoane*) (m.F.B.d.d.)   1
    (*b*) Maternal aunt's daughter (*ngoana' mangoane*) (F.B.w.si.d.)   2   3
3. Classificatory cross-cousin (*motsoala*)
    (*a*) Class. m.B.d. (*ngoana' malome*) (F.B.w.B.d.)   2
        Class. m.B.d. (*ngoana' malome*) (m.B.w.B.d.)   2
        Class. m.B.d. (*ngoana' malome*) (m.F.F.si.S.S.w.B.d.)   1
    (*b*) Class. F.si.d. (*ngoana' rakhali*) (m.si.H.si.d.)   1
        Class. F.si.d. (*ngoana' rakhali*) (F.F.B.d.d.)   2
    (*c*) Miscellaneous (m.B.w.si.d.)   1
        Miscellaneous (brother and sister marry cross-cousins
        si.H.F.B.w.B.d.)   1   10
4. Classificatory sister-in-law (*soare, ngoaneso*)
    Sister's husband's sister   7
    Class. sister's husband's sister (si.H.F.B.d.)   4
    Class. sister's husband's sister (si.H.si.H.si.)   1   12
                                                                                     ——
                                                                                      36
                                                                                     ——

(b) Mother's Generation

1. Classificatory mother (*'me*)
    (*a*) Father's cross-cousin (*motsoala' ntate*) (F.m.B.d.)   1
    (*b*) Mother's cross-cousin (*motsoala' 'me*) (m.F.si.co-w.d.)   1   2
2. Classificatory father's sister (*rakhali*) (F.F.F.B.S.d.)   1   1
3. Classificatory mother's sister (*nkhono* or *mangoane*) (F.B.w.F.B.d.)   1   1
                                                                                      ——
                                                                                       4
                                                                                      ——

(c) Daughter's Generation

1. Classificatory daughter (*morali, ngoana'ka*)
    (*a*) Paternal ortho-cousin's daughter (*ngoana ngoaneso*) (F.B.S.d.)   1
    (*b*) Maternal ortho-cousin's daughter (*ngoana ngoaneso*)
        (m.co-w.si.S.d.)   1
    (*c*) Father's cross-cousin's son's daughter (*ngoana ngoaneso*)
        (F.m.B.d.co-w.S.d.)   3

APPENDIX III

    Father's cross-cousin's son's daughter (*ngoana' ngoaneso*)
    (F.m.B.S.S.d.)   1   6
2. Classificatory uterine niece (*mochana, ngoana' khaitseli*)
    (F.F.B.S.d.d.)   1   1
3. Classificatory cross-cousin's daughter (*ngoana' motsoala, ngoana'ka*)
    (F.si.S.d.)   4
    (m.F.si.S.S.d.) 1; (m.B.d.H.B.d.) 1   2   6
4. In-laws
    (*a*) Brother-in-law's daughter (B.w.B.d.)   1
    (*b*) Class. son-in-law's sister (B.d.H.F.B.d.)   1   2

                                                                     15

                               Total 65

APPENDIX IV

In the tables below are summarized cases tried in Bereng's and Mosuoe's courts. The former cover the period Aug. 1933–Jan. 1934 and were taken from the court record book, to which Chief Bereng kindly gave me access. The latter cover four periods: Oct. 1935–Dec. 1936, and exactly twelve months, April to March, in the years 1946–7, 1947–8 and 1948–9. The 1935–6 cases were compiled from notes kept by my assistant and myself and are not quite complete; the 1946–9 cases were taken from the official court record books, which the court president, Mokete Lethunya, generously put at my disposal during my flying visit to Mokhotlong in August 1949.

These cases are classified according to the principal or ostensible matter in dispute, neglecting all subsidiary matters that might have arisen and been dealt with during the hearing of the case. Thus, where a person sued another for *bohali* cattle and it was found that the latter had taken some without a stock removal permit, the case is recorded as a civil dispute over marriage-cattle and not as a criminal *bewijs* case, even though the offender may have been punished for the offence.

To facilitate presentation, these cases have been compressed into certain wide categories, which therefore do not present the full range of matters covered by the courts. For instance, "theft" includes attempted theft and accessory to theft; as well as actual theft; "assault" includes brawling, fighting, threatening as well as downright assault; "administrative orders" covers a very wide field, from contour ridging to burial of the dead; "ownership" includes disputes over inheritance as well as other forms of property dispute; "damage" includes malicious injury to property, damages to crops by grazing animals and arson. In some cases, the nature of the physical bone of contention is important, as in the theft of different kinds of property, and this is shown in the table of theft cases given below.

An analysis of the types of cases taken on appeal might have led to interesting conclusions, but as this would have needed a far wider range of courts to be of any value, I have not attempted it. But for the sake of interest, to indicate the degree of variation that occurs, a few examples and a general summary are given below.

SUMMARY

Court	Civil Cases Decision Accepted	Civil Cases Appeal	Criminal Cases Decision Accepted	Criminal Cases Appeal	Total Accepted	Total Appeal	Total
Bereng	68	2	48	1	116	3	119
Mosuoe (1)	Data incomplete (see note, p. 340)				(115	69)[1]	243
Mosuoe (2)	90	45	80	22	170	67	237
Mosuoe (3)	115	59	149	30	264	89	353
Mosuoe (4)	74	22	155	49	229	71	300

CIVIL CASES

Date	Court	Bohali cattle	Family Domes. disputes	Misc.	Adultery and Seduct'n	Slander	Owner-ship and Inhrtnc.	Property Damage	Vic. Damage	Lands	Contract and Debt	Admin. istration Jurisdiction and Orders	Pound and Mabo-ella	Initiation	Total
1933–4	Bereng	5	6	—	9	—	1	7	2	8	15	15	1	1	70
1935–6	Mosuoe	5	12	6	10	17	3	17[1]	2	23	34	17[2]	3	2	151
1946–7	Mosuoe	13	5	12	7	5	4[2]	16	2	8	12	4[2]	8	1	135
1947–8	Mosuoe	35	6	9	12	5	43	10	2	21	10	11[2]	9	1	174
1948–9	Mosuoe	28	1	4	7	1	25	15	2	4	6	2[2]	—	—	96

[1] Includes two cases of arson.
[2] Includes five, two, four and one cases respectively, of disputes over jurisdiction, succession to a position of sub-chief or headman, and placing.

CRIMINAL CASES

Date	Court	Assault	Insult	Robbery	Theft	Forgery	Political orders	Bewijs	Stray Stock	Contempt of Court	Obstruct. and Disobedce	False Witness	Misc.	Total
1933–4	Bereng	7	—	—	13	1	—	5	—	—	15	—	8[1]	49
1935–6	Mosuoe	10[2]	—	2	45[3]	1	13	—	4	—	14	—	3	92
1946–7	Mosuoe	20	6	—	41	—	18	2	3	3	3	3	3	102
1947–8	Mosuoe	34	6	1	64	—	37	3	3	4	14	3	10	179
1948–9	Mosuoe	47	13	1	78	—	36	1	2	6	11	3	6	204

[1] All eight cases were prosecutions of subordinate authorities for maladministration.
[2] Includes one case of homicide.
[3] Includes one case of "theft and arson" and one of "theft and forgery", the forgery being of earmarks on a sheep.

The low proportion of appeals taken from Bereng's court is, I think, indicative of the awe in which people hold authorities of his importance and of the fear that the Paramount Chief's court will not readily reverse the decisions of so powerful a chief (Bereng was the then Paramount Chief's favourite son). It also indicates that the higher the court the more authoritative the decision. I was in no position to judge whether this court gave juster decisions than Mosuoe's. The smaller proportion of appeals taken from Mosuoe's court in 1947-8 and 1948-9 as compared with 1935-6 and 1946-7 may be attributed to the improved functioning of that court under the new system, due to the District Commissioner's supervision—the personnel of the court remained unchanged. There are other possible explanations, but as I was unable to pursue them, no definite conclusions can be made.

The right to appeal is unfettered and some dissatisfied litigants are quite prepared to appeal against the court's decision in trifling matters. But as the taking of an appeal does involve the appellant in a good deal of trouble and possible expense, and nowadays requires an initial outlay of at least a few shillings, most people tend to appeal only in important cases, where the dispute concerns a good deal of property or where the appellant was fined unduly heavily. This is reflected in the above summary, which shows that the proportion of appeals is higher in civil than in criminal cases. The following table gives a few more details in categories having an appreciable number of cases.

Court	Bohali Cattle		Ownership of Stock : Lands				Contracts and Debts		Theft		Assault		Political Orders	
	Ac.	Ap.	Ac.	Ap.	Ac.	Ap.	Ac.	Ap.	Ac.	Ap.	Ac.	Ap.	Ac.	Ap.
Mosuoe (2)	8	5	24	5	3	5	10	2	32	9	17	3	14	4
Mosuoe (3)	4	1	10	1	11	10	9	1	53	11	31	3	31	6
Mosuoe (4)	23	5	8	4	2	2	6	—	54	24	38	9	31	5

Land disputes are the only ones where the issues are consistently important and complex; on the other hand, contract and debt cases mostly concern petty amounts and the issues are simple: it is noteworthy that the former have a consistently high proportion of appeals and the latter a low proportion. In assault cases the penalties are usually low, whereas in theft they vary considerably, depending on the quantity of goods stolen; in the former the number of appeals is consistently small, in the latter they vary slightly. The other categories are too variable to yield any clear-cut conclusions on the figures given without further analysis, and this, unfortunately, I am not in a position to give.

Finally, the types of theft cases are briefly analysed in the following table. "Mixed" cases refer to a combination of stock or food with other

Several cases were delayed for witnesses and not subsequently followed up, and some were not completed. One hundred and eighty-four records of completed cases were obtained, from which sixty-nine appeals were noted (see Summary, p. 338).

APPENDIX IV

THEFT CASES

Court	Stock	Food	Mixed	Misc.	Attempted	Conversion	Accessory	Total
Bereng	8	1	–	2	–	–	2	13
Mosuoe (1)	33	1	2	7	1	1	–	45
Mosuoe (2)	26	4	1	6	1	–	3	41
Mosuoe (3)	43	2	1	13	–	–	5	64
Mosuoe (4)	51	4	1	16	–	–	6	78

items, e.g. theft of sheep and wool; "Misc." refers to implements, saddlery, clothes and other such property. The table clearly shows the great preponderance of stock thefts. Deeper analysis of the records would almost certainly have revealed more cases of attempted theft, theft by conversion and separate trial of accessories. Where accessories were tried with the principals no separation of cases is made. "Food" refers to grain, meat and other foodstuffs, but not to animals which are stolen and then slaughtered for food—these fall into the group "Stock".

APPENDIX V

NATIVE AUTHORITIES: MOKHOTLONG DISTRICT AND WARD, 1949

Title	Name	Area or Areas	Taxpayers	To Whom Subordinate	Remarks
Principal Chief	'Mantsebo Seeiso[1]	Mokhotlong	117	The Paramount Chief	To act until further notice
Headman	Vacant	Linotsing, ha Mahlomola	83	The Principal Chief of Mokhotlong	
Headman	'Manthako Thetela[1]	Mechalleng	87	,,	
Headman	Seabatha Lerotholi	Maboloka	123	,,	
Headman	Absalome Letsie	Liphakoeng	114	,,	
Headman	Mabina Lerotholi	Maphiring	133	,,	
Headman	Napo Moshoeshoe	Linareng, ha Napo	60	,,	
Headman	Abia Khoeli	Liraoheleng	28	,,	
Headman	Gamoqane Kubutu	Matsoaing	66	,,	
Headman	Nkherepe Lebopo	Mahesheleng	43	,,	
			854		
Chief	Matlere Lerotholi	Motsitseng	120	The Principal Chief of Mokhotlong	
Headman	Mohlaoli Maketekete	Sekoka	47	The Chief of Mostitseng	
Headman	Tsenyehelo Makhabane	Linotsing ha Makhabane	25	,,	
Headman	Mosiuoa Lerotholi	Senqu ha Mosiuoa Lerotholi	90	,,	
Headman	Makae Nkuebe	Senqu, ha Seotsa	75	,,	
Headman	Moshe Moqeneheli Posholi	Mphokojoane	47	,,	
Headman	Vacant	Makeneng	31	,,	
Headman	Khethisa Molapo	Bothakhisantja	92	,,	
Headman	Molahlehi Manyokho	Tlhanyaku	68	,,	
			595		

Headman	Makhahlela Lerotholi	Masaleng	125	The Chief of Motsitseng
Headman	Senkoase Matete	Moremoholo, ha Senkoase	161	The Headman of Masaleng
Headman	Sofonia Makara	Limapong	83	,,
Headman	Nkuebe Letsie	Mangaung	54	,,
Headman	Ramabotho Makoetje	Thabantso	49	,,
Headman	Vacant	Linarong, ha Makhahlela	52	,,
			524	
Chief	Kemuel S. Matete	Ntlholoetsane	184	The Principal Chief of Mokhotlong
Headman	Molefi Phakisi	Bafali	126	The Chief of Ntlholoetsane
Headman	Setha Matete	Moshemong	80	,,
Headman	Jeremiah Lepipi	Phutha	29	,,
			419	
Chief	Abia Matete	Mateanong	222	The Principal Chief of Mokhotlong
Headman	Mekhoa Posholi	Sanqebethu ha Mekhoa	52	The Chief of Mateanong
Headman	Leutsoa Litsoane	Masueneng	18	,,
Headman	Motlalepula Ralefatla	Sanqebethu ha Ralefatla		,,
			292	
Chief	Lerato Rafolatsane[1,2]	Molumong	369	The Principal Chief of Mokhotlong
Headman	Taelo Monyaka	Tsekong	37	The Chief of Molumong
Headman	Mothoasebaka Mosenki	Tsoenene	82	,,
Headman	Vacant	Fanyere	75	,,
Headman	Moeketsane Moeketsane	'Muela	195	,,
Headman	Motebang Lekhotsa	Libibing	46	,,
Headman	Mfana Kemuel Morojele	Molalana	62	,,
Headman	Letlatsa Rafolatsane	Komakoma	85	,,
Headman	Mohale Tsita	Bobatsi	58	,,
			1009	

343

Title	Name	Area or Areas		To Whom Subordinate	Remarks
Chief	Letsoile Rafolatsane	Nkokamele	142	The Chief of Molumong	
Headman	Liokhoane Leuta	Likhameng	163	The Chief of Nkokamele	
			305		
Chief	Sejakhosi Rafolatsane	Mankeng	156	The Chief of Molumong	
Headman	Tsoenemotho Mokhachane	Linakeng ha Mokhachane	154	The Chief of Mankeng	
			310		
Chief	Mosuoe L. Sekonyela	Malingoaneng	732	The Principal Chief of Mokhotlong	Administrative powers to be exercised by Kariki Sekonyela until further notice
Headman	Ntjabokone Sekonyela	Manakane's	38	The Chief of Malingoaneng	
Headman	'Matoka Makoro Rameleke[1]	Paballong	275	,,	
Headman	Maharasoa Montoeli Khothe	'Meta's	117	,,	
Headman	Qatsa Lehema	Khubelu	29	,,	
Headman	Meno Tsoeu	Nqechane	110	,,	
Headman	Molefi Alotsi	Maitsi	176	,,	
Headman	Mohoebi Lesesa	Mahaoleng	179	,,	
			1656		
Chief	Toeba M. Sekonyela[1]	Semenanyane	368	The Chief of Malingoaneng	
Headman	Thotofeane Sekonyela	Likomeng	354	The Chief of Semenanyane	
			722		
Headman	Solomon Sekonyela	Liseleng	183	The Chief of Semenanyane	
Headman	Malebitso Khubetsoana[1]	Matsoku ha Hlolo	434	The Headman of Liseleng	
			617		

Headman	Takalimane Sekonyela	Mpokochela	222	The Chief of Semenanyane
Headman	Leruo Tello[1]	Lihloahloeng	164	,,
Headman	Khakhachane Mathaba	Liphofung	256	,,
Headman	Marumo Letima	Bobete	339	,,
Headman	Hemi M. Sekonyela	Makhuleng	140	,,
Headman	Maramane Maramane	Methalaneng	241	,,
			1362	
Chief	Kariki Sekonyela	Mapholaneng	385	The Chief of Malingoaneng
Headman	Liselo Lethakha	Sebera	88	The Chief of Mapholaneng
	(Tlela Lethakha)			
Headman	Solomon Lebaka Lethunya	Mofolaneng	190	,,
			663	
Chief	Moloki Sekonyela	Molikaliko	380	The Chief of Malingoaneng
Headman	Leshuta Leshuta	Senqu ha Leshutu	165	The Chief of Molikaliko
Headman	Vacant	Mpharane	110	,,
Headman	Moholi Sekonyela	Metlomo	42	,,
Headman	Noosi Mahasane	Limonkaneng	64	,,
			761	
Chief	Khomoatsela Khatleli	Popa	411	The Chief of Malingoaneng
Headman	Makhutla Khatleli	Tsilantso	411	The Chief of Popa
			822	

[1] These are women. [2] Acting for 'Mankata Rafolatsane, who is also a woman.

BIBLIOGRAPHY[1]

(a) General

Arbousset, T., *Voyage d'exploration aux Montagnes Bleues*. Paris, 1932.
Ashton, E. H., "Political Organisation of the Southern Sotho", *Bantu St.*, *12*, 4, 1938; pp. 287-320.
"A Sociological Sketch of Sotho Diet", *Royal Society of S. Africa*, Vol. 27, 2, 1939; pp. 147-214.
Medicine, Magic and Sorcery among the Southern Sotho, Capetown University, 1943. (Communications from the School of African Studies. New Series, No. 10.)
The Social Structure of the Southern Sotho Ward, Capetown University, 1946. (Communications from the School of African Studies. New Series, No. 15).
"Democracy and Indirect Rule", *Africa*, *17*, 4, October 1947; pp. 235-51.
"The High Commission Territories", *Handbook on Race Relations in South Africa*, Ed. E. Hellman. Oxford, 1949.
Barnes, L., *The New Boer War*. London, Hogarth Press, 1932.
Casalis, J.-E., *Mes Souvenirs*. Paris, Société des Missions évangéliques, 1882; nouvelle éd., 1922.
Les Bassoutos: ou Vingt-trois années d'études et d'observations au Sud de l'Afrique. Paris, Société des Missions évangéliques, 1859; nouvelle éd., 1930. (English translation, *The Basutos*, London, 1861.)
Christol, F., *Au sud de l'Afrique*. Paris, 1897.
L'art dans l'Afrique australe. Paris, 1911.
"Les Bassoutos", in *Le Lessouto*, q.v. infra.
Dieterlen, H., *Portraits et Souvenirs du Lessouto*. Paris, Société des Missions évangéliques, 1923.
Pourquoi les Missions? Paris, Société des Missions évangéliques, 1920.
Pourquoi les Noirs ne tuent plus certains enfants, Recits Missionnaires Illustrés, Paris 1926.
François Coillard, R.M.I. Paris.
Eugène Casalis, Paris, 1930.
La Médecine et les Médecins au Lessouto. Paris, Société des Missions évangéliques, 1930.
Dieterlen, H. and Kohler, F., "Les Bassoutos d'autrefois", *Livre d'Or de la Mission du Lessouto*. Paris, 1912.
"Les Bassoutos d'aujourd'hui", *Livre d'Or de la Mission du Lessouto*. Paris, 1912.
Dutton, E. A. T., *The Basuto of Basutoland*. London, Jonathan Cape, 1923.

[1] This is not an exhaustive bibliography of the literature dealing with Basutoland but is a list of works that have been consulted. For a comprehensive bibliography see Schapera, I., "Select Bibliography of the Southern Basotho" in *Bantu Tribes of S. Africa*, by Duggan-Cronin, Cambridge, 1933; *Select Bibliography of S. African Native Life and Problems*, Oxford, 1941, and *Bantu Studies*, 8, 1934; and a short, interesting bibliography in Smith, E. W., *The Mabilles of Basutoland*.

BIBLIOGRAPHY

Duggan-Cronin, A. M., *The Bantu Tribes of South Africa*, Vol. II, Section III, "The Suto-Chuana Tribes", Cambridge, 1933.
Ellenberger, D. F. and MacGregor, J.C., *History of the Basuto, Ancient and Modern*. London, Caxton Publishing Co., 1912.
Ellenberger, V., *Sur les Hauts-Plaieaux du Lessouto. Notes et Souvenirs du Voyage.* Paris, Société des Missions évangéliques, 1930.
Gallienne, G., *Thomas Arbousset, Missionnaire.* Paris, 1904.
Goiran, H., *Une action créatrice de la Mission protestante française au Sud de l'Afrique.* Paris, Éditions "Je sers", 1931.
Hodgson, V. M. L. and Ballinger, W. G., *Indirect Rule in Southern Africa*, No. 1 Basutoland. Lovedale Press, 1931.
Jacottet, E., *The Treasury of Ba-Suto Lore*, Morija: Sesuto Book Depot. London, Kegan Paul, 1908.
   Contes populaires des Bassoutos. Paris, E. Leroux, 1895.
   "Moeurs, Coutumes et Superstitions des Ba-Souto", *Bull. Soc. Géog.*, 9 (1896-7). Neuchatel, 1897.
   "Note ethnographique sur les Bassoutos", *Livre d'Or de la Mission du Lessouto.* Paris, 1912.
Lagden, G., *The Basutos*, 2 vols. London, Hutchinson, 1909.
Laydevant, F., "La Poésie chez les Basuto", *Africa, 3*, 1930; pp. 523-35.
   "Étude sur la famille en Basutoland", *J. Soc. Africanistes, 1*, 1931; pp. 207-57.
   "Initiation du médecin-sorcier en Basutoland", *Ann. Laterensis.*
   "Religious or Sacred Plants of Basutoland", *Bantu St. 6*, 1, March 1932; pp. 65-9.
   "Praises of the Divining Bones among the Ba-Sotho", *Bantu St. 7*, 4, Dec. 1933; pp. 341-74.
Le Lessouto. Roneoed publication of Commission Missionnaire des Jeunes. Paris, Laforce, 1929.
Lestrade, G. P., Introductory article on Southern Basotho in *Bantu Tribes of South Africa*. Cambridge, 1933.
Mabille, A. and Dieterlen, H., *Sesuto-English Dictionary*, 6th Edition, Morija, Sesuto Book Depot, 1937.
MacGregor, J. C., *Basuto Traditions*. Cape Town, Argus Pub. Co., 1905.
Mackintosh, C. W., *Coillard of the Zambezi*. London, Fisher Unwin, 1907.
Martin, M., "Basutoland, its Legends and Customs", *Folk-Lore, 14*, 1903; pp. 414-18.
Mofolo, T., *The Traveller of the East* (trans. H. Ashton). London, S.P.C.K., 1931.
Norton, W. A., "Puberty Rites of Basuto", *S. Afr. J. Sci., 6*, 1909; pp. 199-201.
Perham, M., "The Basuto and their Country", *Geographical Magazine, 1*, 2, 1935.
Perham, M. and Curtis, L., *The Protectorates of South Africa*. London, Milford, 1935.
Phillips, E. P., "A Contribution to the Flora of the Leribe Plateau and Environs", *Annals S. Afr. Mus., 16*, i, 1917.
"The Protectorate Question", various authors, *Race Relations*, Vol. 2, No. 3. 1935.
Ramseyer, P., "La circoncision chez les Bassouto", *Rev. d'Ethnog. et Trad. Pop., 9*, 1928; pp. 40-70.
Sayce, R. U., "An Ethno-Geographical Essay on Basutoland", *Geog. Teacher, 12*, 1924; pp. 266-88.

Société des Missions évangéliques, *Livre d'Or de la Mission du Lessouto.* Paris, 1912.
Sechefo, J., "The Twelve Lunar Months among the Basuto", *Anthropos,* 4, 1909; 5, 1910.
Smith, E. W., *The Mabilles of Basutoland.* London, Hodder and Stoughton, 1939.
Theal, G. M., *Basutoland Records,* 3 vols. Cape Town, W. A. Richards, 1883.
van Warmelo, N. J., *A Preliminary Survey of the Bantu Tribes of South Africa.* Pretoria, 1935.
Widdicombe, J., *Fourteen Years in Basutoland.* London, 1891.

(b) *Vernacular Publications*

Dieterlen, G., *Mareng Meso.* Morija, 1933.
Jacottet, E., *Litsomo tsa Basotho,* 2 vols. Morija, 1911.
Litaba tsa lekhotla la sechaba (Proceedings of the Basutoland Council). Morija.
Mangoela, Z. D., *Hara Libatana le Linyamatsane.* Morija, 1913.
  Lithoko tsa marena a Basuto. Morija, 1928.
Mapetla, J., *Liphoofolo, Linonyana, Litaola le Lithoko tsa tsona.* Morija, 1928.
Motlamelle, *Ngaka ea Mosotho.* Morija, 1938.
Motsamai, E., *Mehla ea Malimo.* Morija, 1932.
Mofolo, T., *Moeti oa Bochabela.* Morija, 1925.
Segoete, E., *Raphepheng. Bophelo ba BaSotho ba khale.* Morija, 1913.
Sekese, A., *Mekhoa le Maele a BaSotho.* Morija, 1931.
  Bukana ea Tsomo tsa Pitso ea Linonyana le Tseko ea Sefofu le Seritsa. Morija, 1928.

(c) *Official Reports, Pamphlets, etc.*

Basutoland.
Report and Evidence of a Commission on Native Laws and Customs of the Basutos. Cape Town, 1873.
  Census 1911. Cape Town, 1912.
  Native Laws of Lerotholi, 1922.
Regulations for Schools in Basutoland. Morija, 1931.
  New Native Court Regulations (Reform proposals and Regulations). Morija, 1935.
Census 1936. Pretoria, 1937.
An Explanatory Memorandum (Basutoland Native Administration and Courts Proclamations). Bloemfontein, 1938.
In the High Court of Basutoland: Judgment—Chief Constantinus Bereng Griffith v. Chieftainess Amelia 'Mantsebo Seeiso Griffith. Mazinod, Basutoland, 1943.
Explanatory Memorandum Basuto National Treasury. Bloemfontein, 1944.
Laws of Lerotholi. Morija, 1946.
  1. Declaration of Basuto Law and Custom.
  2. Rules issued by the Paramount Chief.
  3. Orders issued by the Paramount Chief.
  4. Native Court Rules
Memorandum of Development Plans. Bloemfontein, 1946.
Report of Education Commission, S. 31540. Pretoria, 1946.

Annual Reports on Social and Economic Progress of the People. London, 1887–1948.
Annual Reports of the Agricultural and Veterinary Departments.
Annual Reports of the Director of Education, 1929–
Harlech, Lord, *Chieftainship in Bantu Africa*. Morija, 1942.
Jones, G. I. *Basutoland Medicine Murder:* a Report on the recent outbreak of "Direëlo" murders in Basutoland, Cmd. 8209. London, H.M.S.O., 1951.
Meyerowitz, H. V., *Report on the Possibilities of the Development of Village Crafts in Basutoland*. Morija, 1936.
Pim, Sir Alan, *Financial and Economic Position of Basutoland*, Cmd. 4907. London, H.M.S.O., 1935.
Sargant, E. B., *Report on Native Education in South Africa*, Part III, "Education in the Protectorates". London, H.M.S.O., 1908.
Staples, R. R. and Hudson, W. K., *An Ecological Survey of the Mountain Area of Basutoland*. London, 1938.
Stockley, G. M., *Geological Survey of Basutoland*. London, 1949.
Thornton, R. W., *The Basuto Pony*. Morija, 1938.
Strong Wheat in Basutoland. Morija, 1938.
Anti-erosion Measures and Reclamation of Eroded Land (reprint of address to S. African Society of Civil Engineers). Morija, 1942.
Urling-Smith, *Report on Native Education in Basutoland*. 1926.

(d) *Unpublished Papers*

Dornan, S. S., Notes on the Geology of Basutoland. (in report of Brit. Assn. 1905.
Jankie, H. E., *Mosotho e motona*.
Laydevant, F., Position sociale des Basutos par rapport à l'augmentation de la population.
Marwick, B. A., *Developments in Native Administration in the South African High Commission Territories*, 1950.

(e) *Literature dealing with other Areas*

Hunter, M., *Reaction to Conquest*, London, O.U.P. for International African Institute, 1936.
Maclean, J. (ed.), *Compendium of Kaffir laws and customs*. Mount Coke, 1858.
Schapera, I., *The Khoisan Peoples of South Africa*. London, Routledge, 1930.
Bantu-Speaking Peoples of Southern Africa. London, Routledge, 1937.
Handbook of Tswana Law and Custom. London, 1938.
Watt, J. M. and Breyer-Brandwijk, M. G., *The Medical and Poisonous Plants of Southern Africa*. Edinburgh, 1932.

SUPPLEMENTARY BIBLIOGRAPHY

The following is a list of books and articles on Basutoland which have appeared since the original Bibliography was compiled. It does not claim to be exhaustive and does not include items listed in: *Basutoland: A Bibliography* compiled by Miss J. te Groen (q.v.); I. Schapera's *Select Bibliography of Native Life and Problems*, Oxford University Press, 1941 (except for Lord Hailey's *Native Administration and Land Tenure*); the Supplement by A. Holden and A. Jacoby, 1950, or the Second Supplement by R. Giffen and J. Back, 1958, issued by the School of Librarianship, University of Cape Town. It is divided into two sections: A—Official Publications, B—General.

(a) *Official Publications*

Annual Report.
Annual Report of the Department of Agriculture.
Annual Report of the Department of Local Government.
Annual Report of the Commissioner of Police.
Annual Report of the Director of Education.
 (Reports for 1960 and 1963 also contained in triennium surveys)
Basutoland Census (1946).
Basutoland (Constitution) Order in Council, 1959.
Basutoland Constitutional Handbook, 1960.
Basutoland Constitutional Conference. Cmnd. 2,371, 1964.
Basutoland Order, 1965: Constitution, Supplement to Gazette No. 3462.
Basutoland National Council: Debates.
Basutoland, The Bechuanaland Protectorate and Swaziland: History of discussion with the Union of South Africa, 1909–1929. Cmnd. 8707, 1952.
Douglas, A. J. A. and Tennant, R. Y., *Basutoland Agricultural Survey, 1949–50.*
Hailey, The Lord, *Native Administration in the British African Territories*, Part V, The High Commission Territories. H.M.S.O., 1953.
High Commission Territories, Law Reports:
 1926–1953. Maseru, 1958.
 1958. Maseru, 1958.
 1959. Maseru, 1960.
 1960. Maseru, 1961.
 1961–1962. Maseru, 1964.
Laws of Lerotholi: Revised Edition, 1959.
Leckie, W. G., Memorandum on "The Adoption of better methods of Land Management and the declaration of Agricultural improvement areas in Basutoland", 1945.
Local Government Handbook: Maseru, 1960.

Morojele, C. M. H., *1960 Agricultural Census, Basutoland*.
  Part 1. Census Methodology. Maseru, 1963.
  Part 2. Households and families. Maseru, 1962.
  Part 3. Agricultural holdings. Maseru, 1963.
  *Part 4. Crop acreages, yield and production. Maseru, 1963.
  *Part 5. Land classification and farming practices. Maseru, 1963.
  *Part 6. Agricultural implements and storage facilities. Maseru, 1963.
  *Part 7. Livestock and poultry. Maseru, 1965.
    (*Private circulation only)
Report of the Administrative Reforms Committee (Moore). Pretoria, 1954.
Report of the Basutoland Constitution Commission, 1963. Maseru, 1963.
Report of the Commission into Education in Basutoland (Clarke). G.P.S. 31540, Pretoria, 1945.
Report on Constitutional Development: Conference held in Nov./Dec. 1959. Cmnd. 637, 1959.
Report on Constitutional Reforms and Chieftainship Affairs. Maseru, 1958.
Report of the Economic Survey Commission, Basutoland, Bechuanaland Protectorate and Swaziland. H.M.S.O., 1960.
Sheddick, V., *Land Tenure in Basutoland*. Colonial Research Studies No. 13. London, 1951.
Taylor, D. H., *Basutoland Population Census, 1956*. Maseru.
Venn, A. C., *Some Results of Agricultural Research in Basutoland*, 1957.

(b) *General*

Anon. (L.T.Ph.) *Lebollo*. (Description of Circumcision) Mazenod (?1963) (subsequently withdrawn).
The Unprotected Protectorates: Fabian Research Series, 1965.
Ashton, E. H., "Protectorates in South Africa", *New Society*. Oct. 31, 1963. pp. 11–13.
"Basutoland: Background papers", *Institute of Race Relations*. London, July 1964.
"Elections in Basutoland", *News Letter: Institute of Race Relations*. London, May/June 1965. pp. 24–30.
Problem Territories of Southern Africa (with Sir Charles Dundas). South African Institute of International Affairs. Johannesburg, 1952.
Ba Re'ng Batho Ha Buka Ea "Lebollo", Letters to the press and the English text of the discussion in the Basutoland National Council, 1963, and 1964 regarding the above pamphlet. Lebollo, Mazenod (?1964).
Basutoland Organisation of Sesotho Authors, *General Report of Third National Conference*. Mazenod, 1962.
Centenary, *Catholic Church in Basutoland 1862–1962*. Mazenod, 1962.
Damane, M., Peace: *The Mother of Nations: The "Saga" of the origin of the Protestant Church in Basutoland*. Morija, 1947.
Doxey, G. V., *The High Commission Territories and the Republic of South Africa*. Chatham House Memorandum, April 1963.
Duncan, Patrick, *Sesotho Laws and Customs*. O.U.P., 1960.
Edwards, Isobel, *Basutoland Enquiry*. Africa Bureau, London, 1955.
Hailey, The Lord, *The Republic of South Africa and the High Commission Territories*. London, 1963.

SUPPLEMENTARY BIBLIOGRAPHY

Halpern, J., *South Africa's Hostages*. Penguin Books, 1965.
"Laws of Lerotholi in Basutoland", *African Studies*, Vol. II. No. 4. 1952.
Laydevant, F., O.M.I., *Morena Griffiths Lerotholi, 1871–1916*. Mazenod, 1944.
"L'Enfance chez les Basutos", *Ann. Lateranensi*, Vol. XII, 1948. pp. 207–79.
"Les Rites de l'Initiation au Basutoland", *Anthropos*, Vol. XLVI, 1951. pp. 221–83. Reprinted. Mazenod.
Lebreton, H., *Litabanyana tsa bophelo ba kereke e katholike Lesotho*. (Notes on the Catholic Church in Basutoland 1862–1874.) Mazenod.
Leoatle, E. A., *Jubile ea Lilemo tsa Lekholo*. The Centenary of the Mission in Basutoland. Morija, 1933.
Lesotho: *Basutoland Notes and Records*, Vols. I–III, 1959, 1960, 1962.
'Mabathoana, M. C. L., *Whetstone of Wits*. Proverbs of Sesotho, English and Latin. Mazenod, 1963.
Makoro, J. C. K., *Histori ea Batlokoa*. (History of the Batlokoa.) Mazenod.
Mohlabani, *Journal of the Marema-Tlou Freedom Party*. Maseru. Various articles, notably "Chiefs and Politics", Vol. 9. Nos. 1, 4, Oct. 1964, Jan. 1965.
Poola, M. Matsetsele, *The Witchdoctor*. Morija, 1951.
Rubin, L. and Stevens, R. P., "The High Commission Territories—What now?" *Africa Report*, Vol. 9. No. 4. pp. 9–16.
Santho, D. M. K., *Bataung*. (History of the Bataung.) Mazenod.
Sechefo, J., *Customs and Superstitions in Basutoland*. Mazenod.
The Old Clothing of Basotho. Mazenod.
Segal, R., *Political Africa*. London, 1961.
Sheddick, V. G. J., *The Southern Sotho*. I.A.I. London, 1953.
Spence, J. E., "British Policy towards the High Commission Territories", *Journal of Modern African Studies*. Vol. 2. No. 2. July 1964.
Stevens, R. P. and Rubin, L., "Southern Africa's Multiracial University", *Africa Report*, Vol. 9. No. 3. pp. 16–18.
te Groen, J., *Basutoland: A Bibliography*. University of Cape Town, 1946. (Rep. 1964.)
"The Sesotho Digest", *Africa Digest*.
Tsiu, A. K., *Lipapali le lithothokiso tsa Basotho*. (Games and Amusements of the Basuto.) Morija, 1954.
Tylden, G., *A History of Thaba Bosiu*. Maseru, 1945.
The Rise of the Basuto. Cape Town, 1950.
Walton, J., *African Village*. Pretoria, 1958.
History of Education in Basutoland. 1958.

INDEX

Adultery, 86, 239, 240, 263, 304
  wife's, 26
Agriculture, 90, 120 ff.
  ploughing, 124-5
  weeding, 127
Ancestors, 111, 113-16, 129
  balimo, 114-15, 283, 284, 285, 289-90, 299
Animal husbandry, 134 ff.
  veterinary knowledge and, 140-1
Assault, 241, 257-8, 280, 338-40
Avoidances, 76-8, 100

Bahlakoana, 17
BaKoena, 12, 13
"Bakoena", 12
Ba-Lefe, 17, 31, 193, 327
Basketry and weaving, 160-1
Basuto, The, books about, vii
  Boer War and, 5-6
Basutoland, 1 ff., 11
  British protection for, 4, 5, 6
  geology of, 120-1
Basutoland National Council, 6, 7, 187, 188, 192, 217, 245, 250
Bathepu, 11
Batlokoa, viii, ix, 17, 46, 202
  See also Tlokoa
Ba-Tsotetsi, 17, 31, 48
Beer, 53, 67, 68, 69, 76, 93, 94, 95, 107, 111, 115-16, 129, 130, 178, 179
  feasts, 111
Behaviour, 94, 249
  patterns of, 20, 21, 76-7, 100
Bereng, Chief, ix, 17, 196-7, 213, 223, 313
Birth, 27 ff.
  first child, the, 27-30
Bone-throwers and bone-throwing, *see under* Divination and diviners
Borikhoe, ix, x, 47 n.1
Boys, 33, 35-7, 38, 60-1
  activities of, 36-7
  initiation, 46 ff.
Burial customs and graves, 102 ff., 133
Bushmen, 2

"Caretakings", *see under* Customs
Casalis, Eugène, vii, 3, 55, 80, 142, 212, 214, 220, 308
Cattle, 14, 134 ff., 172, 173, 179, 180, 204, 212, 245, 246
  mafisa owners and, 181-2, 213, 272
  marriage (*bohali*), 30-1, 63, 64, 65,
  66-7, 71-3, 82, 87, 177-8, 194, 262, 263, 339, 340
  payment as damages, 255, 260, 261
Ceremonies, ix, 35-6, 48, 95, 205, 284-5
  first-fruits, 128, 212
  funeral, 102 ff.
  purification, 28, 109-11
  wedding, 66 ff., 96
  See also Feasts; Rites
Charms, 31, 129, 306, 320, 321
Chastity, 40
  bridal, 75
Chiefs and chiefship, 2, 6, 18, 19, 95, 98, 115, 151-2, 154, 169, 172, 175, 184, 188, 193, 202, 204, 206 ff., 212 ff., 220-21, 222, 235, 244, 245, 247, 249, 252, 275
  administration and, 199 ff.
  advice and, 215-16
  authority of, 222 ff.
  courts and judicial
  duties and functions of, 209
  hut of, 23
  income of, 207-8
  initiation and, 51, 52, 55, 56
  marriage and, 62-3
  medicines and, 305
  messengers of, 214-15
  officials of, 213-14
  National Council of, 217-18, 219
  personal qualities, 220
  political organization and, 186 ff., 190 ff.
  privileges of, 206-8
  property and, 173, 184-5, 207-8
  sub-chiefs, 187, 193, 208, 211
  succession and, 193
  villages of, 21, 22
  wives of, 63, 79, 80-1, 213
  See also Paramount Chiefs
Children, 41 ff., 46, 58, 84, 87, 128, 179, 194-5, 242
  clanship and, 14, 15
  clothes and, 33
  continence in, 39-40
  death of, 102
  education of, 41 ff.
  feeding and food of, 33 ff., 42
  names given to, 32-3
  punishment and, 44-5
  chobeliso (elopement), 65-6, 259-61, 262
Christianity, 8, 24-5, 86-7, 95, 116 ff., 296, 305-6, 313, 316, 334

355

INDEX

Circumcision, 49, 56-7
Clans, 12-17
   clan names, 12-13, 92
Conception, 26-7
Councils, 196
   district, 219
   family, 225
   "Sons of Moshesh", 5, 184, 196, 197, 205, 217, 309
Courts, 7, 210-11, 214, 222 ff., 252, 253, 254
   cases tried in, 338 ff.
   divorce and, 86, 87
   evidence in, 238 ff.
   Native Court Rules, 227, 228, 233, 236, 237, 238, 247, 251, 253
   procedure of, 232 ff.
Courtyard (*lelapa*), 24, 28, 29, 31
Crops, 121, 122, 123, 126-7, 128 ff., 148, 274-5
   ancestors and, 114
   "evaporation" of, 109
Culture, viii, 8
   change in, vii
   European contact and, 4-5, 7-8, 9, 55, 94-5, 161, 166
Customs, 22, 107-8, 119, 129-30, 135-6, 204, 249
   caretakings, 199 ff.
   marriage, 63, 64, 67-8, 74

Daily life, 88-99
Dancing and dances, 39, 48, 52, 54, 95-6, 97, 98, 123, 132, 284, 285
   mohobelo, 95, 96, 97
   mokhibo, 39, 95, 96, 97
   mokoratlo, 48, 53, 54, 67, 95-6
   motjeko, 96
Death, 101-2, 113-14
   legend about, 100-1
   gifts and, 101-2
   mourning for, 125
Defamation, 265-6
Dieterlen, vii, 66, 115, 287, 289, 300, 315, 316
Divination and diviners, 283-6, 288, 291-2, 296-300
   bone-throwing of, 296-300
   mokoma (*bakoma*), 283-6, 288
   seers, 283-6
Divorce, 85, 86, 87
Doctoring, 123, 141, 171, 212, 300 ff.
   of initiation huts, 49
   See also Medicines
Doctors (*ngaka*), 282 ff., 309, 314
   fees of, 288-9
   plants used by, 318-22

Economics and economy of the Basuto, 164-5, 166 ff., 172 ff.
   present position in Basutoland, 175-7

Education, 41-61
   See also Schools
Ellenberger and MacGregor, vii
Elopement, *see chobeliso*
Emblems, 12, 13
Etiquette, 91-2

Family, the, 17 ff.
   biological, 18
Feasts, 47, 48, 93-4, 95, 107, 110, 111, 116, 284
   See also Ceremonies
Fines, 131, 146, 170, 173, 201, 207, 210, 222, 224, 225, 226, 228, 231, 237, 238, 243, 245, 246, 247, 257, 258, 259, 260, 261, 263, 264, 268-9, 270, 271, 272, 273, 276-7, 278, 308
Fokeng, 2, 12, 13, 14, 16, 17, 18, 21
   Bafokeng, 11 13-14
Folk-tales, 3
Food, 88, 89, 93, 166, 175, 176
   at initiation periods, 50
   guests and, 90-1

Games, 35, 38, 39, 46, 59, 98-9
Gifts, 177-8
Girls, 33, 38-9, 45, 47, 60, 61
   activities of, 37-8, 179
   initiation, 38, 57-8, 96, 97
   modesty of, 38-9
Goats, 134-5, 138, 284
Grasses, 153
Griffith, Chief, 81, 84, 85, 104, 193, 195, 196, 201, 221, 252, 335

Headmen, 22, 55, 59, 144, 145, 146-7, 148, 151, 208
   political organization and, 186, 187, 188
Herd-boys, 36-7, 45, 97, 98, 134, 135 ff., 151, 158, 245, 272
Homicide, 255-7
Horses, 134, 138
Hospitality, 90, 92
Hunting, 158
Huts, 22, 23-4
   initiation, 49

Infant betrothal, 64
Inheritance, 182-5
Initiation, 46 ff., 94, 116
   aspects and uses of, 54-5
   boys and, 46 ff.
   courts and, 225-6
   girls, 38, 57-58, 96, 97
   horns, 308
   lodge (*morphato*), 45, 46, 48, 49, 50 ff., 55, 57
Insults, 243, 263-4

INDEX

Intermarriage, 15, 20, 335
Iron and ironwork, 158-9

Jonathan, Chief, 6, 80, 173, 212
Judicial organization, 222 ff.

Kaffir-corn, 122, 129
  "evaporation" of, 129
Khatla, 13
Khoakhoa, 16, 190, 202
khotla, *see Lekhotla*
Kinship terms, 20-1, 43, 78, 324-6
Koena, 2, 13, 14, 15, 16, 17, 21, 53, 76, 80
Kraals, 25

Lagden, vii
Land tenure, 144 ff., 174
  arable holdings, 146
  disposal of, 149
  disputes about, 154-7
  pastures, 150
  rights of, 147
Law and laws, 222 ff., 249 ff.
  criminal, 253 ff.
Laws of Lerotholi, 144, 185, 193, 218, 230, 250-1, 252, 253 ff., 259, 260-1, 266-7, 268, 270, 274, 276
Laydevant, vii, 14-15, 245, 247, 296
Leather-work, 159
Legends, 10-11, 100-1
Lekhotla, (khotla), 23, 25, 36, 48, 54, 75, 88-9
Lelingoana, 4, 55, 79, 82, 115, 185, 200, 201, 202, 208, 212, 214, 327, 331, 332
Lerotholi 5, 80, 190, 196, 218
Letsema, see Work-parties
Letsie, I., 4, 5, 80, 185, 197, 200
Letsie, II., 105, 193, 196
Levirate, the *(kenela* custom), 83-5, 182, 184
Levy, 208
Lineages, 16
Literature, vernacular, 8
Love philtres, 303-4

Makhaola, 195
Mahlape, 11
Mantatisi, 2, 198
'Mantsebo (widow of Seeiso), 7, 197, 199, 202
Marriage, 62-87
  Basuto view of, 66
  bride's trousseau, 73-4
  clanship and, 15
  cross-cousin, 63
  family aspect of, 82
  kinship, 327 ff.
  mala and *seantlo*, 81, 82-3
  marriage to the grave, 195-6
  modern, 195-6
  preferential, 63, 331, 335
  wedding ceremonies, 66 ff., 96
Matebele, 11, 327
Meals: breakfast, 88
  evening, 89
Medicines, 24, 25, 26, 27, 28, 30, 55, 78, 81, 102, 104, 108, 115, 126, 127-8, 129, 131-2, 140-1, 160, 205, 212, 282 ff., 287 ff., 301 ff., 313-16
  initiation, 48, 49, 53, 57
  lenaka, 15-16, 306, 307, 311
  mohlabelo, 282, 285, 305, 306-7
  moupello, 49, 123, 292
  ritual murder and, 307 ff.
Migration and labour, 162 ff.
Minerals, 153-4
Missionaries and missions, 3-4, 7-8, 55-6, 57, 58, 72-3, 83, 96, 104, 116, 119, 124, 217
mohoha, 107, 110, 113
Mokotjo, 105, 111, 185, 192, 195, 197
morphato, see under Initiation: lodge
Moshesh, 3, 4, 56, 80, 87, 152, 185, 193, 197, 199, 209, 216, 230, 249, 250, 252, 291, 292
  lineage of, 104, 196, 202, 247
Mosololi, 194
Mosuoe, 79, 82, 185, 190, 192, 201-2, 204, 205, 223, 245, 263, 288, 335
Motsoene, 80, 197
Musical instruments, 37, 97-8

Nation, the, 10-12
National Treasury, 7, 208, 223 n.,1 247
Nguni, 2, 3, 11
Ntsuanatsatsi, 10, 13, 113, 118

Offences, 228, 243 ff., 254, 255 ff., 278-81, 300, 339
  criminal, 275 ff.
  liability for, 243-6
  property and, 266 ff.
  sexual, 259-61
  vicarious liability, 244-5
Old age, 100
Oxen, 68, 124, 125, 182

Paramount Chiefs and chieftainship, 5, 6, 7, 12, 144, 149, 184, 186, 187, 205, 208, 218, 222
Patrilinearity, 18, 19
Peete, 193, 195
Peli, 2
  Bapeli, 113
Phetla, 2, 11, 12
Phuthi, 2, 3, 11, 12, 13, 14, 16, 29, 46, 49, 50, 52, 76, 83, 108, 132
  Baphuthi, 105, 202
Phuthing, 2, 12, 13, 16, 17
Pitsos, 96, 197, 204, 216, 217
Polane, 2, 11, 12

INDEX

Political changes, 7
Political organization, 186 ff.
  districts, 186 ff.
  duties and functions in, 209 ff.
  sub-districts, 186 ff.
  wards, 186 ff.
Polygyny, 79 ff., 86-7, 200, 213, 334-5
  property and, 179-80, 182, 183-4
Pottery, 160
Prayer, 117
Property, 154, 172 ff., 238
  damage to, 273-5
  household, 179-81
  offences against, 266 ff.
  personal, 110-11, 177-9, 181
  private, 177
  will and, 185
Punishment, 45, 51, 246-8, 254, 256, 270-1, 273, 278

Racing, 98
Rafolatsane, 198, 200, 201
Regents and wards, 198
Relationships, 17 ff.
  in-laws, 19-20, 69, 76-78
  marital, 78-9
  mother-in-law, 75
Religious beliefs, 112 ff.
Rites, 48, 69, 114, 135, 283
  babies and, 31-2
  burial, 105 ff.
  childbirth, 27-8
  koae, 75
  rain-making, 115, 132, 212
  See also Ceremonies
Ritual murders, 7, 15, 212, 245, 286, 304-5, 307 ff.

Sacrifices, 114, 115, 116
Sanctions, 44, 118-19, 223, 253
Savings, financial, 172-3
Scarification, 302
Schools, 8, 22-3, 45, 58 ff.
Seeiso, Paramount Chief, 7, 56, 81, 84, 85, 101, 186, 190, 196-7, 201, 204, 222, 223, 252, 253, 335
Sekese, 74
Sekonyela, 3, 4
Sexual intercourse, 26, 30, 109, 259
  premarital, 39, 40
Sheep, 134-5, 138
  customary and ritual use of, 27-8, 29, 30, 54, 68, 69, 74, 83, 109-10
Sia, 2, 12, 16, 17
Sickness, 115, 299, 300-1, 302-3
Sociology, 10 ff., 176-7
  four chief groups, 10 ff.
Soil erosion, 124, 125
Songs and singing, 48, 53, 95, 97, 123, 131, 284
  initiation, 2 n., 3, 48, 49, 50, 51, 52, 57

praise-songs, 14, 27, 50, 54, 97, 131, 142
Sorcery, 24, 26, 27, 32-3, 48, 108, 112, 113, 141, 240, 247, 250, 282, 283, 289-93, 299, 301, 305-6
Spirits, departed, 26
  witches and, 294
  See also Ancestors
Suckling, 41, 42

Taboos, 14, 28, 29, 30, 45, 49, 67, 76, 78, 100, 133, 141, 160, 280-1, 285
Taung, 2, 3, 12, 13, 17, 31, 122, 193, 194, 202
  ba Moletsane, 14, 16
Theft and thieves, 239-40, 241-2, 243, 245-6, 247, 266 ff., 276, 280, 304, 338-41
Thepu, 16, 17
thokolosi, 295-6
Tlokoa, 2-3, 4, 11, 12, 13, 14, 15, 16, 17, 18, 21, 29, 31, 46, 47, 48, 49, 50, 51, 55, 70, 71, 72, 74, 76, 78, 79, 83, 84, 85, 94, 98, 105, 106, 108, 109, 111, 116, 117 and n.1, 119, 122, 123, 127, 128, 129-30, 132-3, 145, 149, 151, 152, 153, 184-5, 190, 193, 200, 202, 204, 212, 217, 226, 249, 253, 285, 327
Tloung, 12, 17
Toeba, 198
Totems, 13-14, 17
Town criers, 214
Trade, 7, 8-9, 166 ff., 250
Trading stores, 167 ff.

Villages, 21-5
Visiting, 90-1

Wealth, 172 ff.
Weaning, 34-5
Widows, 83-5, 146, 149, 184
Witchcraft and witches, 81, 102, 112, 216, 240, 279, 286, 293-6, 312
  familiars of, 294, 295-6
  smelling-out of, 286, 291
  witch-doctors, 321
Wives, 77, 179, 181, 193-4, 198, 213, 291
  co-wives, 77, 81
  senior, 63, 81, 83, 193, 194, 197, 198, 226, 331, 332
  See also Chiefs: wives of
"Wolves", the, 45 and n., 51
Women, 91, 123, 255
  bakoma and, 285-6
  courts and, 226, 233, 234
  land and, 149
  motsoetse, 29-30
  property of, 111
  purification rite of, 109-10
  rain rites and, 132

regency and, 198–9
sterility and, 26, 27
thokolosi and, 295
witchcraft and, 294
work of, 78-9, 89-90, 130, 160, 163, 178
Work, 88-9, 90, 130-1, 160 ff., 178-9
  agricultural, 163, 164, 165

men's, 89-90
mining, 162, 163, 164-5
peddling and hawking, 161
unpaid labour, 208
wood and stone and, 181
  See also Women: work
Work-parties, 94, 96, 127, 129, 131, 207, 280-1

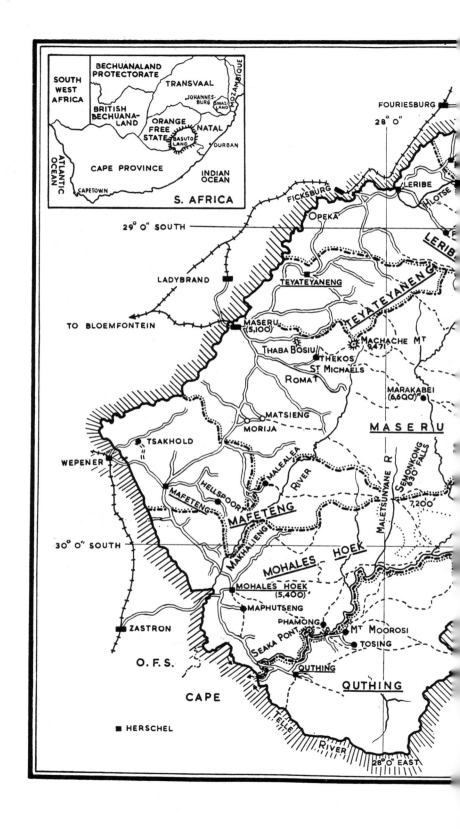

BASUTOLAND

SCALE OF MILES